# Unquiet World

Count Potocki of Montalk
drawn by Jadwiga Walker at a dinner at the Ognisko Polskie,
London, 1945

# Unquiet World

The Life of
Count Geoffrey Potocki
de Montalk

Stephanie de Montalk

Victoria University Press

VICTORIA UNIVERSITY PRESS
Victoria University of Wellington
PO Box 600 Wellington
www.vup.vuw.ac.nz

Copyright © Stephanie de Montalk 2001

ISBN 0 86473 414 X

First published 2001

This book is copyright. Apart from
any fair dealing for the purpose of private study,
research, criticism or review, as permitted under the
Copyright Act, no part may be reproduced by any
process without the permission of
the publishers

Published with the assistance of a grant from

Printed by PrintLink, Wellington

# Contents

|  | Illustrations | 6 |
|---|---|---|
|  | Author's Note | 11 |
|  | Introduction | 13 |
| ONE | Meeting Potocki | 19 |
| TWO | Ancestry and Early Childhood | 40 |
| THREE | Boyhood and Adolescence | 65 |
| FOUR | Manhood and Marriage | 79 |
| FIVE | The Early London Years | 100 |
| SIX | Return to New Zealand | 122 |
| SEVEN | The Trial | 131 |
| EIGHT | The Appeal | 158 |
| NINE | Imprisonment | 179 |
| TEN | New Zealand | 197 |
| ELEVEN | The Later London Years | 204 |
| TWELVE | Katyn | 227 |
| THIRTEEN | Draguignan and Dorset | 241 |
| FOURTEEN | Realisation | 263 |
| FIFTEEN | Resolution | 277 |
| SIXTEEN | Final Impressions | 295 |
|  | Sources | 318 |
|  | Acknowledgments | 325 |
|  | Index | 326 |

 Illustrations

*Between pages 96 and 97:*

Geoffrey Wladislas Vaile de Montalk, aged twenty-one, at the time of his marriage to Lilian Hemus in 1924.

Count Józef Franciszek Jan Potocki the Polish insurgent, 1800—1863 (Geoffrey's great-grandfather) (right), with his younger brother Herman (left) and a cousin (centre). (*Les Polonais et les Polonaises de la Révolution du 29 Novembre 1830*, Stavzeioicz)

Count Joseph Wladislas Edmond Potocki de Montalk, 1836—1901 (Geoffrey's grandfather), Paris circa 1865.

Joseph (also known as Edmond) around thirty years later, as professor of Modern Languages, University College, Auckland, circa 1896.

Joseph and Alexandrina (Macalister) de Montalk and seven of their twelve children, at their home, Clovelly, Mount Eden, Auckland, circa 1901. Back row: Henry, Judith, Joseph, Alexandrina. Front row: Alexander, Jane, Emily, Ethel (wife of Edmond), Edmond, Victoria. The absent children are Robert, John, James, George and Margaret.

Robert Wladislas, 1871—1942, and Annie Maud (Vaile), 1867—1908, de Montalk (Geoffrey's parents).

Annie de Montalk.

Geoffrey (right) with his brother Cedric, Auckland, 1906, about eighteen months before their mother's death.

Geoffrey, 1910, aged seven, at Vallombrosa, Remuera, Auckland.

Dulce, Geoffrey's sister, circa 1918, at the family's home in Majoribanks Street, Wellington.

Lilian Hemus, at the time she met Potocki. (Wanda Henderson)

Wanda, daughter of Potocki and Lilian, at around the time of Potocki's departure for England in 1927. (Wanda Henderson)

A.R.D. Fairburn.

R.A.K. Mason. (Hocken Library)

Douglas Glass, the New Zealand friend with whom Potocki was arrested and charged in London in 1932 with uttering and publishing an obscene libel entitled 'Here Lies John Penis'.

Potocki, newly arrived in Paris, 1928.

Lithuanian Idyll, 1929: Potocki in the grounds of Terespol Palace.

With Count Adam Chrapowicki, Terespol.

Zinka, Countess Chrapowicka (Adam's sister), for whom Potocki wrote the thirty-eight poems he published as *Lordly Lovesongs*.

Potocki and Zinka, Lithuania.

*Between pages 160 and 161:*

Potocki and Cedric in London, 1932, after Potocki's release from Wormwood Scrubs prison. Potocki is dressed in the first of his Richard II style tunics.

Potocki taking an oath in the name of Apollo at his 1932 obscenity trial. This illustration appeared on the front page of *La Stampa*.

Potocki, printing his literary and political journal, *The Right Review*, on his proto-Adana press, London, 1939.

Insterburg, 1933.

Warsaw, 1934.

Near Warsaw, circa 1935. One lover is said to have liked waking in the night to find Potocki's hair around her shoulders.

Potocki with 'family member' Franco, London, circa 1939.

With Odile, probably at the time of their 'official' marriage in London in 1940. Odile was Potocki's muse during his epic translation of Adam Mickiewicz's poetic drama, *Forefathers*.

Odile, with her sons at the time of her divorce from Potocki in 1955.

London, circa 1945: Potocki with Dorli, who would be his intermittent 'secret wife' for more than twenty years.

Potocki, circa 1945, wearing the bespoke corduroy suit he based on the uniform of the Polish army.

Dorli.

Potocki at his flat in Islington, 1946. (Photo taken by the New Zealand poet John Male)

Provence, 1949. Potocki carrying out repairs to the Shack, the olive harvester's hut near Draguignan that was his first home.

The Countess de Bioncourt, Potocki's benefactor from 1949.

Potocki, Marysia (Potocki's Polish housekeeper, immediately to his right) and the twins Potocki denied fathering, Draguignan, circa 1953.

Theodora (adopted daughter of T.F. Powys and natural daughter of Potocki), Potocki and Zlota at Lovelace's Copse, Dorset, in front of Theodora's garden hut, formerly the revolving sanatorium of Llewelyn Powys, circa 1961. (Photo John Powys)


*Between pages 224 and 225:*

Potocki in royal regalia in the grounds of the Villa Vigoni, Draguignan. The silk robe was spun near Warsaw in 1933 and later embroidered by Odile.

Potocki typesetting at the Villa Vigoni.

Potocki in a Draguignan café, with an unidentified female companion, circa 1968.

Potocki with Cathleen , who lived at the villa for seven years and gave birth to her son Gwilym (not Potocki's child) there.

Cathleen and Gwilym.

Potocki holding one of his eight Siamese cats in the back garden at the Villa Vigoni, circa 1973.

Frederica, Potocki's lover for over thirty years, and into old age.

Frederica at Ventimiglia, possibly late 1970s.

The Villa Vigoni (top storey, back view) in the process of renovation at the time of my first visit in 1968.

Potocki wearing his chased silver crown, with William Broughton at the Villa Vigoni, July 1970. (William Stevenson Broughton papers, Alexander Turnbull Library, Wellington, MS-Papers-3976-2)

Potocki with me (and child's hand—lèse majesté!) in Edinburgh, 1983.

Potocki at a Victoria University student orientation programme in Wellington, 1984, where he read poetry with Gisborne poet Gary McCormick and told a lunchtime audience that he strongly disapproved of conventional men's clothing. (*Evening Post*, 4 May 1984)

The launch of Denys Trussell's biography, *Fairburn*, Auckland, 1984. Potocki is in the front row, next to an unhappily seated Eric McCormick. (Anne Noble, *Metro*)

Potocki and the Austin 1800. (Anne Noble, *Metro*)

Filming the TV1 documentary, *The Count—Profile of a Polemicist*: Rod Cave, Ian Paul (director), Potocki and Malcolm Cromie (sound recordist) in the lounge of our 'hospitable mansion', Wellington. (Not in shot: Richard Bluck (camera operator) and Don Duncan (camera assistant).)

Potocki with my husband, John (Miller), in the bedsitter at Hamilton.

Potocki, Draguignan, July 1996.

The burgled and scattered contents of the bindery and archive in the Villa Vigoni at the time of my last visit in July 1996.

*Unless otherwise noted, illustrations are from the author's collection, or from Potocki's archive.*

For John

# Author's Note

This biography/memoir traces the life of, and records my friendship with, my cousin Count Geoffrey Potocki de Montalk: poet, polemicist, pagan and pretender to the throne of Poland. It is drawn primarily from my conversations, taped interviews, and correspondence with Potocki, my diaries, and Potocki's own poetry and prose. The reader may assume that any quotes for which sources are not given in the text have been taken from conversations with Potocki, who frequently spoke almost exactly as he wrote.

Potocki, in fact, was a man born out of his time; he would fit in perfectly in Casanova's *Memoirs*.

Roderick Cave, *The Private Press*

No one can write a man's life except himself. His inner mode of being, his true life, is known only to himself . . . he presents himself as he wants to be seen, not at all as he is.

Jean-Jacques Rousseau, *Confessions*

# Introduction

*Wellington, October 1997*
I'm sitting in the high-backed chair of an eye surgeon and I'm tense. There's a huge meibomian abscess inside the lower lid of my left eye and the surgeon is about to carry out an unspecified procedure on it. But I think I know what the procedure is: he's sterilised an instrument which looks suspiciously like a curette. He's told me the procedure will be painless after the needle, and it's that needle, that injection of local anaesthetic, I'm waiting for. He's drawing it up out of sight, flicking the plastic barrel, expelling the air, holding it discreetly to the side of his thigh as he shines a spotlight onto my face. I stare at a smudge on the ceiling. The room is close. This is the eighth serious bacterial infection in less than a year—every six weeks an antibiotic and an angry one-sided face—and the situation is worsening. This week my eye has been hidden in swollen tissue somewhere between my mouth and my brain. The GP says the bug could get into my head. I wasn't aware of it at the time, but now it occurs to me that the first infection developed about a month after I started examining the contents of my cousin's archive, which I had recently repatriated from France.

In July 1996, during a visit to Count Geoffrey Potocki de Montalk at his cottage, the Villa Vigoni, in the countryside in the south of France, John (my husband) and I salvaged a significant portion of this archive. At the time of our visit we found that Potocki, then ninety-two, although weak and confused, was being well cared for by a neighbour, but his records, which encompassed self-printed books and pamphlets and a vast amount of correspondence—including copies of his own letters since early adulthood—had been left to moulder. They lay carelessly about the small stone rooms known as the archive, bindery and printery, beneath his bedroom, trampled into the damp earth floor by burglars or scattered between smashed trays of type, broken glass and the battered suitcases and boxes in which they had once been stored.

Before he had returned permanently to France from New Zealand in 1993, Potocki, who had been moving between summers for the past ten years, had made John and me the trustees and executors of his will. Now, in view of the archive's ruinous state, John believed we should gather it up and send it to safe-keeping in Wellington. Initially I demurred. Although Potocki was no longer aware of his archive, or his basement, or a world beyond his bedroom, somehow it didn't seem right to separate an elderly man from his papers, the tangible evidence of his past, to despatch them to the other side of the world as though he no longer existed. But John, legal, practical, had no doubts. 'The trustees are liable,' he said, 'and it's what he would have wanted. Didn't he worry about leaving them here? Didn't he repeatedly ask us if we'd store them ourselves if he could ship them to Wellington?' So I reluctantly agreed, and we ordered forty large cartons and many rolls of wide brown tape from the Claret *déménagement* (removal) company in the town of Draguignan nearby, and had them delivered to the villa.

Over the next three days we packed the archive. There was no time for sorting: we had a train to catch and a plane to connect with in Nice. It was quite a task. The rooms were dim, and thick with congealed cobwebs, cramped, musty, cluttered with printing and gardening equipment, water bottles, gas containers and hardened bags of cement. Part of the problem was knowing what to take. There were Christmas cards, cheque butts, envelopes carefully opened so as not to disturb details of postage, draft manuscripts in a script so tiny they were almost unreadable, diaries ditto, pieces of old card (the sides of tea packets were favourites) painstakingly cut to size and secured in neat piles with rubber bands for use as markers and lists. Documents of obvious significance had been thrown together with what seemed to be trash. Or was it? In the end we packed everything: invoices, old newspapers, the lot. An inventory would need to be made but I could do this later in Wellington. Meanwhile John and I had reached a compromise: the cartons would remain in a warehouse in Draguignan until the time felt right to send for them.

\*

Introduction  ❦  15

I sent for the papers at the end of 1996 when Potocki was admitted to hospital, and for the past ten months I've transported them weekly, one carton at a time, from a storage vault to a small rented room in the city, where, working from a groundsheet on the carpet, I've sorted them and repacked them in fresh boxes. In the meantime Potocki has died.

Sometimes the papers have been damp, and I've had to spread them in patches of sun or alongside the radiator to dry. Sometimes they've been completely eaten away by mice. One promising bundle of letters had absolutely no centre: the words had been hollowed out, thousands of words, layer on layer, as far as the margins of each page. I've found mouse droppings, dead insects, red earth and what I assumed to be rodent urine. And mould. Black mould, white mould. I've wiped the mould or brushed it into the air with a pastry brush. I've given up wearing gloves: after an hour my hands were swimming out through the fingers, and I couldn't type through a layer of latex. And I've needed to type, fast, because in addition to listing the contents of each box on the computer, I've been compiling a chronology of Potocki's life should I decide to write his biography. I think I've found a life worth examining; stories ready to emerge from the long years of exile. I've also been entering essential correspondence in case the vault goes up in smoke, or I find myself fastened to cardboard for ever. The paper masks weren't helpful either: they kept wriggling upwards. Anyway, what exactly was I protecting myself against?

I leave the surgeon with white gauze in place. For the past week I've been on a high dose of antibiotics and I'm feeling queasy. This staphylococcus is a nasty bug. I see on the Internet that it's sensitive to *Melaleuca alternifolia* and wipe my computer keyboard with tea-tree oil, as the antiseptic is otherwise known; my computer table, my chair, the radiator, door handle, anything strong enough to take it. I wash my face with tea-tree-oil soap, throw out the groundsheet and pastry brush and stay away from the archive, even though five cartons have still to be cleared. I wonder why John, who has also been handling the papers, has never been affected.

*December 1997*
The infections have ceased. Now I'm making inquiries as to how I should proceed with the remaining cartons. An archivist inspects them,

sees the mould and says I'm at risk. She offers me the use of the Hygiene Room at the National Library, and I wait for it to become available.

*April 1998*
I'm gowned, gloved and masked. My hair is covered with a scarf, my eyes goggled, and a small blue bottle of tea-tree oil is balanced nearby. I carry out a rushed job on the boxes on a bench in the Hygiene Room, beneath a perspex hood through which an extractor fan sucks out the suspect dust and less obvious air, and hurry home for a shower.

*October 1998*
I'm confident, and infection-free. I wonder aloud whether I should make a start on the biography, even though this will mean a return to the archive. A newspaper article speaks of the curse of Tutankhamen's tomb, and I'm interested to read that new evidence suggests a bacterium was responsible. As I put down the paper, there's a sharp pain in my lower right eyelid, and an hour later the familiar redness and swelling. Does this mean there's a metaphysical dimension involved? I haven't been near those papers for six months. Does this mean 'the sleeping and the dead' are not really 'but as pictures', as the Scottish play would have us believe? A doctor at the after-hours clinic writes a prescription. 'If it develops at this rate I'd hate to see it tomorrow,' he says. I mention the archive and the tomb; he tells me about houses built above plague pits in London, and the fates of owners who fossicked about in their basements. I'm spooked; he can understand why. Later, a paper conservator from Sydney advises that it's not possible to fumigate the archive effectively without destroying the papers. I feel trapped, like a bad dream in a painting—a Blake watercolour of Job comes to mind.

*November 1999*
I'm restless, I need to start writing, but I'm beginning to feel as if forces beyond my control have been making me wait, dictating the terms of the project as if to order, steering me away from the papers. What do they want, Potocki's immortal gods? There were no problems when I packed the archive in France, before I mentioned the possibility of a biography. I'm not superstitious by nature—this could all be coincidence—but now I'm wondering if Potocki is opposed to the idea of a conventional biography: the scholarship, the intense detail, the

time it will take; all those years to discover. Is he worried his quicksilver life will be buried and lost in methodology? I toy with a novel, and an epic poem, but his life was too strange for fiction, too full to condense. I move in the direction of memoir—our conversations, the taped interviews, the vividness with which he imprinted himself on my mind. Now I can see him more clearly. He's no longer close to the skyline, resistant, defiant. No longer the fervent inhabitant of Blake's strange dark painting.

WLADISLAVS QVINTVS

MCMLXXVI

POEM FOR THE FEAST OF SATURN
AND THE REBIRTH OF THE SUN

Cover of a poem printed by Potocki at the Villa Vigoni, Provence,
featuring the Polish royal coat of arms he designed for himself

# ONE

 Meeting Potocki

*The course of my life is an indictment of the whole dishonest racket which calls itself democracy.*

I first met Potocki in the summer of 1968. John and I were travelling and camping in Europe, and as we planned to be passing through the French Riviera, only a short drive from the town in Provence where he had been living since leaving London in the late 1940s, I had made arrangements to meet him.

I had written from Scotland before we left. My father, who was his first cousin, had been receiving his hand-printed poems for the Feast of Saturn each Christmas for some years, and knew where he could be found: the Villa Vigoni, Chemin de St Martin, Draguignan. Potocki had replied immediately, without preamble, and in a style which would become familiar:

Dear Stéphanie,
What do you mean, I have probably never heard of you? I printed your name in the BLOOD ROYAL referred to in the enclosed pamphlet . . .
    It is nice your having heard of 'my activities in London in the l930s' but what was much more important was my activities during the war. My so far unpublished book about it is called My Private War Against England. You doubtless know that I claimed the Polish Throne, but I wonder if you know that I was the only person with the guts to publish the truth about the Katyn massacre in English during the war (naturally the English government knew perfectly well that this massacre was committed by their criminal allies, the Soviets).

Also, I broke the English censorship of the Polish papers in England, by the simple method of asking the Polish politicians what was in the censored spaces, whereupon I printed the gist of it in English without asking the permission of the censor's office. This enabled the Poles to take each matter up with the English, and ask: Why is this British-born Count Potocki allowed to print this, if we aren't? Naturally the English couldn't say to the Poles: 'Well, we can't do anything with Potocki. He doesn't ask our permission.'

Details of my great-grandmother's descent from Alexander, Earl of Dunfermline, followed. They were of some interest because at the time I was nursing the Earl of Elgin, and John and I were living in on his sixteenth-century estate only a few kilometres from Dunfermline. He went on:

> I can probably put you and your husband up, that is if the new room is finished, which it probably will be. How will you be arriving? Are you driving a car? You should try to arrange in full detail for me to meet you in Draguignan, for though this place is only two miles from the town, it is difficult to find the first time. Otherwise I had better send you very full sailing directions as to how to get here. How well do you speak French?
> You are descended as my book shows, from the most famous generations of Chiefs of most of the great Scots clans, but not Bruce, the Chief being the Earl of Elgin & Kincardine. But I haven't yet done the Sutherland side of the pedigree, and Bruce may be there for all I know.
> Best wishes to your husband. I hope he is a Scot at least?
> Your affectionate cousin, Potocki of Montalk.

My knowledge of my cousin was limited. For as long as I could remember, the de Montalk family in New Zealand had dismissed him as an embarrassment. He had left his wife and small daughter unsupported in order to 'follow the golden road to Samarkand', to live abroad, to be a poet. He was 'eccentric'—the word was usually delivered in a disparaging tone; a 'pagan'—the tone faltered here as if at the edge of evil; someone who worshipped Apollo and sunbathed naked. He was a man who wore sandals and robes, and grew his hair; a 'madman' who claimed the throne of Poland. And together with his brother Cedric, who had also left New Zealand and remained abroad, he used the family name in full, retained the title of count, and not only acknowledged his aristocratic Polish ancestry but flaunted it. One didn't do such things. If it was good enough for Count Joseph Wladislas Edmond Potocki de Montalk to dispense with his title and diminish his surname to de Montalk on arrival in New Zealand from France in 1868, it was appropriate his antipodean descendants did likewise. Moreover, Potocki's obscenity trial in London in 1932, his subsequent imprisonment, his pro-German stance during the war—my father, who had fought in Greece and North Africa, regarded him as a traitor— and his ongoing appearances in the British courts and press, had impugned the family name and the wider family wanted nothing to do with him.

But I was of another generation. At college I'd been secretly delighted by the sporadic, albeit disparaging, reports about him in the New Zealand papers—photographs had shown him to be a handsome and provocative man—and I'd been amused and even flattered when my mother, frustrated by my teenage rebellions, had exclaimed: 'You're just like the Count!' Later, I'd observed that with his long hair, sandals and robes he was likely to be a man ahead of his time. And, intrigued by his trial, I'd taken the trouble to read about it. In fact, I'd discovered sympathetic discussion of both the facts of the case and the six-month prison sentence in Alec Craig's *The Banned Books of England*, which I'd obtained from the public library and read on a day off from the hospital while sunbathing on a Wellington beach. I'd decided that a relative responsible for an event described by Craig as 'a sensational obscenity case', and the recipient of a sentence that W.B. Yeats spoke of as 'criminally brutal', certainly merited further investigation.

I wrote again and, encouraged by Potocki's sense of political vigour, ventured my opposition to the war in Vietnam and included a naïve piece of poetry on the subject. A second letter followed:

Dear Stéphanie,
It is a long time since I wore my hair down to my waist. After all in those days I was a beautiful young man, and am now to put it mildly much older. I enclose the photograph of my latest passport (which Hindenach has unnecessarily signed on the back, thereby making it unsuitable for use on the passport). He is a celebrated Harley Street surgeon, and was with me at the Christchurch Boys'

High School. He, German, and I, were the two foreigners in the class, and the only ones with real brains.).

A paragraph detailing my grandfather's descent from Polish nobility followed. Potocki continued:

> According to the Polish system, your Father is likewise a Count Potocki and you were born Countess Potocka. As for the English system, I don't recognize it, it is on the way out anyhow. But according to the Polish system you lose your title by marrying someone who hasn't a title—otherwise in a few generations everyone would be a Countess. Of course, if I ever become <u>de facto</u> King of Poland, you can come to Poland and I shall give you a title.
>
> I see you have written: Steph. I hope you mean Stéphanie, for my brother Cedric, who is a most awkward character—when he was in Poland he got himself baptized a Cartholic [sic] and took the additional Christian name Stefan—might think you were trying to cash in on his absolutely inexistent fame. I may say his writings are very much worse than worthless.

He then swerved into a diatribe on Vietnam: '... why is there all this fuss about the atrocities in Vietnam,' he fumed, 'when there wasn't a word of protest about all the filthy Allied lies about the Nazis, nor about the burning alive of 135,000 women, old men, foreign workers, prisoners of war and refugees from the bolsheviks, in one single night at Dresden—by the English? ... "One law for the lion and for the ox is oppression," wrote William Blake, "but so are two opposite laws for two similar lions."' He denounced Americans in Vietnam 'and anywhere else' and asked, 'WHY is there nothing about Katyn, and all the other soviet atrocities? WHO would ever think that the bolsheviks starved millions of families to death? Etc.!' Calmly, he continued:

> Anyway I hope you will stay here more than two days. And if you want to get brown, you can sunbathe naked alongside this house (if you want to) and nobody can see you. It's what I do, and it is one of the reasons why people say unanimously that I look twenty years younger than my pious Catholic brother, who is in fact younger than I am. When he married his son off at the Catholic Church Leicester Square, London, at the banquet afterwards at the Ogniski

Polskie, everyone said they thought he was the elder brother, but he very honestly (in view of my presence) told them he wasn't. I said to him: 'I've always told you, it is because my Gods are better than yours.'

In conclusion he was glad to hear my husband was a Scot, and hoped my poems that were not about Vietnam were better than those that were. 'Try to get here in time for your [twenty-third] birthday,' he wrote. 'May the immortal Gods favour you.' I was intrigued by my Polish connections, and by the prospect of his cottage in the Provençal countryside. Draguignan and its environs sounded promising.

We entered France cautiously from Spain. A month earlier, as we'd driven down the west coast from Boulogne to the city of San Sebastian just across the border, the country had been in crisis. A major student riot at the Sorbonne had provoked unrest at other universities, active dissatisfaction with de Gaulle's Fifth Republic had spread to workers, and strikes were rolling across France, paralysing most of the country. I had written in my diary, 'Car ferries on strike, petrol like gold, services at a minimum.'

Our main concern had been petrol. It was being siphoned from unattended cars, and thieves posing as students had been holding up vehicles and demanding to drain tanks. Some radical factions were openly seeking revolution, tourists were being advised to stay away, and the consuls were unable to cope with those already stranded. Two days before we arrived in Spain, we'd been stopped on a side road by an English motorcyclist who had waved us down, saying he'd been relieved of his tent and petrol by robbers. He'd leant heavily on the car, close to the window and, surmising he had been attracted to the jerrycan strapped with our tent to the roof, we'd sympathised, wound up our windows and hastily made for a highway.

We were a fortnight behind schedule. Problems within the Spanish postal service had delayed us at our poste restante pick-up points, and as our budget was tight and mail meant postal notes from New Zealand, we'd had no choice but to wait for it. Meanwhile, Potocki was impatiently anticipating our arrival. In accordance with his horoscope he was due to leave Draguignan in a couple of days for the home of Fritzi (Frederica, also known as Honey) in Chesières, Switzerland. He and Fritzi had been lovers, living separately, for nearly twenty years.

'I would have left Draguignan earlier,' he had written to her, 'but I was expecting the visit of my cousin Stéphanie Potocka de Montalk, and her young Scots husband John Miller. However, they rushed straight through France and went to Spain and Portugal and mail communication between us was interrupted. I am waiting until they turn up, in case I can be of help to them if there are barricades, lack of petrol etc. She is a granddaughter of Henry Potocki de Montalk, buried at Tolaga Bay.'

We left Andorra late in the day, after the arrival of the mail, and wound our way through low cloud and high winds out of the Pyrénées and down the side of the mountains into France. The road was well surfaced and we were hoping to get as far as the coast, but the mist closed in and the steep gusty conditions meant the going was slow. In three hours we covered only a hundred kilometres. Also, by now the sharp changes in altitude had caused John to develop earache, so we decided to stop for the night in Quillan, where we could camp free of charge in a rugby park. We finally reached Draguignan, stiff and tired, on 18 June at 6 pm. The short route of around 600 kilometres had taken us away from the coast, and the weather, although cloudy, had been humid and hot.

We approached the town with guarded anticipation. A few weeks earlier, in Portugal, we had met Potocki's younger brother, Count Cedric. We'd found Cedric, who had settled in Faro on the hot dry coast of the Algarve, living in a state of genteel poverty in a suite of bare rooms overlooking a communal courtyard noisy with roosters, cats and small children, and, although he had been welcoming and charming, he'd presented us with such an exhaustive list of health problems and difficult times that we'd felt obliged to feed him for a few days in his favourite café, and leave a donation in a cup in his bedroom. We had, moreover, been warned by Cedric to be wary of his brother. We were sitting in the forecourt of the café in the muslin shade of a jacaranda tree at the time, sharing a meal with Cedric's tall, tanned, American friend, a widower. The friend had been telling us about the injection of testosterone he'd been given that morning by the local male nurse. He didn't know what testosterone was. 'I think it's some sort of euphoric drug,' he said. 'The nurse believes I need it from time to time.' As I didn't consider it my business to enlighten him, I shifted the subject to our plans for departure the next day, but Cedric, who had surely picked up on the hormone, put his hand on my arm and said, 'Be careful of

Geoffrey, he thinks of nothing but sex.'

Draguignan is a large market-town inland between Nice and Marseille, in the administrative region of Var, a *département* of forests, vineyards—some of the oldest in France—and immense blue skies. In summer the air in the Var is thick with cicadas, wild herbs and resinous trees; the landscape shimmers. In winter, when the mistral blows down from the north for days, even weeks at a time, the hearths of the stone cottages come into their own; I have heard it said that writers like the mistral—its powerful bite, its persistence, its strong poetic force. Built on the site of a former Roman military post in the fifth century AD, Draguignan was named after a dragon which lived in the marshlands and was said to have terrorised the townsfolk. As the crow flies, the town is only around twenty kilometres from the coast, although the journey by road or rail takes over an hour.

I have no clear memories of Draguignan in the summer of 1968 beyond an impression of old stone and men sitting in squares. In the fading light of a long day it looked like any of the small towns we'd passed through *en route*. Today it is a busy commercial centre, part-modern, part-medieval, servicing sizeable wheat-, olive- and grape-growing communities and, on the outskirts of the town, near the turn-off to the St Martin district, France's largest artillery academy. There are pavement cafés on shaded boulevards, covered markets, a museum and, on a hill above the narrow streets and bent walls of the old quarter, the seventeenth-century clock tower for which the town is noted. A large number of brass plaques in the main streets suggests that Draguignan is well served by medical specialists. Last time I was in the town—after Potocki had died—a taxi driver told me the specialists like to live there because the restaurants, wine and climate are good, and it's close to the coast.

I do remember, though, that we had difficulty making ourselves understood. Although Draguignan is close to the Côte d'Azur, it is not on the tourist route, and in 1968 almost no one spoke English (I had only School Certificate French, and John the Scottish equivalent). It took for ever to locate Potocki. The Chemin de St Martin (later renamed Chemin des Faïsses) was not on our street map, and Potocki was not in the phone book. We should have made arrangements to meet him, as he suggested, but with postal services uncertain and our plans changing daily we had decided to chance it. Finally, a gendarme was able to give us some directions but, when we drove out into the countryside, there were no signposts. We spent the next two hours among sloping wooded hills making fruitless ventures in diminishing light down unmarked and unsealed roads. Eventually, our accidental wanderings led us to the town dump, where a couple pulling garden rubbish from the boot of a late-model car recognised Potocki's name, and led the way to the residence of the Controller of Lands. This was a lucky break, because the controller happened to be a personal friend of Potocki and was able to take us straight to him.

We approached the turn-off to the Villa Vigoni slowly along a thin lumpy road between low stone walls. It would have been easy to miss: for a kilometre or more the land had been overgrown with no obvious signs of habitation. However, as we pulled up behind the controller's car, just beyond a small wood, we saw that well back from the road there was a narrow, double-level dwelling, with a terracotta tiled roof, hiding in long grass. The controller, who confessed to a fear of dogs, was unwilling to approach the building on foot and so, unsure of the exact whereabouts of the driveway, we pressed on our horn and waited with him at the side of the road. After a few minutes there was a shout of welcome and a figure appeared waving and striding, and motioning to a point at which we could turn onto the property. We made our way carefully through the high grass, our Austin Minivan chewing unevenly along an uncertain track. It was difficult to know where the driveway stopped and the lower levels of the property started. If Potocki owned a vehicle it wasn't a large one. As the villa came more closely into view, we could see that it was a somewhat ramshackle stone cottage on which attempts at renovation with the aid of bottles, rocks, slabs of marble, wiring and piping—materials Potocki was later to refer to as 'deliberately chosen rubbish'—were still being made. A small car stood to one side— a Citroën Deux Chevaux, early model, bottle green with British and French identification plates. His standard—a small flag bearing the *Piława* or coat of arms of the Potocki family—hung limply from the front right-hand bumper.

We stopped the van short of the villa, where Potocki was waiting, and were greeted by a slight man wearing a red, long-sleeved, open-necked shirt which might have been silk, a pair of light-coloured riding breeches, and sandals. Although he was then sixty-five, he moved easily, with the energy of a much younger person, and there was something about his appearance that was at once elegant and compelling: the hair swept back from the forehead, perhaps, the assurance, the manner of speaking—he spoke with what would have been described at the time as an 'educated English accent'. He greeted us graciously and with warmth, shaking us by the hand, kissing me lightly on the cheek, smiling, inquiring. I was the first person from the New Zealand branch of the family, including the daughter he had abandoned when she was a child, to meet with him in more than forty years. The controller invited us all to join him for dinner, but Potocki declined. He explained that we would eat later, at the restaurant of a friend.

That evening we dined in a dimly lit stone room on a hillside on the outskirts of Draguignan. Potocki was welcomed with obvious pleasure by the female restaurateur, who seated us at a small table, brought local red wine and bread, and, after consulting with him in French, plucked a guitar solo from the record-player and replaced it with a classical track. After a while she produced a menu—the same sheet of paper she'd been taking table to table. It listed only a couple of items, entered by hand, and she waited as Potocki glanced at the page. He touched her arm. 'The food is so good, selection's simply a formality,' he said, ordering chicken. Her dark looks—she could have been Spanish—and the stone room—its roughly plastered walls, the candles—made me think of Hilaire Belloc:

Do you remember an inn,
Miranda?
Do you remember an inn?

The main course was served. I recall burnished portions of chicken topped with parsley, mushrooms and croutons, served at the table, straight from the pot in which they had simmered with onions, wine and the steam of fresh herbs. And the rhythm of 'Tarantella':

And the tedding and the spreading
Of the straw for a bedding,
And the fleas that tease in the High Pyrenees,
And the wine that tasted of the tar?

I remembered that around the time I first read this poem, as a teenager, I had first seen Potocki's photo in a newspaper in Wellington—the famous photo in which his hair falls below his shoulders and he wears a beret and cloak, and holds the black cat he called Franco.

Soon, warm with wine and rich food, he began to speak of his past. And he spoke as he had written, in twists and turns, darting from subject to subject with passion and wit and frequently with bitterness, but with little sense of exchange. He spoke of events, people and times in his life of which we had little or no knowledge, without explanation, without context. He spoke almost ceaselessly, pausing only to eat, drink and exchange smiles with his female host. John and I sat entranced. From time to time we glanced at each other and shrugged, discreetly. Did he know we were there? When dessert finally arrived we were heavy with stories of self-proclaimed genius, political and legal intrigue, personal persecution and glorious ancestry. He had given a superlative performance. Much later we were to hear the stories again, and again, frequently word for word, with the same tilt of the head, the rage and softening of the blue eyes, the preoccupation with plot and counter-plot and his own unrecognised genius. The devastating smile.

'Miranda' served sugared raspberries and cream, and coffee, and joined us for liqueurs 'on the house'. At around midnight we drove back to the villa. We crawled into our sleeping-bag with our heads spinning, the candle-yellow room going around and around

>Glancing,
>Dancing,
>Backing and advancing,
>Snapping of the clapper to the spin
>Out and in—
>And the Ting, Tong, Tang of the guitar!

Who was 'Driven Mud'? What was 'Katyn'? Why was he a neglected literary figure? 'How is it possible,' we asked ourselves in whispers, 'for someone to have been so consistently wronged?'

The next day was wet. We rose early to find him already at work, pedalling the huge iron press which stood in the rough brick and stone side room he called the printery. We had declined his invitation to sleep indoors—the cottage, although double-storeyed, was cramped—and had pitched our tent on a patch of flattened grass to the side of the house. Between breakfast and lunch and for most of the afternoon he printed on the 100-year-old Marinoni platen machine. We also stayed inside, comfortable in the living room, reading, cooking on bottled gas, and looking through his files and huge library. There were thousands of books. The cottage was dark and restful, its silence broken only by the muffled sound of the rain and the creaking of his press.

The downstairs room, which also served as kitchen and spare bedroom, was cosy, homely, somewhat dusty, more a room of working clutter than outright disorder. It had a low, beamed roof and a concrete floor, and small windows which, I sensed, would on a fine day face away from the sun. The walls were covered with books, and every available surface seemed to have been given over to paper—blank printing paper, hand-corrected proofs, labels and cardboard for covers. There were a couple of shabby but soft chairs by a brick fireplace, a divan for guests, and two waist-high dressers with drawers, which served as kitchen cupboards and bench. Above the bench, to one side, a glass-fronted wall cabinet contained the pantry: tins of tea and biscuits sent by friends from abroad, cheese, eggs, smeared bottles of vinegar, red wine and olive oil. The rest of the wall was studded with hooks and nails from which saucepans and other cooking utensils hung, and woven containers holding vegetables and strings of garlic and onions, and bread. There was no plumbing, no kitchen sink, no electricity, no telephone. The lines and mains from Draguignan had not yet travelled this far. Potocki had his drinking water delivered in huge bottles of green-tinted glass, drew his household water from a hand-pump well halfway between the cottage and the road, and washed his dishes in a plastic basin on the dresser bench. He cooked with bottled gas, lit the room with a paraffin lamp, and showered outside in the summer, in water still sun-warm from the hose he had somehow connected to the well.

On our arrival he had taken us on a tour of the villa, and we had inspected his arrangements with interest. Adjacent to the living room was the printery, The Mélissa Press. It was poorly lit, the stonework was rough and the floorboards incomplete. Clearly, it would be cold during winter. Above the living room, with access by a steep and narrow set of wooden stairs, was his bedroom, which also served as a study. This room too was low-roofed and the chief impression was of a haphazard preoccupation with paper. The walls were lined with files and books—a quick glance suggested hundreds of volumes of poetry, dictionaries in dozens of languages, antiquarian publications, classical works, genealogical and astrological texts. (I don't remember any individual titles, but a subsequent visit by John Macalister, whose article 'Count Potocki of Montalk, a private library in Provence', appeared in *The Private Library* in 1984, revealed that, among the modern poets in a collection of more than 700 books of poetry, Yeats, Roy Campbell and Edgell Rickword were 'well-represented'; that the 'pornography shelf' held *Lady Chatterley's Lover, Lolita, The Kama Sutra* and *The Perfumed Garden*—titles 'unexciting by today's standards'; and that the library was 'low on novels, perhaps to be expected from one whose idea of true literature is poetry'.) There was also a well-blanketed double bed, with a polished wooden headboard on which the Potocki coat of arms had been skilfully carved and painted, and, at the foot of the bed, an upright piano. Alongside the door to the garden, Potocki had pushed back a curtain to reveal a niche in which he had set up a small table as the altar at which he worshipped the god of the sun. Then he had opened the bedroom door onto concrete steps leading to the unshaded upper level of the property optimistically spoken of as the back garden. 'Winston Churchill's down there,' he said, indicating a steep set of steps to a shelter below and to the side of the cottage. 'You'll have to excuse him—he's a bucket.'

At some point during the day he ran short of paper, so we drove him into Draguignan to replenish his supply, and buy steak for the evening meal. On the way home we stopped off at his other properties: an overgrown holding in the suburb of Flayosc, and 2000 square metres of olive grove in the Vallon de Gandi, close to the villa. There was a small building, previously an olive harvester's hut, in the valley, and we clambered about in the wet grass inspecting the dark derelict rooms in which he had first lived after leaving England. We learnt that he also owned land in Dorset, England.

That evening over dinner, the tales of heredity and history resumed. We sat around the table tantalised by more tales of injustice, half told, never explained. As previously, we were reluctant to appear uninformed, to intrude upon the performance. Contrary to Cedric's concern, there was no untoward mention of sex. We lingered with him until well into the evening. The lamp softened the room and deepened the red wine in our glasses. Time and place seemed slightly unreal. I could see us all as if from a distance, laughing and talking in a small circle of light in the dark countryside. In the midst of a revolution in France, here we were meeting with a true revolutionary. 'He gives me hope for older age,' John said later.

In honour of our visit, and my recent birthday, he presented us with a copy of his publication, *The Blood Royal of Ireland Scotland Wales England and other Countries in the House of Potok through*

*Macalister*, a study published 'as a Smack in the Eye to the conceited, arrogant, and on the whole thoroughly mediocre present-day English Uppish Classes' and, as Macalister's article notes, partly 'to prove to the British establishment that he is by no means a two-a-penny Polish noble'. The foolscap-sized genealogy, issued by The Mélissa Press in 1966 and bound in red cloth, is an astonishing tabulation. It establishes 212 descents from Edward III through Potocki's paternal grandmother. It also illustrates the extent of his obsession with heredity. In his six-page Avant-Propos, Potocki wags a finger at the then current thinking on heredity: 'To try to pretend that heredity does not matter,' he writes, 'is just plain ridiculous, or hypocritical. It is so utterly ridiculous that it does not improve one's opinion of the Human Race that such an idea can be raised at all . . . Nor is there the slightest truth in the two-faced assertion, that man is in this respect different from the animals. You positively cannot get a great man out of sixty-four quarterings of dolts, nor a beautiful woman out of thirty-two hideous families.' He quotes W.B. Yeats, who was 'accused of being a Fascist' for having written such lines as:

> I lived among great houses,
> Riches drove out rank,
> Base drove out the better blood,
> And mind and body shrank.

and offers the opinion of a Mr J. A. Allen, a bookseller just behind Buckingham Palace who had published a £50 book of horse genealogies, and whom Potocki had asked whether any general conclusion could be reached from the equine data. 'Yes,' Allen confirmed, 'you will be interested to hear that it is exactly as in human life, and certain strains are endowed with the will and ability to win.'

Potocki then gave us some advice. Pointing to the listing of England on the cover after the alphabetical arrangement of Ireland, Scotland and Wales, he said: 'The English only respect those who boot them up the backside.' (As a Scot, John was interested to hear this.) Then he told us: 'Always use humour when writing to public officials. You will make it difficult for them to complain about you. Poke fun. It sounds good when it comes out later in court.'

At midnight we said our goodbyes and went to bed, leaving him to find his Siamese cat and pack his car for their departure for Switzerland, as ordered by his horoscope, at three in the morning. When we awoke, there was a patch of bare ground where the Citroën had been. The wet weather had lifted, the cicadas were singing and the grass was steaming in the heat. Herbs, bees, huge green-eyed wasps and early summer flowers had sprung from the land. The setting felt magical. His horoscope had been right: it was a great day to travel.

We tidied and locked the villa and lay in the sun. We discussed his advice about humour as I wrote up my diary and wondered why it had been of so little assistance to him. We agreed that people probably took him more seriously than he took himself. 'He has an impish grin,' I said. I looked through *The Blood Royal*, re-read the foreword on heredity and examined his photograph opposite the title page. It was a studio portrait, taken in Draguignan, and an excellent likeness. Beneath the photo were the words 'Count Potocki of Montalk', and at the bottom of the page the comment 'absolutely un-retouched'.

Our visit to Potocki in the south of France left a strong impression. Later, we would ask ourselves whether we had responded solely to the dramatic and compelling presence of Potocki himself—his good looks, his colourful past—or whether we had also in part been seduced by Provence—the hot sun after a damp week in a tent in Andorra, the colour after the arid Spanish coast—and the charm of an unconventional lifestyle. Fresh from the orthodoxy of New Zealand, had John, the social worker, and I, the rigorously trained nurse, also been swept away by the perceived freedoms of Potocki's easy villa, his long summer holiday?

Whatever the reason, the afternoon we left Draguignan, with its red earth, orange tiles, vivid sky, we felt strangely elated. All the way to the coast, and in Nice, sitting on a marble-hard beach, swimming in the fine pebbled sea, eating salade niçoise in large buns, we discussed his difference, and the way in which he and Europe had not seemed out of place together.

Over the years, as Potocki moved in and out of my life, the question of his difference remained. Unanswered. Busy with my own life, I accepted him as he was; as I accepted the weather; as I understood that, like the Provençal climate, he was intemperate yet appealing: a combination of heat waves, calm days and unseasonal rains. And I also became aware that, despite the mellowing effects of age, he remained as individual as the province. As unpredictable.

He wrote to us after we returned to England, inviting us to return for an extended period the following summer, and even offering to assist with our fares. But we were recalled to New Zealand in the spring of 1969, when my mother developed a brain tumour and needed surgery, and I didn't see him again until 1983. We corresponded, of course. I sent letters which reflected my preoccupation with the mortgage, making ends meet and raising a family, while he sent his Christmas messages for the Feast of Saturn, self-printed booklets, pamphlets and poems, and wrote splendid and amusing letters decrying his detractors and detailing the altercations of the day. They were usually signed 'Your affectionate cousin, Władysław R.'

On his failure to secure a Burns Fellowship, he wrote on 30 December 1969:

> ... they turned down my application in favour of one Middleton. On this subject I had a letter from Professor Kenneth Hopkins of the Department of English, Southern Illinois University, the poet, critic and imaginative author, in which he says:
> 'I duly wrote a recommendation to the University at Auckland (or wherever it was) and they duly wrote back saying they had given the job to somebody else: which is the way with these people, they very seldom know what is good for them, even when responsible persons like myself take the trouble to give them guidance gratis. However, we don't want you rusticated to New Zealand.'
> ... I suppose my dear cousin Kenneth [my father] is shocked at the letter I wrote him. I thought a post-Victorian member of the House of Potok would know better. I was telling him it was not my late Father's fault if I were not completely bats, and after describing how Father sold us to the step-mother, I added: 'And all because he wanted a bit of cunt, my dear cousin.'

(My father had certainly been shocked. Under the influence of my favourable reports he had begun to warm to Potocki. He had even written to him, telling him he was relieved to hear that he was 'a regular relative', but now he and my mother believed the family had been well advised to stay clear of him, and I was encouraged, unsuccessfully, to do likewise.)

And this, from 19 May 1970, on taking the Polish Cultural Foundation to court for publishing his translation of the Polish writer Adam Mickiewicz's acclaimed poetic drama *Forefathers* with unauthorised alterations:

> ... The hearing of the Polish Cultural Foundation Case in London was extremely amusing. There was quite a bit of laughter in Court, which as you know is never allowed in these inhuman courts of England unless the Judge happens to crack a joke. But I was able to 'get away with' saying a lot of things about the defendants and about the case, that no lawyer would have dared to say, and the Judge was holding his face between his hands half the time so as not to burst out laughing himself. On the morning of the case to my own very great surprise, I had some really excellent publicity in—would you believe it—THE TIMES!

There was also comment on Lord Longford's report on pornography, written on 2 October 1972:

> ... I must tell you before closing that in the Sunday Times of the 24th September there was an article by Cyril Connolly on the Longford Report. The Longford Report has met with a somewhat jeering reception—and quite rightly too—to which this article is no exception. Cyril Connolly is one of the few present-day writers who really knows Latin and Greek and I suspect he is really an Irishman. He says 'heroic figures like Baudelaire, Zola, D.H. Lawrence, Joyce, Gide, and Henry Miller, not to mention Radclyffe Hall and Count Potocki de Montalk (the most monstrously treated of them all) were confronted by desiccated old puritans on the Bench ...' This is not the first time Cyril Connolly (whom I have never met) has put in a word in print for me in London.

On 30 January 1982, 'Anniversary of the murder of King Charles I, and of the Nazis taking power in 1933', there was an update on the villa and an invitation to visit:

> Since you were here the Villa Vigoni has been somewhat improved. The room with the piano is now quite comfortable, with a wide matrimonial bed. The kitchen has a Swiss heater which keeps it

quite warm even in winter. I myself sleep in a small bedroom over the garage. The bed in the small room to the South could perhaps accommodate two small children, but only one big one. The bed in the kitchen is quite comfortable and is a bit bigger. There is also a tent. Naturally I should be pleased to see you all at the Villa Vigoni.

His invitation was timely. John was planning a period of sabbatical leave in Edinburgh in 1983, and we hoped we might include a visit to France. We even considered the possibility of staying at the villa—clearly it had been improved since we were there. As he wrote on 12 November 1982:

> There are by now, forty electric light and heat points. There's quite a good 'fridge.' There are plenty of points for radios, razors, tape-recorders, vibrators and the like. There is a large, wide, comfortable bed in the top room, with a modern mattrass [sic]. The floor is carpeted, and the carpet is in relatively good state. I myself usually abide in the little room over the garage, where is likewise a wide modern mattrass. This room did not exist when you came, I think. But as regards the children, things would be easier in the warmer weather, for there is a tent, and children like living in a tent. Otherwise there is a comfortable single bed in the kitchen, and it could be widened by getting a typical modern mattrass say three inches wider on each side. There is a similar bed in the little room to the South. And there is a bed four feet long in a cubby hole behind the bed in the kitchen. How long is the shortest of the children?

The bathroom facilities sounded fairly basic still, for, although municipal water now reached the property and there was a bath, the tap was located outside the door and water came in from a hose. On the other hand, there were heaters, and the fragrant fire was appealing:

> The two main rooms are extremely well heated by two Swiss oil heaters, that is to say, the oil is heated by electricity, and it cuts out as soon as whatever heat is reached, as has been set. There are a couple of minor electric heaters as well. Moreover in the kitchen, there is an excellent fire-place which lights easily and heats the place well. There is a good supply of olive-wood, which of course smells nice.

In the end the trip to France was not possible. Potocki, however, had made arrangements to be in Britain in April 1983, and came to see us instead. He arrived at our apartment in Edinburgh towards the middle of the month, in a little green Renault, in remarkable form having driven from France via Fritzi in Switzerland and printing-related matters in London. He was now nearly eighty, smaller and more stooped than I remembered him, but as alert and energetic as ever.

He settled in, typing letters on his portable Olivetti at the dining-room table by day, and in the evening drinking red wine and retelling fragmented stories from his past. His range of interests was exhaustive. He moved through language (in addition to French and Provençal, he spoke, wrote and/or read Latin, Greek, Polish, Hungarian, Italian, German, Sanskrit), ancient and modern European history, religion, politics, printing, literature, music, art. As his letters had indicated, he was equally comfortable discussing the more practical realities of life. He had, after all, modernised the Villa Vigoni—built walls, put up beams, laid concrete and installed the electricity—himself.

In an effort to reconcile the so-far confusing order of his life, and aware of the need to retain some permanent record of this complex and highly unusual relative, I started to record interviews with him on tape. Once he had finished his correspondence for the day—usually after lunch—we would sit at the dining-room table and I would attempt to disentangle the stories and names that were now becoming familiar from the thicket of what appeared to be incidental detail surrounding them. It was frequently difficult for me to form a complete picture. He ordered his life discontinuously, and in snatches. One minute we might be in a palace in Lithuania, the next in an agricultural camp in Northumbria. We could be speaking of Fritzi in Switzerland or Dorli in London when suddenly an Edwina or an Odile would be mentioned, or I might find myself somewhere between a pamphlet on apartheid and the incompetence of the Polish Cultural Foundation. The children would arrive home from school, tea and biscuits would be called for and the tape would run on, recording taps running in the kitchen, doors banging, a cartoon on television and my own increasingly distracted line of questioning as yet another Potocki digression wound itself uninvited into the conversation.

After a couple of weeks, having assembled a sketchy chronology, I drove him to a studio in the teaching aids department at the University of Edinburgh, and conducted an interview on video. He was at ease on camera, and his facility for expression, timing and an amusing turn of phrase, together with his seemingly flawless recall, made me aware of his potential as the subject of a documentary. His tendency to digress and talk on was a problem, but a good editor would take care of that. I contacted the Television New Zealand arts programme, *Kaleidoscope*. Interest was expressed, and correspondence ensued.

Meanwhile he ate well—his enjoyment of food was evident—making liberal use of both butter and olive oil, and eating large quantities of whatever was offered. He accepted beans, bacon, sausages, eggs—the full Scottish breakfast; and meat, mash and two vegetables—the full family dinner. Nothing was declined. Everything was well chewed. Each meal began with a private grace: before eating he bowed his head and quietly gave thanks for the meal, in Latin. The children took to imitating him as he sat at the table long after they had finished, carefully despatching his crusts, dentures clicking. He didn't mind. 'Mead inside, olive oil outside,' he would tell them, helping himself to a spoonful of honey, later patting his face with oil and eau-de-Cologne. Now and again they joked with him. 'Who was Kasimir the Great?' they would say, feigning interest. Or, 'Look what someone's done to your papers!' as a teaspoon, bought at the local joke shop and apparently covered in raspberry jam, would be left on a genealogical tracing or horoscope chart. He referred to them as 'the brats', but was amused by them. Dylan's tendency to call for his attention, and then lose interest in his reason for doing so, used to cause him particular amusement.

Dylan, then aged five, would call out, 'Geoffrey!'

Potocki would patiently put down his paper, turn himself slowly around and, finding the child over the tops of his spectacles, ask, 'Yes, what is it?'

Dylan, oblivious to the inconvenience caused, would reply absent-mindedly, 'Doesn't matter.'

'When I was coming out on the boat,' Potocki would say, 'the grown-ups would complain about the noise the children were making, and I would tell them it didn't matter about the noise the children were making, what was worse was the noise they were making themselves.'

For the most part he dressed conservatively. He wore a plain brown home-made cotton jacket with matching trousers and silver buttons crafted by hand, a green or red shirt, a green woollen scarf, a black beret, long socks and sandals. Jonathon, then aged fourteen, asked him to dress as a 'mere mortal' when his friends came around, and

Potocki was amused and happy to oblige. In the evenings he would change into a plain crimson garment for dinner. When we dined out, he dressed in what he referred to as 'the royal robe'—a wine-coloured tunic with tapestry trimming, which he wore with a broad leather belt with a huge silver clasp, and a white long-sleeved undergarment resembling a night-shirt. Heads hardly turned as we took our seats in the restaurant. There was never any suggestion of ridicule: the Scots take things as they come. An acquaintance arriving at our door one evening to find Melissa, then thirteen, and Donovan, twelve, having a row in the hallway and Potocki in full regalia, moving from room to room in search of his spectacles, simply said: 'Your place is like the set of a stage play.'

Twice a day, morning and evening, he prayed to his heathen gods at the small altar he had set up on his bedside table. He said: 'I always say my prayers to the sun, and to the planet of the day, in the morning in Polish or Hungarian. And in the evening I say some general prayers in Latin. I think using a dead language has some effect in magical matters. I used to say all my prayers in English, but I was so enraged with the English that there were many years when I wouldn't think, speak or write in English.' The ritual included burning candles and incense, and the intermittent tinkling of a small brass bell. He sat, or knelt, before a silver-framed photograph of his Scots-born grandmother, on his father's side, and a couple of idols—tiny bronze figures of Eastern appearance—a low chant audible behind his closed door. After the morning ceremony he would appear in the dining room, bow fractionally, and greet us with 'Good morning, cousins, I hope you slept well?' In the evening, flushed with red wine and conversation, he would bow again, wish us the protection of his immortal gods, and retire to his room with a mug of hot milk and whisky. At dinner there was always the toast: 'Your good health, cousins.' The toast is still with us today: 'Your good health, cousin,' John and I say when there is wine on the table.

His bedroom was next to our entrance and we wondered what the genteel Edinburgh widows who also lived in the building were making of our strangely garbed guest, not to mention the smell of incense in the lobby. They had nodded to us as a family, but now, *en route* to the Safeways supermarket with their trundlers or afternoon tea at the House of Fraser in Princes Street, they chatted easily with Potocki. He liked to be among women, and they seemed keen to respond to him.

The longer he stayed with us, the less demanding he was to live with. After a couple of weeks the need to speak seemed to ease, and he settled into a routine of writing, reading and seeking out good second-hand bookshops. We in turn developed the ability to excuse ourselves from monologues mid-sentence, knowing he could talk on without us. He also visited friends, most notably Dorli, of whom he had spoken inconclusively on tape. Dorli had been traced to a tenement flat in a hard-faced housing estate on the outskirts of the city. She was found to be a small, smoke-wizened woman in a jumble of belongings, of which a hand-carved camphor-wood screen and a delicate tea-set appeared to be the remnants of a more comfortable life. She had once been his sweetheart, his 'secret wife', a woman with whom he had had a charged and erotic relationship. But I didn't know any of that then. I only knew that he visited briefly, and didn't speak of her again.

The only uneasy note was an intolerant remark about Jews—an intolerance he'd alluded to previously in a letter. Uncomfortable, we moved the subject along. He also railed against communists and Christians. He was elderly, eccentric . . .

In mid-May, with the end of our sabbatical leave in sight, Potocki finally began to think about leaving. He had been hoping for word from *Kaleidoscope*, but by now it was clear that the producer was stalling. 'I'll have to write a proposal, raise finance and produce the programme myself,' I told him, adding 'this will take time'. So he repacked the back seat of the Renault with paperwork, filled the bottle in his glove box with whisky, and headed cautiously out of Edinburgh. But he left expressing a desire to return to New Zealand. In the fourteen years since we had first met him, interest in his strange life had been growing. Other family members had been making detours while travelling in Europe to meet him; people fascinated by his seemingly extreme but ever-independent line of thinking had also been calling; and librarians, private printers, collectors of rare books and academics—especially in American universities—had become increasingly interested in obtaining his work. 'If I'm still alive,' he said, somewhat wistfully, 'I may come to New Zealand for my eightieth birthday in October. I would like to try to whip up some interest in my literary and other work . . . now that it's finally being admitted that I exist.'

TWO

## Ancestry and Early Childhood

*May not all this dispense with the need for psychoanalysis?*

In 1997, after Potocki's death, as I worked through his archive cataloguing, cleaning and reading his papers, the question of his difference returned. Faced for the first time with the firm detail of his life, aware of the extent to which distortion surrounded him—as, given his eccentricity, it inevitably would—I found that now I needed to know about his strangeness, to separate the fact and the rumour; to reconcile his life. To decide whether he had been a sometimes heroic figure, or simply a figure of fun.

His unveiling became a process of reflection. At times this process was relaxed and easy—a journey of factual discovery and assessment; at others it was an insistent clamour—the clamour of my own voice and experience of Potocki, against the more neutral voice of biography. It began with considerations of identity and the spectrum of difference in society, a spectrum which includes those talented and free-thinking yet harmless individuals who force us to question so-called normality, who all too often inhabit 'the suburbs of human contempt', as Quentin Crisp so poignantly put it. And the manner in which many who are unusual or gifted are also thought to be 'mad'.

Increasingly, I came to understand that, in the case of Potocki, an insight into the phenomenon of perceived madness, or eccentricity, was going to be pivotal, and so I started to follow leads in this area. To begin with, progress was slow: the research appeared to have been sporadic and inconclusive. But then I heard about a major study undertaken by David Weeks, neuropsychologist at the Royal Edinburgh Hospital, between 1984 and 1995, involving a thousand people in Britain and America identified as eccentric. This study, published as *Eccentrics*, and favourably reviewed in *The Spectator*, which found that it 'matches the subject in an ordered and lucid fashion', and the *New Scientist*, which observed that this was the first time eccentrics had 'been subjected to scientific study', confirmed most immediately my own finding that 'there is nothing to be found on the subject of eccentricity in modern scholarly literature'. It also confirmed that, in addition to embracing strangeness, flouting convention and rejecting conformity, eccentrics thrive on creativity, are typically opinionated, outspoken and convinced they are right and 'the rest of the world is out of step', and frequently possess a mischievous sense of humour. Many are also aware from early childhood that they're different. As I read on I felt as if I had stumbled on a portrait of Potocki.

Weeks was positive about eccentricity. He concluded that because eccentrics are willing to follow their unique visions—even at the risk of being labelled weird—they enjoy enhanced levels of aliveness and health, and that, far from being aberrant and unhappy, they experience much lower levels of stress because they do not feel the need to conform. They are 'essential for the health of the social organism,' he wrote, 'for they provide the variety of ideas and behaviour which permits the group to adapt successfully to changing conditions . . . all intellectual evolution depends on new ideas; they are the essence of science, of exciting new art, indeed of all intellectual progress.' The *New Scientist* agreed, noting that, while their hopeful dispositions suggest 'a self-belief that perhaps borders on the pathological', they provide 'a chastening contrast to our debilitating, postmodern propensity for overwrought self-analysis. If we can learn anything from eccentrics', it said, 'it is that being in the world but not of it is not solely the vocation of the mystic.' Added *The Spectator*, '[Eccentricity] is not a disease but a state, a complex personality trait characterised by people who are imaginative, resourceful, forthright, assertive and bright.' I found such positivity reassuring. Conditioned by my parents and the conservative New Zealand press to believe Potocki's behaviour was worthy only of suspicion and ridicule, I also felt a sense of relief: a response similar to the elation I experienced in France in 1968 when I realised that, outside New Zealand, Potocki's diversity was tolerated, sometimes celebrated.

The report validated my own response to his eccentricity. Having had Potocki, the self-invited house guest, stay with me and my family for long periods (sometimes months at a time), having known him, I had discovered that, although the sentiments of the press and wider family were understandable, particularly given his provocative and on occasions extreme point of view, there was also much about him to like, even enjoy. I had learnt that, as with the difference Thoreau writes of in *Walden*, his idiosyncratic behaviour was not solely an affectation, but appeared to come from deep within him. 'If a man does not keep pace with his companions,' says Thoreau, 'perhaps it is because he hears a different drummer. Let him step to the music which he hears, however measured, or far away.'

The question now became what had caused his eccentricity, his music, and why his particular brand of strangeness? His flamboyance, for instance: Weeks had found that the eccentrics he studied 'by and large were not at all exhibitionistic; that is, overly self dramatising, over-emotional, histrionic, or attention-seeking'. Had inherent characteristics been responsible for Potocki's behaviour? Like many of Weeks's eccentrics, he'd been aware from early childhood that he was different. Did this mean a genetic component was involved? That he was a natural-born rebel? Or was his situation more complex? And what of his environment? Somehow it didn't seem possible that he had been born simply to rise up one morning and announce to himself that henceforth he would dress in a medieval manner and disengage with the world in a single-minded and spectacular way.

Weeks had concluded that true eccentricity is a comparatively rare phenomenon. He had found that 'classic, full-time eccentrics' number only about one in 10,000 people and that, as they tend to be at the opposite extreme from those who are anxious, hostile and depressed, and frequently enjoy good health, they rarely presented for assessment. Dr Louis J. West, professor of psychiatry at the University College of Los Angeles, agrees, noting in the Internet article 'Wilder at Heart' that defining eccentricity in clinical terms is difficult as 'generally speaking, they're not unhappy, and they're not out of touch with reality', so they seldom seek treatment, psychiatric or medical. To what extent, I wondered, had Potocki, arguably New Zealand's greatest eccentric and only once psychiatrically assessed, also been shaped by life: by chance and unfortunate coincidence? By society: his trial and imprisonment, his childhood?

One morning as I sat on the floor of my small room in the city, slitting the brown tape on yet another box from the archive, wrenching back the cardboard and peering with anticipation and despair at yet another collection of dishevelled and discoloured paper, I found a sturdy, stained typescript with a faded turquoise cover. The pages had been hand-tied with what was now a dusty green cord, and on the front cover there was a gummed label with the typed title: RETURN TO APOLLO by Count de Montalk. On the next page, in Potocki's hand, in thin blue-black ink, there was a second title: IN THE HALLS OF ADMETOS, and 1937 in Roman numerals. Turning this page I found, also in Potocki's hand: 'The following are dead: Uncle Bert/Aunt Blanche', and what appeared to be a note to himself: 'Any "obscene" words could if necessary be merely represented by blanks or asterisks.' There was a third title-page: RETURN TO APOLLO THE LIFE-STORY OF COUNT POTOCKI OF MONTALK MCMXXXVI, in well-spaced type, with the words MEDUSA THE GORGON handwritten above in faded blue ink. Immediately before the story began, there was a typed dedication to his mother:

To the lovely and sustaining
memory of
Maud Vaile de Montalk
Countess Potocka
my mother
and the Goddess of My Muse.

The dedication was followed by a faint sentence in ink pencil, which seemed to read: 'At rest in error patient Dear.'

I moved the computer to one side and lifted the document to my desk. It was only mid-morning, but I switched on the light: a storm was blowing in from the south, and I sensed I had serious reading in hand. The script appeared to have been drawn from a manuscript started in England in 1928, and completed five years after Potocki's release from prison. It was heavily altered in pencil and ink, and the first twelve pages were missing. It began abruptly after the death of his mother, examined the traumatic aftermath of this, hailed his Polish ancestry and his special place in the family as oldest child and 'heir', and, regular digressions aside, provided a detailed account of his childhood and youth. Injustice, hunger and the ill-treatment of himself and his younger brother Cedric at the hands of his stepmother were endless themes. Ever since I had known Potocki he had spoken of an unhappy childhood, but, aside from angry statements about 'starvation' and a 'mingy wicked stepmother', he had supplied few details. Assuming harsh child-rearing practices to have been common at the turn of the century, even in supposedly enlightened households, I had believed his situation to be a tale of the times. Now, faced with the detailed account, clearly typed, double-spaced, at times heavily corrected by hand, I began to feel as a parent might who, having dismissed the grizzling of an infant, has now found the reason.

The draft ran to 169 pages, at which point it stopped as abruptly as it had started. I did not find a published copy of the typescript, but I assumed that the incomplete account of his childhood which he later began printing in serial form in his right-wing political and literary journal, the *Right Review*, and in older age in Polish as a series of booklets, had been transcribed from this early work (to my knowledge the autobiographical booklets never progressed beyond his childhood). Certainly the brief account of his early years given in the collection of essays, poetry and interviews published in 1993 as *Aristo, Confessions of Count Potocki de Montalk* had been drawn from this document.

As I sat at the desk reading, the seagulls raucously escaping the harbour, the day like the typescript growing darker, and afterwards, when I returned to the carton from the Draguignan *déménagement* company—at the sight of which, and given my task, the word derangement was frequently coming to mind—I wondered whether I should use this draft, whether working from the unfinished material would be intruding beyond a limit Potocki might regard as acceptable. The draft was not a journal—an acceptably careless form—and the absence of journals, diaries and other forms of personal record in the archive suggested that Potocki had written or preserved very few. It was possible they had once been there and he had lost them—as he had lost so many of the documents he had piled loosely on the back seat of his car as he travelled within New Zealand and Europe, and in his baggage backwards and forwards across the world—but the daily records I had found tended to be financial and so devoid of personal detail as to be incidental. I wondered whether he had preferred to record himself for posterity more deliberately in letters, pamphlets and poetry, and if so whether he would have considered the typescript, in its current form, suitable for public scrutiny.

Then later, with the manuscript balanced alongside my keyboard as I pieced together the chronology of his early life, I found myself ignoring the corrections and typing the original words—the most spontaneous words—onto the screen, and wondering again about the level of my intrusion. Biography and memoir are intrinsically intrusive, but I was writing as a relative, as someone to whom the manuscript had been entrusted. At times the original words felt almost too unrestrained to read, more personal even than his letters, which had after all been carbon-copied and carefully preserved, presumably not only as a record for him but also with an outside reader, or an audience, in mind. There was a sense of private, unresolved grief in the dedication to his mother, and in the act of writing itself—an act which I sensed was in part an attempt to understand and exorcise the turns his life had taken by bringing the burden of loss to the surface: the loss of his mother and the carefree years of his early childhood, the loss of his dignity and freedom following his obscenity trial and appeal, the loss of his love of England and his acceptance as a poet.

And what of the phrase MEDUSA THE GORGON handwritten above the title? How personal was this? What did it mean? Did Potocki see himself as Perseus, defender of his mother, Danae, from the lustful ruler Polydectes to whom he showed the severed head of Medusa, thereby turning the king to stone? Or was he Medusa, his hair turned into serpents by Athena out of envy for his beauty? Or Medusa again, a lock of whose hair was said to have the power to repel an army? In 1930 he had started growing his hair, and now, in 1937, it almost reached as far as his waist.

I could have the Polish booklets translated . . . I could work from the *Right Review*, or from *Aristo*, or an earlier book, *Recollections of My Fellow Poets*. But the published works felt deliberate and distanced. There was an intimacy about the stained, hand-corrected typescript that made it breathe, brought it alive. Finally, the fact that he had sought to preserve the document in an archive so extensive it had surely been accumulated with biography in mind settled the issue. When I re-read the opening paragraph, which speaks of the death of his mother, and checked it with the versions where the words were tight and crisp on the page, I knew I would work from the typescript.

But first there was the matter of his Polish ancestry to untangle.

Count Geoffrey Potocki of Montalk was born Geoffrey Wladislas Vaile de Montalk, in Auckland, New Zealand. He was the eldest son of Robert Wladislas de Montalk, an architect, who was the eldest son of Paris-born Professor Count Joseph Wladislas Edmond Potocki de Montalk, who was the only surviving son of Polish-born Count Józef Franciszek Jan Potocki, the Insurgent, of Białystok. Józef—Geoffrey's great-grandfather—was the son of Count Jan Alojzy Potocki and Princess Marjanna Czartoryska; and Jan was the son of Count Piotr Franciszek Potocki, Lord of Białystok, who married his close cousin Krystyna Potocka, daughter of Princess Teresa Sapieha.

Beyond his great-great-great-grandparents, the family reached back through Piotr's parents, Count Józef Potocki, Castellan of Lwów, and Pelagia Potocka (granddaughter of Feliks Potocki, the Castellan of Kraków and Grand Hetman of Poland) to Count Alexander Jan, Prince Palatine of Smolensk. Immediately beyond Alexander there was Count Paweł Potocki, Polish ambassador to Pope Alexander VII at the Holy See, who married the Princess Eleanor Soltykoff, cousin of the Tsarina. Paweł, who was the son of Count Stefan Potocki, Lord of Zahajpol and Palatine of Bracław, and Princess Mary of Moldavia, was created Hospodar of Moldavia in 1595 and, following the death of his older brothers, Palatine of Bracław. Stefan was the second of the four sons of Mikołaj Potocki (born c 1500), a nobleman descended from the Lords of Potok (c 1200).

The individual stories of Geoffrey Potocki's ancestors are as fascinating and as extravagant as the times. His great-great-grandmother, Marjanna Czartoryska, was a descendant of the poet Wacław Potocki, a writer of improper verse. Feliks Potocki was wealthier than most of the crowned heads of his day, with more than 20,000 armed retainers, a royal court at Tulczyn—where the foremost poet of the time, Stanisław Trembecki, was poet laureate—and a garden so beautiful it was the subject of Trembecki's masterpiece, *Sofjówka*. It was said of Paweł Potocki, ambassador to the Holy See, that he had all the horses of his suite shod with gold in order to show the Italians what it meant to be a Polish *pan* (lord).

The wider *Piława* Potocki family, one of the oldest aristocratic houses of Poland, included army commanders, senators, diplomats and scholars. Delfina Potocka, the black sheep of the family, who lived in Paris and smoked opium, was a mistress of Chopin, and it was 'a Madame la Comtesse Delphine Potocka' to whom Chopin dedicated the Valse in D flat, Op. 64, No. 1, and the Piano Concerto in F minor, Op. 21. Alfred Potocki's palace at Łańcut was known before the Second World War as the show-place of Poland. And Potocki connections with Pushkin included Artur Potocki, officer and author, and acquaintance during Pushkin's Odessa years, who had famously replied, '*J'aime mieux m'ennuyer autrement*' (I prefer to be bored otherwise) when asked to go fishing.

*Piława* is the name of the Potocki coat of arms. It distinguishes the primatial family from Potockis of less noble birth, including those who have purchased the name. The *Piława* Potocki line, which originally featured a silver cross, became two branches in the late sixteenth century—*Piława Srebrna* (silver) and *Piława Złota* (golden)—when Stefan Potocki, Lord of Zahajpol, built a new city, Złoty Potok (Golden Brook), on his lands and changed the silver cross on his arms to gold. Geoffrey Potocki was descended from the golden line. Its coat of arms presents a golden cross with three crossbars. Above the bars there is a count's crown and a helm with five ostrich feathers; below, the motto *Scutum Opponebat Scutis* (One Shield Against Many).

The former position of the *Piława* family within Poland's once 'all powerful oligarch of magnates' is extensively documented. 'By the mid-eighteenth century,' writes Norman Davies in *Heart of Europe: A Short History of Poland*, 'a handful of magnatial families—the Radziwiłł, Potocki, Branicki, Czartoryski, Zamoyski, Lubomirski, and Sapieha broods among them—had cornered most of the hereditary offices of state and had accumulated landed fortunes larger than that of the Crown itself. . . . Their private "states-within-the-state", populated in some cases by hundreds of thousands of serfs, exceeded the dimensions of many a German principality or of an English county, sustaining self-sufficient economies and private armies.'

Today the romance of the family remains and, while the Polish Potockis live modern, practical lives, some traditions, such as marriage between aristocratic families, continue. In an article on the descendants of Poland's nobles seeking to define their role in the Third Republic, the *Warsaw Voice* reported in 1996 that although, unlike their grandparents, young aristocrats do not have live-in nannies and tutors, few speak fluent French and the wealth and power of the families is largely a thing of the past, these descendants feel like members of a big family and believe they should still play a special role in society. This role is variously defined. Some families dream of retrieving and developing land and palaces which are falling apart; others speak of encouraging the aristocracy's tradition of bilingualism. Those who see the social group slowly fading away, because 'the communist regime sought to destroy everything that had roots', now feel compelled to re-establish roots and traditions. The young Potockis interviewed defined their patriotism as practical: 'It's reflected in our hard work. We've been told since childhood that we must be the best.' The report also notes that most of the families have relatives abroad and that 'interestingly, aristocratic background is much more important abroad than in Poland. Foreign aristocrats address each other with their titles and wear signet rings (to attest to their blue blood)' whereas 'In Poland such behaviour provokes laughter.'

The early source of Geoffrey Potocki's information about his ancestors was his father, Robert, who frequently reminded his children that his own grandfather was Count Potocki, 'an exceedingly great nobleman'. 'In fact,' Robert would add, 'in Europe even today instead of saying "Caesar's wife", they say "as a Potocka".'

However, like the rest of the New Zealand family, who were perhaps more concerned with relating to the new world than the old, Robert does not appeared to have pursued his ancestry. This task would fall to Geoffrey and Cedric, who, between 1933 and the Second World War, would carry out a considerable amount of genealogical research, including collection of certified documents, in Poland and France—research which after the war was regularly, some might say incessantly, released by the brothers to bewildered and largely uninterested relatives for whom post-war Poland was communist, behind the Iron Curtain and out of sight.

Indeed, it was not until Poland re-emerged as an independent nation in 1989, and I started to look seriously at Potocki's life, that his endless certificates, letters and conversations on the subject, and the huge rolled pages of family history assembled by Cedric (who on 26 May 1937 was acknowledged by the Polish authorities to have been born a Polish citizen by reason of his 'proven legitimated descent from Count Józef Franciszek Potocki') became of any real interest to me.

And I found that Geoffrey and Cedric had been thorough. The family tree, previously patchy, was now impressively complete, and vague stories and seemingly strange family habits were suddenly starting to make sense. Habits, I would joke, like my fascination with small beaded caps before I knew that my great-grandfather had worn one, and my father's unconscious manner, when young, of clicking his heels together when turning. There was also my own and my father's cross-over teeth. 'You've got the Potocki teeth!' Cedric had exclaimed on meeting me in Faro. 'All that intermarriage,' John would now laugh.

I learnt at this time that the New Zealand branch of the family was established as an indirect result of the Polish insurrection of 1830, following which Potocki's great-grandfather Józef and his younger brother Herman, condemned to death by the Tsar for their part in the uprising, fled to permanent exile in Paris, their inheritance, said to be a chain of properties stretching from Kiev in the Ukraine to west of Warsaw, confiscated.

I also learnt that Józef and Herman, having been arrested *en route* from Poland to France by the Austrians at the request of the Russian government, and imprisoned and treated badly for six months in the fortress at Brno, had made their way when released to Italy, where they recovered at the 'palazzo' of the third Marquess Townshend, on the Lago di Como. It was here that Józef met Geoffrey's great-grandmother, Judith Charlotte Anne O'Kennedy (also known as Kenedy), who, together with her sister Norah, was being raised as a niece of the marquess, but was in fact his foster daughter and said to be an illegitimate daughter of George IV.

Later, I found a letter to my father's sister, Eva, dated 25 October 1948, in which Geoffrey explains events further, including the origins of the name de Montalk. He writes that, having 'abducted' Judith from the villa at Como, Józef

> took her to Belgium and married her under the auspices of Mrs Trollope, the mother of the celebrated novelist, who was at that time occupying the chateau D'Hondt at Bruges. It would appear he did this under the more or less false name of 'de Montalk' . . . The name 'de Montalk' appears to be an attempt to translate into French the word 'Białystok' (White Mount). Need I point out that the correct form, Montalbe, is virtually impossible in French. It happens also that he was Lord of Białołówka (and of many other places) but he actually lived at Białołówka and maybe this is what he had in mind for 'de Montalk' is certainly a sort of equivalent of it. [An archival note dated 1973 advises that 'Montalk was a

village belonging to my Great-grandfather in the North-Western Ukraine.']

Additional details emerged, completing the French link in the story of the family's migration. In Paris, Józef had resumed life as a military offer, serving as Chef d'Escadron (Commander of the Cavalry) in the Spanish army and taking part in the Mexican expedition of General Prim. And he and Judith had had two children: Joseph (Geoffrey's grandfather) and Christine.

Joseph, godson of Anthony Trollope, was born on 17 February 1836, studied at the Sorbonne, completing a B. ès L. (Bachelor of Literature), and began a medical degree at the University of Naples, which he abandoned to join Garibaldi's campaign of 1859. Following the famous march on Rome, during which he was wounded, he was decorated with the silver Medal for Military Valour (the gold medal of which was the equivalent of the Victoria Cross). *The Cyclopaedia of New Zealand* reports that he was also awarded a Knighthood of the Military Order of Savoy.

Especially intriguing was the matter of Joseph's Potocki inheritance. Not long before the death of his father, Józef, in 1863 in Paris after a long illness, the Polish properties of Józef's father, Jan Alojzy Potocki, bypassing the insurgency-tainted Józef and his brother Herman, had passed to the untainted generation of Joseph and Herman's son Stefan (Józef and Herman were never pardoned for their part in the insurrection, and were excluded from the Tsar's Letter of Pardon of May 1856).

At this point I was disappointed to find Geoffrey and Cedric's reconstruction uncertain. For an undisclosed reason, Stefan was said to have presented himself as the primary heir to the estate of Jan Alojzy Potocki, as a result of which Joseph, the rightful heir (by now a widower with a small son and daughter), was obliged to negotiate a financial settlement on condition he took himself off to the antipodes and did not return. Also undisclosed was the reason for an entry on Józef's death certificate, which stated that he died *célibataire*—an entry at odds with the information recorded on his son's birth, baptismal and first marriage certificates—and suggested that perhaps a marriage certificate had not been produced when the death was recorded. Although, as Geoffrey wrote in the *Right Review*, June 1947: 'in French law the words "son épouse" in the *Acte de naissance* of Our Grandfather, constitute proof that the marriage certificate was produced to the authorities issuing the birth certificate, and raises a presumption of marriage which has to be rebutted by any contrary party'.

Examining Geoffrey's records more closely, I initially speculated that this ousting of Joseph—which appeared to have taken place with the support of the extended family—occurred partly because the marriage of Józef and Judith was perceived to be morganatic—'In fact', Geoffrey continues in the *Right Review*, 'the present-day Potockis have caused their pawns to say as much'—and partly because the Potockis' strong Polish Catholicism rejected the civil nature of Józef's marriage to Judith in Belgium. There was also the breakdown of this marriage in 1840, following which Judith had Joseph and his sister, who had been baptised as Catholics, re-anointed as Protestants and raised them to speak English and French, but not Polish.

More recent investigations, however, have raised the possibility of less principled considerations. A genealogical Internet site has revealed that a church marriage took place between Józef and Judith in Paris on 25 May 1857, six years before Józef died. And careful re-examination of Cedric's records has shown that the identity of the signatory to Józef's death certificate, Konstanty Count Branicki, was none other than the husband of Jadwiga Potocka, sister of Joseph's ouster, Stefan.

Joseph would later tell his New Zealand-born family that attempts were made by Judith, his mother, to obtain his inheritance, but that Alfred Cock, the QC she consulted in Paris, advised her that the Potocki family—recorded in the *Right Review* as 'The "big" Potockis, who stayed behind in Poland and curried favour with the enemies of their country'—was too powerful to fight. As Stefan is said to have died without heirs, and the New Zealand descendants of Joseph disappeared into history, this line is now believed by some Polish Potockis, despite Cedric's 1937 proof of ancestry, to be extinct.

The emigration of Joseph Potocki de Montalk to New Zealand is a more straightforward matter of record. In 1868, after travelling in Germany and Italy, Joseph left Europe under his 'gentleman's agreement' with Stefan. He arrived in Wellington on 23 July 1868 on the SS *Mataura*. On 30 April 1869, at the age of thirty-two, and having reduced his name to de Montalk, Joseph (also known as Edmond) married Alexandrina Williamina Sutherland, eldest daughter of Robert Stewart Macalister of Caithness. In the same year he took up a position at Wellington College. *The Early History of Wellington College* records that 'In 1869 Monsieur Joseph E.W.P. de Montalk, B. es L. (Paris) was appointed professor of Modern Languages at the School. He was of Polish descent and ranked as a Count in his own country.' He then moved to Nelson, where he taught at Nelson College, and from there to Otago University College, Christchurch Boys' High School, Christ's College, Canterbury University College and, in 1894, Auckland University College. Between 1877 and 1891 he was an interpreter and protector of European colonists on the Special Settlement Scheme at Jackson's Bay, Okuru, on the West Coast of the South Island, where he set up a store and repeatedly called for a road, a doctor, 400 immigrants and a sawmill.

Joseph de Montalk was author of *The Elements of French Literature*, published in Christchurch in 1879, and founder and president of the Alliance Française in Auckland. He became a member of the Société de Linguistique de Paris and, as an Officier d'Académie, was a recipient of the Palmes Universitaires (an award made 'to those who have specially distinguished themselves by eminent services in connection with teaching, and to learned, literary and scientific men who have done particularly brilliant work'). It was perhaps on this account that he was accorded a salute of cannon on the Waitemata Harbour during the visit of a French warship to Auckland.

Potocki remembers his grandfather, who died in 1901, as being venerated for his knowledge of languages—particularly Greek, Latin, Italian, French and German—his fine tenor voice and his sense of humour. He was also respected for his humanity, and for his habit of visiting the gaols out of kindness in order to speak in their languages to foreign prisoners who had no one to whom they could talk.

Joseph and Williamina had seven sons and five daughters. Potocki's father, Robert Wladislas, and my grandfather, Henry Potocki, were the first and third sons respectively.

Potocki's maternal side, although less historically compelling, was moneyed. His mother was Annie Maud Vaile, the daughter of Samuel and Annie Vaile. Samuel was a wealthy Auckland 'merchant and land agent' His father, George, is described by his grandson, E. Earle Vaile, in *Pioneering the Pumice* as having arrived in Auckland from England in 1843 with seven 'young children to face the cannibal and the desert'. A committed Baptist, George came to New Zealand rather than 'submit to the dominance then held and exercised by the Church of England'.

It was Samuel Vaile who loaned Robert de Montalk the sum of £6000, without interest and without security, with which he purchased and built a home at Vallombrosa, the park-like estate in Remuera where Potocki was born. 'The story went,' writes Potocki in the typescript, 'that this astonishing ten acre park had been planted long ago by a man mysteriously referred to as an "absentee" for his wife, who refused to live in such an outlandish part of the world. Probably the estate kept on growing wild till my father bought it at the beginning of this century.'

Geoffrey Wladislas was born at Vallombrosa on 6 October 1903. His brother, Cedric Earle, was born two years later and a sister, Dulce Maud, in 1908. 'The Golden Idyll', as the *Right Review* terms the first five years of his life, began with 'brilliant and powerful stars'. Born at the exact moment Mercury crossed the meridian, he believed his birth to have been of considerable astrological significance:

> The Sun was five degrees from the meridian; Saturn, in trine to these, was rising in 2 degrees 41 minutes of Aquarius; Mars in conjunction with Antares, was in sextile to both groups; the Moon was at full in Aries, and was approaching an eclipse; Jupiter in Pisces, in sextile to the ascending 21 degrees of Capricorn, was opposed by Venus in Virgo; and Borelli's comet, whose ascending node had coincided with my Ascendant, had reached perihelion at the point occupied by my Venus while the figure of the perihelion at my birthplace shewed [sic] my Ascendant once more rising.

'Those,' he dryly observes, 'who take the trouble to erect this theme and study it in the light of objective astrological knowledge, based on strict comparison with known horoscopes in the past, will come straight and do their homage of their own free will.'

'Then,' he continues in the *Right Review*, 'the skies began to cloud over, and the dream was troubled, and gave place to a most frightful nightmare, such as is almost impossible to believe; and it seemed interminable, but at last with adolescence I began to waken, and slowly to live . . . Since I reached manhood my goal has been to incorporate the Golden legend of my Dream into my Life, for the Dream and the Nightmare are still struggling for the mastery in that other world, which dominates or is dominated by this world of sense.' He was speaking of his mother's death as a result of thrombosis on 24 May 1908, nine days after the birth of his sister, and of its aftermath. He writes in the typescript:

> I never saw my Mother dead: nor have I ever to this day seen anyone dead. (Death is a Thing I have not yet seen, except incarnated in folk who are deemed to be alive). I remember wandering about the house after Mother's death and meeting my Father in the hall. I asked him where Mother was? He answered with some lofty Victorian evasion, and sent me to sit in the window-seat of the living room. He looked out into the garden. Later he had the window nailed up and filled with stained-glass leadlights. The Golden Idyll was over.

The effects of the death of a parent, and the abrupt loss of maternal love, on a child not yet five are incalculable: the sense of abandonment and uncertainty, the child's unspoken concern that it might be in some way to blame, the tendency to regress or to fall back on fantasies, the physically and emotionally stressful term of adjustment which in unresolved cases can become indefinite. Potocki was an adored, privileged and perceptive first son, who was living in a 'strange and lovely place' in a close and secure relationship with his mother. He remembers in the *Right Review*: 'My Aunt Blanche in later years repeatedly told me how my Mother adored me, and what hopes she entertained of me; and in a weak moment she even confided that my Mother's dying words to her were, that *she feared no one would understand her Geoffrey*.' He reflects that from an early age his mother had encouraged the strong sense that he was special, that he was 'destined to be a person of intelligence and talent'. He had believed he was 'a little prince . . . and had always been treated as such and dressed as such'. Looking back, he has an image of himself as 'strong, healthy, well-built, swift, and supple', as 'plump and formidable-looking'. He also recalls his early relationship with his father with fondness. 'Wladis', as his wife called Robert, was not often seen, but when available he was, like Annie Maud, 'always kind'.

It seemed to Potocki that Vallombrosa, the estate on which he was happily growing up—the four-hectare park in which his mother sat 'under the camphor laurel, and over the grave of the totara tree', which he used to climb—had been created especially for them 'by divine providence'. He writes in *Aristo:* 'Apart from shrubs . . . the garden was full of exotic monkey-puzzles and Morton-Bay [sic] figs in full growth, and even Old World trees . . . In one of the wild, luxuriant valleys, an enormous pear tree stood among the tall juicy grass: in another a dead kauri was covered with grape gone wild.' There were also 'big pohutukawas . . . sacerdotal mystic trees, whose foliage of silver, grey and green, and whose gnarled limbs, recall the sacred olive.' Most of his earliest memories are of this 'luxuriant, untidy garden'. In the *Right Review* he recalls 'running lithely about the leaf-strewn "Serpentine", which made a complete circle under the tall trees that surrounded the main lawn . . . that lovely Lady sitting on a Kaiapoi rug under the camphor-laurel, while seas of golden sunlight poured over the mountainous tops of the trees, on to the wide lawn, which on the far side was allowed to grow into forests of tall grass, high enough for us to hide in with ease . . . a hydrangea bush of prodigious size, that is about twenty feet in diameter, which looked like a bowl of lapis lazuli turned upside down on the grass.' He romped with Cedric in 'thickets of periwinkle, or in the forests of nasturtium', and hid inside 'the huge bushes of tekoma' where they had 'palaces where we escaped from our nurse, and could not be found'. And the house into which he capered across a verandah, through a lobby, into a large hall and onto a balustraded stairway, 'with long clear-golden locks flying behind me in the air, aware rather than conscious of being beautiful', was large, and light with his childhood energy.

Although he did not remember his mother 'very distinctly', scenes remained:

> I recall her sitting at an easel in the ball-room which my father had built on to the house for her. She is wearing a long black dress of her own design, in which she looks truly royal: for she has the beauty and the bearing of a Queen. She is painting a clay road skirting a forest. She had quite a reputation as a painter, but it is so long since I have seen any of her work that I can offer no opinion of its quality. It is perhaps worthy of note that one of her favourite subjects was a River, which I always took for the Waikato . . . Yet maybe rather she was thus painting our ancestral name: Potok, that is Stream, Torrent, Flood—the mystic River of Life.
>
> Another time I remember being alone in the house with her.

She is in a different, more homely dress of white linen. The servants are out, and she has cooked some lentils for me to eat. I say petulantly: 'I hate lentils, Mummy!' She replies that, seeing she has cooked the dinner for me with her own hands, I am a naughty boy to complain, and by way of punishment, we are going to finish our meal in the scullery. So we solemnly remove from the spacious kitchen into the scullery.

But I distinctly remember thinking to myself, 'I do not see how Mummy makes out she is punishing me, as she is coming to keep me company in the scullery herself.'

I also remember her habit of saying, when the doors opened of their own accord (from air pressure in the house, I suppose) that the *fox had done it*.

His last memory of his mother, however, is very clear: '. . . my Mother took me down to the barber in Newmarket and had him cut off my golden curls. I remember quite well this visit to the barber, who gave me a clay pipe to blow bubbles out of. My Mother was with me all the time in the barber's shop: I am sure she was not pleased with the transaction. Probably she had been browbeaten into it.

'"Maud, how much longer are you going to let that kid run round like Little Lord Fauntleroy out of a fairy story?"' Less than a month later his mother was dead.

The typescript tells us that the 'curse fell slowly', that the first thing that happened was the arrival of his paternal aunts Judith, Emily Littre and Victoria, and their mother—his Scots grandmother—who abandoned 'their gloomy dwelling at Mount Eden, and installed themselves at Vallombrosa'. It seems that in the beginning the children were well treated and 'respected as the victims of a great sorrow', but the considerations did not last:

> My Grandmother was an old tyrant, and I confess I never liked her. She was one of the Macalisters of Ascog, Buteshire, and as such descended from Angus, Lord of the Isles . . . She wore her hair in 'sausages' and had a 'frost-bite' in her nose. She used to sit in state in my Mother's bed and 'do' Madame la comtesse. The latest French newspapers were always very conspicuously displayed about her . . .

He remembers that once she declared his neck was dirty, and ordered him into the dressing room adjoining the Blue Room '(Mother's bed-room)' to wash it. When he returned she was not satisfied, and sent him back numerous times to wash it again.

> I washed my neck more and more carefully, and kept coming back to report, as if I were a recruit reporting to the sergeant, instead of being the heir of the house. There was no question now of being little Lord Fauntleroy, nor little Count Potocki either. At last Aunt Emily Littre happened to come in, and said to her mother: 'For God's sake leave off tormenting the boy, Ma. Can't you see his neck is sunburnt?'

But Aunt Emily is not remembered as 'guiltless'. Although she was a schoolteacher of some distinction, who studied the Montessori system in Sydney and, after her death, was remembered with a monument in the grounds of Mt Albert School inscribed 'Child, hear the music of her soul', she appears to have engaged in some disturbing behaviour at Vallombrosa. 'Her superiority to the other members of the family', writes Potocki, 'lay in the fact that she sincerely meant well, but fell a victim to her own passions. She was a first-class woman gone wrong ...' Her passions, as Potocki perceived them, 'had a profound influence' on his mind. 'For it is an eminent example', he says, 'of the wickedness of what passes as morality. What lack caused this horrible tragedy? Sex of course. At once all hands are held up in holy horror ... '

> She was passionate. Her hungered pulse raced when she saw such a chaste and beautiful boy and in consequence she used to whip me mercilessly round the back of my bare, attractive knees with switches of tekoma or with my Mother's riding whip. Afterwards I would find her kneeling beside her bed in the former nursery, asking God for forgiveness. I do not accuse her of hypocrisy in this. There is nothing as tragic as sexual frustration. I declare that if she had taken stock of her inmost desires, and carried them out intelligently, there would have been quite infinitely less harm done to herself and others than was done by her allowing her desires to be repressed regardless of the fact, that this inevitably led to desires which were worse, more harmful, and less pleasant in fruition. If the reader thinks I do not mean what he thinks I mean, then he is mistaken.

Potocki spends some time thinking about the strange behaviour of Aunt Emily. He rings two paragraphs and marks them 'later if at all'. One states that she was not married, that 'she ultimately went mad, and thus died', and that hers was 'the only case of insanity I have ever heard of in our family—and I may be conceded to know rather more about my ancestors, than is usual'. The other resurrects William Blake—'He who desires and acts not breeds pestilence'—and asks: 'Is it not certain that he was right? Christ taught us that the tree is known by its fruit (Luke VI 43,44.) Do the Christians perhaps think He was wrong? Are they sure they do not consider His teaching Jesuitical?'

A third paragraph, marked 'USE LATER', reads:

While on the subject of Aunt Emily, I may as well tell the reader that years later she was put away in the Avondale lunatic asylum, but after a while recovered . . . This must have been some seven or eight years after the War . . . At last she fell ill again, and one day I talked to her as she lay in bed. She went out of her way to ask my pardon for the way she had treated us at Vallombrosa. I fear I was not as gracious about it as I might have been, for I did indeed feel she had treated me badly, but I was touched also, for although most all of the members of our family have at one time or another treated me scurvily, Aunt Emily was the only one who ever had the goodness to ask pardon. And this will be put to the credit of her account by the Recording Gods. I pray that she will get in her next life on earth, all that was denied her this time.

Although Potocki spoke to me of being whipped as a child, he never widened the context, and I always assumed he referred to the thrashings his stepmother had given him. In the late 1980s, therefore, when I was working as a video examiner with the Video Recordings Authority and asked him how he felt about depictions of sexually explicit sado-masochism for home entertainment on video, I was surprised by his response. I had assumed that his horror of censorship would make for an interesting discussion, but his reply was unexpectedly brief. 'It should be banned,' he said emphatically. 'It'll give people ideas. They'll only want to copy it.'

Interestingly, while Potocki finds Emily and her whippings to have had a profound (but unexplained) effect on his mind, it is Judith, the less attractive, Christian aunt, he remembers with the most loathing. Described as the aunt 'whose very appearance showed how dangerously close our family had been sailing to the Mendelian wind', she is uncharitably remembered as being of dwarfish appearance with muddy eyes, hair like a fuzzy mop, and a disagreeable complexion. 'I cannot imagine which of our more immediate ancestral quarterings she represents,' he writes, 'but it was certainly none of the Polish ones.' As 'the star Christian of the family', who never had a conversation with or wrote a letter to him 'without preaching a sermon in it', Judith is seen as having been instrumental in encouraging him to become 'disgusted with Christianity'.

> When we were helpless children she used to drag us up into an alcove which was by a turn in the stairway, leading up one side of the 'hall', from the ground floor to the upper storey of our house, and there she would read us 'stories from the Bible'. This performance invariably filled me with loathing and disgust, and I intensely longed to escape. I am not sure that aunt Emily's whippings were not preferable.

Potocki believed Aunt Judith 'emanated a bad magnetic influence, which was depressing and unwholesome', and he felt this bitterly: 'She shed a blight on her whole surroundings, beautiful as they were . . . In these circumstances the fact that she was consistently put forward as the "good" woman of the family, might have had disastrous consequences moral or "psychological", had I not had an inborn love of the Good, which was proof even against aunt Judith.'

Reading about his early sensitivity to beauty, or, as in the case of Aunt Judith, an absence of beauty, I found myself wondering whether this was a window into Potocki's later preoccupation with the themes of beauty that underpinned so much of his poetry and seemed to pervade his thinking? The account of his early life as published in the *Right Review* suggests this period of his life was flooded with (and he was sensitive to) images of beauty: a mother loving and accomplished, a park glorious and carefree, the pampered life of a little prince. I wondered how real was this idealistic remembrance, this dream? Photographs of the two boys before Annie died certainly suggest indulgence: Geoffrey and Cedric dressed when small in 'short white linen frocks, cunningly embroidered little girls' drawers of white linen and lace'; Potocki when older in a 'well-designed suit of brown velvet'. And his description of this little suit in the *Right Review* even hints at his later, adult dislike of 'modern men's clothes', his preference for cloaks, sandals and medieval tunics:

> The wide collar and cuffs were overlaid with handmade lace. Round the waist was a broad silk sash of old-gold colour, with a fringe of tassels at the ends. The pants were short and showed at the knees. A pair of brown cashmere socks turned down below the knee, matched my neat little tan sandal-shoon. This with my golden hair made an image of real beauty—which is the one supreme natural end of man's desires.

'Any biographer,' he adds in brackets, 'or critic of my life who does not consider in its pride of place, my consuming love of beauty under all her forms, will be at the best an unjust hypocrite.'

I also found myself asking how enduring was the influence of the 'Golden Idyll', how precious during the dark years of his stepmother; and how far were those dark years responsible for reinforcing this preoccupation with beauty, for rendering the earlier childhood experience all the more memorable and precious? 'My environment,' he would write, 'consistently tried to kill this beauty in me—and only succeeded in strengthening it.' And how black were those years really, and how golden the idyll, the 'glow of well-being, of scented sunshine, and of maternal love' that had made Vallombrosa 'seem eternal, seem Heaven'? In 1939 he had written: 'And now nothing remains of Vallombrosa as I then knew it, but the impression its beauty left upon my mind.'

Searching for confirmation that Potocki's memories of his mother were not only the idealised notions of absence and loss, I came across a letter from Robert to Potocki, who had been seeking details of his mother, sixteen years after her death. Robert had written:

> ... As my sweetheart and wife—just incomparable—she was my real mate and we never kept the smallest thing unknown to the other—the good with the unfortunate alike—she was very timid yet very brave if the occasion warranted—She would have gone into a lion's den and thro' fire to save me from any harm or to save you or Cedric (she only knew her little Dulce for 9 days.) She was

a sweet, loving, brave, useful loyal woman of the effeminate type of female, a darling. If anyone ever went to heaven she did. God bless her loving soul for ever and ever amen.

I found that Robert's further descriptions of Annie Maud's grace and charm placed her convincingly in the idyll that Potocki remembered as Vallombrosa:

> She was medium height and dark and with a good and graceful bearing and good looking—handsome. She could do [anything] whatever—I often used to tell her that she could build a battle ship if given the material. In the house a splendid housewife, great cook of anything from first to last which even can be put on a cake—and did all this economically: She could and did design and make her own dresses . . . Was most artistic in arranging the house and could make nice furniture out of a cardboard box or two and some soft material. Was a very fair painter in oils particularly—better than most . . . could play violin and concertina . . . really so much she could do. She was a loyal friend to her friends and was often consulted by them as she had such a clear understanding—she was a born diagnoser of diseases and a born nurse . . .

And what of Vallombrosa, the paradise of his childhood—Blue Room, Terracotta Room, Ballroom—the 'fairly large house' designed by architect Robert, with its 'great crimson curtains' and steep Marseille tiles? What of the romantic park, purchased to entice a wife to the other side of the world? Was there a paradisal clue in the name: a town on the northern slope of the Pratomagno mountains, a valley east of Florence? I'd never thought to ask Potocki when he was alive. Browsing through the first of his three autobiographical volumes in Polish, I found mention of Milton, and the sense of Vallombrosa I was seeking in the strangely appropriate *Paradise Lost*, i.303:

> Nathless he so endur'd, till on the Beach
> Of that inflamed Sea, he stood and calld
> His Legions, Angel Forms, who lay intranc't
> Thick as Autumnal Leaves that strow the Brooks
> In Vallombrosa, where th'Etrurian shades
> High overarcht imbowr;

Despite the sometimes misguided ministrations of Grandmother de Montalk and the three aunts (the third aunt now in residence was Victoria, who was 'a typist and was at that time completely innocuous, as a typist should be'), life at Vallombrosa seems to have continued in an otherwise secure manner for the first four years following the death of Annie Maud. The typescript reports that the other members of Potocki's father's large family visited, he saw members of his mother's family, and holidays were taken. It recalls especially a holiday he had in the home of Aunt Jeannie in Opotiki, where he enjoyed one of his 'few experiences of a kindly human atmosphere . . . so rare a thing from that time on, that it glimmers still in my memory'.

In 1910, at the age of seven, he started school at nearby King's College, a private Anglican grammar school. Here, he enjoyed the opening of school with prayers in Hall, and in particular the prayer 'Prevent us, O Lord' on account of its beauty. He was also 'enormously delighted by the tasselled banner of red and gold' which figured in the football competitions, even though he never, at any time of his life, willingly took part in football or any other sporting activities.

At about this time, Potocki decided that he was a poet by Divine Right. 'I did a lot of wondering about words when I was a child,' he once told me, 'trying to find out in what way they might be associated with their meaning.' He also experienced feelings that he was special: 'When I was quite young, by Grandmother's side,' he said, 'and they sang in church "And thou, child, shalt be called to the prophet of the highest, and thou shalt go before the face of the Lord to prepare his ways", I always considered that that referred to me. And it never entered my head that it referred to anybody else in the church.' He believed this response to have been a sign of the 'general sense of consecration and destiny' that from then on pervaded his life. Weeks's study of eccentricity reports that most eccentrics became aware that they were different when children because 'they were constantly searching for underlying answers', noting that at least two-thirds of his sample became aware or were told that they were different between seven and nine years. It seems that how this happened, why they felt it and how they acted on it is almost invariably a defining moment in the life of an eccentric. Weeks also found that, although sometimes a chance event was sufficient to trigger the notion, situations which caused children to feel isolated 'often contributed to the development of their eccentricity'.

At the age of eight Potocki began to write poetry. His first poems, written lying on the dining-room carpet in front of the fire, were about 'the matters that exercised my mind—the Battles of La Haye Sainte, Quatre Bras, Dettingen . . . I rimed Sainte with faint'. His father commended him on his poems and gave him a silver threepence, telling Potocki he was glad he was so clever, and he was rewarding him because he wanted to encourage him always to do everything well. 'Unfortunately my Father was not satisfied with giving me threepence. He gave me some free advice on making Poetry as well. He counted the syllables in each line of my poems, and persuaded me that my good natural rhythm was wrong. Later, for Christmas of 1913 he made me a present of a fairly complete Tennyson. He told me that this was to put me on the right track in Poetry, and was a further reward for the verses I had begun to write some time before.'

On one occasion, he was caned for admitting he had not learnt the required reading lesson at home. In vain he tried to explain to the headmaster that as he already knew it there had been no need, but he was caned none the less. In class he found the pace slow and tended to be bored. There was also an incident which he was later to view as significant. In the typescript, he recalls the afternoon when, having left his ruler at home, he asked the boy he sat next to in class if he could borrow his ruler.

'I'll lend it to you if you write fuck on your blotting-paper,' was the reply.

'All right,' said Potocki.

'Write it very small, so small you can hardly see it.'

Potocki obliged and, as he had to borrow the ruler many times that afternoon, he wrote the required word neatly, many times.

That evening at home his father pounced on the blotting-paper, and said: 'Who wrote this, my boy?'

'I did, Dad.'

'You did?'

'Yes.'

'I don't believe you can write as small as that.'

'Yes, I did write it, Dad. I can write very small.'

'Well, let me see you do it again.'

So Potocki took up a pen and wrote the word again.

A couple of days later his classmate was brought before the assembled primer school and caned. 'He was hoisted up on some sort of desk for the purpose. I distinctly remember having viewed the whole thing with that familiar sense of unreality. Nor had I had the notion that I was in any way responsible. When I come to think of it, it must have had a fine effect on my popularity at College (not that a trifle of that sort would worry my Father).'

Meanwhile, at Vallombrosa, Geoffrey and Cedric—although now less loved, less indulged and, in Geoffrey's case, sometimes thrashed—remained in settled and familiar routines: the milk boy still delivered milk in large pails from the Jersey cows which lived in the valley at the edge of the estate free to the Baptist orphan home nearby, the entire park was still theirs to play in and, after a period of mourning, the balls were revived. Potocki remembers: 'The Ballroom was draped as before with flags and festooned with lycopodeum, women danced past in their rustling dresses . . . Chinese lanterns hung on the trees.' One morning after such a ball he took a tour with Cedric 'round the huge tables still spread in the dining room. We ate some of the trifles, soaked as they were with wine, but the wine itself, which we sipped out of some glasses that had stood overnight, we did not care for.' There was still no doubt in his mind that, despite the absence of his mother, he remained a special eldest child, he retained his place as the 'Heir'.

# THREE

## Boyhood and Adolescence

*Life in New Zealand is a wonderful training for a future King—a superb lesson in 'How a nation ought not to be governed'.*

In 1912, life at Vallombrosa took 'a sudden turn for the worse'. Grandmother de Montalk died on 29 December 1911, and Robert, who was rebuilding the Cargen, a large hotel in Auckland, met a Miss Evelyn Hickson (a boarder in the original hotel), took her to Wellington, and married her.

'One day of evil omen—though a sunny day—they came back,' writes Potocki in the typescript. 'It was the summer (I think October). They came slithering down the preposterous gravelled declivity called "Westbourne Road", in a large, uncomely grey touring car with the hood down. I stood up on the stump of a huge tree near the gate, and waved a handkerchief in welcome (my God!) and then I clambered down, and opened the gate for them.' The new reign was introduced by Robert leading Geoffrey and Cedric, one in each hand, through the high velvet curtains of the hall into the drawing room, and having them kiss a recent 'distasteful enlargement of Bartlett's fine photograph' of their mother. Robert then told them they were to call the new lady 'Mummy Darling', the result of which was that, although Cedric called her Mummy, or Mum, Potocki refused to call her anything but Mother.

The typescript paints a dismal picture of the new order. For reasons never explained (perhaps financial misfortune was a factor), Evelyn (or Lulu as Potocki's father called his new wife) 'lost no time in beginning to starve us'. The first meal she served the children on taking over the management of the household was 'scanty' and had to be eaten in the kitchen. 'We were permanently relegated to the kitchen from the very day of Lestes' [Evelyn's] arrival, and except for Sundays were fed (or starved) in the kitchen, until 1918.' Then, after a few days, the children were put on what was remembered as a régime of proper starvation rations for keeps: 'Before this she had cut up a lot of bread and put it on a plate in the middle of the table. Now however she alleged that I took the "lion's share" and in order to rectify this injustice she gave us a permanent and equal allowance per person (three of us) the total amount of which did not come to half the former amount. From this time on, we had a ration, like prisoners, fixed by immutable law.' The equal allowance took no account of the children's ages: Potocki, an active and hungry nine-year-old boy, received the same serving as Dulce, aged four.

The restrictions on food, writes Potocki, together with a deepening loss of good will at the formerly harmonious Vallombrosa, 'shocked and annoyed the servants', who left and could not be replaced. 'No one would come to be entertained, she offended everyone, and in this way my Father as an architect was quickly ruined . . . In this connection the very just annoyance of the Vailes was of great importance, but quite apart from this, "Lestes" [a robber, a plunderer], as I christened her when I began to learn Greek, made it impossible for my Father to have friends or to entertain even in a small way. Clearly this would ruin any professional man.' With the servants gone, Geoffrey and Cedric were now required to carry out household chores: shoe cleaning, washing up, preparation of vegetables and sweeping and scrubbing the floors. They were also required to spend any time they had spare doing the gardening, and in deference to their newly perceived status as servants they were dressed in 'the most horrible caricatures of clothes that could be thought of . . . not just old shorts and patched shirt like working-class children. Far from it. She conscientiously contrived every possible means for making us look undignified, grotesque, and scare-crow like . . . ' This humiliation, bitterly felt by Potocki, was to have lasting consequences:

> I was by nature beautiful, talented, trustworthy, and kind . . . and a violent reaction against this, a determination to raise my head *coute que coute* [cost what it may], and to raise it higher than ever is the only explanation (taken with heredity) that is necessary for my subsequent tactics . . . I fear it is impossible to convey to readers, who have not the same fierce love of beauty, the agony it was to me to feel myself dressed in such degrading clothes . . . Of course if

visitors arrived—a rare enough event in those days—the beldame would say: 'Go on, skidaddle, you kids, and put your good clothes on.' Then we would appear all nicely dressed, and very polite, and people would think: well, one hears funny rumours, but they seem to be well looked-after, and they don't say anything.

Early in 1913, a year after Evelyn's arrival, Potocki and his brother were removed from King's College and sent to the state school in Remuera. Here, Potocki met the future poet Rex Fairburn, who, because of a change in school zoning, had temporarily transferred to Remuera Primary School from Parnell. 'I well remember one day when Fairburn walked home with me. We halted by a grove of butterfly-lit grass in Westbourne Crescent, not far from Vallombrosa, while he explained to me lucidly his opinion of algebra. His definition would almost do for an Encyclopaedia—something about manipulating unwieldy masses of figures, by using alphabetical symbols in their stead.' It was a definition Potocki 'heard and remembered, but understood not a whit'. Fairburn later professed to have an equally quirky first memory of Potocki. 'He [Fairburn] says we met one day in the latrine in the school grounds. It appears I attacked him with an etymological problem. "When you say, Miss Norton's crabby you mean she has a bad temper. But really it means she has crabs crawling all over her. Just the same if you say, Mr Crawshaw's ratty, you mean he's got a bad temper. But it really means he has rats running up and down him."'

At home, Potocki continued to be haunted by hunger:

The starvation kept getting worse and worse . . . We used to empty the tea-pot (which was part of our duty as household slaves) into a coffee tin, which we kept in a hole in a huge tree that had been felled years ago and still lay between the kitchen and the fowl run. Then when we were feeling our hunger too much, we used to go and drink some of these accumulated stale tea dregs. But it so happened that Lestes' sister, Hessie, and her husband, a schoolteacher named White-Scott, came to stay for a fortnight at Vallombrosa . . . She [Hessie] was a pleasant person, well-built, and of a kindly mien; and the same applies to her husband . . . At all events, she kept her eyes open to such good purpose, that she discovered our secret vice . . . She was horrified. Of course we were drinking almost pure tannin. But she must have said something pretty scathing to Bob and Lulu, for hardly a word was uttered to us except: 'It's a wonder you haven't got ptomaine poisoning.' (Although as a rule breaches of discipline were punished with a rigour to which prison is milk.) And Bob and Lulu were strangely subdued about the whole business.

The rigour with which Evelyn responded to her stepchildren is typified by her reaction when Cedric became ill with the mumps. Cedric, having his tea, suddenly felt sick and vomited into a pot he had grabbed from the table. In his haste, however, he knocked cubes of dry bread from his plate into the pot. Evelyn then demanded he eat the wet cubes so as not to waste them. 'My blood boils when I think of that,' Potocki had added by hand.

Many pages in the typescript are taken up with memories of hunger and with the injustice of being singled out for meagre rations in what Potocki believes was still an affluent household. On Robert's perceived ignorance of the situation, he remembers that on Sundays, when he, Cedric and Dulce were permitted to eat in the dining room and his father, and perhaps an occasional guest, could see what they were eating, Evelyn went to some trouble to create an impression that their helpings were more generous than they actually were: 'for instance she would lay a piece of bread on a wide plate, and pour a thin hash of mincemeat and gravy over it'. Also that she 'always cut the bread in quadrangles tending to triangular shape, so as to get four out of a slice from a tin loaf'. On not asking for more, he explains that 'It could not be done without occasioning a first-class "row", the effects of which lasted for weeks.'

Potocki recalls his stepmother as intimidating. He describes her as a dark-eyed, dark-haired and sallow-complexioned woman, well built, and 'of a stiff and artificial carriage, [who] when on show looked quite aristocratic in an unpleasant manner'. Her features are remembered as 'good—though distinctly semitic' (this last comment added in ink), her expression as unpleasant—'at best a quizzical grin, and at worst, a horrid scowl'—and her neck as always covered with a lace net, 'supported with concealed bits of whalebone'.

She is charged with innumerable acts of pettiness. For instance, she is believed to have cancelled the Sunday visits of the children to the home of the Vaile grandparents and the two aunts, Blanche and Evelyn, to whom they had become so attached. Potocki had found the Vailes' home, Twyford, also designed by Robert, to have a 'beneficent aura, and a good spell [which] was most real'. Here, since before the death of their mother, amid the 'beautifully stuffed Bird of Paradise in a dome-topped cylindrical glass cabinet', their grandfather's sword, an array of table silver, bowls and trays, they had been served Sunday dinner cooked by Aunt Blanche, 'a first class cook'. Blanche, whose outlook was strongly royalist, 'had some marvellous Satsuma vases in her room, and used to tell me how a "little Jap" spent a whole lifetime making one, beating tiny bits of pure gold into it, till it was finished'. He believed that Evelyn, who hated the idea of their getting one huge, good meal a week, arranged for them to visit Twyford after school on Thursdays so that no meal was involved. Nevertheless, he and Cedric spent a good deal of time in the pantry, eating lumps of brown sugar or sugared lemon-peel. Blanche, who was likely to have attributed their presence in the pantry to boyish gluttony, would say to them: 'I always call my pantry your Happy Hunting Ground.' But the boys never told her of their predicament. 'The fact that we did not tell her of our woes,' says the typescript, 'shows how completely terrorized we were.'

Evelyn also kept them close to the house, laying down boundaries beyond which they were not permitted to pass, so that they rarely played in, or even got to see, the 'exciting gullies and thickets' on the outer reaches of the property. And she instituted a 'diabolical piece of torture [which] she would certainly pretend if taxed with it, was actually for our benefit'. Each evening she required the boys to do arithmetical calculations 'running into the millions'. If one answer was wrong, two more sums had to be done in its place, and no reading was permitted until the task had been completed. While Cedric later told his brother that these sums gave him no trouble—'at a later stage of his career he could add up five columns of pounds, with shillings, pence, and farthings, simultaneously in his head'—they caused the more creatively wired Potocki 'much anguish'.

For a time it was possible for me to assume that the inhospitable household, the departure of the servants, the restrictions on the children's food and the other problems during Evelyn's first eighteen months at Vallombrosa were indeed financial in origin and not wholly of her making, or necessarily as vindictive as Potocki perceived them to be—particularly when the typescript revealed that, in May 1914, Robert came to a realisation that as an architect he was facing financial ruin.

As I read on, however, there seemed little doubt that Evelyn, a single woman who came to the marriage with no children of her own, and did not subsequently have any, resented and was threatened by the responsibility of stepchildren. I concluded that these tensions, together with Robert's newly straitened circumstances, led to an approach to child-rearing which was not merely misguided but frequently deliberately abusive.

This situation was not uncommon for children of this period. Tuberculosis and childbirth claimed many young mothers, and my own mother frequently spoke with sadness of the pervasive effect of the emotional neglect and coldness of her own stepmother. Furthermore, as Robert's letter to Potocki had shown, Robert had been deeply in love with his first wife, and remained so as long as sixteen years after she died.

I also found myself wondering whether, framed against New Zealand at the turn of the century and its attitudes to raising children— boys in particular—Potocki's childhood was in fact markedly harsher than that of many others. The country was, after all, emerging from sixty years as a frontier society. The concept of male character and colonial vigour, with endurance and hardship essential components, was still strong. Given this setting, were the effects of Potocki's boyhood likely to have been unduly profound? But I wondered only briefly. Having sat with the typescript, its painful account in my hands, I felt that generalised comparisons were distasteful. They ignored individual states of emotional fragility and all-important considerations of context; and they took no account of the complexities of temperament, or heredity—to call in Potocki's old war-horse. Of more pressing concern was the extent to which cruelty or disregard might have an impact on a psyche still stunned by the premature death of a parent, particularly a mother.

The typescript offers no reason for the downturn in Robert's fortunes, apart from Potocki's assumption (based on information 'communicated' to him by Robert's 'confidant, Cedric', in 1933) that Evelyn's inadequacies were in some way to blame. Perhaps Samuel Vaile's financial assistance, previously available to his son-in-law if and when architectural assignments were lean, ceased when Robert remarried. The maintenance costs of a property as grand as Vallombrosa would have been considerable, and the small income from Grandfather Vaile's trust which provided for his grandchildren's 'maintenance, education, and advancement in life' was unavailable for such use. But was there a lessening in architectural assignments? At first I thought this unlikely—by all accounts Robert was a competent and innovative architect who was particularly remembered for his pioneering work with concrete. Then I found several references to Robert's career in *Cast in Concrete*, a book by Geoffrey Thornton, which introduces Robert as having been 'interested in concrete construction from the turn of the century', confirms that in 1912 in Auckland 'the New Zealand born Robert Wladislas de Montalk designed and built the Hotel Cargen in reinforced concrete', and states that 'At the time the Auckland Master Builders' Association strongly opposed the use of this method as a new fangled idea and its members engaged in a boycott for a period.' As there was no further mention of Robert's career until 1919, when 'he produced a design for an interesting concrete house in Wellington'—a house which was 'innovative in having a total concrete concept' with walls, columns, beams, rafters and roof tiles all concrete—it did not seem unreasonable to conclude that Robert's financial downturn might have been connected to controversy over his preference for concrete over wood or brick as a building material.

The only other comments I found on the subjects of Robert's solvency and architectural career were Potocki's statement in an article in the *Wanganui Chronicle* dated 3 March 1984, following a visit to Mangaweka, that his father 'turned from architecture to farming and the family's prosperity faded badly'; and a remark in a letter to Potocki from Uncle Ted Vaile in 1936: 'His judgement in business affairs is worse than useless and has reduced his own substance to starvation point.'

It is possible that Potocki explained the downturn in his father's fortunes in a manuscript I have not yet seen. It is also likely that he found it convenient, if not gratifying, to attribute responsibility to his stepmother, and to leave his father, who he believed had betrayed him— and continued to do so by denying Potocki's pain and his complicity— in an ambiguous and incompetent role. What does finally emerge, however, is Evelyn's financial interest in Vallombrosa through Robert's 'second marriage settlement', entered in pencil by Potocki as '£1,250 if I remember rightly', and the possibility that financial considerations had in part brought about their marriage.

Whatever the reason, in May 1914 Robert sold his practice, Vallombrosa was leased to a printer, and the family was relocated on a hundred acres of farm at Alfriston, a small rural settlement south of Auckland, a few kilometres inland from Manurewa, and, coincidentally, a short distance from the new site of a former neighbour, the Baptist orphan home. Robert, who had purchased the land, planned to farm it himself.

The typescript offers a bleak description of the family's new home. Potocki, who by now was a stressed child very possibly suffering from depression, perceived 'The whole place, in fact the whole district [to be] bleak and desolate.' He remembers the farm as long and narrow, the homestead as 'a miserable dwelling of about five rooms, with some contiguous outbuildings in which our farm hand slept', and the area around the house as 'a paltry field of mangolds, and a bit of a vegetable garden, in which stood a large apricot tree'. A handwritten note in ink in the margin of the typescript advises that Robert had paid 'too much for the land, and was cheated over the cattle'.

Life at Alfriston is described as 'a perpetual nightmare of misery', from which Potocki's only relief was 'the solemn loveliness of the native forest' or 'looking for the curious green orchids, or sitting blissfully on top of a nikau palm, like Brahma on his lotus'. The cattle were 'unlovely', the starvation 'bad' and Geoffrey and Cedric, who were forced to go barefoot even in winter in frost-covered grass, developed chilblains, cracks and then sores on their feet, and 'as a result of starvation naturally became horribly constipated'. Evelyn was unsympathetic. 'Come on, you,' she would say roughly when treating the painful lesions on their feet, 'put your foot up there.'

Each morning the boys rose at six from 'a squalid little room off the kitchen', and carried out work, as allotted by Evelyn, before breakfast. This work, the need for which may have resulted as much from a shortage of farm labour following the outbreak of the First World War as from financial shortfall, was resumed on return from school, a walk of several kilometres each way. One of the worst jobs was grubbing—cutting blackberry, or gorse with its tough woody branches and stems, out by the roots with a mattock made for a full-grown labourer. Harry, the farmhand, is said to have pitied them—their daily struggles with the huge mattock and brambles, their jarred wrists, their underfed state—'for though he was mighty badly fed himself, he used to give us some of the ridiculously small potatoes which formed part of his diet'. Also remembered are the sips of his mushroom ketchup that Harry gave them. 'It was maybe one of the worst sins of my life,' writes Potocki, 'that when dying with hunger I used to run into his shed like a hunted rat, and drink some of his ketchup without his permission.'

School too was unsatisfactory. The building itself 'consisted of one fairly large room and a porch, standing in the usual dreary acre, which however, actually boasted a few macrocarpa trees', and the teaching was mostly undertaken by pupil teachers. And there was scandal. Knowledge of sexual assignations in the nearby forest, in which Potocki, then aged eleven, claims he was far too green to take any part, resulted in Cedric, aged nine, boasting that—as Potocki has discreetly typed in the script—he had '------' someone. A school friend asked the brothers, now deemed to be experienced in such matters, if they would take a message to the oldest girl in the school and ask her if 'she would let him swive her'. The girl in question replied that she would like to but was fearful of becoming pregnant.

The matter came to the attention of Robert and Evelyn when the boys discussed it at home one Sunday morning and were overheard. Potocki was called to his parents' bedroom and by threatening means had the story extracted from him. 'It was the same as the King's College affair, only much worse. They did not succeed in getting the word ---- out of me. The most they could earn was by way of the circumlocution, that Cedric "got on top of" the girl concerned.' Cedric was then called to account, but on giving evidence he attempted to normalise the situation by saying 'Geoffrey got on top of Lukaszewski [a classmate] too,' as indeed he had, when wrestling in the playground.

The result was that Potocki found himself 'saddled with a monstrous and unjust accusation of homosexuality . . . Thus, the one success I had scored in withstanding their brutal third degree, that of substituting for the word ----, the phrase "get on top of", was turned to my own and everyone's worst disadvantage.' His father, picturing the school as a 'hot-bed of sodomy as well as mere fornication', reported the matter. The schoolmistress was suspended, an education board inquiry was held, and the children were removed and made to attend the school at Manurewa.

Holidays with the de Montalk cousins were also stopped because the boys were told 'I had "got on top of" Lukaszewski.' This was a serious matter, as such holidays had hitherto constituted the 'only relief from the Hell we were living in'. The year 1914 was recalled by Potocki as one of the worst of his life. He was frequently beaten by Evelyn, who 'continued and aggravated the tradition which she had inaugurated at Vallombrosa, of whipping us ferociously and sadistically on the slightest pretext or on no pretext, with our Mother's riding whip.' (He wonders here whether comments 'made about aunt Emily' do not apply 'in a more sinister nuance'.)

Always hungry, he incurred her wrath by complaining to his father about the lack of food. He would waylay Robert and complain that they didn't get enough to eat, or that they were starved, as a result of which there would be a row. Cedric would stand in with him during the rows but, as the more placid middle child who as a follower was not as inclined to attract the attention of Evelyn, he would later make peace with her. Potocki, as the eldest and hungriest, and forced to take the role of instigator, bore the brunt of family discipline. He would sulk afterwards, sometimes for weeks.

Part of the food problem was that, as at Vallombrosa, each of the children continued to be served exactly the same portion. In 1914, Potocki was eleven, Cedric nine and Dulce six. Having never known her mother, Dulce was brought up by Evelyn to believe she was her daughter, and in these circumstances is said to have received nurturing and sufficient food. But the boys were forced to steal raw porridge, treacle and dripping from the pantry whenever they could, and particularly when their parents drove with Dulce to Papakura. They did not attempt to slice the bread, for this would have been noticed, but the dripping was cut, carefully, following the edges of previous cuts. One day they climbed an apricot tree and ate until they 'nearly burst'. When Robert suggested he learn how to milk, Potocki, sensing a nutritional opportunity, quickly learnt to do so and drank when he could from the bucket. From this time on, he had a passion for milk. Later, milk and cows assumed a godlike status in his life: 'Is not Vach, the melodious cow, the Mother of Music? Is not Lakshme, whose name is milk (lait, mleko, milch, milk) the same Goddess as Aphrodite.'

At Manurewa school their classmates made donations of food from their lunches, and children from the Baptist orphan home gave them their 'fat sandwiches of melonjam'. The walk to school is remembered as a particular misery. Although the distance of five kilometres was not great, it was painful and therefore interminable, for, while Dulce was taken in the cart, Geoffrey and Cedric, always hungry, walked in all weathers in bare feet: feet 'frozen, bloodless' and perpetually covered with stone bruises. 'I once got a stone-bruise so bad that a doctor had to be called in to lance it,' writes Potocki.

On one occasion Evelyn struck him on the forehead with an iron poker. The wound bled profusely, as head wounds do. Hoping that if he could present his bloodied face to his father some sort of justice would be done, he made a rush for the door. But Evelyn made a furious dash for the door also, and stood there 'with arms akimbo, brandishing the poker'. Potocki was driven into the bathroom and made to wash away the blood and wait for the wound to settle. When it had dried he was sent out to find his father and complain. But by this time the injury, although dangerously near the temple, 'had no journalistic value' and Evelyn, 'knowing what to expect, was all ready with cajolements and sex. They held one of their Beds of Injustice and I was betrayed.'

Issues of injustice and betrayal were starting to assume importance in Potocki's thinking amid 'misery that seemed to have no visible ending', the deliverance from which in being 'grown up seemed a literal eternity away'. He wanted to write to his mother's family, the Vailes, and complain about their 'pitiful state' but, understandably, he did not believe that anyone would support him against the authority of his father. And he constantly devised schemes for running away. He retreated into fantasy, and a determination grew to 'incorporate into my heart every image of beauty' and to pour onto himself 'the loveliness of Poetry'.

Years later, writes Potocki, without any complaint from his side, his uncle Edward Vaile told him that he had come to the conclusion all was not well and had asked Robert if he would allow Vaile to take his nephew from the farm, bring him up and 'ultimately send him to Oxford'. Robert had agreed, but only on condition that Vaile, who was developing his huge estate, Broadlands, in the central North Island (described in Vaile's account of the venture, *Pioneering the Pumice*, as 'one of the largest freehold estates in New Zealand'), sent his nephew to school in Christchurch. 'Had my uncle had me educated at Auckland, with holidays on his estate—53,000 acres [21,000 hectares] near Rotorua—everybody would have known exactly what had happened.' Vaile, who lived ten kilometres from his nearest neighbour, and twenty-two kilometres from post and telephone facilities, had been uncertain as to the best course of action, and had let matters be.

The new venture at Alfriston also created tension between Robert and Evelyn. The children witnessed frequent rows, most of which were about money, and in which Evelyn would refer to Vallombrosa as a white elephant. Potocki recalls a terrible row in the backyard, during which she taunted Robert with 'When I married you, you told me you had a thousand a year. If you hadn't told me that you know perfectly well that I would never have married you!' That evening she told the children that the printer who had leased the property did not pay the rent, and that she had to pay the interest on the mortgage, the rates and taxes, and the repairs, just the same, and would be better off without 'bally old Vallombrosa'. Shortly after this row, Vallombrosa, which Potocki describes as 'morally our property as being bought with Mother's dowry, [and] legally our property by virtue of my Father's second marriage settlement', was sold 'for a figure so low, as to amount to a fraud' and subdivided.

Evelyn was also scornful of the Potocki heritage and, when her husband was not present, lost no time in telling the children that Polish counts didn't count, and that in Poland counts were two a penny. She would refer to their great-grandfather, Count Józef, as 'a Greasy Pole or a Dotty Dalmatian', and she dismissed their mother as 'a common woman, the daughter of a shopkeeper'.

In October 1915, Robert de Montalk managed to exchange the unprofitable farm at Alfriston for a small holding, which included a fruit farm and some letting cottages, at Mangaweka, a small rural community near Taihape, in the Rangitikei district. Potocki terminates the typescript account of his childhood at this point and moves briefly to 1921 and young adulthood. Presumably the years between were less stressful and, as he grew older, the power of his stepmother lessened and the tension and depression lifted, for he writes less of them (although there is his statement that he had been fed, or starved, in the kitchen until 1918, at which time he had matriculated and was about to start work as a student teacher). The principal facts to emerge from this period are that Potocki, aged twelve, made his first literary connection in the person of the editor of the small weekly newspaper the *Mangaweka Settler*, and had his first poem published. When asked once, he was unable to remember anything about this poem, apart from the fact that 'The editor improved it, to my knowledge—that's what editors do.' The following year he topped the country in the examination for entrance to secondary school. A letter sent by Potocki in 1919 to the education board in Christchurch, seeking a position as a junior teacher, states that he achieved this distinction with 716 marks, 'which was 79 marks more than those gained by any other candidate'.

It was something of a relief to come to the end of Potocki's account of his childhood. The emotional intensity of the years in which he had been most vulnerable to and affected by 'Lestes' had made uncomfortable reading. I was surprised, therefore, to realise, when I started noting the chronology of events, that the most relentless section of his childhood had in fact encompassed only three years. This led me to reflect on the strangeness of time, which is long and stretches for ever in childhood and remains so in the memory even as adulthood shrinks and becomes but a moment; and on his later imprisonment in Wormwood Scrubs, viewed now in the light of his childhood; and on the extent to which the helplessness and hunger of his imprisonment would have held special significance for him.

I also thought about the nature of memory—its disorder, its transience, its capacity for attracting stray information—and the truth of memory—the way in which one person's remembered truth differs from that of another—and about the elusive nature of the man whose truth I had just been reading: his large sense of himself, his reputation for self-presentation. Apart from some letters sent by Robert rejecting his son's recollection of events, I had no clear means of assessing the veracity of Potocki's account of his childhood, and in particular the harsh account of his stepmother. All the other immediate witnesses to this period of his life—Evelyn, his brother and his sister—are of course dead. Yet despite the absence of balance there was no question of my not considering it. Yes, it is subjective; yes, it is very likely to be selective, and some of the details may not be as others might have remembered them. Nevertheless, completed as it was in the stress of his life following his trial and imprisonment—in his need to understand his non-conformity, its origins, and his increasing rejection by society—and extending beyond this stress to his eccentricity as it was now developing, I believed the account to be an important aspect of his reconstruction. These were things he had known in his bones and felt in his heart. They were his truths, and as such truths I could work with.

In any case, could there ever have been independent verification? Robert, facing financial ruin, unable to resolve the loss of his beloved Annie Maud, appears to have either not noticed or closed his mind to the events of those years, while Cedric, two years younger, less consciously aware of the death of his mother, less hungry, less harshly treated, perhaps as the middle child more pragmatic, appears to have made his peace—at least outwardly—with his stepmother (although Cedric did leave his son with the impression that his childhood had been a hard one). Only Dulce, raised as Evelyn's own child, seems to have left a firm acknowledgment that this was an unhappy time. In 1955, in a letter sent to Potocki, then living in France, Dulce, who had gone on to train as a nurse, had written of their childhood: 'I consider it a very great asset in life since it enabled me to learn so much of the human mind.'

Independent verification aside, however, it seemed to me that the childhood connections to his later preoccupations and aspects of his eccentricity were too compelling, too truthful, if you like, to ignore. I wondered, therefore, to what extent the unconscious foundations of Potocki's eccentricity lay in his childhood: in his long hair, the cutting of which was the last memory of his mother before her death; in the archaic and unconventional clothing designed by a mother whose devotion made him believe he was special, princely, even kingly; in the nurture of Vallombrosa and its beauty, heightened for ever in his mind by the treatment of his stepmother; in the need to retreat into fantasy, to seek the solace of poetry. There was also Evelyn's denigration of his ancestry: perhaps this helped to give rise to his obsession with his aristocratic connections. And there was his young boy's sense of helplessness and adult betrayal: perhaps this resulted in the rebellious and anti-establishment stance which started in young manhood, and achieved free reign on his release from prison.

FOUR

## Young Manhood and Marriage

*The sun is out at Lammastide, and in the sky
the first aeroplane of spring.*

In 1917 Robert moved the family again, this time to Nelson. That year Potocki, now a boarder at Christchurch Boys' High School, won the IIIA form prize for excellence in English, French, Latin and history. He appears to have been happy at Boys' High. Doubtless the headmaster, C.E. Bevan-Brown, a classical scholar, described in *The Years Between: Christchurch Boys' High School 1881—1981*, as 'a companionable man' with a friendly face, the common touch and an infinite capacity for putting his students at their ease, both assisted and influenced him that year.

In 1918 they were in Wellington, where Robert set about re-establishing himself as an architect, and Potocki attended Wellington College, referred to in *Recollections of My Fellow Poets*, without further explanation, as 'that perfectly horrible school'. Here he won the Eichelbaum Literature Prize for Form IVA and a Senior Free Place without exam. He also sat and passed the Matriculation exam 'from IVA, which according to the master who took the entries (one Fritz Renner) was unheard of. It was at least one class too early, and he tried hard to prevent me from putting my name down for the examination.'

A neatly written letter from Potocki to 'Auntie Evelyn', sent from 61 Majoribanks Street, Wellington and dated 2 January 1919, presents Potocki as a polite and perhaps somewhat unworldly fifteen-year-old boy:

Yesterday, New Year's Day, went for a swim at Oriental Bay. I have never had a swim at a beach before, as I only learnt to swim last Xmas . . . it is quite different from swimming in the baths, the water being fresher, and besides the gentle swell of the waves is rather nice. There were a good many people (mostly children) bathing, and still more looking on. I think that perhaps the nicest place to bathe is in a shingly slow moving river. Did you bathe in the Waikato? Ced and I used to fish on the wharves here and at Nelson, but we caught only 'spotties' (perch). With love from Geoff, thanking you very much for your postal note, which helped to buy a watch.

In February 1919, and still only fifteen, Potocki, having matriculated, became a pupil-teacher at Berhampore School. Here, still wearing short pants, he was put in charge of 'Upper Standard III'. He also started studying Greek at Victoria University College, privately, in the study of Professor Dettman. At the end of the year, eager to be independent and with pleasant memories of Christchurch, he applied to the secretary of the education board there for a position as a junior teacher:

> Being an old boy of the Christchurch B.H.S. I am desirous of continuing my studies at the Canterbury College so I would like to be placed on your list of candidates for the position of (1st Grade) Junior Teacher. I wish to be appointed to a Christchurch city or suburbs school, (not over about 4 miles from the Square if possible).

The headmaster of Berhampore School, on 12 November 1919, provided a reference which confirmed his 'literary powers' and observed that 'At present he has not shown that he has the power of control highly developed. This is his chief lacking quality—which however, has somewhat improved. Rather than recommend his removal from the service I would rather he be placed in another school where he might have a new sphere of action to further test his ability. As far as I know his character is good.'

Responding to the question of his ability to control a class, and perhaps showing early signs of his later preoccupation with perceived personal injustice, Potocki immediately asked the education board not to 'lose sight of the fact that I went to Berhampore straight from Wellington College—<u>a boy in short trousers</u>'. He continued: 'I think that this had some considerable bearing on this matter, especially in the early months. I have noticed a great deal of difference since I assumed men's clothing, as is indicated in the testimonial.'

The following year he took up a position as a junior teacher at St Albans School, and studied Greek, Latin and English literature at Canterbury University College, where, finding the lecturer to be boring, he left off studying.

In 1921, during a holiday visit to Auckland, Potocki, now 18, decided to 'chuck teaching' and study law at Auckland University College. He was persuaded in part by his disillusionment with teaching, which he was finding tedious, and in part by his godfather, Uncle Bert (Hubert Earle Vaile), with whom he had developed a sympathetic relationship. It would appear that, despite his academic successes, the 'Lestes' years had left Potocki with low self-esteem and what he would later describe as a 'general lack of confidence in myself', for at this time he confided to Uncle Bert, a real estate agent of means whom he saw almost daily at times, that he had been depressed so low that he believed he now needed to soar as high as he had been pushed low in order to restore himself. Uncle Bert prescribed what Potocki refers to in the typescript as 'the magic of sex'—a prescription it appears that, despite considerable contemplation, Potocki would not benefit from until he met the girl he would marry. 'I took the Christian religion very seriously when I was young,' he told me, 'and continued to stick tenaciously to the magic of religion.'

His uncle also set about arranging a placement for him as a registration clerk with Auckland law firm Earl, Kent and Massey. 'Massey was the son of the Prime Minister, and it was a very good firm, and I was paid more than any law clerk in Auckland who had a similar position, on account of Uncle Bert's influence.' In the course of his duties, searching title-deeds and presenting mortgages and conveyances at the public counter of the Land Registry Office, he met Maxwell Billens Rudd, a young man also of poetic persuasion who was similarly employed by the Public Trustee. The two started meeting for lunch in the restaurant at the top of the Milne and Choyce department store 'sky-scraper in Queen Street' where, Potocki recalls, Rudd was 'rather fond of saying: FUCK ALL IRELAND!', repeatedly telling Potocki that he was 'envious of my person' and declaring that in his next life on earth he was going to be an aristocrat. 'He said that the only thing he had which was better than mine, was his ears. His ears were in fact very pretty and small, and almost like a baby's, and a "superstition" exists that when a man has such ears, he will die young.' Potocki believed that Rudd, who sadly did die young, aged twenty-two or twenty-three, and wrote only a small amount of poetry, was significantly gifted and original. He believed the same of poet R.A.K. Mason: 'all these people—Rudd, and Mason—they were original, not because of printing their poetry all across the page or something funny like that, or tricks to make themselves appear original, they just were. That's my opinion at any rate.'

In around 1923 Potocki met Mason—who had recently published a 'remarkable booklet of poems, "The Beggar", and had ultimately tipped five hundred of them from the wharf into the harbour, from sheer indignation that the book had not been appreciated'—at a talk on literature at the YMCA and invited him to join the group, which by now also included Rudd's 'hanger on, the inevitable Sweetman, who wrote the most frightful rubbish'. Earnest discussions were held on the top floor of Milne and Choyce on a range of literary topics, including work in progress, the work of English, French and Italian poets, and the scanning of English poetry. Under Potocki's influence, group members believed themselves to be a poetic aristocracy through which the now-decadent traditions of English poetry would be revitalised. W.S. Broughton writes in *New Zealand Profiles: A.R.D. Fairburn* that Potocki claimed this vitality would flow from 'the qualities of their sensibilities' and 'the vigour of their antipodean colonial environment in which the decadence of the "old world" had been eliminated by the close proximity of man to nature'. The same year Potocki published his first collection of poetry in the form of a leaflet, 'a somewhat youthful thing' of four pages entitled 'The Opal Studded Diadem'. He also made the acquaintance of Douglas Glass, whom he first met at John Court's draper's shop in Queen Street where Glass was a salesman: 'Glass was very chatty and wistfully anxious to converse about literature. He explained to me his great ambition in life was to write a booky essay such as Half Hours With My Library and it was going to be one big plagiarism.'

At around this time Potocki put his career in law on hold, and entered the College of St John the Evangelist in Auckland to study theology. In fact, as he told me, he was dismissed from his law firm for indiscreet remarks made in a bar in Queen Street about a will he had prepared. He had decided he liked the idea of being a priest. He did not feel he had a calling—'no more than any of the others had'—but he did have a liking for the ritual and literature of the priesthood. 'It was an extremely picturesque college really, you know. We used to have meals in hall, wore our gowns and got into the habit of putting your arm underneath your sleeve so it wouldn't get in your porridge while you reached for the milk or something.' In the course of his studies he was introduced to the printing of the early missionaries in New Zealand, an introduction he later claimed was the foundation of his interest in private printing. 'If some stupid missionary could do this,' the theological student said, 'why not I?'

Before long, however, college discipline and restrictions became a problem, so he resigned to seek ritual and literature, and if possible a living, elsewhere. He told me: 'I left the college because a Shakespeare company came to Auckland, and they were going to play all the plays of Shakespeare. I asked the warden for permission to go to them, and he gave me permission to go to only one of these plays, and I was so indignant I left the place and got myself a job teaching at two country schools. You had to go between the two on horseback, and I couldn't manage the animal that was available, which was rather a wild mare, and that job also came to grief, for that reason.'

Rather than continue with teaching—a profession he would later describe as 'a fashionable way of prostituting a good hereditary brain'— Potocki returned to the law. He also joined a Theosophical Lodge. Under the influence of Uncle Bert, who had urged him to 'get rid of all this bloody old women's rot about Jesus Christ', he was beginning to view the restraints of conventional worship bleakly. Although he remained enamoured of the ritual and literature of Christianity, he regarded as ridiculous a religion which sought to extinguish rather than encourage the senses. The typescript reveals Uncle Bert's considerable influence in this matter. 'There's a God all right,' he told his nephew, 'but who knows anything about him? Not the fucking old Parish parson . . . fucking old hypocrites! You ought to know better than to believe the old bastards.' He had also said that it was 'a damned shame to see a young fellow' with his brains 'wrapped up in all this nonsense about Jesus', and that if he would 'go and fuck some nice young girl' he would begin to see sense. 'You're trying to disobey Nature,' he would say, 'which is the same thing as disobeying God.' The affection and respect with which Potocki regarded his godfather, who took the time to listen and talk to him, is obvious. He especially remembers Uncle Bert's 'two really great virtues . . . namely a Good Heart, and a Total

Absence of Hypocrisy', observing that 'If we liked to use a religious phraseology, we would call these Love and Truth.'

Having joined the lodge, he met John Ross Thompson, a first cousin of J.M. Barrie. 'And one day a young lady came up to his house, where I was staying, to give back her father's masonic regalia following his death. Her name was Lilian Hemus. Not very long after this—in November 1924—I married her.' It would appear that Lilian had by no means been his first love, nor would she be his only love in the course of their brief marriage. In his first collection of poetry, *Wild Oats*, published in 1927 in Christchurch, poems written between 1924 and 1926 praise several women. And a letter from his father in 1924 indicates serious interest in a 'Hilda' the year he married Lilian. The letter also demonstrates a controlling side developing in the hitherto uninterested Robert:

> My dear Geoffrey,
> ... Very glad of description of Hilda. She will not take it amiss from me when I say that to improve her carriage she should stand or rather walk some time every day with a walking stick behind her back. To do this she should have an ordinary walking stick—held in front, parallel or rather level and at the waist height—hand clutching stick at each extremity. In that position raise the stick head high and bring it over her back below the shoulder blades without removing hands from original position of stick. Stand or walk in this position often—she will soon walk straight as a reed. This will add dignity to her. You can give her my love and tell her that I welcome her as my daughter of whom I hope to be proud. I hope to be proud of the pair of you: She shall be exactly as my own and I hope and trust that she will accept me as her father ... she can consult me on anything and I will be frank with her.

The letter finished: 'If you try to live up to the ideal standard of your dear mother and I think you are aiming that way—you will make an ideal husband to Hilda.' As an afterthought Robert had added: 'Stick to study, but do not overdo it.'

Although initially it did not occur to me that the amorous adventures of a young man were a matter for speculation, a poem I found written some years later, in Paris, addressed to his mother on the anniversary of her death, gave me cause to reflect on Potocki's considerable interest in women:

> If in this world there be like you another
> may the high gods give me her for a wife!

I found this significant. On the one hand, it seemed that not only was his mother, whose death was 'the great disaster' of his life, responsible for the high ideals he sought in a wife, but happily it was through her, and not his stepmother, that he related so readily and successfully to women. As his poetry shows, he worshipped women—romance, libido and love, one and the same. On the other hand, I wondered, could he have been like Rousseau, who wrote in his *Confessions*: 'If my aroused senses demand a woman, my agitated heart demands, still more urgently, love.' Could his attachment to women also have had a poignant side?

Potocki married Lilian Hemus on 23 November 1924 at St Paul's Church in Auckland, without the blessing of Lilian's family. Lilian, who was a first-year English student at the university, had been raised to take an interest in the creative rather than the domestic arts, and her family had hoped she would have a career as a teacher before settling down. Her father had owned his own store in Newmarket, her mother employed a maid and, although family members were keen patrons of the arts and members of the Shakespeare Society, as respectable middle-class Aucklanders they did not view the unsettled poet as a suitable match for their daughter.

At first, life with Lilian was agreeable. A naturist, she encouraged him to take naked sunbaths—a habit he continued into old age—and she soon became pregnant. But as domestic responsibility began to conflict with his need for freedom and his greater calling as a poet, Potocki became disillusioned with married life. Inevitably, the expectation that he as husband would ensure the financial security of his small family became a problem, particularly when Parr, Blomfield, Alexander and Burt, the law firm for whom he was working before he married, declined to continue his employment on the ground, according to Potocki, that they were not comfortable employing a married man on a law clerk's wage.

When, almost immediately, a milk run was offered for sale, Potocki, spurred on perhaps by his fondness for cows and the importance milk had assumed during his underfed childhood, bought it. But before long he realised that he was no businessman. His lack of interest in figures, apparent since childhood, together with the fact that 'I didn't have the heart to follow up on the poor families who owed me money', meant that he found himself getting ever deeper into debt. And there were practical problems. He couldn't catch and bridle the milk horse in the morning—his impatience caused it to run away—and the pregnant Lilian would have to rise early, coax it into submission, and harness it to the milk cart. He argued with the customers. Then the Ford truck he purchased in place of the horse proved unreliable. After a year, in debt and unable to sustain the venture, he was forced to give up.

In the meantime, in September 1925, Lilian, soothed in labour by Potocki playing Beethoven's 'Moonlight Sonata' on the piano, gave birth to Wanda. Christened Maud Wanda, the baby was born a month early and weighed only two kilograms. Hospitalisation was urged, but Potocki, unwilling to entrust Lilian or Wanda to what he considered to be unproven expertise, insisted she stay at home. Convinced of the efficacy of olive oil even then, he purchased a large quantity, which he warmed and used to soak the flannels in which Wanda was wrapped. The midwife was instructed to continue the treatment.

In January 1926 he moved the family to Christchurch, where, although he resumed his legal studies, his real commitment was to writing poetry. 'Yes, I went back to the law in Christchurch. I was employed by R.L. Saunders, who was an awfully nice chap, but he had his papers in the most infernal disorder. And I catalogued the whole lot of them for him. I got it so that you could put hands on So-and-So v So-and-So in two minutes. And then I would say to him, "Look here, Mr Saunders, So-and-So hasn't paid his bill. Now he owes you seventeen guineas. If you don't do something about it, he'll never pay you. Why don't you send him a bill?" And he'd dictate a letter, and he would say, "We must do that again because there's a split infinitive in it." And I would say, "Who is the poet here, Mr Saunders, and who's the lawyer? It's got to go off." And so I would send it away. I created no end of money for him.'

A letter from Robert in February that year reveals that by now, despite his wage as a law clerk, a gratuity from grandfather Vaile's settlement and regular sums from Uncle Bert, Potocki remained in debt. Robert's letter chides his son for having failed to repay the 'substantial monies' loaned him by one of his father's 'oldest and dearest friends', and for having left Auckland without even making arrangements for repayment by instalment. 'What sort of man are you?' asks Robert:

> Have you not a motor car, and does it not cost a lot to run it . . . don't you realize that you should have sold the car and have paid your debts or part of them and that you should not own another car until you are free of debt and can afford to run one. Don't you think it would be manly and honourable to work for a living and not use your wife's money . . . If you go on in this wise the time will surely come when the law will place you under restraint—you know what I mean. I have a letter here addressed to Mr Potocki de Montalk, Dairyman: Now one thing the Potocki and their wives, the Potocka were renowned for was Honour—To be 'as a Potocka' is, in Europe, almost as well known as saying as to be like Caesar's wife . . . Do you realize that in bearing this name that you should make it honourable. It is a name to be proud of. It should not be associated with dairymen but with the highest calling in the land.
> . . . I hear you are keen on becoming a priest—God help the Church. I no longer believe in the church—most probably this is because there are so many men in it of your loose standard with regard to the rights and wrongs of things. You are not the sort of man for the Church—You will never get on in it. You are totally lacking in 'tact'—you cannot learn tact—You will never possess it . . . You have no tolerance and this is again an essential. I would like you to think of your dear mother and do what she would like— one of the things would be to be dutiful to me and one to be always honourable. It did not injure me that you deliberately did a mean and petty thing in not coming to see me yourself and in taking away the baby—but it made me sorry for you and for the baby that it had such a mean father. You should now try to be a real man for the sake of your wife and child.
> Your affectionate father R.W. de Montalk.

Presumably Robert's tone awakened Potocki's unhappy childhood, for his reply (not found among his papers) appears to have called into question his father's right to speak to him of honour. On 3 March Robert wrote at length and with much bitterness to Mrs Geoffrey de Montalk at 24 Hewitts Road, Merivale, Christchurch, from Anne Street, Highland Park, Wellington:

Dear Lilian,

I am in receipt of a long letter from Geoffrey, such a disgusting one, full of lies, resentment—altogether disgusting—if you are unaware of its contents, then so much the better . . . It is a falsehood what you describe at Geoffrey's mother's deathbed and as I was the only one present I know—the dear soul died very suddenly and had but time to say good bye to me—Let her name not be desecrated any further. But she would be sore indeed if she knew her son's attitude to me and to the world. At the time of your marrying, Geoffrey proposed to love me very greatly—was loving to my wife also—So why this break—Was this a lie too?

Robert went on to remind Lilian of the gift of £30 he had given Geoffrey as a deposit on a house at a time when he himself received only £180 a year. 'Only since March last have I been in better circumstances or we could not contemplate a trip abroad.' He continued:

His non-success is because he thinks he is different to or better than the general ruck and because he will not heed advice nor will he be governed by others. To help him is to actually hinder him . . . Do not look to me for money—not after the letter I have just received from Geoffrey . . . Geoffrey's letter to me, the malicious lies he told Uncle Ted about my wife, and what he wrote me on that head, I can never excuse, although after proper retraction I may pardon. Geoffrey was the apple of my eye and I once had hopes that he would become . . . one of our first and most respected citizens . . . My son has severed himself for all practical purposes from me and from nearly all his relations—all of whom were fond of him and wished at least to help him . . . I think you ought to watch Geoffrey very closely for your own sake because I do not think he is right in his mind . . . Finally, please try to believe that as my wife is not a very wicked woman, that neither am I a very wicked cruel man—and this may do you good, which is my wish. If either of you have any kindness of heart and (alleged) Christian charity, try and understand that I am not well.

There was a postscript to the letter:

... Geoffrey has accused me of behaviour the most vile during his childhood and up to the present. He has accused my wife likewise and both in the most offensive terms. I am not aware of any ill behaviour of mine to him not at any time—I have never known of the offences said to have been committed by my wife and I do not believe them. But if I did, I could not permit them to vilify my own soul for all time—but would rather forget them and forgive ... Geoffrey's mind is obsessed with wrong premises and ideas—His only cure is to <u>dismiss this subject</u>. And even if true to forget them for all time and to forgive. You can sell the car, also save cost of running—you can both walk the short distances to and from the city—thus, you can get and save money to buy food.

Potocki was indeed increasingly unwilling to 'heed advice' or 'be governed by others'. He stubbornly ignored his father's exhortations to become a conventional citizen, and remained committed to his calling as a poet.

In July 1926, he received a letter from his former primary-school friend, Rex Fairburn in Auckland, who had recently started writing poetry himself. 'Dear de Montalk,' he wrote, 'You probably won't remember me. I belong to a time in your life of which I should think you recollect very little. However, the dead past having buried its dead, I shall attempt to do a little body-snatching.' Fairburn enclosed a number of poems which Potocki described as 'Brookey', or in the style of Rupert Brooke. The two resumed their friendship via a continuous correspondence, which included sending each other poems for criticism. Fairburn wrote, for instance: 'As regards your poetry, I should like to make a few criticisms. In the first place, you must widen your conception of Beauty. Beauty is just as much to be found (by the searcher) in a dead rat in a gutter or a drunken prostitute as in orthodox lovely things.'

Later that year Fairburn, who was spending five months on Norfolk Island, wrote the first half of a Petrarchan sonnet which he sent back to New Zealand for Potocki to complete. 'Which I did, and in this way it became the beginning of his literary career, for I published it in *Wild Oats*.'

By now Potocki's own literary career was beginning to burgeon. He was publishing poetry in the Christchurch *Sun*, and his first collection was nearing completion. But his married life was increasingly under pressure. Only two years after they were married, he and Lilian agreed to separate. Two days later Potocki found himself in the Christchurch Magistrates' Court on a charge of assaulting his wife.

Lilian's point of view can be pieced together from the various newspaper accounts of the case. She is reported as having told the court that the trouble with Potocki in the role of husband was that he infused too much poetic idealism into the home, and failed to contribute sufficient cash. When the milk business failed, he compromised with his creditors and she lost £1000 of her own money. When they moved to Christchurch he decided to build a house, and erected a temporary home in the form of a garage, but he only ever got as far as laying the foundation-stone of the house. Later, when they moved to Hoon Hay, near Spreydon, their relationship became troubled. He wouldn't work. He simply sat at home all day writing poetry. Meantime they had nothing to live on. One day he said he was leaving and did so, taking their motorcar. Asserting her right to the vehicle which had been purchased with her money, she accosted him in the street in front of the court, where it was parked. A scuffle ensued, during which she fell to the ground and appealed to a nearby sergeant to arrest him on a charge of assault.

In court, Potocki told the magistrate that this was 'a tale of dire adversity'. His life had been ruined by a woman, he said, and was this not happening every day? He explained that they had been living on the proceeds of the milk business, which he had had to give up through his being fool enough to regard everybody as honest, including his wife. He had wanted to drive by car to see his counsel and friend, Canon Jones. The car, which he had been sleeping in for two nights following their decision to separate, was the only place he had to sleep in as his wife had taken the bedding.

'What is his occupation?' the magistrate asked Lilian.

'Come on, say it out,' Potocki called from the dock as she hesitated.

'He is a poet,' she replied.

'Does your husband make a living by writing poetry?'

'No, we have been living from hand to mouth lately. We have been living on some money I received a few months ago. Prior to coming to Christchurch in January last we had a milk business in Auckland.'

The magistrate was kindly. He found that there were special circumstances surrounding the assault, in particular the age and temperament of the parties, and he did not want to do anything which would widen the breach between them. As Potocki had already spent the night in a cell, he dismissed the case and suppressed their names (Potocki appears in print as 'the young husband' and 'the writer of poetry', Lilian as 'the young wife'), hoping the poet and his wife would be brought together again.

Despite the magistrate's hopes and Lilian's entreaties, Potocki steadfastly continued to be a poet, and an absent husband and father. He had decided some time ago that he did not wish to remain in New Zealand, even though this would mean abandoning his wife and child. In January 1927, an aunt had written in a false panic from Sussex:

> My dear Geoffrey,
> I heard from your aunts in Auckland that you were on your way to England. I cannot help thinking that you have made a mistake in doing so. There is a great deal of unemployment, and poets, here, are as thick as peas in a pod! . . . Even if you get a publisher to accept your poems you will not get enough to live upon until you make your mark in the world . . . I am very sorry but I cannot ask you to stay here but I live with an aunt who is quite ill and she cannot have anyone in the house to stay. You were only three when I saw you last so I would not know you if I saw you.

Meanwhile, at Easter 1927, at the age of twenty-three, he published his first collection of poetry: *Wild Oats*, 'A Sheaf of Poems by Geoffrey Wladislas Vaile Potocki de Montalk, Prince Potocki, from Clifton, Sumner, in Christchurch.' Two hundred purple-covered copies were printed by The Sun Newspapers Ltd, Christchurch. 'Without apology,' he said in his introduction, 'I send out this first book of poetry to that New Zealand audience, not so very small, of my friends and acquaintances. . . . This little collection is, of course, the fruit of my youth, and I shall not wait for the critic to tell me it shows signs of immaturity. Let it be compared with the work of say, Coleridge, at such an age.' The volume, which is 'Dedicated to my friend and fellow-poet, Rex Fairburn', collects some forty poems, including sonnets, songs of wonder, love and desire, and reflections on religion and death.

There is a poem in memory of Maxwell Rudd, who had died young, as predicted, the previous year:

> And you'll be back with wizard chimes
> And tunes upon your tongue—

And sing us, with strange coloured rhymes,
The songs you leave unsung.
(from 'In Memoriam, Maxwell Rudd, Poet, *obit* 23rd Sept., 1926')

And a response to Fairburn's suggestion that he widen his concept of beauty:

A dead rat in the gutter at Baghdad;
A sleek green carrion bird;
A sweeter song, oh Ishmahad,
Than you have heard.
(from 'The Song of the Dead Rat')

The collection is optimistic. It is also frequently rich with celestial imagery and the majesty of love. It speaks of crowns, princes, jewels and kings. It closes with the Petrarchan sonnet written jointly with Fairburn.

The dual personality of this poem reveals the differing temperaments of the two poets. Fairburn's octave, written on Norfolk Island about November 1926, after a period of imprisonment following involvement in a brawl, is tied to the land. Later to become the editor of a farmer's journal, Fairburn is diminished and depressed by the sea:

There are no flowers upon the Ocean's mead,
No yellow grass to lay me in the sun;
There are no hills where lazy cattle feed,
Nor pools to splash them when the day is done.

Down in that green old world there is no sound
Of music or of dancing. In the Deep
Never a table, happy faces round,
No twilight rooms where tired men may sleep.

The sestet, on the other hand, written on 'Virgin Lucy's Day, December 1926', shimmers. Potocki is elusive. He considers the possibilities of the sea. And he is unconventional, shifting the mood not only of the poem and the sea, but also of the form of the sonnet itself. Fairburn's form in Shakespearean rhyme is now turned to a Petrarchan sestet:

But fishes there slip by the weeds and gleam
Like God's ideas before Creation's dawn—
Say His dim reverie of worlds like ours,
A universe of lazy-moving dreams,
Green bubbles for cities, bright fishes stars unborn,
Wind-billowed grass—before God thought of flowers.

Mason appraised the collection in candid terms. Writing to Potocki in London in 1930, in an 'Extended Diary Style Letter' (possibly never sent and published in 1986 as *R.A.K. Mason at Twenty-five*), he found some sections to be 'immature' and spoilt by 'obtrusion of your own pet fads and fancies' or a 'littleness of spirit'. But he declared himself impressed with others, noting that 'A Lyric' of which he now knew every 'splendid line . . . is about as good as anything I know', that 'Flecker seems to suit you for I love "A Tone Poem"', and that 'The Songs of Useless Beauty' are often fine (but don't drive a man too often to the bloody dictionary, life's too short for that)'. He concluded: 'none of what I have seen since is as good as the best of those I have named, and I don't ask for more.'

'A Lyric', which had previously been published with an illustration in the *Sun*, Christchurch, was one of Potocki's most recent poems:

Like light that falls on temples below the morning star
The children of the morning are panoplied for war:
The light on breasts of steel and over brazen helms
Gleams like the threads of sunrise a-laughing in the elms:

The blazing banner flaunting its consecrated crest
Long will not leave the lances asleep upon the rest;
The eager trumpet's war-blast leaps like a flame at night,
Burns like a brand of battle the early amber light.

Within the old grey city the bells ring out for Mass
In strongholds where the weary from shades of war may pass:
And yet like light that glitters on temples from afar
The children of the morning are panoplied for war.

Although *Wild Oats* collected the writings of youth and, in keeping with a young man's follies, contained moments of extravagance and grandeur, it was nonetheless one of the starting-points in the development of New Zealand's poetic identity. It placed Potocki among the generation of writers who would lay the basis of New Zealand literature as it developed in the 1930s. 'The early work of D'Arcy Cresswell, Mason, Ursula Bethell, the youthful Fairburn and de Montalk in the 1920s', writes W.S. Broughton in *A.R.D. Fairburn*, 'was the first stage.'

But, while the work of Fairburn and Mason among others would develop to mirror and question New Zealand society, Potocki, who would remain abroad, would retain his archaic and royal tone, and the dreams of traditions and earlier ages—retreats since childhood—would continue to inform, and limit, his work.

Soon after *Wild Oats* was launched, Fairburn wrote:

> Dear Geoff—I regard Wild Oats as the test. If they accept that and support it, I will consider that they deserve to have other stuff printed here. If, however, they don't take much notice, I will vow never to publish anything in N.Z. myself, never to lose any opportunity of dissuading others from doing it, and in general take no notice whatever of my native country.

He then successfully submitted the joint sonnet to the Auckland *Star* for publication, and in June 1927 wrote to Potocki:

> Dear Geoff—You know our Siamese-Twins Sonnet—the one you included in 'Wild Oats' well about 6 weeks ago I sent it to Mulgan of the 'Star' among some others, and I have just had a note from him today saying he is going to use it—or, as he says, it is going to use him.

The *Wild Oats* 'test' started promisingly enough. Poetry critic Ian Donnelly wrote to Potocki in September 1927:

> I think *Wild Oats* is the most significant thing that has been done in New Zealand by our generation. There is imagination and thought in the work, and on the technical side you have a subtle mastery which will probably grow greater as time goes on. As a first effort it fills me with the highest hopes for your future, and I have a feeling that those who are jeering at you now will be glad to applaud as the years go by.

Despite Donnelly's favourable response, *Literature and the Arts: New Zealand* (1947) reports that *Wild Oats* was rejected by 'the literary editor of one of the large dailies [Alan Mulgan], [who refused] a review because the author was in the process of dissolving his marriage'.

The strangleholds of colonial convention and the absence of cultural enrichment continued to intensify. On 5 July Fairburn had written to Potocki:

> Dear Geoff—I am absolutely, completely, damnably, and utterly sick of this intellectual rat-hole the geographers mark 'Auckland' on the map. It is a spiritual cesspool, an ethical sink. It's the very devil to have spent the larger part of a lifetime of 23 years in a place which is in itself beautiful and which has a sprinkling of people you can love in it, yet to be driven to hate it. The ground rots from under one. I am quite ready to pack up my toothbrush and a few books and chortle gleefully as Auckland fades into the mists.

Potocki had replied: 'Poets are as badly treated in this land of white savages and All Blacks as they are feted and laurelled and crowned in Merrie England.' And earlier Fairburn had warned: 'By the way, when writing to my home address, don't put 'poet' on the envelope. The old man . . . can't stand a bar of R.A.K. [Mason]; so if he saw an envelope lying around addressing his son as a poet, well, the red rag to Bonzo wouldn't be in it.'

Still, there was Christchurch Cathedral, where Potocki attended choral evensong nightly. And on 17 June 1927 there had been the concert by visiting Polish pianist, composer and statesman, Ignacy Paderewski. There had also been dinner with Paderewski. When the pianist announced that after his tour of Australia he would give a few concerts in New Zealand, Potocki had written to him saying that, as a great-grandson of Prince Potocki the Insurgent, he hoped Paderewski would be kind enough to receive him when he was in New Zealand. 'I was still working with Saunders at the time, and around mid-morning an envelope addressed to me was brought to the office, and I was asked to dine with Paderewski at Warner's at 1.30.'

Potocki describes the encounter in his essay dryly entitled 'Celebrities Who Have Met Me, I. Paderewski' (Draguignan 1953):

He [Paderewski] wore a heavy great-coat. His carriage was impressive and characteristic, and his face massive, fairly youthful, and leonine . . . There was just the slightest awkwardness, when Sir Ignacy relieved it by asking me whether or not I spoke Polish. No, I said—I know only about six words. What are they? he asked. Oh, I said, probably I mispronounce them frightfully. Never mind, he said, let's hear them. He agreed with Good day [and] corrected me on Good night. What are the other two, he said. They're swear words—I cannot say them! So he patted me three great fatherly pats on the back.

The party went into dinner: the virtuoso, his wife, his female secretary and Potocki. Paderewski asked about his father, his profession, where he lived. There was discussion of the Polish aristocracy, including the Potocki family: 'The Soviet,' said Paderewski, 'has confiscated the lands of Potocki, as these lands lie in provinces under the present domination of Russia. However, they have some property in Poland.'

There was also discussion of current Polish politics, and the building and subsequent dismantling of the Russian cathedral in Warsaw: 'They chose a lovely site,' said Paderewski. 'The building was the tallest in Warsaw, the first thing to meet the eye, and was put there expressly to show the world that Poland was a conquered country.'

During the meal, the party spoke a good deal of Polish between themselves. Potocki noted that 'it sounded a very sweet and beautiful tongue' and was 'inspired with a desire to learn it'. He was asked what his ambitions were. He replied: 'It may seem foolish, but I am going to London, with not more than £30 in my pocket, to try to conquer the world of letters, or die in the attempt.'

'Splendid, splendid,' murmured Paderewski.

Afterwards, the Christchurch *Sun*, in which Potocki 'was in the habit of publishing poems and some little prose', asked him to write an account of his dinner with the great musician and statesman. 'They were flabbergasted when I refused. I was not there as a reporter, but as his guest. They suggested publishing it after he had left NZ so that he wouldn't know about it. But I was adamant. I said, "You know perfectly well he has refused to give interviews. He invited me as a member of the Potocki family born in exile. It isn't a question of Paderewski not knowing about it. It's a question of honour."'

\*

Geoffrey Wladislas Vaile de Montalk, aged 21, at the time of his marriage to Lilian Hemus in 1924.

Herman Potocki   Vladimir (Włodzimierz) Potocki   Józef Potocki

*Above:* Robert Wladislas, 1871–1942, and Annie Maud (Vaile), 1867–1908, de Montalk (Geoffrey's parents).

*Right:* Annie de Montalk.

*Opposite, top:* Count Józef Franciszek Jan Potocki the Polish insurgent, 1800–1863 (Geoffrey's great-grandfather) (right), with his younger brother Herman (left) and a cousin (centre). (*Les Polonais et les Polonaises de la Révolution du 29 Novembre 1830,* Stavzeioicz)

*Opposite, left:* Count Joseph Wladislas Edmond Potocki de Montalk, 1836–1901 (Geoffrey's grandfather), Paris circa 1865.

*Opposite, right:* Joseph (also known as Edmond) around thirty years later, as Professor of Modern Languages, University College, Auckland.

*Opposite, bottom:* Joseph and Alexandrina (Macalister) de Montalk and seven of their twelve children, at their home, Clovelly, Mount Eden, Auckland, circa 1901. Back row: Henry, Judith, Joseph, Alexandrina. Front row: Alexander, Jane, Emily, Ethel (wife of Edmond), Edmond, Victoria. The absent children are Robert, John, James, George and Margaret.

Geoffrey (right) with his brother Cedric, Auckland, 1906, about eighteen months before their mother's death.

Geoffrey, 1910, aged seven, at Vallombrosa, Remuera, Auckland.

Dulce, Geoffrey's sister, circa 1918, at the family's home in Majoribanks Street, Wellington.

Lilian Hemus, at the time she met Potocki. (Wanda Henderson)

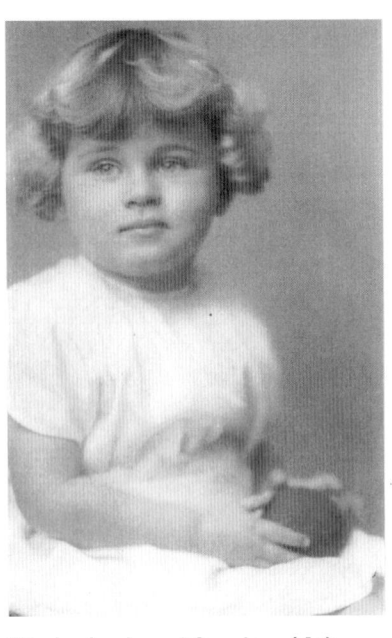

Wanda, daughter of Potocki and Lilian, at around the time of Potocki's departure for England in 1927. (Wanda Henderson)

A.R.D. Fairburn.

R.A.K. Mason. (Hocken Library)

Douglas Glass, the New Zealand friend with whom Potocki was arrested and charged in London in 1932 with uttering and publishing an obscene libel entitled 'Here Lies John Penis'.

Potocki, newly arrived in Paris, 1928.

Lithuanian Idyll, 1929: Potocki in the grounds of Terespol Palace.

With Count Adam Chrapowicki, Terespol.

Zinka, Countess Chrapowicka (Adam's sister), for whom Potocki wrote the thirty-eight poems he published as *Lordly Lovesongs*.

Potocki and Zinka, Lithuania.

In early September 1927, Lilian, believing the increasingly absent Potocki to be on the verge of deserting her, applied to the Supreme Court for restitution of conjugal rights.

'You are anxious for your husband to return and live with you again?' asked the judge.

'Yes,' Lilian replied. 'I think it will be good for the little child, whose age is so young.'

A letter written by Potocki to Lilian, who had suggested they return to Auckland, was read out in court:

> I note that you mention Auckland . . . Well, surely you must know that I would not live in that intellectual rat hole (as the poet Rex Fairburn calls it) while the Holy City, Christchurch, the lovely and fair, is still on the map of New Zealand.
>
> It is not true (of me at any rate) that 'Love goes lightly on' even if the immortal Rupert Brooke did say it; but for all that I am afraid it will be another incarnation before we live together again.

In a second letter, also read out, Potocki advised that he was headed for a place where poets are appreciated:

> As a matter of fact I shall be leaving for England almost immediately. I also have two prose books under way, and shall complete them on the voyage. You cannot imagine, surely, that I would allow you further to interfere with my work in life . . . I do not particularly want to see you, but can you arrange for me to see the little girl before I go?
>
> I cannot understand you continuing this action as I do not intend to come back to you. This 'Poet and Peasant' idea apparently isn't a success. Next time it will be with a woman with a Royal body and a Royal mind, or there will be no next time.

'One ought,' the judge observed, 'to be indulgent, at any rate, to a citizen who is good enough to describe Christchurch as the "Holy City".' Lilian was then granted the order, and Potocki was asked by the court to assume once more 'the sadly commonplace role of husband within 30 days'.

A couple of weeks later, however, he filed for divorce and left for Auckland in order to make arrangements to flee the country's 'suffocating philistinism', to 'follow the golden road to Samarkand'. Lilian accepted the inevitable. Although married life had been uncertain and stormy—Wanda says her mother spoke of Potocki as having a temper, of 'furious rows', following which he wouldn't speak for days— she had been very much in love with him, in love with his 'strength and his fineness'. She wrote:

> Dear Geoffrey,
> ... It was a lonely drive home after you left by the train—I hope you had a good trip and I suppose by now you will have seen most of your friends in Auckland. How soon are you going to leave N.Z.?
> The baby loves the music and is very interested in all the 'goggies' on the records. She will certainly appreciate your gift to the full. Hoping you have a successful time and a pleasant voyage—
> Love from Lilian.

Life would be difficult for Lilian. She would go without food so that Wanda might be fed. She would be obliged to take a series of live-in housekeeping positions, in the course of which she would be cited in a divorce case and suffer the ignominy of a mention in *Truth*. She was an attractive woman and, to avoid the attentions of the men in whose homes she was housekeeping, she would have to keep changing jobs.

Potocki, unwavering in his search for poetic identity, unrepentant about the abandonment of his wife and child, emerges from his marriage as single-minded and selfish. His father, less readily assuaged than Lilian, was immediately concerned about the good name of the family. On 7 October 1927, while on vacation in Nice, he wrote:

> My dear Geoffrey,
> I wish you many happy returns of the day and as you are now 24 and should be acquiring some commonsense I hope you will try and acquire some. I see no reason why you should not write to the papers—if you write sense—your first letter to the Sun on milk was sensible—the others were in execrable taste. I have great objection to your using Count and Prince ... There is a Prince Potocki—a real man in Europe—if it should come to his ears that you are using his title you will either be <u>put in gaol or in a lunatic asylum</u> ... I hear you have obtained a passport in the name of Count de Montalk—<u>do get this altered at once</u> ... You have no

right to leave New Zealand without your wife and child. You are not a gentleman. No amount of assertion will make you one . . . you have brains and no <u>balance</u>—you should try and acquire the latter . . . there are no openings in England for such as you—all the young men who can are going out to the colonies—there is just starvation in England—Don't go . . . Try and get some suitable occupation in N.Z. qualify at the University—go like the snail, slowly and surely. Go back to your wife and child and lead the life of a decent honest humble man.
R. W. de Montalk.

In Auckland, Potocki spent much of his last month in New Zealand at Rex Fairburn's home in New Lynn. He also saw a good deal of Mason. This was the first time he had met Mason and Fairburn together. Denys Trussell notes in his biography *Fairburn* that 'Mason found him an attractive personality who thrived on ridiculous quarrels, fighting with everybody, but somehow remaining likeable'. Of this time Potocki writes in *Recollections of My Fellow Poets*: 'Discussion of poetry and its scansion reached a peak, and of communism likewise.'

Towards the end of October 1927, having turned twenty-four only weeks earlier, he left for England via Sydney, where, while Lilian resigned herself to life as a housemaid, he spent 'an amusing month, sunbathing and all that'. He was farewelled in Auckland by Rex Fairburn and his brother Geoffrey, and Mason. 'As the ship began to move,' he remembers in *Recollections*, 'I, still under the influence of mediaeval ecclesiastical ceremonial, made the sign of the cross over them in the air, as they stood below on the wharf. Rex then ostentatiously made the sign of the Crescent Moon in the air.'

FIVE

## The Early London Years

*I'm not very enthusiastic about Bohemia—I'd accept it if it were thrown at me.*

'Well, N.Z. for a poet, well, it was the last place in the world. I mean, the attitude of people towards poetry in those days was that you were an anti-social waster, there's no doubt about it. And it was the same in N.Z. House in London. We were all treated like anti-social wasters, including the great Fairburn. Since then they've had his verses in the great glass window, but when he was here he was treated like a dog, the same as we all were.'

Potocki travelled to the 'Old World' on the SS *Oronsay*. He arrived in London on 19 January 1928 and was met at Kings Cross Station by Douglas Glass. (Glass, a book buying and selling enthusiast with a special interest in the work of Samuel Butler, was working as a draper's assistant. He would later become a respected portrait photographer for the *Sunday Times*.) Potocki's initial impressions were not favourable. He was horrified by the sight of what he described as 'all those miserable little houses between Tilbury and St Pancras—grey and all that', and disappointed to find that Glass, who had invited him to stay in his apartment, in fact had no apartment but was living in an expensive boarding house. Not only this, but a couple of days later Glass was taken into custody for stealing from the menswear shop at which he was working, and Potocki was obliged to befriend him. This was an inauspicious and foreboding beginning.

He found himself going around London trying to get bail for Glass, only to discover that no one would have anything to do with him. 'I'd said to him when he told me he suspected he was going to be arrested—

he showed me a great trunk full of goods he'd stolen from John Barker's—for goodness' sake, Douglas, you've got to get rid of this stuff. *Chuck* it in the Thames. Put it in the left luggage at Victoria Station, anything you like, but *get rid of it*! Then tomorrow morning go to your employers and say, "You haven't given me that rise that I asked for and which I deserve, and so I'm leaving." And they'll think "Good riddance to bad rubbish" and you'll hear no more of it. But he didn't and what happened? Within a couple of days he was behind bars.'

Disinclined to remain in London after Glass had gone to prison, Potocki made plans to go to Paris. He had been told by a friend inherited from Glass—a gentleman known as Old Splash, and otherwise referred to as Sunshine—that he would find life inexpensive there and be able to support himself teaching English. The friend, who was also listed in *Burke's Peerage* under the Baronetcy of Dashwood, and would become one of several benefactors, male and female, offered to assist the impecunious and charming young poet with a pound a week. 'So I went and in fact got jobs teaching English, met a lot of Poles, and started learning Polish, and he did in fact send regularly some small sum, which just made all the difference, because in those days you could sell a pound in Paris for 125 francs and some centimes, and you could get a meal—a three-course meal, not very good quality, but still it was three courses and wine thrown in, and service—for three francs fifty.'

When Glass, who had been sentenced to six months in prison, was due for release, Potocki returned to England. 'I announced that I was going to come and meet him at the prison gates, and Old Splash did everything he possibly could to persuade me to drop him for once and for all. But I said, "Well, you don't drop a friend when he's got himself into trouble," so I went and met him at the gate of Wandsworth Prison. We had a cup of tea at the Church Army Store opposite, and we found a place in Chelsea—a great big room with two beds in it, and really rather tastefully furnished, on Kings Road—and we were living there. But it all became a bit too expensive, so I went back to France.'

In Paris, Potocki met a young Polish nobleman, Count Adam Chrapowicki. Chrapowicki gave him lessons in Polish and invited him to his chateau in a Polish enclave in Lithuania. Thus it happened that, during September and October 1929, Potocki found himself a guest in a genuine Polish palace. An account of his visit appeared in the *New Zealand News* on 28 January 1930.

Count Geoffrey de Montalk, whose title is an ancient Polish one, recently paid a visit of two months to Lithuania. 'The Lithuanian lords, who are, of course, all Poles, since Lithuania is part of the historic Poland, have had,' he states, 'most of their land confiscated. The nobles are still the only people who live in a civilised way, and when we went out in the lordly carriage, or even on foot, we were always greeted with low bows, and "Good Day, Mighty Lords".'

He was surprised to find a country 'in such a medieval state of growth. Take away the palaces and the lords,' he told the *News*, 'and what is left would be something appreciably lower and far less interesting than the Maori culture. The very cabins of the peasants are far below the level of a decent Maori pa. The nobles showed a consuming interest in all my pictures and explanations about New Zealand, and were astonished to find that in many ways our country should be so far ahead of theirs.'

From New Zealand, Robert de Montalk had continued to harangue his son. He had remonstrated about debts not paid. He had not found his son's publications list praiseworthy, nor had he been impressed by his living arrangements. And as ever he was concerned about his son referring to himself as a count, and the effect of his 'pretensions' on the good name of the family. From time to time, probably in desperation, he had even raised the likelihood of 'gaol', as in a letter written on 17 February 1928:

> Your life pains me really. No other of our name was ever dishonest. You have been so all your life. You will find in England that your misdeeds in N.Z. will follow you and if you do not go straight you will soon be in gaol.

He had asked the Guardian Trust to pay Potocki's debts from the small allowance the latter had been receiving from his grandfather's estate, and he had declined to forward a list of relatives abroad. 'You are a nice Count and Prince—both bogus—and you are a bogus gentleman,' he complained.

On 25 February 1928, Robert had written of another debt to be paid from Potocki's allowance, and again there had been a forecast of prison: 'So if you continue to live the dishonourable manner of the past you have much better chances of living in a very strongly built and guarded stone house of large dimension than of in a pretty little thatched cottage near London.' A month later, on 27 March, he wrote: 'You carefully omitted to tell me of the life you are living and how you have managed to live in London for 2 months in a good place for 2/7 halfpenny. Of course I don't believe it. I wish you success but in your own name of W. Geoffrey de M. only.'

Robert's futile attempts to restrain his son and obtain information from him continued:

*9 April 1928*
Dear Geoffrey,
I am sorry for you in London with little cash . . . still it is your own fault and you left your wife—a woman with a small child—penniless in N.Z.
   You must not look to me for money . . . I shall always be glad to hear from you, but instead of quoting a string of all the authors' names you know, which are quite well known to me—I would prefer that you told me what you are doing and that you told me the truth. To tell me you arrived in London with 2/7 halfpenny and that you stayed some weeks in a good lodging house is just not reliable. . . . If you must write, drop poetry and write prose. Go in for writing about clean things and in good English.

*23 April 1928*
. . . Reflect on your life: 1. You are nearly 25 and so far have never earned what I call a decent living salary. 2. You have been in about 8 occupations; in all save one, 'milk', by now you could have been at the top of the tree if you had only stayed in one of them. 3. You spent some £1200 of your wife's money—and after you deserted her and your child. 4. On two occasions you have dropped the family name in the mud for all the world to hear of . . .

*3 June 1928*
. . . I suppose you have found out that I was right in my advice to you not to go to England . . . I miss Cedric, who is in the Herald in Auckland, for whom he is now one of the junior reporters. . . . I hope by now you are in a billet and that you will make Poetry your hobby in spare time and not your life work . . . Your late wife and child passed through I think from Auckland to Christchurch on

Tuesday last. I caught a glimpse of her and the little girl in Lambton Quay . . . I am sorry for her and child. However that is part of your life which like similar things you appear to be proud of—but no one else thinks likewise. . . . You could have been someone honoured and well paid all the time. Perhaps some day you will learn but I don't see that day coming . . .

For his part, Potocki continued to lament his traumatic childhood and the hypocrisy of a father who spoke of honour yet had not only deserted him but refused to acknowledge the pain this had caused. It would seem the more Robert marginalised those difficult years, the more Potocki played out their drama. Had either been willing to unbend, to discuss their differences, so much might have been different. Instead, calls of 'How could you?' echoed between them, and the two men remained locked in competition for the moral high ground.

*7 June 1928*
Dear Geoffrey,
. . . You had better rid yourself of the idea, whether true or otherwise—but actually otherwise—for the cruelties put on you between the years of 7 and 14, now 12 years ago . . . What sort of a man do you call yourself who at 26 complains of the manner of his life when 7 to 14. You ought to be ashamed of yourself—but no, you will not. Of all my family you have been the most favoured. You have had chance after chance . . . and every time you have thrown away the chance . . . You are looked upon as a charlatan . . . one who ill treats his (once) wife and dishonours himself and relatives . . . I have always told you that writing prose was a commercial proposition and I am sure you could make not only a living but a name if you kept to pure English and wrote clean stuff. . . . I advised you years ago not to waste your time on poetry and I knew what I was saying . . . the greatest distinction you have attained is that of an ass—the public who know you, know you for a 'great ass' and not a 'great Poet' and the greater ass because you have the ability to be the opposite.

This letter continues in tones of grave disappointment. Shortcomings are reiterated, responsibilities recalled. 'I want you to become a man— a decent honourable sensible man and not a vain crowned ass,' Robert pleads. 'I do not think that Governments should subsidize poets. If the workman is worthy of his hire the people will pay as they pay the labourer.' Finally there is the threat of withdrawal of financial support. 'I have told you the terms of Vaile's trust and having nothing to add. You complain to the Trust and that will be the end of your portion. That is all. . . . I wish you well as always. Your father, R.W. de Montalk.' As usual there is a postscript: 'How have you lived in London and gone to Paris too—4 months on 2/7 halfpenny . . . not one word of what you have been doing in London and Paris.'

In September, an uncharacteristically brief letter was sent to arrive in time for Potocki's birthday in October:

Dear Geoffrey,
Just a line as I am very busy with patents. Your last letter is sickening . . . You may think you are very wonderful, but none of the decent people which this country has will ever fall down and worship you . . .
 I wish you many happy returns of the day and cannot afford to send you a present.
 . . . Give up this nonsense of re-incarnations etc. It leads to lunacy. I would rather any of mine dead than that. Yes, believe me—the two who love you best and truly only are myself and Cedric.
Your affectionate father, R.W. de Montalk.

Robert may have been losing patience with his son, yet it is difficult to imagine how he thought his tirades would have any effect other than to push him into even more unacceptable behaviour. His was the classic parental dilemma. On the one hand he was saying, 'What are you doing? You're my son. What is this 2/7 halfpenny? Please tell me about your life.' On the other he had a son who, to his mind, was behaving oddly and irresponsibly, and for whom he could see only disaster ahead. Potocki, like any youthful adventurer safe at a distance, simply went his way, hoping to impress but writing selectively of his activities.

Cedric, less affected by his stepmother and therefore closer to his father, had also written in disapproving tones. As a cadet reporter at the *New Zealand Herald* in Auckland, he had spotted an article about his brother in a London newspaper, the contents of which he had not found pleasing. The article, dated 17 July 1928 and headlined 'DINERS TURNED AWAY—COATLESS NEW ZEALANDERS—EXPERIENCE IN WEST END', had described an incident at a restaurant in which Potocki and Glass had been refused service because they were wearing silk shirts and grey trousers without coats. Describing Potocki as 'a poet from New Zealand who has only been a few months in England', it revealed that Mr Geoffrey de Montalk and Mr Douglas Glass had entered the restaurant 'Attired in belted trousers and immaculate silk shirts, with a collar and tie complete', and the manager had refused to serve them. 'He [the Manager] admitted the two were neatly dressed, but stated that if he allowed them to disregard the conventions, others less well dressed might take off not only their coats and waistcoats, but their collars and ties as well.'

Cedric had sent the article to Potocki with a letter dated 27 July:

My Dear Brother,
Nothing terrible or shameful—that I grant you—but conventions are conventions—damn them! And do you realise it hurts and harms! Some people have no tact—not referring to you and your note about tact being another name for hypocrisy . . .

The winds are rustling in the trees at Terespol:
the insects are singing their last summer song
and the first colours of autumn's gorgeous blazon
shine on the leaves. The young nobles loll
on the palace verandah, and the day goes like a long
Elysian dream. Here haste were a treason.
(from 'Praeludium', *Lordly Lovesongs*)

By 1931, Potocki had found it possible to be a poet. Assisted by the small remittance from his grandfather's estate, occasional donations from Uncle Ted, part-time positions in Parisian schools teaching English, and from time to time the financial assistance of benefactors such as Old Splash, he had managed, by living frugally, to feed himself and pursue his calling. The *Sun* newspapers in Christchurch and Auckland were publishing his poetry and regularly commissioning feature articles (including accounts of his meetings with the English poet Humbert Wolfe and American poet Walter Lowenfels), and his poetry was being accepted by the leading outlets of the day: the *Observer*, *Country Life*, the *Irish Statesman*, *Poetry* (Chicago), *Voices* (New York).

Although his early poetic standing, and dream of a place in New Zealand literature, would dissolve in the wake of his obscenity trial and disappear as his eccentricity intensified, there seems little doubt that, prior to his trial in 1932 and as his publications list grew, Potocki was regarded as showing literary promise. Would he have enjoyed some degree of success? Is it conceivable that, had he not gone to prison and emerged for ever angry and embittered, the England of which he had written with 'sentimental adoration' in 1929: 'No wonder the English language is like the voice of the wind/the voice of the trees, of the mountains, of the sea', would have remained easy in his mind, his politics and poetic vision likewise?

His father might not have thought it likely. Much of Potocki's poetry at this time was written in praise of women, and on 30 June 1929 Robert expressed dissatisfaction with his son's choice of subject:

> My dear Geoffrey,
> ... I see occasionally some of your work. It does not please me either as to the poetry or the matter. I don't like hips, kisses, breasts, warm bodies, etc. Perhaps one poem on these lines is excusable, but not repetition after repetition. On the other hand I believe you have very strong literary talents and if you go in for good clean work—something elevating—in choice English—and avoiding the general use of words unknown to the million—and use plain words—that you could make your mark ...

Robert also poured scorn on the recent innovation of a small crown on Potocki's letterhead, reminded him that his 'dear mother', who was an artist of some ability, had often said 'if I had to earn my living I would be a dressmaker or milliner as there is no money in painting', and disagreed with his favourable assessment of Katherine Mansfield, dismissing her as 'very ordinary'. He returned as always to the question of an orthodox occupation: 'You are a born teacher. Why not qualify for a Professorship in Languages ... after which you could get a post in N.Z., Australia, Africa, Canada in one of the universities at £1,000 a year.'

Disdain is a powerful disincentive to compliance, and parental disdain, particularly that of a parent perceived as flawed, the more so. On discovering that Robert's disapproval now extended to 'kisses, breasts, warm bodies', I began to wonder if there was a suggestion of rebellion, as well as daring, in Potocki's progression from the mildly erotic verse he had been writing to the ribald work and translations for which he would soon be tried. Had Robert, in all his understandable parental concern, his desperate predictions of imprisonment, and now what Potocki might have seen as his hypocritical declaration of puritanism, inadvertently encouraged his son to move in a more sexually frank direction?

During this period Potocki made the acquaintance of New Zealand poet Walter D'Arcy Cresswell. 'I had a letter from him, inviting me to visit him. He had a very small bed-sitter in Stourcliffe Street, on the top floor, and in the end I visited him there many times. You knocked loudly with the knocker—one knock for each storey, and in the case of Cresswell three—and he would put his head out of the window and throw down the key.' In *Recollections of My Fellow Poets*, Potocki remembers that 'The room was definitely rather sordid':

> There was a large double bed, made up in the usual way for that sort of place, with one of those, as it were, honey-combed white cotton spreads with white cotton tassels all round. The fire place was in cast iron, and 'shaped like a tomb-stone', as mentioned at the head of one of his poems. It was painted a shiny black. This had however one advantage. For each week Cresswell would inscribe with white chalk thereon a line of poetry by one of the great English poets, which at the beginning of the next week he would obliterate in order to replace it with a different verse.

Despite his less than salubrious surroundings, Cresswell was always hospitable and Potocki was usually presented with afternoon tea when he called. It was some time before he realised Cresswell was homosexual. He writes:

> Reverting to the big bed: one day I met at Cresswell's place a young man designated as "Edward" . . . After Edward had gone, Cresswell explained in a purposeful tone of voice, that he did not

really love Edward until he slept with him. But in spite of glances toward the bed, I was, shall we say, so dense about such matters, that it was not until some time later that I tumbled to what he meant by this to me, cryptic remark. I fear he was like so many British members of that confraternity, so aggressive about it that to him people who did not happen to be employed that way—were scarcely human. It even comes out in his posthumous poetic play, or mystery, called *The Forest*, which is otherwise very good.

Afternoon teas aside, however, Potocki considered Cresswell to be aggressive and arrogant 'and school-marmy on many subjects besides this', and very much concerned with bagging the title of 'Only New Zealand Poet', an attitude he did not find in the other New Zealand poets, all of whom showed a friendly interest in each other's work. He also considered Cresswell's determined door-to-door selling of poetry to be in poor taste, even though at sixpence a poem, or half a crown a set, it proved to be financially rewarding: 'In those days', he told me, 'a silver halfcrown would buy a meal at the Diner Français, in Old Compton Street, which would last you two days. Or two three-course meals at Poggioli's. Or twenty-four half-pints of milk.'

Cresswell's attitude caused Potocki to self-publish a long satire entitled 'Against Cresswell, A Lampoon'. The lampoon, which was started one evening while walking back from Cresswell's flat in Marble Arch to his basement flat in Earls Court, and completed at four o'clock the following morning, was 'Like most of my satirical efforts . . . purely and simply a truthful account of what happened.' After the poem was printed, Glass took a copy to Cresswell. 'According to Glass's report,' Potocki writes in *Recollections*, 'Cresswell began by taking the poem in his left hand. He contemplated fixedly the outside cover: which he then struck with the back of his right hand, exclaiming: "There ought not to be a full stop after the word CRESSWELL."' To which Potocki responded: 'I would agree, but this comes of not printing the thing with one's own hands. All the same—how britisch—to fix on some truly irrelevant detail!'

The poem was reviewed in Poland by Dr Marjan Z. Arend of Poznań, in *Kurier Poznański*, January 1931, in an article which starts: 'Count Geoffrey Potocki de Montalk, that name will at once intrigue a Pole.' Arend continues:

Cresswell, with the arrogance typical of a man belonging to the new colonial countries, offended Potocki by the assertion, that he (Potocki) does not know how to write serious poetry, a field that ought to belong to him (Cresswell) . . . [Potocki] points to his own origin . . . and proclaims himself

> . . . a bright bloom of a glorious line
> from which the Muse was now about to shine
> for the second time in fullest power—
> Wacław Potocki was the former flower
> in whom a races of princes turned to song—

Describing Potocki as 'a young man—for the whole tenor of the work betrays youth', Arend finds that, although 'the literary quarrel of the two young New Zealand poets concerns us little, the really important thing in the meantime is, that G. Potocki de Montalk has already published some collections of poems, which have met with friendly criticism, and still further, that he intends to opine his future creating in Polish themes, wishing to spread the knowledge of Polish affairs in the Southern hemisphere. On that road it befits us to wish him success.'

Meanwhile, two collections of poetry had been building. At Easter 1930, *Surprising Songs*, 'An Odyssean tale in poetry', was published in London, in hard covers, by Columbia Press. In his foreword Potocki decries 'Christianity and democracy', against which he raises 'the banner of the aristocratic gods, and their sons, the kings and the poets'. He says of New Zealand: 'It is true that in some ways that superb and lovely land is a very bad place. For me it was Hell from which I fled at the very first possible moment.' He also declares:

> The writing of pretty little verses is a waste of good time (and print). Let us talk less about poetry and more about the Poet. It is useless to imagine that all this tame Georgian verse will live. At the back of the written poetry must loom the great spirit, the outrider of the hordes of men, the king proclaiming his kingdom, the avatar bearing in his own being a light against the darkness.
>
> For poetry without the Poet is as stale and empty as a land without a king.

The collection, which is dedicated 'To My Friend The Count Adam Chrapowicki', comprises sixty pages. Many of the poems were reprinted courtesy of prestigious publications in New Zealand, England and the United States, and the final arrangement had been decided with the assistance of Walter Lowenfels.

The songs are a surprising mix of subject and tone. Self-righteous formalists are taken to task:

> You are not to be trusted—your misuse
> of Christ's Own life shows this, since you have bent
> the Jesus of a forged New Testament
> into an argument for self abuse.
> (from 'Credo In Unum Deum Omnipotentem')

Homesickness is acknowledged:

> The Seine flooded to within a foot of its quays
> reminds me often in a secondhand way
> of the Waimakariri, whose island willow-trees
> are the city-isle of the Louis.
>                     The sunny day
>
> shines a cold blue behind black gothic towers.
> My heart cries for Kaianga willows (dreary
> rows of hotels reply) Kairaki firs
> and pines and sand, and the wide Waimakariri.
> ('Paris')

And the ceremony of high church, including evensong, which Potocki attended nightly whichever city he was in, is celebrated:

> Do You, Lord Christ, when evensong is rung,
> walk back and forth in the triforium
> listening quietly to antiphon
> and Magnificat and Nunc Dimittis sung
>
> in this imperial Abbey in the afternoon?
> (from 'Evensong')

A number of poems are written in praise of women: Lilian, Avice, Elsie, Evelyn, Rose, Clare, Ada:

> Did you not feel upon my mouth the glow
> of lilac clouds in sunsets I have loved,
> of summery dreaminess in the South, a row
> of arched gothic silent pines, where moved
>
> only the swish under the cliff of the soft sea?
> (from 'Evelyn')

Twelve copies of *Surprising Songs* were printed on hand-made paper, for people who had been encouraging or financially helpful. They included Walter de la Mare and Charles Lahr.

The following year *Lordly Lovesongs*, a collection of poems written almost daily, and sometimes several times a day, during and for a time after his stay at Terespol Palace in Lithuania in 1929, appeared from the same press. Dedicated to 'Zinka Countess Chrapowicka', sister of his host, the verses, a number of which had previously been published in *Country Life* and *Poetry*, woo the countess until finally she permits him to kiss her. They remember her after he returns to London: 'What shall be done with these?/The memories of you leaning with tender grace/against the wall', and hope that when they are reunited they will 'steal the very eyes of the gods'.

Reviews of the two volumes were favourable. Of *Surprising Songs*, Dr Zbigniew Grabowski wrote in *Ilustrowany Kurier Codzienny* (Kraków):

> In the sum of these poems, written with eminent mastery and craftsmanship . . . and immense economy of words, there is no lack of declarations of love nor of confessions of faith in life. His erotic poems are lit through with thoughtfulness . . . not blurred pastel, but decided sweeps, revealing everywhere a tendency towards synthesis alike in image as in thought. He enriches English poetry with his own valuable qualities, as much in imagery as in command of words.

Arend, in *Kurier Poznański*, was similarly enthusiastic:

Here rings both the beauty of classic language and form, and the splendour of warm colours. And nota bene, how many poets in Poland could write such verse? Youth, sureness, warmth of feeling, a good literary style, as in the English classics of the Elizabethan and following ages, besides an undoubted lordship over form, seem to foretell for Potocki an uncommon future.

Humbert Wolfe is quoted on the promotions page of subsequent Potocki publications—available 'at many of the best bookshops in London'—as having said:

> It did seem to me that here was work which deserved attention, and in which I personally found promise of something very definite . . . His work is eager, it is sensitive, it is as prehensile of some aspects of life as a monkey. There is life here! . . . A bright, chaotic mind.

Similarly cited is Walter de la Mare, who wrote:

> Full of enthusiasm and colour (perhaps with an excess of this) . . . a genuine gift of expression but . . . at times technically erratic . . . in my small opinion of it [*Surprising Songs*] showed definite literary promise for the future.

In New Zealand, Ian Donnelly wrote in the *Sun*: 'A provocative and original thinker. He is a writer with universal interests, and amazing examples of large sympathy and varied interests are to be found in his poetry.' While the perceptive Cresswell told Potocki: 'You will take my advice, I sincerely hope, about scrupulously regularising your verse for the purpose of satire. I think you may make a name for yourself if you do and delight us all.'

If there were direct words of criticism, presumably Potocki did not keep them. The only negative notes in his archive came from his family. Uncle Ted's comments were typical:

> Dear Geoffrey,
> Your letter carrying news of all your literary doings and projects and prospects has been with me about a week. The two copies of *Surprising Songs* are also to hand and I have read a good many of the poems. I must confess that I do not understand most of them.

In August 1930 Cedric arrived in London, having left New Zealand against the advice of his father. He too had poetic aspirations, and doubtless envied his brother's freedom. Uncle Ted wrote from Auckland:

> You know that I got him a job with the 'Herald' and that he did his best to show the proprietors and the staff how the paper should be run—with the inevitable result that he got run himself. I very much fear that poor Cedric has not strength either physical or mental to battle his way in London. I dread to hear that he has died of starvation.

Rex Fairburn followed in the autumn. In the two years since Potocki had left, Fairburn's disenchantment with New Zealand had increased. On a personal level he was unemployed, and his uncertainty with women had seen him unable to sustain romantic attachments. Creatively, he felt isolated and directionless. His article for the *New Zealand Artists' Annual* of August 1929, upbraiding the culturally barren populace for its neglect of the new poetic voice of Mason, summarised his position: 'There seems to be very little of hope of establishing a native literature in New Zealand as long as the people continue to ignore the claims of talent of this sort.'

Mason, however, had not been persuaded that he also should leave New Zealand. Although he observed that 'Rex looks worried and (sounds silly to say it) is ageing. Seems to be worrying, just sort of slops along without any ambition', he himself had given up teaching in favour of outdoor work in the country and was on the verge of increased creativity. In January 1930, in the letter to Potocki which was possibly never sent, he had written:

> I often think of you as I roam by some secluded and delightful solitude; with affection not unmixed with a sense of arrogance that after all perhaps I have made the better choice. At the moment I happen to be staying with an elderly maiden aunt at a quiet little country settlement where I have spent at least 6 years of my life. When the sun shines it is absolute Paradise . . .
>   I must admit that the prospect of England appals me . . . Of

course, I should like to see it, but I fancy a very little bit would give me a belly-ache. After all, this is my own native-land and all that . . .

I hope this finds you as lusty and unabashed as of old. Wish I could see you occasionally . . .

By now Potocki was a distinctive and familiar figure in the streets of Soho. He wore a cape, and leather sandals without socks, and he had allowed his hair to grow. He had adopted the cape on returning from Paris at the end of 1929, at which time he still dressed 'as a very proper young British person', even though it had always been his view that everything was wrong with conventional clothing: 'It was hideous: bad colours, bad shape, an insult to the human form.'

He explained to me that the cape came after his 'very modest and well-made gentleman's overcoat in navy-blue woollen material wore out'. Lacking sufficient funds to replace it, he had his Swiss girlfriend, Marcelle, make up a cape in cotton. When this wore out, 'Minnie, who I was living with at the time, and was a marvellous seamstress, made a second cape from a marvellous great length of crimson cloth which was really curtain material.' He had found men's shirts 'particularly hideous', although he believed they improved under the influence of the Japanese. 'They would only open so far down, and one had to go to Harrods or some place like that in order to get a decent shirt. Before Fairburn arrived I bought a shirt from Harrods—an expensive shirt—and I can't remember for what reason, but I had cause to complain about it. So I got my private secretary, Dorothy Cannibal, to write to Harrods concerning the grievance, following which they sent a replacement shirt and an apologetic letter. Dorothy Cannibal was an invention, and Fairburn, who arrived soon after the incident, was very taken with the idea of her. Then I discovered many years later that he had appropriated her and made considerable use of her in his own publications, as if he had invented her himself. Perhaps by now there's some copyright in personal secretaries. But as far as the cloak was concerned, I wasn't going to go around dressed like a poor person who couldn't afford an overcoat, so I therefore preferred to have a great big crimson cape, you see.'

Potocki's abhorrence of 'modern men's clothing', resulting in the adoption of cloaks and robes, has been seen by many as a manifestation of narcissism—a condition attributed in *Heinz Kohut and the*

*Psychology of Self* to problems that arise when the child's natural process of becoming aware of itself as a child, separate from its mother, is upset. These problems, Kohut believes, offering the example of the premature death of a mother, can lead to the development of traits of 'omnipotence, grandiosity and exhibitionistic narcissism'.

I found Kohut's theory compelling: Potocki had himself said that the death of his mother was the great disaster of his life. But, while it appeared the cause might be correct, I was not so sure Potocki was wholly narcissistic. Thinking further about his preoccupation with himself—his 'famous vanity', as he once jokingly dismissed an 'impertinent' suggestion of self-worship—it seemed to me that, although his behaviour before I met him certainly suggested an intense psychological preoccupation with himself, in his later years at least he was driven day to day as much by caprice and his original view of the world as by self-absorption.

I found him to be as relaxed in and about his robes as a wearer of a kilt or caftan, and I knew that, were he still alive, he would have something very strong to say about Kohut and his theory. Potocki had no time for the 'sect of pretenders who call themselves psycho-analysts, psychologists and the like—quacks for the most part' or their theories, which he dismissed as 'dogmatic and arbitrary as the most far-fetched religious beliefs, and far more illogical'. On analysing his life, he had written in the typescript that part of its purpose was to show that his childhood could be explained satisfactorily without the condescending aid of so-called experts, and that 'All that is needed in order to get at least as far as they get, is brains, penetration, and insight. After that,' he continues, 'astrology and religious myth will provide more fruitful clues, than any they have to offer.'

Fairburn's arrival was greeted with enthusiasm. The two had corresponded regularly for the past two years, and Potocki's affection for him as a fellow-poet was undiminished. 'I'm looking forward to taking you all over Europe, Poland included,' Potocki had written in February 1930. 'And if you stay here a year or so, I daresay you'll never go back.'

In the foreword to *Surprising Songs* he had referred to his friend as a 'poet of the great line' and 'my very beautiful young friend'. He had also dedicated a poem in the collection to Fairburn, 'one of the three I love most in the world'. Entitled 'Rex', the poem could be read as a song in favour of Fairburn:

> Flaunting your golden cape, at last you come,
> stirring more than girls or wine can do
> blood that after the long gloom is numb.

These words were, however, in praise of the sun god, Apollo, as the last lines of this first stanza confirm: 'You are a little late, we have stayed for you,/my Lord the Sun.' Much later, these references to Fairburn were to rebound on Potocki. Some would argue that there were elements of a homosexual attachment in their relationship, suggestions which Potocki hotly denied: 'It was very foolish and naïve, I agree,' he told me, 'but there was never any suggestion of any such thing. All my references were to the sun. This was a poem of sun worship, not Fairburn worship.'

To begin with, Fairburn lived with Potocki, who introduced him to other poets, including Edgell Rickword and Humbert Wolfe, and to artists, and eager female company. But the closeness the pair had enjoyed in New Zealand, and during their two years of intense correspondence, would not be sustained in London. 'Of course I lost no time in dragging him to Westminster Abbey, but he could not be induced to obey the rules. He preferred music drifting from afar, in the pursuance of which, while Glass and I sat down in the choir stalls for evensong, Rex mooned around in the Poets' Corner.'

It appears that, as much as Fairburn was excited by the idea of London at first—'It's a lovely old place—my breath is taken away a hundred times a day by its sheer beauty,' he wrote to Mason on 13 October 1930—he rapidly tired of city life. And to Potocki's disappointment he did not share his own enthusiasm for cultural enrichment, for places like Westminster Abbey and the 'wonderful music' that was to be heard at some of the sung services; nor even for the *Book of Common Prayer*, which Potocki considered to be 'one of the high peaks of European literature, until our degenerate bishops in our time abolished it'. When Fairburn confessed, six months after arriving, that he still had not been to see St Paul's Cathedral and wondered whether a visit would be worth the trouble, Potocki's opinion of him was certainly not improving. He replied scornfully: 'Oh no! I shouldn't bother if I were you. It's only the greatest Renaissance church in the north of Europe, that's all.'

There was also the 'extended course of sedulous pub-crawling' which, to Potocki's disgust, Rex embarked on, to the exclusion on one occasion of Potocki's birthday, and on another the Trooping of the Colours. 'I will say that some of his pub-crawling was done with Edgell Rickword, who to my way of thinking was about the only good English poet of the time (in spite of his being an active communist, as in the case of R.A.K. Mason). I will also say that in England it is almost impossible to get anywhere without pub-crawling. As against which, he did not get anywhere anyhow.'

On occasion Potocki was embarrassed by Fairburn's boorish behaviour. He describes such an instance in *Recollections of My Fellow Poets*:

> One day Rex, Douglas Glass, and I went to visit Edgell Rickword, who had a top storey flat in Cathcart Road, or was it in Finsburough [*sic*] Road round the corner. There he abode with Betty May. The door of the house was opened by the landlady thereof. She was a typical frumpish and totally unattractive proletarian London landlady, except that she seemed to be a good-natured person.
>
> Fairburn promptly engaged her in a juicy conversation about fucking. It was obvious that he thought himself very daring using various forbidden words, particularly 'fuck', with this faded frump. I had the impression that she was pleased enough to hear this magical word proceeding from the mouth of this handsome young nit-wit, but was somewhat embarrassed also.
>
> Afterwards, I had to ask him, not for the last time, if he seriously thought he was imitating me and Glass.

Given Potocki's flamboyant attire and aristocratic preoccupations, moments of embarrassment were almost certainly experienced mutually.

Towards the end of 1930 Potocki encouraged Fairburn to arrange for the Columbia Press (Potocki's own publisher) to print his first collection of poetry, *He Shall Not Rise*. Despite their joint interest in the publication of Fairburn's collection, as 1931 wore on—and Potocki moved closer to his obscenity trial—the pair drifted further apart. Fairburn entered into a serious relationship with a fine arts student, New Zealander Jocelyn Mays, and married her at the end of November. Now he faced fatherhood, domestic responsibilities, and increasingly a social conscience. When New Zealand friend Clifton Firth suggested that Potocki's early poetry was superior to his, Fairburn replied angrily on 23 December 1931:

> Monty is an example of the dissipation of self, not the concentration and refinement of self. His mediaeval, sentimental, Chopin, droit du seigneur, prick-obsessed, Polish love stuff is *not* as good as mine. I had the sentimentality natural to youth, and have since lost most of it. Monty has not.

In New Zealand, the de Montalk family were similarly impatient. Potocki's mail from home was a litany of disapproval. Uncle Ted asked of the lampoon on Cresswell: 'What object is served by the publication of a lampoon on a perfect nonentity?' He also had something to say about the unsatisfactory reports of the 'indolent, dishonest, and generally disreputable' life his nephew was leading:

> You are of age and must decide for yourself what sort of life you lead but I am certainly not going to help you to keep mistresses instead of paying your debts. You cannot therefore look for any further financial assistance from me.

Potocki, incensed but undeterred, answered:

> ... I should hate you to think I want to whitewash myself, for I'm damned if I do; but you may as well have the facts right. I can hardly go into your accusation that I lead a slothful life, because I do not know what your conception of this term is. I am very energetic and industrious in my own way, but I have no desire to deny that I read or study into the small hours of the morning (to catch up with the education I missed by being born in N.Z.) and then sleep till noon, but I don't see in what way this concerns you.
> As to debts, you seem to have the idea that I am living on my debts, as I did my last year in New Zealand. As a matter of fact I have struggled and starved to keep out of debt ... it is true I have run into debt, but very little since the debt you are talking about is the only one I owe, except three or four smaller debts which I am doing my best to reduce.

He added that he did not squander money on mistresses:

I hope to be able to be more generous with my girl friends when I am a lot richer than I am now, but in the meantime let me tell you that since I have been in Europe I have spent no money on girls beyond an odd shilling or two when I am well enough off to be able to afford some little present such as a few flowers. Don't let me be misunderstood: I have <u>girl</u> friends, I don't mind if you call them mistresses, concubines, wives, anything you like: but I do <u>not</u> spend money on them except in infinitesimal quantities. I am at least too much a man to be obliged to pay for love.

Unwilling to place himself at financial odds with his uncle, he finished on a conciliatory note, invoking vague plans for the welfare of Wanda:

> . . . I am half disposed to sell my interest in both my father's settlements, in any case I am going to raise enough money on them to buy a house in England and I am quite determined to have Wanda over here and see her decently educated in languages, literature, and made into a cultured woman generally. I realise too well what I missed, to be willing to see her waste her youth where she is now. Best of love to yourself and Uncle Bert, also Aunt Evie.
> Your affectionate nephew Geoffrey.
> P.S. Please don't get the idea I want you to send me money. G.

By now Potocki, in the manner of many who, when tantalising details of their forebears start coming to light, need to know more, was intensely interested in his genealogy. Attracted by his ancestral 'gleam of splendour', he was also advancing a tentative claim to the vacant throne of Poland—a claim which, although fanciful, was not completely without foundation. He told me: 'I began expressing claims to the throne of Poland round about 1930. I don't know why, apart from the fact that I'd had ancient and royal convictions since childhood. It was just one of those things. No, it wasn't a gimmick at that time. Certainly not. And even now I should have thought my claims to the throne of Poland would be not at all foolish except for one thing and that is I'm not a Roman Catholic. That's the only real obstacle to it. Cedric was interested all right, but then he was the younger brother. And my father was only interested in boasting that he was the son of Count Potocki.'

At this time Potocki based his claim on his descent from Polish aristocracy, and a Polish tradition of elective monarchy from within the ranks of nobles. Three years later, in Poland, however, he found that he could strengthen his royal assertion by virtue of his descent from the House of Piast, one of the great ruling dynasties of Poland. His claim then became based on the marriage of his great-great-grandfather, Count Jan Alojzy Potocki, to Princess Marjanna Czartoryska, a descendant of the Silesian Piast family: 'What happened was that Sybillia Piast married the aristocrat Gerhard Denhoff; his great-granddaughter, Teresa, married Prince Czartoryski of Korzec; and their eldest great-granddaughter was Marjanna Czartoryska. The Piast family reigned over Poland as a whole, and then over parts of the kingdom, including Silesia, until the middle of the seventeenth century, when they became extinct in the male line. The Jagiełło dynasty, which had muscled in about 1400 AD and intermarried with the Piasts, also became extinct, and as there were no Jagiełłonian descendants, I believed I could make a claim. It's true I claimed through the female side, but the Polish system allows this.'

Although he would pursue the throne in a spectacular and often light-hearted fashion, acquiring a small silver crown, devising ceremonies in Latin, and bestowing knighthoods on admirers and other worthy recipients, the basis of his claim remained a serious matter. He became convinced that, in the wake of elective kings (following the abdication of Jan Kazimierz in 1668), 'Poland had practically ceased to exist' and that the elective system 'was the principal and only really fundamental cause of the destruction of the Polish State'. Accordingly, he prepared complex tables and other documents of proof supporting his descent from the hereditary king, Kazimierz IV, through the Silesian Piasts. 'Our claim is therefore,' he would write in a 'Legal Basis' of claim drawn up for Richard Aldington on 10 October 1955, 'that We are the best possible representative of the elder dynasty Piast, and We are merely renewing the claim of Our Ancestress, the Countess Denhoff, put forward during one of the elections.' In the light of this evidence, he concluded, he might therefore consent 'to be the last elected and first new hereditary king' of Poland.

# SIX

## Return to New Zealand

*However undoubtedly pleasant Ao tea roa may be to live in, it is only the taking part in the growth of culture in New Zealand, that can justify a person like myself in establishing himself there.*

It is summer in Wellington, 1984, and a ceremony is taking place in our house in Kelburn. Potocki is standing in the middle of the lounge in a long garment of Polish hop silk, and the loose leather sandals he wears in summer with bare feet, and in winter with the woollen socks he draws up to his knees and refers to as stockings. The sun is low, and Eastbourne on the other side of the harbour is reflecting back the last bright light of the day. There is the low sound of an incantation in Latin and the dry smell of incense. A young man in a kilt is kneeling in front of Potocki and a student poet with long hair is sitting on the window-seat, an official witness to the ritual.

Potocki dubs the young man with the blade of his silver Louis XVI sword. Jonathon, Donovan and Dylan eat pies and watch television in the dining room on the other side of the glass doors. Melissa, breathless in trainers, bursts into the lounge without knocking. 'Geoffrey,' she says, 'I need my sweatshirt.' She lifts it from the sofa, and leaves the room without closing the door—as if the induction of a liegeman of life and limb as Lord of Sidra in our lounge at sunset is an everyday occurrence.

Potocki pauses, raises his eyes above the top of his spectacles and watches her—probably with pleasure, since she's wearing shorts.

In late winter 1983 I received word from France that finally, after an absence of fifty-six years, Potocki would return to New Zealand. He planned a six-month visit during which he would rent a small flat, reunite with his family and 'try to whip up some interest in [his] literary and other work'. He advised that, in accordance with his horoscope, he would leave France by car early on 8 September 1983, for Switzerland. 'If all goes to plan,' he wrote, 'I should arrive via Nouméa, at Auckland, 10.45pm on the 29th of September.'

On 18 October, however, he was still in Switzerland, safely indisposed, courtesy of the horoscope:

> ... What happened was that as soon as I arrived in Switzerland I was taken ill and it was diagnosed as a case of acute appendicitis. I certainly never expected to have appendicitis, especially when just off eighty. Anyway I was rushed off to the hospital and operated on virtually at once (as soon as they had time to do the usual preliminaries, the same night). I was then confined to the intensive care unit. During the fortnight I was there I was no good for anything, but since I have been convalescing with Frederica looking after me, and I seem to be getting almost back to normal.
>
> A young Polish nurse who took an interest in my 'case' said that the appendix itself was burst, hence the peritonitis, and it certainly appears that had I not been operated on at once, I should not have survived.

He arrived in Auckland on 9 November 1983. A week later he wrote to me:

> Several days of parties, readings and the like followed as well as two articles in the Herald, somewhat spiteful though they may be useful as publicity, and an interview on 1ZB which I consider satisfactory, although it was interrupted with publicity on the first occasion, but not on the Sunday. Doubtless the Lord does not like publicity, in which case I entirely agree with him.

The publicity had been generated in part by the recent publication of Potocki's slim volume of essays, *Recollections of My Fellow Poets*. The essays, dated 1 June 1983, had been published by Donald Kerr to coincide with Potocki's return to New Zealand. Conversational in tone, they recall New Zealand poets Maxwell Rudd, R.A.K. Mason, Rex Fairburn, Walter D'Arcy Cresswell, Alison Grant and, briefly, Carl von Straubel. Potocki's recollections of the poets are characteristically incisive, irreverent and amusing, and Kerr as editor had wisely 'maintained a policy of non-interference, trying my utmost to present the essays to readers as they were to me'. He had made only 'one or two very small changes but nothing that would change the true sense of what is written'.

The *Herald*, however, which pre-empted Potocki's arrival in Auckland with a feature article on 29 October prompted by the recollections, had published a somewhat skittish review of his life. Readers were told that 'Oral history records that during his youthful days in New Zealand he brightened the drab streets of Auckland and Christchurch by his regal garb of flowing crimson cloak and matching crimson velvet cap adorned with the Polish royal eagle and the escutcheon of the feudal house of Potocki', and, in a reference to his aristocratic ancestry and claim to the throne of Poland, commented that the royal palace in Warsaw is now probably a tractor factory.

'More lies!' Potocki no doubt exclaimed, as he did whenever confronted by myths about his behaviour. In fact, there was no cloak or crimson velvet cap in New Zealand, and the royal robes—self-made after researching medieval dress in the British Museum—were not worn until after his release from prison in 1932. The quip about the palace was similarly misplaced. Potocki palaces still existed in their own right both within Poland and in those parts of the former Polish Ukraine which were then part of the USSR, while the (late baroque) Pałac Potocki in the Krakowskie Przedmiescie, Warsaw, which was reconstructed after World War II, far from being a factory was part of the Ministry of Arts and Culture.

But Potocki, accustomed to an unfriendly New Zealand press, moved on. He purchased a car, attended a number of literary occasions, and rounded up relations and other interested people, leaving in his wake phone calls and flurries of correspondence about his capacity for conversation.

At Christmas we received the customary poem for the Feast of Saturn from Tauranga, where he was staying with his daughter, Wanda, last seen in 1927, when she was two. The poem had been hand-printed. Even in the midst of returning home, he had managed to track down a small press. The absence of punctuation was unusual—typesetting limitations, perhaps—as was the wistful tone:

> Places where I would like to be
> and have not been

places which I would like to see
and have not seen
Kajurahu and Angkor Wat
and Udaipur
temples and palaces wherefrom
visions of light endure.

On 28 December, at six pm, after ringing for off-ramp instructions from Palmerston North, he arrived at our address, a small figure at the wheel of a weathered blue Austin 1800, his standard on the bonnet, firm in the Wellington breeze. As he sat down to a meal of spiced sausage and rice, apricots and ice-cream, he declared that he had found New Zealand to be even more beautiful than he remembered. 'The exception is Auckland,' he said. 'Much of the architecture is in poor taste, and parts of it have been changed beyond recognition.' He added: 'But the drive between Paeroa and Waihi has to be one of the most beautiful in the world.'

He appeared to have taken his reunion with his daughter and her family in his stride. He had enjoyed picnics and other family gatherings over Christmas, admired his descendants and argued with Wanda's husband—a returned serviceman—about the war. But now that he was in Wellington there was a literary life to pursue.

I was interested to know how Wanda had responded to her father. There had been correspondence between them. Lilian, her mother, had spoken of him—she had been very much in love with Potocki when he left her to 'follow the golden road to Samarkand' in 1927, and had found the social stigma and financial insecurity of solo parenting hard—and Wanda had been aware of his controversies and the tendency of the wider family to shun him.

'He was like a stranger,' Wanda said when we spoke about Potocki some years after his death. 'And he wore me out. Looking back, I suppose this was because in a subliminal sense he made me feel like a kid. I was fifty-six, I had a husband and children, I was a free-standing woman—I made my own decisions—and suddenly he'd come home, and the house had to revolve around him. This took me down. He was pleasant when he wasn't fighting the war with Bob, which he did every morning—and I had to keep the peace—but it was too late for the family to be subservient to a patriarch.'

His arrival in Wellington coincided with a very busy time for me.

Only two weeks earlier John and I had taken over the wardenship of Weir House, a large multicultural university hall of residence in Kelburn, and had moved the family from Karori to a tired though spacious house alongside the hall.

There was much to be done at Weir House, home to 230 students from twenty-six countries—not only to the Warden's residence, but also to the hall itself. The furniture and furnishings were in an advanced state of disrepair, standards of student behaviour had broken down, and funds for setting things right were minimal. Even though the comparative quiet of the summer vacation had descended on Kelburn and there were only small groups of international students in residence, I was deep in catering and cleaning contracts and the costing of a major maintenance programme. I was also wrestling with the finer points of student discipline for the coming year. How did one deal with drunken vomiting in the corridors, urinating into rubbish bins, feeding friends from outside flats free in the dining room? Fighting at drunken parties? What would it take to break the pattern of false fire-alarms in the middle of the night—twenty-nine the previous year—and the disregard for property? Any day now vans would be arriving from goodwill shops to remove damaged wardrobes and beds. A row of bins in the car park awaited badly stained carpets and leanly upholstered chairs, and the chef was still insisting, despite strong advice to the contrary, that the contingent from the People's Republic of China did not have a problem with curried eggs once a week for lunch.

Potocki, however, undiminished by his recent surgery, air travel and full schedule, seized on what he declared to be our 'ideal arrangements' close to the cable car, city and university, and installed himself in a bedroom vacated by Jonathon for 'a week or two, three at the most'. Out came the familiar scent and sound of the altar; the typewriter at which he clattered, seemingly without pausing to think, edit or draft; the piles of papers and books. Interested people arrived to visit and sip whisky with him in Jonathon's bedroom. At meal times he made his way eagerly to the dining hall, where he ate everything on offer—especially the curried eggs—and tested the conversational skills of the summer students.

A suitcase and a tea-chest full of manuscripts and books arrived, and were unpacked. An acquaintanceship with Rod Cave, Professor of Librarianship, was renewed, and access to the old Arab platen press which was housed in the original buildings of the university was arranged.

The possibility of a New Zealand pension was canvassed. And, although he said he could not very well stay at our place for ever, and would much rather live up north than in Wellington, for in Wellington he 'would pretty well have to get a much smaller car', we started to become aware that the term 'short visit' was meant to be measured in months.

A few weeks after he arrived, he decided to rediscover the South Island and took temporary leave, departing early one morning, before we had risen, to catch the car ferry to Picton. On 22 January he wrote from Christchurch:

> This morning I went to Christchurch Cathedral. They carried on like a gang of Baptists. I told the main priest that they were not Anglicans but Presbyterians. He said: 'I couldn't agree with you more.' And it turns out that in his own church he has one service on Sundays (St Barnabas) at which the old Book of Common Prayer is used exactly as in the days before they invented all those wicked improvements.
>
> The choir, like everything else in New Zealand, has gone into the Deep Freeze for December and January. On Wednesday I am to have tea at the university with the professor of Latin and Greek, and I mean to ask him whether the university would accept a thesis in Latin for a doctorate. But I think I shall write the thesis in any case and I shall probably find some university which will accept it. On Monday morning if all goes well, I propose to set out for Dunedin and if all goes well shall stay there a couple of days. After that I shall try to get myself invited to Invercargill.

In Dunedin he inspected the Hocken Library's holdings of his poems and translations, gave readings of his work, and found friendly interest in his writing and unusual life. The *Otago Daily Times* described him as 'vigorous, learned and cosmopolitan', as 'an avowed royalist, and an enemy of democracy' and reported him as declaring '"The whole thesis on which democracy is based is totally unjust . . . like one man, one vote"', and '"The biggest idiot can have a vote whereas a valuable person also has one vote." Eyes sparkling,' it continued, 'this fiercely independent man said he did not care about public opinion because the public were stupid.'

On his way back to Wellington he broke the journey with some of our 'extremely helpful friends'. Would they remain so? we wondered. 'If I possibly can I shall try to extend these breaks still further,' he continued, 'for I like the idea of getting back to your hospitable mansion on the 12th February, and with luck, a day or two after that Dr Cave's printing press will be ready for use. There has been some good weather, but I do not think much of it for a New Zealand summer.'

In May, with a New Zealand pension a strong possibility, he drove to Auckland, put his car into storage and flew to Europe for six months, where he wrote to Rod Cave from Switzerland:

> I am a bit tired after all my voyages, but I do expect to be back next week at the Villa Vigoni. It is very nice being up here with my Swiss lady friend, but the atmospheric pressure at sea level, or nearly so, suits me far better than up in the Alps. No one would ever see me up in these parts were it not for her.
>
> It will be something to be able to eat European bread instead of the perfectly frightful rubbish they sell in New Zealand. And to drink something more like real milk, than what they sell there, in a country with hundreds of thousands of pure-bred Jersey cows (with their tails cut off by white savages.)

He planned to return in August. In the meantime, the Broadcasting Corporation of New Zealand had approved my proposal for a television documentary, and I was dusting off the interviews I had recorded in Edinburgh and trying to make some sense of his writing and all those disparate stories. The documentary was to be a first for me—my previous film-making experience had been limited to dressing sets and managing the production of television commercials—and for John, who had agreed to assist with the financial and legal aspects of the production. It was also a first for director Ian Paul, a lighting cameraman working mainly on commercials, and for Rod Cave, who had been corresponding with Potocki since the sixties and would step in as interviewer.

Cave's acquaintanceship with Potocki had come about in 1961 through an exhibition, 'English Private Presses 1757–1961', at the Times Bookshop in London. Potocki's *Prison Poems*, published by the Montalk Press for the Divine Right of Kings, had been included in the catalogue, and Cave, who was living in Trinidad at the time, had been intrigued by a catalogue note stating that 'the author was sentenced to a term in gaol as a result of information laid by the printer of some of his poems'. He had investigated further. He had found the account of Potocki's trial and imprisonment in *The Banned Books of England*, and, when on leave in Britain in 1962, had discovered that several of Potocki's books were listed in the General Catalogue of the British Museum. In *The Private Library* (spring 1967), of which he was honorary editor, Cave recalls that 'several were reported to me as missing as a result of war damage, but those I managed to see impressed me'.

Potocki was obviously a poet of real if minor talent; in politics he had apparently moved to the extreme right wing during the thirties in the way that other antipodean writers such as Jack Lindsay had moved as far left. His publishing history seemed confused in the extreme.

In his introduction to *The Private Library*'s feature story, 'Geoffrey Potocki and His Press', Cave writes of his search for Potocki and the fascinating acquaintanceship which followed:

> Over the next two or three years, when I was back in the West Indies and later when I was in Nigeria we engaged in a correspondence which gradually petered out in the way such exchanges so often do. It was splendid, but always alarming to receive one of his letters as he was always free in expressing his extreme right-wing views on self-rule for the colonies, what should be done with Dr Jagan etc. and one felt that if the letters fell into the wrong hands one would find oneself unceremoniously on the next plane home.

Cave reflects that while it lasted their relationship was full of interesting things. 'And even fuller of unanswered questions.' Why, he wonders, if there are so many stories about 'this strange figure from the literary world of the thirties and forties . . . a good poet, a splendid pamphleteer, a magnificent enemy', so little about Potocki has appeared in print?

I spread out my pages of transcriptions and scribbled notes on the floor. Where to start with Potocki's unanswered life? Something concrete, like his trial? He relived it constantly and I'd recently obtained a copy of the transcript. Internment? A poet in prison? Imprisonment had visual possibilities: Potocki in his robes between the lines of disused shelving in the old Hunter Building law library at the university, in the stone-block severity of the private printing room, the windowless typesetting room; in a crisp white printing apron, with Cave, and the steel body of the Arab platen press. A smoke machine. Narrow windows. Light filtering through.

SEVEN

# The Trial

*I was getting my poetry published in the* Observer, Country Life, Poetry Chicago, Voices *of New York, the* Irish Statesman, *and so on, and then I was put in prison over 'Here Lies John Penis', and after that no one would have anything to do with me. And it wasn't that they didn't agree with me. That was the funny part of it, you see.*

At the end of 1931, Potocki, who had been dividing his time between England and France for four years, translated François Rabelais's well-known poem 'Chanson de la Braguette', wrote a parody of Paul Verlaine's 'Idylle High-Life'—both ribald poems readily available in France—put them together with three sexually frank verses he had written about an amorous adventure involving Rex Fairburn, and took them to a typesetter so they could be set in linotype. He didn't ask the typesetter to print the poems, he simply asked him to set them so that he could take the type home and print them himself by hand on his kitchen table. He planned to distribute the collection, which he had dedicated to his French friend François Vernon, privately among his literary friends, and he had no intention of selling it.

He had undertaken the translation and parody very seriously, 'as sincere works of literature, as a literary experiment, if you like.' He was particularly pleased with the translation of 'The Song of the Braguette' (codpiece), in which a lady arms her husband for battle. He believed it preserved the original metre, rhyme and exact meaning of the poem, and was emphatically better than any other translation. And he considered the parody of Verlaine, which he entitled 'In the Manner of Paul Verlaine, Roman Catholic Poet', to be similarly satisfactory. It was also his view that it would be appreciated only by students of literature because of the subtlety with which it duplicated the original poem, and that only a student who had studied Verlaine's work in its original language would appreciate the manner in which he had captured the poet's style. In fact, he had written the parody with the purpose of attacking the obscenity of Verlaine's work: Potocki wanted to show him up as a hypocrite, as a Roman Catholic who wrote obscene verse. He told me: 'He may well have been one of France's great lyric poets, but he was also very decidedly a pervert, for he engaged in vicious sexual practices, and published his poems in such a way that no one could buy them without buying other poems of a most vicious nature. I should say that "Idylle High-Life", although saucy, was by far one of his less ribald poems.

'As for the short verses, they were written in the first place because of Fairburn. He published this thing *He Shall Not Rise*, and then on top of that he kept telling Glass and me that he was very badly in need of a wahine, and he was telling us the practical results of not having one, and could we get him one? And I said, "Of course we can. What's wrong with Edwina's friend, Jean?" And her name happened to be Jean Luck. So, you see, as the second short verse says: "Here lies a poet/who never had a fuck:/let's hope in heaven/he'll have much better luck!" And there was a footnote, "P.S. He has since, Editor", and the judge was infuriated by that.'

He continued: 'And we found this girl for Fairburn, and we gave him instructions as to how to behave, for in spite of his beauty he didn't know which end to pick up a girl. That's the principal fact about Fairburn. He was a *very* good-looking man and very well built, and everything like that, and all the girls were dying to be attacked by him, but he didn't have the *guts to do it!* And we told him what to do when he got this girl up there. I said, "Well, first of all, when you get the girl in there, you lock the door very ostentatiously, and you make some idiotic remark such as 'The bold bad baron locks the girl in.' That's the first thing you do, so she can see that the landlady can't walk in on her. But you're to leave the key in the door so she can see it's still there and she can get out whenever she likes." And then I said, "For the love of God, don't try to *undress* her. Get undressed yourself first." And I quoted John Donne at him—Dean of St Paul's—"To teach thee I am naked first, what needest thou more covering than a man?" Of course she hadn't got an Eiffel Tower sticking up in front of her, so I said, "You set her a good example and you'll have no difficulty whatever. She'll take her clothes off at once after she's seen you naked. You don't believe it, but she's just as anxious to see you naked as you are to see her, if not more so, and that's normal, it's just natural, but on top of that she's told us that she would love to see you naked. So go ahead, get undressed, and all will be all right."

'Instead of that, he had seven candles lighted on the mantelpiece: a mystic number. And he put the electric light out—he had these seven candles burning there—and he tried to take her clothes off, *contrary to all our sermons!* And when he failed to get her clothes off, he took one of these candles, and he presented it to her and he said, "Oh, very well, you'll need this, then." And I said to him, "Look here, Rex, do you *really* think you're imitating us?" And then I went and wrote this thing about his never having had a fuck.

'Of course English literature is littered with words Christians choose to call obscene. It goes without saying that Shakespeare is bawdy and *quite right too.*'

In addition to having some fun with Fairburn's unsuccessful adventure, the verses were significant for the play they made on the title of Fairburn's first book, the recently published *He Shall Not Rise*. Fairburn had taken the title from a poem in the book, 'Rhyme of the Dead Self', which read as a rejection of his youthful work: 'He is dead pale youth and he shall not rise'. Potocki, who had been disappointed with what he described as the 'Georgian flaccidity of some of this work', had used his short verses to proclaim to his friends that Fairburn would indeed rise again.

As the collection was not such as Potocki 'would show indiscriminately to all persons', he delayed publication in order to make his arrangements discreetly. Finally, however, on the morning of 13 January 1932, he and Douglas Glass, filled with the charm of their own existence, went in frivolous mood in search of a compositor. Glass, who was living in Thakeham, Sussex, had been summoned to London by Potocki the previous week to attend the singing of King Henry VIII's anthem 'O God the Maker of Alle Thing' at Westminster Abbey and a performance of Bach's Christmas music, and was staying with him in his room at Hammersmith. It was a mild morning—unseasonably so— and the pair were dressed as if for spring, in shirts of coarse silk and sandals without socks. Potocki, who wore his hair long, had his crimson cloak across his shoulders, and a heavy scarf, sewn by hand, carelessly about his neck.

Uncertain as to their precise destination, they asked a policeman on duty on the steps of the Old Bailey for directions, telling him the poems were spicy and contained the words *de foot* and *de con* (as in 'De foot et de coun', spoken also in jest by Alice and Katharine in Shakespeare's *King Henry the Fifth*, III.iv), as well as explaining what the words meant 'in the King's plain English'. In *Whited Sepulchres*, the 47-page treatise he would write on his trial, Potocki recalls that the policeman, who either had a penchant for practical joking or did not understand 'these two popular vocables', referred them to an address 'which turned out to be that of the printers of the *Methodist Times*', although they were not aware of this when they presented themselves. Here, the pamphlet tells us, 'a charming, dapper old gentleman of the polite, anxious sort' bowed them out, 'said several times in a most apologetic manner: "I'm afraid we couldn't undertake a job of that sort, Sir" (of course I was "Sir", not Mr Glass)', and directed them to the premises of Comps Ltd, Kirby Street, Hatton Garden.

At Comps Ltd, Potocki showed the booklet of five poems to the manager, Leslie de Lozey. He explained that, with the assistance of Glass, he intended to print off a hundred copies himself 'in a primitive way, the reason for this being that they contained words which the Philistines chose to consider obscene', and that as this would be his first attempt at printing it would be helpful to have the manuscript in linotype.

De Lozey spent some time inspecting the manuscript and informed them that he would undertake the commission, but couldn't do the job for the usual price. Potocki remonstrated. De Lozey asked him how much he expected to pay, and Potocki replied, 'Well the trade price is 1/3 a thousand ens.'

'But this is unusual stuff,' de Lozey declared, 'and I can't give it to my men—I'll have to stay behind after they've gone and set it up myself. And as I'll have to do it myself, I'll have to charge double the rate.' He decided, in the end, that he would want a pound for the job.

'But there are only seventy-five lines, and the proper price would be closer to seven shillings,' argued Potocki. De Lozey, seemingly keen to obtain the commission at the inflated rate, then 'advanced the fact' that he had had the opportunity of setting up D.H. Lawrence's *Lady Chatterley's Lover*, but had had to turn it down because it was too risky, being a bulky work and at that time very much in public view. 'You ought to have set it up,' Potocki told him, 'and boasted about it to the end of your life because it was a very great work.'

'At this point,' he recalled in conversation with me, 'Glass, who had been venturing anti-Jewish remarks in asides—I didn't know what the devil he was on about, I had no idea that de Lozey was a Jew, nor did I mind—entered the conversation and delivered de Lozey somewhat of a sermon on obscenity along the lines taken by D.H. Lawrence and Richard Aldington. That is, the freedom which should be allowed for the publication of such works.'

De Lozey, who appeared to remain interested, showed no signs of being shocked by either Glass's anti-Semitic remarks or his over-enthusiastic lecture on obscenity. He would not lower his price, however, and was told by Potocki that, since he could not afford to pay over double the normal rate, he would try to get the job set more cheaply elsewhere. 'Failing that,' Potocki said, 'I will buy some moveable type, and a typesetting stick and set it up myself.' De Lozey then suggested that Potocki leave the manuscript with him and, if he couldn't arrange a better price, he could telephone de Lozey and instruct him to go ahead.

Shortly after they left the premises, de Lozey took the manuscript to the police. A warrant was issued for their arrest, and five days later, at 11.30 am on 18 January, Potocki's room at 83 Edith Road, Hammersmith was raided and a number of books were seized, including two volumes of Potocki's own poetry—*Lordly Lovesongs* and *Surprising Songs*—and *The Well of Loneliness*, by Radclyffe Hall, recently deemed by a magistrate to be obscene.

The astonished Potocki 'heartily urged the Detective Inspector to confiscate the Bible also', which he assured him was 'full of obscene tales, and Shakespeare, who was abominably smutty, and Rabelais, who was present both in French and in Urquhart's English translation, and Chaucer'. 'Don't you know "The Miller's tale"?' he asked the detective inspector railingly, quoting him, as a typed account of his trial found in the archive circumspectly reports, 'a few verses of the passage beginning just before the lines':

Abak he stirte, and thoughte it was amys,
For wel he wiste a womman hath no berd.
He felte a thyng al rough and long yherd,
And seyde, 'Fy! allas! what have I do'?

and the inspector laughed sheepishly.

Matters moved swiftly. Potocki and Glass were arrested and jointly charged at the Clerkenwell Police Court with uttering and publishing an obscene libel entitled 'Here Lies John Penis'. They were told by the magistrate, to their considerable surprise, that they would be remanded in custody at Brixton pending arrangements for bail—'An incredible decision,' writes C.H. Rolph in *Books in the Dock*—and then, without further preamble, were bustled out of the court and through the back doors of a police van. 'Naturally we were horrified,' Potocki told me, 'but once we recovered from the shock, we were quite willing, once inside, to see what Brixton prison was all about.' (Glass had previously been in Wandsworth Prison.)

They found Brixton was chiefly about bad food, and exercise twice a day in a yard with oval concrete paths between which some of the prisoners attempted to grow flowers. It was also about feeling cold. 'Robes?' he said when I asked him how he was dressed. 'No, they came much later, after the Scrubs. In Brixton I was dressed in a handmade suit of blue serge, with trousers cut square at the top and supported by a leather belt, a tussore silk shirt, without a waistcoat, and a pair of sandals without socks. I also had the voluminous woollen wine-red cape I wore in winter for warmth. It was taken away from me on admission, but as I couldn't do without it, even though the winter wasn't particularly cold, I applied to see the Governor and asked to have it back. It was returned to me by an officer, folded on two outstretched arms, and I was permitted to wear it at exercise time.

'It's possible that conditions in Brixton then were better than they are now,' he continued, 'because there was no television, and everybody was in a cell by himself, but the food really was very bad. I, however, being a descendant of William the Conqueror, managed to digest it!' Anticipating a short stay, the pair found moments of humour possible. In *Whited Sepulchres*, Potocki recalls the night of their reception, when, together with a number of other prisoners, they were put through a questionnaire:

> When it came to my turn and the officer asked: 'What's your religion?' I truthfully replied: 'Pagan'. The officer began to write it down, and spelt it out wrongly. 'P-A-G-A-N' I explained. Next came Mr Glass. 'What's your religion?' 'Pagan.' This was duly written down. After us came an unfortunate Cockney debtor in a bowler hat, a sort of petty Macawber [*sic*], a hopeless and resigned

recidivist where debts were concerned. He was of shortish stature, a little bent; and moderately cheerful in the best tragical Cockney manner. He was about forty-five, and characteristically kept his hat on his head. 'What's your religion?' asked the Officer. 'Pagan,' said the Cockney proudly. Everyone looked up and smiled, including the officer. A ray of Apollo's brightness had penetrated 'Reception'. But all the same, the officer would not allow mere Cockneys to arrogate themselves the religious luxuries claimed by literary prisoners or aristocrats. Mr Glass, being with me, was allowed to be a Pagan, but to the debtor the officer said with humorous severity: 'You were Church of England last time. Religion, Church of England,' he repeated as he wrote it down.

Personally, I confess that in spite of my amusement I was annoyed at this snobbish injustice. Why shouldn't the poor debtor have the fun of being converted to Apollo's faith during his drab incarnation?

Bail, however, was not immediately forthcoming. Detainees were not permitted to use the telephone and friends were unable to ring in because the prison number was not in the directory and could not be obtained on inquiry. Potocki was therefore obliged to write to a girlfriend, and to Cedric, who was still living in London, and wait three days before his release could be arranged. Once released, he set to work finding bail for Glass, who had no friends willing and able to sign for him. Glass had found incarceration more taxing than Potocki, and had been continuously ill on the prison diet. 'Finally, a certain Scotch Nationalist, who wanted to lease a house I was renting in Thakeham— in addition to my room in London—in the event of my going to gaol, and was consequently willing to impress me with his wealth, bailed Mr Glass although he didn't know him from a soapy bar.' The Scot was poet Hugh MacDiarmid.

Less than a week later, they again appeared at the Clerkenwell Police Court for a preliminary hearing and disclosure of the Crown case against them. A friend had contributed £2 towards their defence, and Potocki had briefed barrister C.J. du Cann, the counsel who had appeared on their behalf at the earlier court proceedings. Despite his three days in prison, Potocki remained in a light-hearted mood. The mood in court— as he recalled in conversation, almost word for word as written in *Whited Sepulchres*—was similarly cheerful:

The Crown Solicitor asked de Lozey to recount Mr Glass's remarks on obscenity, which, in my opinion, were irrelevant to the alleged misdemeanour, and de Lozey replied: 'He said, Your Worship, that we say eat, and drink, and walk, and swim, and ride, and breathe, and why not say . . . must I say the exact word, Your Worship?'

'Certainly.'

So de Lozey began again, in slower tempo: 'He said we say eat, and drink, and walk and swim, and ride and breathe; and why not say fuck?" The Word fell on the expectant air with a soft thud. Mr de Lozey said it carefully in the most courteous and refined tone of which he was capable, and the Magistrate, it seemed to me, smiled faintly.

Potocki's appearance in court attracted the attention of the press, and the *Empire News* of 24 January 1932 was only one of several newspapers which described his proceedings. Beneath the headline 'THE COUNT IN SANDALS', it reported:

> A young Polish Count of British nationality and of strikingly handsome appearance appeared in the dock at the Clerkenwell Police Court yesterday on a summons charging him with publishing an obscene libel to a printer in Finsbury.

Identifying Potocki as 'Count Geoffrey Wladesled Vaile Potocki De Montalk', it continued:

> He entered the dock arrayed in a flowing brick-coloured cloak over which flowed a wealth of thick fair hair. He wore a heavy silk scarf which fell down over a velvet coat, black trousers, and almost touched his bare feet, for he wore sandals which left his ankles and toes exposed to view.
>
> His pale, handsome face seemed to twitch with excitement when the evidence against him was being given, and he turned round occasionally to discuss points that had been raised in the case with another remarkably handsome young man who figured in the summons with him . . .
>
> In the well of the court were many young women, who gave the impression of belonging to an artistic circle.

The magistrate, Bertrand Watson, having considered the Crown's submissions, committed Potocki for trial by jury at the Old Bailey, and admitted him to bail in the sum of £50, or two sureties of £25. Glass, as second defendant, was discharged on the ground that no reasonable jury would convict. Potocki had said to du Cann, 'The main thing is to get Glass cut out of this, because I don't want to stand trial with him with the sort of sticky past he has. I've always disapproved of it, as he knows perfectly well.'

As he writes in his typed account of the trial, he had elected trial by jury believing nothing would come of the case:

> I thought no judge in his right mind would convict me. After all I was being accused of publishing these things when I had not published them. And whereas I had intended to publish them, the English law says 'the thought of man is not triable for the devil himself knoweth not the thought of man'.

A friend donated £5 towards his legal fees, and Potocki, satisfied with du Cann's performance at the police court, retained him for his appearance at the Old Bailey. As the magistrate had appeared reasonable, even amused, he was confident of a triumphant outcome. Over the next two weeks his solicitor prepared a brief of the evidence for his defence. The brief, which included a statement by Potocki that he shared the opinion of 'many great writers of today that there should be frankness in discussion on matters of sex', observed that the circumstances of the case were somewhat unusual:

> It is not a case where a sexual maniac has lost all control of his sense of decency, and makes an obscene observation, or where there is an attempt to corrupt the morals of any one of the general public.
>
> The Accused is a man of superior education, and a student of literature. He is a linguist and has studied and is conversant with medieval works as well as modern works of English and French authors.
>
> He is a Poet and has published collections of poems as well as having contributed to Newspapers and Journals in all parts of the world. His writings are upon diverse subjects and have been very well received by the Public and Literary circles. 'Evensong' in his Book, 'Surprising Songs' has been very favourably commented upon.

Just how unusual this case of obscene libel would prove to be—
and in terms of its effect on Potocki how far-reaching—neither Potocki
nor his solicitors could have foreseen. They could never have known
that in matters of fairness, and for all its rhetoric about British justice,
the London judiciary would demonstrate so convincingly that it was
still shackled by Victorian prejudice and conformity, that censorship
commentators would be outraged, with C.H. Rolph describing the
case in *Books in the Dock* as 'the most extra-ordinary obscenity trial
of the century'; and that, as Potocki himself would later observe: 'The
joke throughout the literary world all over the globe was who was libelled?
And the answer was John Penis.'

HERE LIES JOHN PENIS
Dedicated to François Vernon

Here lies John Penis
buried in the Mount of Venus.
He died in tranquil faith
that having vanquished death
HE SHALL RISE up again
and in Joy's Kingdom reign.

Here lies a poet
who never had a fuck:
let's hope in heaven
he'll have much better luck!
    N.B.—He has since—Ed.

For . . . and his girl, on leaving them the key of my room.

Herewith the key to the heaven between her thighs—
take it, and in its use be stern and wise.
May Eros leave his fiercest dart in her
and fill her cunt with burning oil and myrrh;
and, not to leave so sweet a thing forlorn,
Apollo give you a stiff splendid horn.
The place is lucky, since the poet's bed
is hallowed with a bleeding maidenhead.

IN THE MANNER OF PAUL VERLAINE,
ROMAN CATHOLIC POET.

The violin
that in the dark
speaketh of sin
in Hagley Park

recalls how lingers
on the Penis
with lustful fingers
the hand of Venus,

Venus-Shop-Girl
whose elation
knows how to swirl
the best sensation,

Venus y-clept,
whose soft hand full
stroked as she wept
the beautiful

cock of the Marquis
Tittle-Dee-Tum
caressed his carcase
and his bum.

You have undone
His Lordship's pants
and think it fun
so loud he pants

when you tug the tool of
Lord Tittle-Tum
and you mouth is full of
lordly come.

O Marquis, deign
to listen to me
(not Paul Verlaine)
—my advice is free:

Don't boast of this shocking
lewd success
when you are fucking
the Marchioness.
    (Parody of 'Taille High-Life')

THE SONG OF THE BRAGUETTE
    from the 'Chiabrene des Pucelles'
    (Translated from François Rabelais.)

The wife who sees her man set out for war
from head to heel, except his cock-box, armed,
says to him, 'Darling, for fear you should be harmed,
arm that, that over all the parts I love more.'

What? And shall such advice be counted queer?
I say no no: because her greatest fear,
when she saw him in lively mood, was lest
she'd lose the tit-bit that she liked the best.

---

Last time I was in London, I went to see the Old Bailey, or the Central Criminal Court as it's more correctly described, wondering if a sense of the past was still there: the infamy of Recorder Judge Jeffreys, the remnants of trials, a sense of Newgate Prison on the site of which it was built and alongside which it later stood, its Justice Hall open to the air so that prisoners would not pass on typhus or gaol fever.

    It was a grey city day and a cool wind blew about its facings of Portland stone and its tower, dome and bronzed figure of Justice, head in the sky. As it was summer I hoped I might see the laying of posies on the floors of the judges' benches and the ledges of the docks—a tradition between May and September from times when flowers were used to lessen the smell and ward off disease from Newgate Prison next door.

Disappointingly, I found little to suggest the ambience of the 1930s. Posies were now carried into court only once a year, and the small session-house in which Potocki had been tried had been extended. Moreover, I was told by a clerk, the courtroom of the Recorder had been rebuilt, following its destruction by bombs during the Second World War.

I wasn't seeking the weight of history, more a sense of place. This was the building Potocki had entered with confidence, having insisted on trial by jury, believing this would be his big moment. He had told me: 'After all, I regarded myself as having been wrongfully arrested and contemplated a counter-attack', a statement which suggested that, had he so wished, he could have dispensed with the jury and chosen the less spectacular route of a defended hearing before a judge. The statement also suggested that *The Well of Loneliness*, found to be obscene in 1928 by a magistrate, without recourse to literary expertise or writers waiting in court to give evidence, may have featured in his thinking. 'Why hide away?' he might have asked himself. 'As a former student of the law, I know my crime has been minor and the worst I can expect is a fine. Why, then, pass up the chance to showcase literature, wrongful arrest, freedom of expression? Myself, as a poet?'

On the morning of the trial, having prayed to his gods, and joined Minnie, his mistress, and Glass, who was also staying at Edith Road, in a breakfast of eggs, bacon, toast and several cups of hot sugared tea, Potocki had dressed—for effect. While a more cautious defendant might have favoured a sober appearance, he had combed out what the *News of the World* would describe as his 'wealth of luxuriant long hair' and settled for his cloak and open-toed sandals: word had gone out and a large crowd was expected in the public gallery—literary figures, censorship experts, reporters and female admirers.

With time in hand and a sharp wind from the north-east scattering snow in the suburbs, he and his friends made their way to the Old Bailey, where they passed beneath the solemnity and occasion of the words of the Recording Angel—*Defend the children of the poor and punish the wrongdoer*—without any particular concern, and ascended to the central hall, two marble steps at a time. Then, after meeting with du Cann, and encouraged by Glass, who would remain in the hall to direct supporters, Potocki kissed Minnie, surrendered to his bail and was taken into custody with a flourish, for the duration of the trial.

He followed a warder to a cell beneath the courtroom, gathered the sweep of his cloak around him for warmth, paced for a moment and then took a seat on a bench. The cell was bare, with toilet arrangements visible from the door, but this did not bother him. Potocki, the prisoner, was simply passing through. Tonight he and his friends and their girlfriends would dine out, order wine, toast his performance. Tomorrow there would be the dailies. At the end of the week, editorials. Beyond that, flattering impressions of fame. He took his fountain pen and some loose sheets of paper from his pockets, and turned his attention to the speech he had started the previous evening.

The trial took place before Sir Ernest Wild, the Recorder of London. It began with Wild's judicially improper warning to the three women who had been balloted to serve on the jury that this 'was a very filthy case indeed'. The Recorder repeated this warning, telling the women commandingly that they need not serve if they did not wish. Two women then retired, but the third, who (as Potocki writes in *Whited Sepulchres*) 'flatly refused to give up the privilege of hearing my very filthy case, told the Recorder firmly that she would "serve"'. As it happened, yet another woman was balloted, so that in the end two women served on the jury.

The facts of the case were not in dispute, and the prosecution immediately established that Potocki and Glass had taken a manuscript of verse to de Lozey, linotype setter, and asked him for a price to set it in linotype. It then set out to prove that the character of the poems was such that their publication in the admitted circumstances was a criminal offence: in other words, first that publication in the legal sense—that is, the passing of the manuscript to another person—had taken place, and second that the material passed in this manner was obscene.

Potocki wrote in his typed account of the trial: 'Regarding the charge, uttering and publishing an obscene libel, I should explain that in the phrase "obscene libel", the word libel has nothing whatever to do with libel. It does not mean defamation or slander, but reverts to its primary etymological meaning, which can be found in any Latin dictionary: Libellus, a little book, small writing, and kind of book or writing or handbill.' Although it was likely that the provisions concerning publication had been fulfilled and the poems had, technically speaking, been 'published', it was by no means certain that a jury would consider publication had taken place.

Or that it would find the words to be obscene. In legal terms, the highly interpretative test for obscenity required the jury to find, in the words of Sir Ernest Wild, that 'the tendency of the matter charged as obscenity is to deprave and corrupt those whose minds are open to such immoral influences and into whose hands a publication of this sort may fall'. What Wild meant, and indeed attempted to convey to the jury, was that Potocki's intention with regard to the poems was not the issue. The issue was, as Wild put it, 'whether the tendency of the publication is to deprave and corrupt not Bishops or respectable people who have got clean minds . . . but people whose minds are open to such immoral influences'.

The jury was also required to decide, should it find publication and obscenity had been proved, whether a defence of public good mitigated these circumstances. Such a defence justified the publication of obscene material if that material was 'necessary or advantageous to religion or science, literature or art, or other objects of general interest'.

These considerations were complex. With all things arguable in law, especially before juries struggling with strange legal definitions, issues of statutory interpretation and their own subjective assessments, a verdict of not guilty was a definite possibility.

It was du Cann's task, therefore, both to enlighten the jury about Potocki's literary background, and to confuse it about the Crown's case. It was also his job to discredit prosecution witnesses, so that the jury, by means of implication and without untoward interference from the judge, might be persuaded that a witness who is shown to be unreliable in one respect may also be untrustworthy in others. In this latter regard, the first of many amusing moments in the trial occurred when, under cross-examination by du Cann, de Lozey admitted that he had not in fact read the poems. Potocki relates the exchange in his typed notes:

> He was then asked by Mr du Cann how he knew they were obscene. He answered that he had turned over the pages and seen obscene words. In point of actual fact he had studied the whole manuscript carefully in our presence. After further questioning, among other things, Mr de Lozey said self-righteously that he would certainly inform if he were offered an obscene Greek manuscript to print; and then looked very foolish when he had to admit he knew no Greek.

Despite the light moment and the point scored, du Cann, who had managed to discredit de Lozey most effectively in this manner in the lower court, then began to lose his assurance, in Potocki's view. Wild had already made clear his personal distaste for the material—and indeed, by his impatient tone, for Potocki himself—and the more he brought these views to bear upon the court, the less ably du Cann appeared to perform: 'Wild refused to allow any importance to be attached to the most glaring details of de Lozey's self exposure, and unfortunately Mr du Cann started to become intimidated.'

Wild's impatience with Potocki—a private impatience which should not have affected his impartiality—was rumoured at the time to have arisen, ironically, because he believed Potocki in his cloak to be a communist. It is equally likely to have resulted in part from the personal and literary challenges the case required of him. As Alec Craig, an authority on literary obscenity laws, observed in *Above All Liberties*, in a chapter entitled 'The Strange Case of Count Potocki of Montalk', Sir Ernest Wild was 'as ordinary, respectable and unimaginative as Count Potocki of Montalk is extraordinary, unconventional and poetic'. Wild, aged sixty-three, was nearing the end of his judicial career: a privileged career as Recorder of London, the principal legal officer of that city, appointed by the Lord Mayor and, as a sitting judge, not required to go on circuit as other High Court judges were. Craig's description invites a picture of an ageing and dull man, presiding over a youthfully confident, sexually aware and good-looking poet, whose appearance could 'only create prejudice in the drab surroundings of modern London and in the grey minds of its rulers'. It is easy to imagine that Wild, while he may have viewed his flamboyant prisoner, dressed to eccentric perfection, with distaste, while he may even have considered him weird and effete, would also have been very aware—given the female admirers in the public gallery—that women knew otherwise.

As Potocki entered the witness box, spectators craned their necks and jostled for a clearer view. Was he wearing socks? Was the cloak lined? Were those velvet trousers he was wearing beneath it?

He refused to take the oath. 'I do not approve of this book,' he said of the Bible, 'and I would rather not swear on it.'

There was silence—a shocked silence from the bench—followed by a discussion between the Recorder, prosecutor and defence counsel as to whether or not pagan oaths should be permitted in Christian courts. Wild was very still. His eyes moved from counsel to Potocki and around the courtroom. Then he said sharply: 'I must be satisfied that it is on religious grounds that you object. You object to being sworn on the Bible because you do not believe in it?'

'Because I believe in other gods, my lord,' Potocki replied.

'Then it is on religious grounds?'

'Yes, my lord.'

'Then you may be affirmed.'

'Why would I swear on the Bible,' Potocki once wrote to me, 'when I am not at all convinced that the Bible is the word of God? I insisted because I was already engaged in worshipping Apollo, the Sun God, and so I demanded to swear by Apollo. When I was finally permitted, to proceed, I lifted my arm in a Roman salute, and intoned a pagan oath. Later there was a full page colour illustration of this on the front page of *La Stampa*, in Italy, but in it I was an aged man, with white hair, wearing a crimson robe with a Roman motif in gold around the bottom.'

Some accounts of his oath taking have him mumbling into the folds of his cloak, both arms raised, and at least one of these claims to be an eye-witness account. He disputed these: 'Either they are lying, or have bad memories, or are copying from previous sources,' he protested. 'Naturally I did not raise both arms above my head! I raised my right arm (like Julius Caesar or Benito Mussolini). It seems to me that these people (like so many others) want to profit by me, to sell their books ... The modern English Uppish Classes are contemptible beyond belief.'

Having previously pleaded not guilty to a charge of uttering and publishing an obscene libel consisting of six sheets of manuscript, he now stated, led by counsel, that he was a British subject born in New Zealand, that his grandfather was a Polish count, and he himself was entitled to that honour. He further stated that he did not regard any of the poems as obscene, except perhaps one, and explained there was a good reason for that. Part of the poem's purpose had been to expose 'the famous French Roman Catholic poet, Verlaine'.

The transcript of the trial, *Rex v G.W.V.P. de Montalk*, is incomplete, a concern which Potocki's solicitors would impress upon his appeal barrister, St John Hutchinson, at the time of his appeal, only to have it ignored. Even so, it confirms not only the perverse nature of Wild's interest in the case, but also the extent to which his conduct was judicially improper. Given the condemnation of Wild's conduct by censorship commentators such as Craig, and Rolph who was in court at the time, it seems likely that, with an appeal pending, the excisions were made deliberately.

Most obvious is Wild's continual interrogation of witnesses, including Potocki, an action most assuredly not the prerogative of judges. Also obvious is Potocki's defiance and sense of theatre in the face of cross-examination. As Rolph observed, 'He had been trained for the law, loved a battle . . .'

Wild: 'There is a modern school who is writing this sort of poetry, is there?'
Potocki: 'I hope so, my Lord.'
. . .
du Cann: 'Is the purpose of writing such poetry to deprave and corrupt, or is it for the purpose of literary experimentation?'
Potocki: 'For the purpose of literary experimentation and also to uplift, if I may say so, my Lord.'
Wild: 'So tell the jury how those four lines could uplift anybody.'
Potocki: 'I think a man who does not make love, if he can be persuaded by any means to do so, is being uplifted.'
. . .
Crown Counsel: 'Are we to take it that you consider sexual intercourse uplifting?'
Potocki: 'Certainly sir. That's what it's all about.'
. . .
Wild: 'You call this poetry?'
Potocki: 'Anything a poet writes in verse is poetry.'
Wild: 'How do you become a poet?'
Potocki: 'My Lord, it is the choice of the gods.'
Wild: 'What gods? Can a man call himself a poet and be a poet?'
Potocki: 'No my Lord, not unless he is.'

Under Wild's direction, the court examined the five poems. 'Sir Ernest eyed the jurymen and women keenly as they turned over the pages. At last he said to me hopefully: "I hope you will not insist on reading these *filthy poems* to the Court," but I had no intention of doing any such thing. I was far too busy thinking about Gods, and my divine mission, and injustice—about whited sepulchres and ravening wolves. So he read one out himself and he read it haltingly, like this: "Here—lies—a—poet—who—never—had—an—F." And later I got my own back on him with that in my pamphlet *Snobbery with Violence.*'

Spirited discussion regarding the definitions of 'obscenity', 'publish' and 'corrupt' took place. Evidence was given on Potocki's behalf by the poet Edgell Rickword, at that time a critic with the *Times Literary Supplement*, who had written on Verlaine and was regarded by many as an authority on the poet. Writes Potocki in *Whited Sepulchres*:

> He was dressed in a sombre brown overcoat (if I remember rightly he kept his hands in the pockets of it most of the time), but as he swayed backwards and forwards with a slight movement very characteristic of him, against the background of a meretricious false-classical oak pillar, he looked very imposing in a whimsical way of his own.
>
> The prosecution tried hard to trip him. 'Mr Rickword, you are a Poet, I understand?'
> 'Yes.' Counsel had another try.
> 'How long have you been a Poet?' Rickword looked into space, swaying slightly, reckoning up the *annorum series*, or for all I know calculating the specific density of barristers. After a moment he replied: 'About fifteen years.' . . . He gave evidence that my translation of Rabelais's *Chanson de la Braguette* was a good one, and that my Verlaine parody was 'a very good version of the original.' Cross examined by Crown Counsel about the other three poems, he answered: 'They're not my style.'

As the trial progressed it became clear to Potocki that du Cann was not only 'much infected by the evident determination of the Court not to let me have justice', but appeared to lack the legal insight necessary to sway such a case. He explains in his pamphlet:

> . . . one of the principal reasons for his failure at the Old Bailey was, that when I interviewed him during the preceding week, he would hardly let me get a word in edgeways. . . . Although I never

dabbled in the modern pseudo-sciences, I know a good deal, by means of general intelligence, intuition, and a logical habit of thought, of what is vulgarly called psychology. And what would be dubbed the psychological side of this case was all-important. Legally, the Crown's case was horribly in the wrong, and a strong defence could have made them look very silly.

Take as a trifling example the case of the boy 'writing up on the lavatory wall', to whom I was compared by the Recorder, and from whom I was differentiated by my own lawyer. What then? Are boys who write limericks on lavatory walls to get six months' imprisonment in future?

But the bullying tone and bias of Wild—as Potocki would say again and again—were his predominant concerns. For instance, despite the evidence brought in support of the merit of the translation and the parody, Wild baldly stated that the poems had no literary merit whatever, and during his summing-up ridiculed the suggestion, pointing out that one of the poems 'did not even rhyme', to which Potocki replied from the dock, 'Even Shakespeare, England's greatest poet, used blank verse.'

When all the arguments had been presented to the court, du Cann addressed the jury. He urged them to remember that de Montalk was a poet, that it was customary in England to regard poets with contempt unless they were dead, 'but it was one of the glories of England that we had had such great and renowned poets'. He told them that they should not be prejudiced because de Montalk came before them wearing a cloak, long hair and sandals, but should remember his business was poetry; that this was not a case of a depraved man seeking to deprave others; that 'his verses were only written for a small circle of literary experimenters, and like great writers such as D.H. Lawrence and James Joyce, he wanted to make words respectable which were regarded as obscene'. He continued:

> Words regarded as objectionable in one age became respectable in another. The most innocent damsel would not blush now at the word 'trousers', yet Anthony Trollope had told how his publisher was horrified because he used the word in his manuscript. In those Victorian days trousers were always unmentionable. Again, another word ['bloody'] was regarded as a terrible expression until Bernard Shaw used it in *Pygmalion*, and Mrs Patrick Campbell astonished

and delighted fashionable London with a phrase in which the word occurred. Then the word became almost fashionable, and it has been used by such a great poet as John Masefield.

Wild summed up. His duty was to impartially assist the jury to interpret the law. But he had this to say:

> A man must not say 'I am a poet,' and publish filth; poets are just as liable to obey the law of the land as ordinary plain citizens, and it is no good for this man to say: 'Oh, I am a poet and therefore I shall do things that nobody else may do.' The sooner the highbrow school learn that the better for the morality of this country.

He told them that they could consider the expert opinion of eminent jurist Sir James Fitz-James Stephen—as submitted by du Cann—that a work containing matter that might otherwise be considered obscene may be published if shown to be for the public good, provided that the publication does not exceed what is required for that purpose, and that the issue of whether or not a manuscript came within these limits was a matter for them to decide. He also said, however: 'What was good enough for the times of Shakespeare and Rabelais is not good enough for us, since we now live on a higher moral plane.' He then asked the jury: 'Are you going to allow a man, because he calls himself a poet, to deflower our English language by popularising these words', and warned, 'Remember, the standard of morals has advanced.'

The jury wished to retire to consider its verdict, but the members were immediately directed by Wild to remain in their seats in the jury-box. *Whited Sepulchres* reports that, despite the obvious need for discussion, 'he displayed great impatience to have a verdict, and when he saw them deliberating rather vivaciously, he said: "You surely can't have read them! You surely can't have read these *filthy* poems!"' Then, when the foreman of the jury rose to deliver their hastily reached verdict, and indicated his intention to reply to the charges in two parts, Wild 'cut him short, and asked him trenchantly in irritated tones' whether Potocki was guilty of publishing an obscene libel or not. The foreman, 'a nervous simple man, awkwardly blurted out "Guilty"', at which point Wild observed: 'No decent-minded jury could have come to any other decision than that the defendant had attempted to deprave our literature.'

Potocki told me indignantly: 'You could have walked out of the court and bought Rabelais's "Cod Piece" in thirty antiquarian bookshops in Urquhart's translation. My translation was better, that's all. And the Verlaine parody, well that really was a bit saucy, but I don't think the judge had any occasion to take it so seriously, especially as he was a renowned smut hound himself. Richard Aldington wrote me twice saying that he, himself, and Wild were both guests of honour at the Odd Volumes Club, and Strauss, the chairman of the banquet, had to pull Wild up several times because of his filthy language, although he was guest of honour.'

As a prelude to sentencing, Detective Inspector Cain of Scotland Yard, on behalf of the Crown, outlined Potocki's background. As there were no previous convictions, he spoke only of his character, informing the Recorder, in prejudicial tones, that Potocki's family had encouraged him to enter the legal profession, but that he had wanted to be a poet and left home. He confirmed that Potocki's grandfather was a count, but, unaware that under the Slavic system the title passes automatically to the son of a count, whether his father is dead or not, he stated, unchallenged by counsel, that Potocki was not entitled to that recognition himself.

In mitigation, du Cann told the court that 'de Montalk had written other and quite beautiful and distinguished verse approved by critics', that he had been influenced by a modern school, and had no intention of harming anyone.

Wild responded by saying that so-called artists and literary people must remember they had to keep within the rules of decency. 'These writings,' he trumpeted, 'were of the filthiest nature, and literature must be protected against offal of this kind.' It would be well, he continued sternly, 'if people who published filthy works could be brought before a jury rather than fined.'

He then turned to Potocki and asked whether he had anything to say.

Potocki replied that he wished to make a speech. He had completed an eleven-page speech while waiting in his cell below, which stated that the case was 'absolutely parallel in principle with the crucifixion of Christ, who was killed (so we are told) because he wished to stir the Hebrew folk from their slothful fears, and to persuade them to face the facts of life in all their terrible loveliness'. He had also planned to tell the court that although he was 'born in New Zealand, where no creative life exists except in animal form, and where all the loveliness of European civilisation exists only in a weird state of caricature . . . All beauty was [his] religion, all ugliness [his] foe'.

'I can only hear a speech in mitigation of sentence,' said Wild.

'I have nothing to say on that subject, my lord.'

'Well,' said the Recorder, 'can't you suggest what punishment you think you deserve?'

Potocki drew himself up and answered that he thought he ought to be sentenced to several years in Buckingham Palace. He was then sentenced to six months in prison, in the second division (without hard labour), and ordered to be taken below.

Edgell Rickword said to him later: 'When I heard your reply, my heart stood still.'

Half an hour after sentence was passed, a constable came to his cell and told him his brother wanted to see him. He was taken to the grating, where he found that his brother was Douglas Glass, who was in a state of considerable agitation, shaking his head and saying that his faith had been shattered, and the sentence was dreadful, and what a shock it had been, particularly as he believed he was partly responsible.

'Don't let it shatter your faith,' Potocki replied, adding, 'I'll scrape along. It can't be as bad at the Scrubs as you've made out. We must turn the situation to some advantage. There'll be sympathy for me, so you should see some literary people, and start whipping up all the support you can for an appeal.'

Absolved from the 'histrionic obligations he felt himself to be under', Glass fervidly agreed to do whatever was necessary—to 'strain every energy, and to leave no stone unturned'—in order to ensure all turned out well.

The trial was widely reported—Potocki's conduct in the face of the English governing class system and stuffy legal ritual with glee by the tabloids, the threat to freedom of expression earnestly by the broadsheets. The unexpected sentence was discussed endlessly. Suddenly everybody knew the count who wore a cloak and sandals, and stories about Potocki surfaced, many of them exaggerated.

The *New Statesman and Nation* on 13 February 1932 accurately summed up the general reaction of outrage, and applied itself to the legal and literary points of view. It reviewed the facts of the case, Wild's conduct during the trial, and the surprising nature of the sentence. 'De Montalk is a poet,' it noted 'who takes his work seriously. (He has published two or three books which have been praised by very competent critics.)'

> ... The case raises issues of very great importance ... Is it the business of the police or of the courts to protect literature against defilement before it is in the usual sense published? The usual defence of our law of obscene libel is that it checks the sale of pornography. Probably most people in this country are in favour of some restriction on grounds of public decency. But I have never heard anyone defend the strict application of the present law. Its scope is indefensibly wide and we only retain it because our authorities usually show discretion in applying it. It is technically an obscene libel to post a letter which includes an 'obscene' word (the words commonly regarded as obscene change with each generation) and, as we have seen in this case, it is technically an obscene libel to take such words to a printer. Obviously the law is in this case reduced to an absurdity. No one's morals were corrupted, no one's sense of decency outraged, no innocent youth contaminated. Therefore, the whole case for applying the law, as defended by its more intelligent advocates, falls to the ground. I hope there will be an appeal and the real issues of liberty and censorship—very far-reaching ones—will be fully discussed when Mr de Montalk's case is again considered.

*Time and Tide* on 18 February wrote: 'This is a far harder sentence than has been given in many cases of quite savage assault.'

Rex Fairburn, similarly outraged, although confused as to the actual details of the case, immediately wrote to Ron Mason:

> I suppose the news about Monty got into the New Zealand cables. I'll get the News of the World (a lousy rag) next Sunday, and send it out to you. I hardly know anything about it. But apparently he had a row with old Durham of the Columbia Press, and D. rang up the police and gave them the MS of some poems Monty had been trying to get him to print. The case was heard in the Magistrate's court first, where Monty and Glass appeared, M. in red cape and sandals, G in black ditto and ditto. Glass was discharged, and Monty asked to go before the Recorder at the Old Bailey ... I'm going to write to the Manchester Guardian

about it. It's the sort of thing that makes my blood boil, and brings all my latent anti-social feeling to a head . . . Oh I could spit blood.

On 22 February he wrote again to Mason: 'I am contemplating a small pamphlet to be entitled THE IMPORTANCE OF BEING SIR ERNEST WILD.' And a week later:

> A little more news about the de Montalk case. I had another letter from Glass this morning, and he says:
> 'Yesterday I received a letter from W.B. Yeats. Among other things he says, "the sentence was criminal in its brutality. I send you a guinea and wish I could send you more but I have calls on my purse here." Augustus John has agreed to contribute five pounds. Today I had lunch with Lord Alfred Douglas and although he is sympathetic in a general way he is afraid to have anything to do with the matter because it would be against the tenets of the Catholic Church.'

Potocki had been shocked by the Recorder's behaviour in court. Later he was to learn that this was by no means the first time Wild had been guilty of judicial impropriety. 'It was fairly widely known that Wild had a reputation as the old lag's friend, because he was very pally with repeated offenders—real proper criminals. He was also, as you've doubtless read in Alec Craig's books, known as "The Blackmailer's Friend" because when homosexuals were up to complain of being blackmailed he asked them such searching questions about what they'd been up to that they preferred to go on being blackmailed. Whereby Sir Ernest Wild nullified the law.'

I wondered about Wild's homophobia, his reputation for an obsessive detestation of homosexuals which saw him arrange for charges against them to be heard by him personally. Was this phobia in part responsible for what was seen by those present at the trial as Wild's personal distaste for Potocki? Did he perceive the poet, with his long hair and cloak, to be sexually ambiguous, to be of interest not only to women but also to men?

Or was there also a wider issue of morality at stake? Was Wild's admonition that the sooner 'the highbrow school' learnt that they were not above the law the better linked to the 1928 ruling on Radclyffe Hall's *The Well of Loneliness?* Although Hall's book had been banned in Britain, it had been released in the United States, and Hall herself had not gone on trial. Furthermore, although considered to be of small merit, the book had attracted the support of literary London, thirty-nine members of which, including Leonard and Virginia Woolf, had attended the hearing. Did Wild see sinister implications here? Did he believe society was being threatened by decadence and subverted by artists and writers? Was he in effect saying to Potocki: 'The author got away last time, and I'm not prepared to see this happen again. You are not a big fish, but you are in my court and you are a catchable one. I will see you convicted, and the sentence will be severe.' Had he in fact set out to extinguish literary experimentation in this area?

Alec Craig, who wote about the trial later in *The Banned Books of England*, looked at the literary merit of Potocki's collection. He found the parody or free translation of Verlaine's *Idylle High-Life* 'capture[d] something of the sparkling (and grossly improper) gaiety of the French', and Potocki's version of the poem by Rabelais 'an improvement on Urquhart because it retains the metre and rhyme pattern of the original'. (Sir Thomas Urquhart, 1611–1660, was also eccentric. His translations of Rabelais were, and are still, considered by many to be without peer.) Craig also thought that the manuscript overall, 'although not everyone's meat, could be of legitimate interest to anyone whose tastes were literary without being prudish', and that 'Neither Rabelais's vigour nor Verlaine's delicate mastery of French verse [was] in any way diminished even when they dealt with subject matter normally found repulsive'. He observed that the short verses were 'quite unsuitable for polite society in twentieth-century England', but it had to be remembered that they were not intended for general publication.

He was scathing about Wild's judicial conduct, writing that when summing up Wild 'betrayed his own opinion in an unmistakable fashion', and about his literary pretensions, noting that he had published, at the age of fifty-nine, 'a volume of very adolescent verse entitled *The Lamp of Destiny* and rather fancied himself as a champion of literature'. Indeed, in *Above All Liberties*, Craig had gone further, stating that Wild's poetry 'argues a state of arrested emotional development or a depravity of poetic taste, both equally remarkable'. The volume's full title was in fact *The Lamp of Destiny or Some Indiscretions of the Long Vacation*, and in it Wild had described himself as 'the meanest bard that ever twanged on Lyre'. It contained verse of this order:

I watched the Sun a-sinking
In the sea;
And oh! I fell a-thinking
All of thee.
and oh! I fell a-thinking
His radiant beauty drinking,
Just as the Sun was sinking
In the Sea.

As Potocki noted: 'Some pretty mean bards have twanged on lyre, but he would have to have been one of the meanest. His poetry has been ridiculed completely. The fact was, he was jealous—the court was full of girls who were ogling me. The whole thing was a tragedy for me, but it was ridiculous and very amusing, I should think, for onlookers.

'The trial? Oh, it only lasted a day. What was really important was the appeal.'

# EIGHT

## The Appeal

> *I was subjected to such a boycott as is unheard of in the annals of world literature. The whole thing had a most unfortunate effect on my life. It extinguished my career as a poet.*

The literary world was outraged by Potocki's conviction and harsh sentence, and the threat to freedom of expression. A meeting was held at the home of Leonard and Virginia Woolf to decide on a definite course of action and, in the four weeks between the trial and his appeal in the Court of Criminal Appeal on 7 March, an appeal fund was opened and contributed to by many of the leading writers of the day.

Questions were asked in the House of Commons. *Hansard* for Thursday, 8 February 1932 (Vol. 261, No 40) records that

> Mr Vyvyan Adams asked the Home Secretary whether he will review the sentence of six months' imprisonment passed on Mr de Montalk, in view of the facts that such publication as occurred was merely technical.

Adams noted that part of the offending matter was a translation and that a limited circulation only was intended. He also asked on what principle of law 'discrimination is made against this gentleman and in favour of all the works of Aldous Huxley and all the books of the Apocrypha'? He was advised by Sir Herbert Samuel that Potocki had applied for leave to appeal and the matter was therefore still before the courts.

The press also kept pace with developments. The *Week-end Review* of 20 February, under the heading 'Censorship of Literature Again', described Potocki's sentence as savage. 'The case raises a question of much importance,' it pointed out. 'De Montalk is a poet of some ability. We have seen two of his books, and in our opinion the poems they contain are genuine and commendable stuff, about as far removed from pornography as possible.'

> But the point is this: Is there moral justification for, or is any useful purpose served by, invoking the law in a case where clearly no one can have been corrupted by the words complained of, as no one but the author and a printer saw them?

Leonard Woolf, who at the time of the appeal was managing editor of the Hogarth Press and from 1923 to 1930 had been literary editor of the liberal weekly the *Nation*, describes his involvement in the case in his autobiography *Downhill All the Way*. He writes:

> The strangest of all the incidents which came out of the *Nation* was the case of Mr Y [Potocki]. It began one morning when I was working at home and I received a telephone message from the office saying that a Mr X [Glass] had called and wanted urgently to see me—he could disclose his business only to me. I told them to tell him that, if he came round to Tavistock Square at once, I would see him for a few moments. Twenty minutes later there appeared a small gentle-voiced man in sandals.

Glass described the 'catastrophe' that had befallen his friend, and Woolf agreed to go into the matter, which he did, carefully. He concluded that the whole thing was 'a monstrous business' and the sentence (which he incorrectly refers to as three months) was a gross injustice, particularly as Potocki was a first offender. 'I knew Mr Y by sight, for he was a well-known figure in the streets of London, and as soon as I realized from Mr X's description who he was, I saw how prejudice would corrupt the incorruptible British magistrate or judge before whom he might appear.'

Woolf conferred with his friend, barrister 'Jack' St John Hutchinson KC, who agreed that the sentence was monstrous and said he would appear in the Appeal Court on Potocki's behalf for a very moderate fee. 'I got donations from seven publishers and more than 20 writers,' recalls Woolf. 'In the end the solicitor's bill was £91, 7s. 0d. and Mr X spent £12, 4s. 0d. so that I had to raise rather more than £100—it cost me personally over £50. The result was extremely unsatisfactory.'

In addition to J.B. Priestley, W.B. Yeats and Woolf, contributors included Augustus John, who gave £5, H.G. Wells, Havelock Ellis, Walter de la Mare, Laurence Housman, Lord Esher, T.S. Eliot, Hugh Walpole, Bertrand Russell, E.M. Foster, Gerald Gould, Rebecca West, Humbert Wolfe and Stephen Hudson. Aldous Huxley, who was in France at the time, responded to a request for assistance from Glass and wrote on 9 March, enclosing 'a small contribution'.

Meanwhile, Potocki, shut away in Wormwood Scrubs and unable to communicate with his solicitor, was not confident the 'projects' of his defence would be adequate without his assistance. Two days after his arrival he set about preparing his own grounds of appeal, arguing that the Recorder was prejudiced and coerced the jury, and disputing the finding of legal obscenity and the weighting given by Wild to his literary standing.

His text, as reproduced in *Whited Sepulchres*, stated that the poems in question formed only a small part of his poetical work, 'and to consider their moral drift is impossible without reading all the rest of my work, a good deal of which is published . . . and though my work tilts at the established morality it uplifts Honour, a much nobler thing, in its place.' He reminded their lordships the King's Justices that 'Poets have been persecuted in other ways, and for this reason Lord Byron and Shelley, among the Poets of the past, and James Joyce, D.H. Lawrence, Aldington, and Roy Campbell among the living, have deliberately chosen to live abroad', and that 'the only reason why the words in question could ever be considered obscene, is that they have so often been spoken by those who thought evil of them. The fact of love is in no way obscene, or if it is, then so is the whole Creation! For the above reasons I appeal against my Conviction and Sentence. Long live the King!'

After the disappointing performance of du Cann in the High Court, Potocki was wary of having another barrister briefed. He believed he would argue the case in the Appeal Court more successfully himself, and in a letter to Glass on 11 February, discussing the notice of appeal, he made this clear:

> I positively will not have ---- [St John Hutchinson] briefed for me. It seems to me the best idea would be to speak for myself, and let a barrister be present with a watching brief from the Authors' Society or some such body. Then he could rescue me if I got swamped in a

Potocki and Cedric in London, 1932, after Potocki's release from Wormwood Scrubs prison. Potocki is dressed in the first of his Richard II style tunics.

*Above:* Potocki taking an oath in the name of Apollo at his 1932 obscenity trial. This illustration appeared on the front page of *La Stampa*.

*Left:* Potocki, printing his literary and political journal, *The Right Review*, on his proto-Adana press, London 1939.

*Left:* Insterburg, 1933.

*Below left:* Warsaw, 1934.

*Below:* Near Warsaw, circa 1935. One lover is said to have liked waking in the night to find Potocki's hair around her shoulders.

Potocki with 'family member' Franco, London, circa 1939.

Potocki with Odile, probably at the time of their 'official' marriage in London in 1940. Odile was Potocki's muse during his epic translation of Adam Mickiewicz's poetic drama, *Forefathers*.

Odile, with her sons at the time of her divorce from Potocki in 1955.

London, circa 1945: Potocki with Dorli, who would be his intermittent 'secret wife' for more than twenty years.

Potocki, circa 1945, wearing the bespoke corduroy suit he based on the uniform of the Polish army.

Dorli.

Potocki at his flat in Islington, 1946. (Photo taken by the New Zealand poet John Male)

Provence, 1949. Potocki carrying out repairs to the Shack, the olive harvester's hut near Draguignan that was his first home.

The Countess de Bioncourt, Potocki's benefactor from 1949.

Potocki, Marysia (Potocki's Polish housekeeper, immediately to his left) and the twins Potocki denied fathering, Draguignan, circa 1953.

Theodora (adopted daughter of T.F. Powys and natural daughter of Potocki), Potocki and Zlota at Lovelace's Copse, Dorset, in front of Theodora's garden hut, formerly the revolving sanatorium of Llewelyn Powys, circa 1961. (Photo John Powys)

sea of Procedure...

There is a suggestion that I am not necessarily entitled to be present at the Appeal, though if I weren't, surely a great outcry could be raised about it. I am quite in favour of the presence of a barrister with a Watching Brief, but unless I can have a really great lawyer I consider I should be much better advised to plead myself.

Give my love to E ----- [Edwina, a girlfriend] and Cedric and kiss M ----- [Minnie, his mistress] for me. May the deathless Gods be with you all: don't lose your heads—'underneath are the everlasting arms'.

In order to act for himself, Potocki needed ready access to legal materials and time in which to prepare his case. As neither could be arranged in prison, for already he was required to work in the brush shop, he hoped to arrange bail. In the meantime Glass had written asking if arrangements could be made to visit him and discuss the various matters, and Potocki, strained by the effects of his isolation, replied:

My dear Douglas,
I got your letter of the 11th yesterday after I returned from work and was very glad to have it. In fact, for the first time since I was a child, I cried properly over it, for though it was very brief I could see how much work lay behind it. Also the note, 'Edwina loves you.'

The Governor is quite in accord with your coming. I explained to him your position in the international literary world, and how you were the only person competent to arrange things so well for me. I don't know whether, in such circumstances, you could get in with the Visiting Order, had it been sent to Sussex. It is all these dreadful details that are worrying, for if it isn't done exactly right, the opportunity sometimes seems to be lost. However I hope the Gods will see to it—Apollo and Hermes must be busier than they've been since the time of the Emperor Julian!

When applying for bail from in here, it seems necessary to offer a reason. As such reason, I said that having taken Law at my University, I desired to be my own advocate at the Appeal; and desired the opportunity to study the case-law on the question of the subject of the Appeal.

The application for bail required funds, legal assistance and the stated support of the literary community, but, as the appeal fund grew and Leonard Woolf increasingly assumed responsibility for Potocki's defence, it was decided that bail should not be sought. Woolf and Glass argued that it was better for him to remain inside, as there would be more sympathy for him if he was languishing in gaol. Although on a practical level it would appear this decision was taken to ensure Woolf retained control of proceedings, in personal terms it seems to have been a less than considerate response, given the grimness of prison life.

As his month in the Scrubs wore on, Potocki became convinced that there was a profound difference of opinion between him and 'the Glass-Woolf clique' as to how his defence was to be conducted: 'Having had a good legal education, and being besides a Poet, I was naturally in the right as the event proved. I said that efforts should be concentrated on the argument that a successor of Homer, Dante, Shakespear and Byron, was being made the victim of something approaching vaticide.' He also believed Wild's illegal behaviour should be emphasised and that the way to win the case was to 'represent to the Court the enormity of sending a Poet to gaol for a trifle of this sort, the more especially as *mens rea* was patently absent'. Furthermore, he argued—quite correctly—what was the First Offenders Act, which restricted the sentence of imprisonment for first offenders, for if it wasn't for the judge to observe it?

Isolated, and without access to his defence team, no member of which came to visit him to discuss the case, Potocki began to believe he was being treated by his 'alleged supporters as a mere pawn of no consequence whatever in the affair, except as a recipient of a sort of charity', although he felt this was not the intention of most of those who had subscribed to his appeal fund. He believed his concerns were confirmed when the case came to court: 'Throughout the proceedings, beginning at the Old Bailey, and continuing in the Appeal Court,' he told me, 'the judges were made to feel that I had no genuine support among the *literati*, who were merely concerned with the principle of the thing. At the appeal, St John Hutchinson, Woolf's barrister, referred to me in a sneering and disparaging manner, and he persistently called me "Mr de Montalk" in spite of my protests, and openly supported the Recorder's view that I was a bogus Poet and a bogus aristocrat.' Exceptions to these accusations were Gerald Barry, editor of the *Weekend Review*, Rebecca West and the *New English Weekly*. W.B. Yeats and Aldous Huxley were also counted as supporters of broader and more genuine motive.

Meanwhile, anxious that the so-called 'Woolf clique' would carry their dislike of his 'Aryan and aristocratic person so far as to damage the case hopelessly', Potocki told Glass that he would appear in person on his own behalf unless he was not only promised an interview with his barrister before the trial, but was able to secure certain promises regarding the legal direction the defence would take (with an appeal pending, he was entitled to a short appeal visit daily). Despite promises made, however, St John Hutchinson did not call at the Scrubs. 'They lulled my suspicions to sleep with the most absolute promises on these matters,' writes Potocki in *Whited Sepulchres*, 'and further played on my good will by pointing out that the case concerned not only me but all writers in England. Consequently I could hardly believe my eyes and ears when I found myself before Annas and Caiaphas, without ever having seen counsel before, and heard all those most solemn undertakings broken in a weak and stupid defence, which omitted every important legal point, and as good as conceded that I was not entitled to even the very lowest rank in the hierarchy of letters!'

Potocki's appeal was heard by Lord Chief Justice Hewart and Justices Acton and du Parcq on 7 March 1932. Potocki did not perform well. In *The Banned Books of England*, Craig explains why:

> Appellants to the Court of Criminal Appeal who have not obtained bail pending appeal suffer considerable difficulties. For one thing, the lowering of effects of prison diet make it very difficult for them to give a good account of themselves unless friends outside send a dinner in to them on the day of the trial. This was not done in the Count's case, and there is no doubt that he made a poor showing.

In his typed account, Potocki recalls that on the day of his second trial, owing to his trip to town, he had a hurried breakfast at the prison and 'It was even more insufficient than usual, particularly as we missed the "Exercise" cocoa and "toak" [the dry piece of bread handed out before drill] which formed quite an important item of our morning food.'

Moreover, Glass, who had promised to send a decent dinner down to the cells, or at least to get someone else to do so, did not keep his word, and by the time Potocki came before the judges, he was 'nearly fainting with hunger, having had only a small piece of bully beef and a bit of bread'. This absence of support depressed him, 'for what was I to think of the goodwill of my friends when they did not even send in some food to strengthen me and cheer me up?' In addition, he was confined from nine o'clock until around three 'in a sort of wooden horsebox the measurements of which I think were three feet six inches, by five feet'.

Afterwards his supporters reproached him for his poor showing, saying, 'You should have smiled up at du Parcq, who was interested in you. You looked bad.'

'Yes,' he replied. 'I felt like a starved and beaten dog, otherwise I should have said: "My Lords! May I dismiss counsel and speak for myself! And may I be given a meal first!'

His poor showing aside, however, Potocki believed that the brief prepared by his own solicitors, with the assistance of his own text, was sound, and had St John Hutchinson presented the case as advised, the appeal would have been decided in his favour. He writes in *Whited Sepulchres*:

> ... the question of my literary status, which ought to have been the principal point on my side, not having been raised at all by my lawyer, was very naturally raised by the Bench. Imagine my astonishment, when I heard Judge Acton say:
> 'One of these poems is alleged to be a translation from Paul Verlaine. I read Verlaine myself. He never wrote anything like that.'
> To this Mr St John Hutchinson did not answer a word, but stood there gaping, even though I had taken care to provide a whole volume of Verlaine full of such poems ... Moreover, had counsel taken the trouble to read the Transcript of the case on which he was appealing, he would have seen evidence of an authority on Verlaine *par excellence*, namely Edgell Rickword, that it was a very good version of the original!

St John Hutchinson erred further. Referring to Potocki's Buckingham Palace retort, he told the court that his client, who had read Socrates at university, had remembered Socrates' famous answer that 'he ought to be maintained at the public expense in the Prytaneum', and had decided that Buckingham Palace would be the next best thing. Potocki was incredulous. 'Of course his explanation-away ... was completely false!

I did read Plato at College, and in Greek too; moreover I was the only non-theolog Greek student of my University years. But I had clean forgotten about beastly old Puritan Socrates and his Prytaneum. Homer, Euripides, Aeschylus, Sophocles, and—Aristophanes—were my men, not Socrates.' Potocki was moved to write:

> 'What are you doing up there,
> In that basket, hung up in the air,
> Mr St John Hutchinson?'
> 'I am treading on air
> And having a stare
> At the sun.'

Justice Acton seized the occasion and challenged St John Hutchinson with 'But you don't seriously compare your client to Socrates, do you?' To Potocki's consternation, his counsel had answered the question by 'turning it into an awkward joke, to the effect that Socrates was an ugly man, and he would not like to compare his client to him', to which the judge responded by pressing the point, and counsel weakly admitted 'that in person and character I was quite unlike Socrates'.

Potocki had hoped that, should such a question arise, St John Hutchinson would have been prepared to confirm he was a poet, at least in the historical sense of the word, but 'The same mummery was gone through (with even less regard for my status) when Juvenal was mentioned . . .'

The appeal was not successful. Apparently ignoring the crucial issue of Wild's illegal behaviour, the Lord Chief Justice held that there was no doubt that 'there was publication—indeed it was not denied that there was—and there was no doubt the material referred to was in the highest, or the lowest, degree obscene.' He also declined to reduce the sentence:

> We see no reason at all for interfering with the conviction . . . With regard to the sentence of six months' imprisonment in the Second Division, which was passed by a learned judge of long experience, we have carefully considered the matter and we see no reason for interfering with it.

The decision, given Wild's judicial impropriety, is disturbing. At the very least there was his refusal to let the jury retire. The appeal brief given by Potocki's solicitors to St John Hutchinson states: 'When movement was made by the Jury to leave the box and confer in the adjoining room [Wild] directed them to remain in the box and consider the matter there.' As any juror will confirm, deliberation is difficult enough in a jury room. How much more problematic the discussion of complex censorship issues in a jury box, under the stern and instructive eye of the judge, and the scrutiny of the court?

And, in considering the censorship issues, how were jury members to decide—in the face of Wild's intolerance of the material, demonstrated so conclusively by his directive remark thirteen minutes into their discussion that surely they could not have read 'these filthy poems'—that the test for obscenity had less to do with how offensive they personally found the poems than with the tendency of the material to deprave and corrupt? How were they to debate the point made by du Cann that the law meant the words 'deprave' and 'corrupt' to be interpreted as to make morally bad, rather than simply to shock and disgust?

There was also Wild's instruction that, despite obvious disagreement between them, the foreman immediately return a verdict. And there was his treatment of the foreman—a well-meaning but inarticulate man—who, when he attempted to add a rider regarding the unresolved situation, was, as Potocki's solicitors stated in their appeal brief: 'at once directed to give answer to the question addressed to him, whereupon he became flustered and sat down without completing his remarks'.

Knowing that Potocki had held reservations about Leonard Woolf's 'motives' regarding the appeal—Woolf's disregard for his need to be involved in, or at least kept informed about, the handling of his defence, although understandable, had been a major concern—I was surprised to find Woolf in his biography so strongly expressing his outrage at its outcome for Potocki personally:

> I watched him [Hewart] 'doing justice' in the Appeal Court for the better part of a day and he seemed to me—and still seems to me—a typical example of a High Court judge suffering from the occupational disease of sadistic, vindictive self-righteousness. His treatment of the unfortunate Mr Y was disgraceful.

Woolf, who had previously served as a judge and police magistrate in Ceylon, believed the reason for the failure of the appeal lay in a 'curious psychological phenomenon' affecting prejudice and justice which he had become aware of during his three years in the colony. He had observed that, if he returned a verdict of guilty in three or four cases in succession, he 'tended to have an overlenient response' to the next defendant, particularly if he had had a moment's hesitation in finding the accused guilty. 'And vice versa, if one had found four accused in four cases not guilty one after the other, one had to be very much on one's guard against being unconsciously over-severe to or prejudiced against the accused in the next case.'

He was interested to detect the same 'mental process' in Hewart, who, however, seemed to be unaware of his prejudice. The case immediately before Potocki's had concerned a man convicted of housebreaking. Woolf had immediately seen that this appellant 'was an old lag'. He noted that the 'evidence against him was overwhelming', that he had been convicted many times, and that his appeal rested on a 'tenuous technical point' on the subject of which his counsel had made a very clever submission. When Woolf heard Hewart dismiss the conviction, 'smacking his judicial lips over the absolute justice of British justice', and telling the recidivist that he had been fortunate in having a barrister who had been able to put his difficult case so competently, he 'felt in [his] bones that British justice having been so magnanimous to the old burglar would probably take it out on Mr Y. It did.'

He notes that St John Hutchinson made an excellent speech showing that the sentence was 'monstrously excessive' in relation to the offence, but that Hewart obviously regarded the barrister unfavourably and disliked Potocki. 'As soon as the case was closed,' Woolf writes, 'he turned to the judge on his right and to the judge on his left and muttered something to each in turn.' The judge on the right, who was seen as having been on the bench 'for so long that he administered justice like a machine', automatically agreed with the Chief Justice. The judge on the left, however, who was much younger, had 'a reputation for being civilised' and was sitting in the Court of Appeal for the first time, argued with Hewart. He also stood up and moved around Hewart to the side of the elderly judge so he could explain his point of view more readily. But, although he remonstrated for some time, Hewart appeared to remain determined and in the end the younger man shrugged and returned to his seat. Hewart then rejected the appeal 'with the same self-righteous self-satisfaction with which he had allowed the appeal of the burglar'.

I was also surprised by Woolf's use of ciphers when referring to Potocki and Glass in his autobiography, and by the absence of their surnames in its index. Was the privacy of the two men a consideration, as it appears to have been elsewhere in the book when a third unrelated coded reference appears? (Possibly in the case of Glass who, after a shaky start in prison, had by now come to prominence as a photographer; less likely in the case of Potocki, who had never stopped railing publicly against the illegality of his trial and the injustice of his sentence.)

Or was Potocki's public post-trial condemnation of Woolf in *Whited Sepulchres*, and later in *Social Climbers in Bloomsbury*—a satire in which he ridicules literary pretension and shallow intellectualism—an issue here? Was Woolf in fact publicly diminishing, rather than attempting to protect, Potocki? Potocki had been very direct in his criticism of Woolf, whose actions he believed were in part responsible for the failure of his appeal, and whose disregard of him while he awaited his appeal in prison had, in his mind, confirmed his standing as a pawn in Woolf's high-profile pursuit of freedom of expression.

In this last regard it may be that, in the wake of the Radclyffe Hall case, the genuine concern Woolf did have for Potocki personally was indeed overtaken by the pursuit of principle. *The Well of Loneliness* had attracted the attention of a mere magistrate, Hall herself had not been prosecuted and members of literary London, in court to give evidence, had been ignored. In Potocki's appeal, however, Woolf had a writer who had been on trial in the Central Criminal Court, with an expert witness, and before a jury and the Recorder of London. As *Whited Sepulchres* reports, Potocki was told at the time: 'The case concern[s] not only [you] but all writers in England'. And as Virginia Woolf wrote during the period prior to Potocki's appeal (*The Sickle Side of the Moon: The Letters of Virginia Woolf 1932—1935*), Potocki was 'an idiotic Polish Count [who] has got himself into prison for writing silly indecent poems'. Furthermore, her reaction to an evening spent discussing the case as 'anger, laughter and utter boredom ... one evening will last me a lifetime with the count', was similarly dismissive, suggesting she at least entertained little sympathy for Potocki on a personal level.

It is also probably worth observing that, had Potocki not been flamboyant and not provoked the Recorder, it is unlikely the case would have attracted such widespread attention. A tame and less opinionated poet would probably have received a small fine and been bound over (ordered to come up for sentence if called on). The very behaviour that seems to have caused Woolf to be wary of Potocki was in fact responsible for the platform on which the debate was able to take place.

So, if the use of X and Y was indeed Woolf's public equivalent of Potocki's snub, then why did this seem inconsistent with his sympathetic tone? Was the sympathy stated for posterity? Interest in Potocki as an adventurous printer and wronged poet—rather than simply a royalist curiosity—was building when Woolf was writing his life story in the mid-1960s. Or did he use the ciphers for protection, concerned that Potocki, by now acutely litigious and often legally successful, would challenge his account of the case?

As for Woolf's explanation for the failure of the appeal, although I found it plausible, I was still bothered. It seemed to me that, given Wild's prejudice and interference, the appeal court should have declared a mistrial. I had no trouble accepting that a jury might reject the defence of public good and decide some of the poems were obscene, but surely the overriding issue for appeal was not the substance of the case, but the judge's conduct of the trial. And, beyond that, at the very least should not Potocki's grossly inappropriate sentence have been reduced to a fine?

'What do you think?' I asked John one night, having spent the day trawling through *Whited Sepulchres* and the various briefs and transcripts and trying to make sense of Potocki's taped remarks on the matter. John is a barrister and lectures on criminal law. Having seen the trial transcript, he too was surprised by the level of Wild's interference. He referred me to the unlikely sounding case of *Jones v. National Coal Board*, in which the trial judge, like Wild, had taken 'a substantial part of the examination out of the hands of counsel for the defendants' and intervened during cross-examination.

On appeal, Lord Denning had declared a mistrial. In his decision, dated 25 March 1957, he said:

> In the system of trial which we have evolved in this country, the judge sits to hear and determine the issues raised by the parties, not to conduct an investigation or examination on behalf of society at large . . . justice is best done by a judge who holds the balance between the contending parties without himself taking part in their disputations . . . Yes, he must keep his vision unclouded . . . Patience

and gravity of hearing is an essential part of justice; and an overspeaking judge is no well tuned cymbal ... Such are our standards ... There is one thing to which everyone in this country is entitled, and that is a fair trial at which he can put his case properly before the judge.

This was relevant material, but I was still no further ahead. 'If Wild was so out of order,' I said, 'why didn't the appeal succeed?'

'Have you checked the actual grounds of appeal?' asked John.

This meant a return to the archive. I purchased a mask, rubber gloves and a fresh phial of tea-tree oil. I was taking no chances.

The document was there, and it damned Wild's conduct. It consisted of a detailed and cogent submission prepared by Potocki himself, together with supporting and additional arguments from his solicitors.

Potocki's submission opens with the powerful statement that the Recorder had been biased and coerced the jury. His other arguments, in summary, claim that the poems were not legally obscene, as they could not corrupt the morals of those into whose hands they were likely to fall, and, even if they were obscene, the defence of public good applied, because they had been compiled for literary purposes. His arguments distil his legal and literary talents and are an indication of his potential should he have elected a career in the law.

His solicitors make the further point that Wild had misdirected the jury three times: that he had failed to point out there must be an intent to corrupt public morals; that there was no evidence on which the jury could find such an intent, as the only person who had complained had been de Lozey; and that Wild had led the jury to believe a number of copies of the collection were to be sold, when in fact there was no evidence to support this.

I was interested to find a further document which revealed that, while Potocki's application for leave to appeal his sentence had been granted, leave to appeal the conviction had in fact been refused. This meant that the hearing in the Court of Appeal had consisted of an appeal against the refusal to give leave to appeal the conviction, together with the appeal against sentence.

'I still don't understand why it didn't succeed,' I said. 'The case against Wild was overwhelming.'

'I'll get hold of Hewart's decision,' sighed John.

The appeal decision of Lord Justice Hewart confirmed my suspicions. The Appeal Court had not considered Wild's conduct. It had merely focused on the issue of intention to corrupt public morals.

'Why was Wild's conduct ignored? Why didn't St John Hutchinson bring it before the court?'

'Gutless counsel?' suggested John. 'An establishment job? A barrister worried about showing Wild up and making an enemy of the Recorder? No worries about sacrificing a colonial. Or perhaps, given the climate of judicial comity, he didn't believe a case against Wild could be won. A successful challenge to Wild's behaviour would not only have discredited the Recorder, but it would have demonstrated the unthinkable: that the British system of impartiality didn't exist. Safer to appeal the case on the more neutral issue of obscenity.'

However, John did not believe this was the whole story. 'There's also the possibility that, together with Woolf, he'd decided to ignore the solicitors' brief detailing Wild's interference and bias, and appeal the case on the issue of obscenity alone because he was hoping to establish a legal precedent for freedom of speech. If he'd won on the ground of judicial bias—which was undoubtedly the stronger legal argument—he wouldn't have created any precedent. Potocki's personal interests were sacrificed whichever way you look at it.'

'Then there was the strange business of the incomplete transcript of the Old Bailey trial. Large sections were left out. The solicitor's brief to St John Hutchinson was very specific about this.' This was also ignored.

John could certainly see why Potocki might have believed there was a conspiracy.

Another point had occurred to me. 'Maybe St John Hutchinson wasn't the man for the job. He was doing Woolf a favour—perhaps he wasn't attuned to what would work best in this case.'

'It's possible he wasn't familiar with criminal law. As a KC, and a friend of the Woolfs, he was more likely to have been a specialist in civil litigation—there's more status and money than in criminal litigation. He'd probably never been inside a prison.'

'No wonder Potocki raged—especially with his legal background. I never took any notice. I got used to it. "Six months in the Scrubs". It just rolled off the tongue.'

'It's appalling Wild's behaviour wasn't challenged,' concluded John. 'An enormous injustice was done. There was clearly a closing of the ranks. The worst thing one can say of a judge is that he's prejudiced. The judge who conducted the coal board case resigned. Potocki was quite entitled to feel that he'd been shafted: by the English, the establishment, Woolf and British justice.'

The establishment, societal standing, a KC concerned about his promotion to the bench? Not relevant, surely? The Woolfs and St John Hutchinson were self-confessed liberals, free-thinking members of the left. Or could it be that an entry in *The Diary of Virginia Woolf: Volume IV* in June 1932 suggests otherwise? Dinner at 'the Hutchinsons' at 3 Albert Park (opposite Regent's Park and the Zoo)? A regular enough occasion with a party member 'back from Cambridge', someone else 'smoking a cheroot' and a certain 'tightness in the talk' necessitating champagne? For although there was mention of a speech to be made 'at a bazaar about the Christian attitude to the unemployment question', the scene was not quite as convincingly left-wing as I might have imagined. Was this because there were footmen in attendance? And 'Desmond and Lord Balniel' were present, and Lord and Lady Derwent? And Lord David Cecil was 'only absent' because he had sprained his ankle, and Lord Chichester was 'ringing up'? Or because 'Jack', who was making small talk about 'expanding Sadlers Wells', was saying, '"So good for Leonard all these Lords"'?

Still I wasn't satisfied. There were doubts about St John Hutchinson, and the closing of judicial ranks around Wild, who had entered the heat of the arena and allowed his eyes to become covered with dust, had been all but exposed. Now I needed to know about Hewart. What of the man who should have dispensed the ideal championed as British Justice? I had Woolf's account of the Chief Justice, but surely there was more. I was convinced, though, that the standard reference texts would speak only of his achievements.

Then, by the greatest coincidence, a couple of days later I opened a copy of the *London Review of Books*, dated 1 June 2000, and there in the top right-hand column of a review of *The Struggle for Civil Liberties: Political Freedom and the Rule of Law in Britain 1914—1945*, was Lord Hewart, recalled, as described by his entry in the *Oxford Companion to Law*, as

> ... perhaps the worst Chief Justice since the 17th century, not as being dishonest but as lacking dignity, fairness and a sense of justice ...

I spent an afternoon in the library looking for Hewart.

In *Judges on Trial* by Shimon Shetreet, I found him described as a most persuasive advocate with an immense capacity and appetite for work. But I also read that 'there have been some dreadfully bad judges. None was worse than Lord Hewart, C.J. . . . He lacked only one quality which should distinguish a judge: that of being judicial.' He was further described as rivalling 'Scroggs and Jeffreys in arbitrary and unjudicial behaviour on the bench', and as lacking 'in a marked degree that deliberation which enables a good judge to keep his mind open until the conclusion of the case'.

Opening *The Great Judges*, I found Justice Gerald Sparrow concluding that Hewart appeared to be wanting in restraint and 'completely devoid [of] wide human experience'. Tellingly, Sparrow observes that, although Hewart was married with six children, his life in Didsbury, Manchester, 'had its limitations [and he was] remarkably ignorant of sexual motivation outside the narrow confines of surburban domestic bliss'.

In the end, Potocki's only consolation was that, although he personally had been unsuccessful, his appeal set the precedent for the defence of public good. *R. v. De Montalk* (1932) 23 Cr. App. Rep. 182, which is still quoted in textbooks on criminal law, provides that in obscene libel cases:

> It is a good defence to the charge that the publication of matter prima facie obscene was for the public good, as being necessary or advantageous to religion, science, literature or art, provided that the manner and extent of the publication does not exceed what the public requires.

Afterwards, a petition which was to have been drawn up and signed by the still outraged literary community did not materialise, although Potocki claimed there were 'hundreds of people, many of them important, simply panting to sign it'.

Potocki was returned to prison. The next day Glass wrote:

> My Dear Geoffrey:
> I tried to get in to see you after the Appeal but failed. I lost track of Mr Meyer while I was talking with Mr Woolf, Virginia Woolf and

Mr St John Hutchinson. After experiencing some foolish opposition by the policeman I lost heart and went off on my own, to be alone, so that I might think clearly and quietly as to the next step. I must say I was so surprised and horrified at the result that I could not look your way when you left the dock or put up much of a fight to get in to see you. I have not lost heart but the result was a severe shock and a blow. I know nothing like it in the history of alleged British Justice.

He advised that he had been in touch with the MP Vyvyan Adams, who had drafted another question for the House, and that Woolf would consult further with St John Hutchinson. He also urged Potocki not to lose heart. 'The chances of doing anything now are very small, but you may rely on me to push those chances to their extreme conclusion.'

> I may have to go over to Holland before the 15th. I shall not stay long but I think it will be in mine and your interest that I do so. I will give a lecture or two and also arrange for a further series of articles to be published there.
> ... The Hogarth Press are now considering your next book, 'How Few Withstand'. I think something will come of it. [Nothing did.] ... Edwina is rather cut up and sends you her fond and sincere Love. She too had hoped and prayed for more justice. Minnie ... well, I leave it at that ... I fear you looked a little too severe while you were in the Dock. Many of your friends commented on this, yet perhaps they would have looked severe.
> You already know how far I was able to get with the appeal so let this give you some confidence that I may be able to reach the Home Secretary with the assistance of those who are interested in this outrageous sentence and conviction.
> Edwina's fond Love and devotion.
> My own Love and Hope,
> Yours, Douglas.

Potocki, who by now had spent nearly six weeks in Wormwood Scrubs, had lost all hope of a just outcome and did not see any point in taking the matter further. He fumed instead about the unsatisfactory behaviour of St John Hutchinson: his failure to consult with him in the crucial pre-trial period, his slighting of him in public by not using his title. Disillusioned but undiminished, and yet to fully realise the extent of his sentence, he looked to his release, vowing never to place himself at the discretion of others again. On 13 March he wrote to Glass:

> . . . I didn't think much of St J.H. for breaking the condition on which I consented to brief him . . . I agreed, in the alleged interests of the literary community (mais l'Etat, c'est moi!) to forgo my right to speak for myself . . . he did not so much as see me before the case, and once, almost inaudibly it is true, during the trial called me 'Mr.' I rely on you to protest. I will not be called 'Mr' by my alleged defenders on any pretext whatever . . . There is no Mister Geoffrey de Montalk, even in Prison. Here I am Prisoner No. 4579, outside I am a Prince of the House of Potocki. The sooner everyone recognizes the unbending intransigence of my character, the better. Either I have my way, whole and undefiled, or I go under.
>
> My main concern now is to have money when I come out: as you know I must go abroad; and then there's Edwina whom I want to take. I am in favour of a trip abroad à quatre if we can manage it.
>
> I charge you with my thanks, except to those who degrade me to the rank of Mister (this nothing can excuse in my eyes) . . . For two pins I'd become a Frog. I am becoming more and more convinced that 'God is a Frenchman'.
>
> I specially resented Counsel's reference to my 'sufferings', though he is quite excused on that point. It all means that once again, I hope for the last time, I have allowed myself to be beguiled into following the foolish counsel of others against the high voice of my own peculiar genius. I have never done so yet, without regretting it.

In the early spring, beyond the walls of his cell, supporters continued to protest the injustice of his six-month sentence. Rebecca West's letter to the editor of *Time and Tide*, published on 12 March, was typical of many:

> He is going to spend six months—March, April, May, June, July, August—in jail. That the law should function in this way seems to raise a moral issue. Surely it is, and ought to be, abhorrent to every human being that the community should send any of his or her fellow creatures to prison save for the protection of its citizens from

serious injury. I must confess that, as a citizen, I should much prefer to be without this protection. I would far rather that Count Geoffrey Potocki de Montalk was allowed to do anything he will with his poems than that I should have laid on me the heavy moral guilt of depriving a human being of his liberty without just cause.

Art, censorship, civil rights, legal impropriety and improper application of the law continued to be debated at length in the press. The *New Statesman and Nation* argued on 12 March that the outcome of the case raised a public issue that intimately and immediately affected every editor, publisher, printer, author or journalist. It spoke of the extreme length to which the law of obscene libel had been stretched: 'It means that any individual who writes an indecent limerick and gives it to a friend is liable to imprisonment if it happens to fall into the hands of the police . . . And [this purely technical crime] may be punished with a sentence that one would usually expect in the case of a crime of violence or of professional thieving.' It continued: 'It was obvious that Montalk had done harm to no one. Yet the judges had to find him guilty of the same offence as some lewd ruffian who prints pornographic literature for sale in the shops of the underworld.' The implications of this decision were described as very wide.

> A journalist who brings an article to an editor with the familiar remark, 'I am not sure whether this is publishable, but you might look,' is liable to prosecution for obscene libel if the editor cares to consult the police. An artist who paints a nude and offends the taste of the hanging committee may find himself in prison if a member of the committee reports him to the police. Every novelist who submits a new work has to run the risk that some person in the publisher's house may turn informer. The publisher may not have submitted an unexpurgated draft, but he may be guilty of an obscene libel in the eyes of the law.
> . . .
> As far as obscene passages go, we know that every copy of the Bible, or of Juvenal, Aristophanes, Chaucer, or Shakespeare is obscene, but we rely upon a certain discretion in the enforcement of the law. Is the discretion in fact exercised? There are whole streets in the West End of London in which every other shop contains blatantly pornographic literature obviously displayed for commercial

purposes. Yet the vendors of pornography are left alone.

...

What is the explanation for the leniency of the police on the one hand and the savage treatment of an eccentric on the other?

Fairburn wrote to Charles Lahr at his shop in Red Lion Street on 21 March 1932, thanking him for a pirated edition of the 'de Montalk booklet'. He liked the Verlaine poem 'very well' and hoped that 'prison won't do Monty any harm [as] he is the sort of person whom it is likely to injure rather than benefit'. Glass, he observed, as 'the supreme opportunist, our modern Autolycus, is quite capable of looking after himself in a den of lions'.

How did so much misfortune really come about? I once asked Potocki. He was in no doubt. 'Glass,' he said.

'Surely not.'

'Oh yes! Glass all right. When we took the manuscript to de Lozey, he began attacking the Jews. As I've said, I didn't know what the devil he was on about because I had no idea that de Lozey was a Jew, but Knott, the publisher, told me when we were outside the court afterwards—the police court—that de Lozey was indignant that Glass had carried on about the Jews, especially as he considered it was obvious Glass himself was a Jew. I don't think he was. Anyway, de Lozey wanted to get Glass arrested, according to Knott, and of course he couldn't get Glass arrested without getting me arrested.

'And you see, in the ordinary way, if de Lozey had gone to denounce me and any other ordinary person to the police, the police would have said to him, "Look, Mr de Lozey, can you tell us who set up in type the illegal edition of *Lady Chatterley's Lover,* or do you happen to know who set up *The Autobiography of a Flea?* Because if you don't know we do, and you had better go home." That's what they would have done normally, because the police aren't that stupid. But Glass was involved, and they'd been trying to arrest Glass, because he was thieving and swindling all over the place, and always slipping out of their hands— he'd already served six months for stealing from John Barker's, the menswear shop in Kensington. So when de Lozey came along with his name, they said "Got Glass at last", you see, and that's why they issued the warrant.

'That's never been printed, but that's the real reason. The police didn't care whether I printed these poems or not, but they couldn't very well arrest Glass without arresting me. So they arrested us both, but Glass slipped away again because I unwittingly instructed du Cann to arrange it.' He continued, bitterly: 'And when I went from prison to the Appeal Court in London, my wonderful friends outside didn't even send me a meal. After all the care I'd taken of Glass when he was in prison, they didn't think to let me have something to eat. I mean, when you're hungry, and you haven't had anything proper to eat for a month, and then your friends don't even send you in some bacon and eggs.'

'What about Wild?'

'As for Wild, well, there was every reason why the appeal judge should have reversed Wild's judgment. But you see Wild already had a thoroughly bad reputation and it would have been a great disgrace for him as he was just about to retire—in fact he died two years later. So I was sacrificed to what I have always described as an "esprit de corpse".'

'And the Appeal Court?'

'The appeal judges, they simply walked over St John Hutchinson. He was hired for me—he was taken on by Leonard Woolf and his gang, you see.'

# NINE

## Imprisonment

*'Moorish castle' indeed! Moorish billiard balls!
No wonder the Prince of Wales has had his
fingerprints taken.*

'I was extremely angry, and I've remained angry ever since. That's why I always look so bad-tempered in all the photographs of me, and the drawings made of me in England. I was, am, and am likely to remain, extremely indignant.'

In 1932 Wormwood Scrubs Prison was, as it still is today, one of Europe's largest penal institutions. Purpose-built by convict labour between 1874 and 1890 in West London on 200 acres—one of the most extensive pieces of common land in London—its exterior was imposing, castle-like, described by its staff as Moorish, and its tiered interior with an arched glass ceiling had a capacity of one thousand prisoners in separate cells.

At the time of its inception, it was a pioneering model of prison reform, reflecting an assumption (held until the turn of the century) that the contemplation of one's misdeeds in solitary confinement was likely to lead to the reform of the prisoner. The result was a régime designed for the infliction of suffering, and a prisoner who would emerge from his sentence shorn and cropped, poorly nourished, mentally numbed and often insane.

When Potocki entered the Scrubs in 1932, menial work programmes had been introduced and the compulsory cropped haircut done away with, but the rigours of a retributive system remained. The diet was still poor, prisoners were flogged, executions were carried out, standards of hygiene were inadequate, and the very buildings were pervaded with a sense of the hardships of their past. As a significant number of the

1400 inmates were serving maximum sentences, it was known as a 'lifer's prison', and it was as grim in the context of its time then as it is now.

Immediately Wild had pronounced sentence, Potocki was hustled out of the dock and, after meeting briefly with Glass in the cells below the courtroom, transferred to a police tender to be taken, with four others, to prison. On seating himself in the van, he was verbally accosted by one of the other prisoners, who stated threateningly that he agreed heartily with the judge and said that if anyone gave filthy literature to *his* little daughter he would do him in.

With a criminal record and a prison sentence, Potocki should have been despondent, but he remained relatively unperturbed. He was convinced that his criminal status would be overturned on appeal, and aware of the need to remain calm so he could ensure that financial support was arranged and an effective legal argument prepared. He was even optimistic that he would yet be a *cause célèbre*. As his pamphlet *Snobbery with Violence* confirms, on arrival at the Scrubs he observed his surroundings with a lucid eye, noting in particular that the gate was 'pompous and pretentious' and the chapel 'one of the stagiest pieces of hypocrisy in England'.

In reception he was relieved of his personal belongings—watch, fountain pen, cash—and taken before an officer in another room, where he was ordered to hand over his clothes, take a tepid bath in an adjoining cubicle, and dress himself in prison clothing: 'grey caricatures of what is already the basest vulgarity—modern male attire—and grotesque to a degree—no item of which fitted, except the boots.' Then he was offered a pint of cocoa and a slice of dry bread, and locked up, with his travelling companions, to await further formalities. In due course his fingerprints were taken. He protested. 'The Prince of Wales has had his fingerprints taken,' an officer said.

'The Prince of Wales wears a bowler hat,' Potocki replied.

Brief meetings with the deputy governor and the medical officer followed, and then with the chaplain, to whom he declared he was pagan and would appreciate a volume of Shakespeare as Holy Writ in place of the customary Bible. Finally, he was given a pillowcase, into which he was instructed to put two canvas sheets, a pair of felt slippers, a tooth-brush, a Bible and a prayer book. He was also handed 'an incredibly stupid tract called the "Narrow Way"', for which he later observed prisoners demonstrating 'their just contempt by destining their leaves, with a quite deliberate symbolic intention, to the basest usages'.

Admission procedures complete, he was marched with the other new admissions to B Hall and locked up in a separate cell, 'for which the gods be thanked! And thank the Lord also there was no television, and you weren't allowed to smoke, although the creatures bought tobacco illegally and smoked it up the ventilation vents and you could smell their rotten tobacco just the same'. As it was now late, he lowered the wooden trestle that was his bed from the wall and, exhausted, went straight to sleep.

Potocki rarely spoke in detail of the months he spent in prison. When I casually asked him about them, he was vague. When I interviewed him on tape, he was only marginally more detailed. I assumed that having documented the experience in *Snobbery with Violence*—having dealt with it—he put it behind him, preferring to save his energy and contempt for those responsible for putting him there, for the 'monstrous injustice' of his punishment. Anger was perhaps a more useful emotion than self-pity.

However, the 53-page pamphlet, *Snobbery with Violence: A Poet in Gaol*, written after his release and published in late 1932 by Wishart & Co, provides a compelling account of his period of imprisonment. Unlike *Whited Sepulchres*, which vociferously condemns his trial and appeal, and which, given the issues of legal obscenity, literature, censorship and English puritanism it argues, is necessarily dense, *Snobbery* is Potocki's incisive prose at its most effective. While the commentary is scathing, the tone is restrained, matter of fact and frequently humorous: although the underlying realities of his sentence are only lightly exposed, they are readily imagined.

Aldous Huxley wrote to Potocki that he found the pamphlet 'a very interesting and at the same time well written account of prison life as it appears to a man of intelligence and sensibility', while George Orwell, lamenting the absence of quality pamphlet prose ten years later in the *New Statesman and Nation* (9 January 1943), described it as one of the 'few good pamphlets in recent years', on a par with D.H. Lawrence's *Pornography and Obscenity*.

Reading this account, thinking about his imprisonment, picturing him there in the clank and grind of the Scrubs—its long narrow halls, its four noisy tiers of cells, the steel of its stairs and projecting balconies—I began to have a sense for the first time of Potocki as a young man. I had known the older Potocki, but the younger man had eluded me. Like the early part of the century he'd lived in, he'd been distant, unfamiliar. Now, in the process of writing this memoir—in the intimacy of memory and imagination, the ease of assumption—I found I was beginning to relate to him.

He was twenty-eight—older and younger than my sons—a young man who was passionate about literature, language and women, and identified with an earlier age. He had arrived in London a 'naïve and sincere young poet', believing he could do anything, achieve everything. He had been impetuous and unwise, but he had also been exciting and bright. 'A bit of colour in an otherwise drab world', as the *Polish Daily* would later describe him. A young man noted for his 'unaccountable retinue of pretty girls', as C.H. Rolph, who attended his trial and had seen him 'quite often' in the streets of Soho, would write in *Books in the Dock*.

I saw him waking each morning at a quarter to six in the overnight stench of his cell block to the loud, insistent ringing of a bell—the signal to rise, take a cold wash from the water which remained in his jug, and tidy his surroundings: a shelf near the door which served as a table, a chair, a trestle bed. I saw him in his sour air, the thin light from his window, getting dressed, waiting for the scrape of key against steel, the shout of 'Slop out!', the narrow shuffle of the queue to the recess (ablution room) where the drains rapidly blocked and the sink and the toilet were brimming—a 'typhoidal affair'. He would fetch the day's washing and drinking water from the same room—'in their own way, the English are the dirtiest race in the world'—his movements awkward in boots, an odd figure with his long hair, lank without the glamour of his cloak, angular in ill-fitting clothes, and return to scrub out his cell, squat on the wet floor, listen, watch the door so he wouldn't miss the delivery of toak (grey bread and cocoa) before drill. He was perpetually hungry and the small snack would be welcome.

He would take his toak, balance it on his chair as he finished his scrubbing, moistening the bread in his cup of cocoa with one hand, wetting the brush in the bucket with the other, wondering if today drill would be a blank file, dressing by the right, his arms close to his body, a white wind freezing the yard, or, like yesterday, a march in the prison grounds staying close to the wall, grateful for the shelter. Either way he'd be on edge lest someone grasped him when the guards were not looking. He had yet to decide which was worse: daytime in the brush shop and yard, or night-time with lock-up at six and access to the recess forbidden until morning.

He'd return from the yard '*At the double!*' and stand beside his door. Breakfast would approach: another slice of grey bread, a scraping of margarine, weak tea in a mug with a crown on it, porridge ladled from a can. He'd sit on his chair, taking the porridge first, spooning it carefully so that nothing was spilt, holding the bowl close to his mouth, wiping it clean with the bread, leaving the tea—colour of a 'clean silk shirt'—until last because only a short time was allowed for breakfast, and food saved in the cell was almost certain to be stolen by cleaners.

Straight after breakfast, having obediently set out his cell in the recognised way (chair in the middle of the room, slippers in front of it one either side of the dustpan, bedding folded neatly 'in a certain order'), he'd march to the brush shop, where brushes for scrubbing the decks of the Royal Navy were made. He'd work until twelve, taking a break of ten minutes most mornings during which he'd be permitted to walk around an exercise ground. And talk—'a privilege to which most prisoners attach the utmost importance, not because they have anything to say, but merely because they want to make a noise'.

At midday he'd be returned to his hall for an hour for dinner. The meal, which for the first half of his sentence was served in his cell, doubled as shaving time. If he'd shaved the previous day, he'd have half an hour in which to read before returning to the brush shop until five.

At six, having eaten his toak—otherwise known as supper—in his cell, he'd be locked up for the night and required to sew dull-red mailbags, by a bad light, even in summer, until eight: work 'ruinous to the eyes'. On Thursday evenings task time would be halved and he'd be allowed to attend lectures—'farcical affairs'—on subjects such as 'dogs, or the Army . . . or Venereal Diseases':

> One disgraceful lecture was on India, in which the Hindu was represented as ignorant, treacherous, dirty, and smellier *than a goat* (a story was told to this effect). The English, on the other hand, were the pure, fine, intelligent, manly Christians, and lantern slides of the repulsively ugly buildings we have put up in India were shown to demonstrate this . . . Either low-caste Hindu or goat would be nobility itself in comparison . . . In the end I left off going to lectures and stayed in my cell reading.

At eight a bell would ring and he'd be permitted to let down his bed. But sleep was usually impossible until nearly ten, for there was a shooting range alongside the prison. Sleep was also disturbed intermittently throughout the night by the warder opening the eye-hole in the door:

> You hear a light click as a rule, and you see an Eye looking at you. Sometimes the Eye asks if you are all right, especially if a prisoner has committed suicide during the week before . . . There were at least two suicides during the four months and three weeks of my actual imprisonment; and, as all measures were taken to hush these up, I am ready to believe there were more.

Before long, the inadequate diet and lack of hygiene caused his health to suffer. When he first arrived in prison he had been so confident about the strength of his stomach, which had been able to digest the diet at Brixton and 'to accommodate itself to the food of different countries and places', that he had assumed he would tolerate the prison food without problems. But, like most others, he succumbed frequently, and on occasion severely, to diarrhoea.

Potocki directs some of his pamphlet's most scathing commentary at the nutritionally meagre and unpalatable prison diet. This he does for all the obvious reasons, particularly its weakening effect in the month prior to his appeal, but also, perhaps, because it revived memories of the hunger of his childhood.

In Chapter 3, 'Disquisition on Dinner', he writes that the dinners 'call for considerable comment, as it is practically impossible to exaggerate the badness of them'. He finds they are barely edible or nourishing and are 'tasteless and repulsive to a degree', noting that in just over five months, he received no fruit and less than half a pound (227 g) of vegetables, excluding year-old potatoes and dried white beans. The meals were made up mostly of stale potatoes, suet pudding and dried beans, supplemented with stale bread and cocoa, which made, he believes, for a diet 'the starchiness of which almost amounts to poisoning'.

Individual dinners, which were 'so insufficient in quantity as to leave every prisoner feeling very hungry, even those with small appetites', are dealt with in detail. He recalls in particular the shortcomings of the bully beef and bacon dinners, but 'the most famous dinner, on account of its villainous bad suchness, is "Sea Pie"'.

> This consists of a frightful cube, about three inches wide, of bread-cum-suet pudding, with suggestions of meat hanging onto it, the while swimming in a thin stock or gravy. On considering the question of this 'Sea Pie' after I was released from prison, it occurred to me that the only thing that 'puts it across' is its name . . . for I believe that even prisoners would not eat such muck were it not for the suggestion of 'something rich and strange' in the title. Words are omnipotent, so this filthy dish suffers a sea-change in the pathetic imagination of the prisoner. Personally, I am not at the moment concerned with what the British bourgeoisie feed their slaves on, but I do think that the makers of English literature ought to be protected from this sort of offal.

Other problems surfaced. He began to experience a peculiar dull shooting pain in his teeth, and pain in his ears, and a sense that his body was being strained beyond the diet of starch, the lack of hygiene and the general 'badness of the food'.

Linking these symptoms to a rumour among the inmates that their cocoa contained bromide, and being strongly opposed to drug-taking of any kind, including even aspirin, he took this concern to the chaplain, who was 'very sure of himself, cock-sure in fact'. When the chaplain reacted to the suggestion with uncharacteristic embarrassment and prevarication, Potocki sought out the senior medical officer. When the doctor merely murmured, 'Ah, yes. Ah, yes', Potocki was convinced of the truth of the rumour:

> Up to that point he had been talking freely and in a friendly way. Now, however, he was absolutely at a loss . . . Surely, if there were no truth in it he could easily have said 'Yes, but of course that's absolutely untrue,' or something of the kind. Of course, the object of giving the prisoners bromide would be to keep them in a subdued state, and to prevent what the Governor lusciously calls 'immorality' . . .

He would have been glad to go without the serving of food containing the bromide, but rumour suggested it was hidden variously in the cocoa, the porridge and the tea, and he could not go without all these things. 'If the authorities *must* use bromide,' he writes, 'it ought to be put in the tea, a valueless article of diet, and this should be made known.

Then prisoners who can refrain from onanising without the aid of bromide, could go without tea and so avoid being poisoned.'

He observes that, 'according to their own confessions and even boasts, most prisoners onanise in spite of the bromide, and this must do them more harm than onanising in ordinary circumstances. One prisoner, a young man who professed to have had some dealings with women, said to me: "As a matter of fact, I won't say I haven't masturbated at all since I have been in here. I have. But only about eight times. That's not bad for five months" . . . *Res ipsa loquitur*, m'lord,' wrote Potocki. 'The thing speaks for itself. You can't stop it from speaking, either.'

Halfway through his sentence, having satisfied behavioural expectations, Potocki was upgraded to D Hall. This meant he could now join other prisoners for meals on the ground floor, attend evening lectures up to three times a week, and receive one visitor and one letter every three weeks.

He found communal dining disappointing. While he appreciated the unexpected custom that permitted flowers to be placed on the meal tables, and had Edwina send in some daffodils—short-lived because they were immediately poisoned with salt by prisoners from the next table—he was unimpressed with the company he was forced to keep, noting that 'instead of being allowed to associate with the most congenial folk you can find, as would be in the interest of a good atmosphere in the prison, you have to associate with any criminals fate happens to place you among'. He was also disturbed by the opportunity mealtimes gave some of the long-serving prisoners, who had been made leaders, to amuse themselves by making life miserable 'for any men whose qualities ought to make them worth protecting'.

This forced contact with large numbers of people he would not normally have mixed with, excluding many of the warders but including the upper levels of the staffing hierarchy, was a particular concern. The staff members to whom he took most exception were the governor, the deputy governor, the chaplain and the medical officers—on the subject of whom he curtly remarks: 'I say Public School, that is all.' The exception was the senior medical officer, whom he found to be an intelligent person. The warders (or officers, as they preferred to be called), on the other hand, he found to be 'mostly decent fellows and quite human':

The prisoners call them 'screws,' and hate them immeasurably. It is taken for granted that you despise the 'screws.' Well, I don't agree. They, with a very few exceptional prisoners, and two or three persons on the higher staff, were the only people I had any respect for there. After all, the 'screws' do not seriously set themselves up to be anybody in particular, whereas some people do.

Heavily disillusioned with all things establishment, upper class and English, he observed: 'What I don't approve of is the half-pie Public School aristocrat in plus fours.'

As for the prisoners, he considered most of them to be appalling people to associate with. A notable exception was the painter George Hann, whom he met in the early stages of his imprisonment, while awaiting his appeal. He told me: 'Hann had been put in gaol for stealing no end of diamond tiaras and things like that, and he was stupidly romantic about it. He kept talking about how he had all this glittering stuff in his room. But unlike me, it did him a lot of good in the end, because when he came out, I fed him at my place, and someone else gave him bits of plywood and paint, and he was able to get by on painting fishes and things on them, and selling them for five paintings for a pound, and slowly getting the price up, until just before the war when he was able to ask thirty pounds for a painting.' Another exception was a Jewish gentleman from Poland who had embezzled the funds of a Polish co-operative. 'He was very entertaining—of course I wasn't anti-Jewish at that stage—and would see to it that some of us got *mutza* from the Jews.' Of the other second division inmates he declares: 'Very few of them seem to be first-rate criminals even, but rather petty coiners, unsuccessful forgers, bigamists, and, alas! homosexuals.'

The long-haired, heterosexual Potocki found the sexual threat and innuendo from inmates he perceived as homosexual alarming: 'From the very beginning,' he writes in *Snobbery*, 'I was made the victim of Nancy-boy cat-calls, kissing noises, and even mild assaults . . . The most frightful obscenities of speech and gesture were to be seen in the Brush Shop.' In particular he was the subject of three unspecified assaults by a young Scots prisoner. 'Note,' Potocki advises at the foot of the page, 'that I have toned down this report by not saying what this man's assaults consisted of.'

The issue of sexual molestation came to a head when a Cockney prisoner, newly moved to the brush shop, was encouraged to prove himself by coming up behind Potocki and shoving his hand between his legs. Potocki reported the group responsible for this harassment to the warder, who initially refused to take down their names, complying only when Potocki threatened to have the matter raised in Parliament.

Three days later he was summoned to the governor to explain his complaint. Making a pyramid shape with his hands, he told the governor:

> The prisoners in the Brush Shop, sir, have a habit of arranging their hands in this shape and then jamming them up each other's buttocks. The prisoners to whom this is done, sir, never object, in fact quite the reverse. I, however, have made it plain that I do object in the strongest way . . . on Friday last, the prisoner [not named] stuck his hand in my buttocks from behind, and then put his other hand in the air, and said 'There's my hand, it couldn't have been me.'

The governor, who had just returned from witnessing a flogging, dismissed the complaint, saying that a sexual interpretation was being placed on a gesture that need not necessarily have a sexual intention.

'It seems to me, sir, that even if it has no such intention, it is nevertheless an extraordinary thing to do,' argued Potocki.

'Yes, but it is quite common in barracks and such places,' countered the governor.

'I quite realise, sir, that while I am here it is my duty to treat the officers and authorities with respect, and I have done my best to do so. But I was not sent here to be assaulted by my fellow prisoners. London is absolutely rotten with homosexuality, sir, and it is really for my propaganda for straight sex that I have been sent to prison.'

'Very well, then,' was the response, 'I will have these men up, but I foresee them denying it and should you be unable to prove everything you have said to the hilt, I will have you punished for bringing false accusations against your fellow prisoners. In the meantime, you will be sent back to C Hall for your own protection.'

'It was not in the hall, but in the workshop that these incidents took place,' argued Potocki. 'C Hall is the maximum punishment for an ordinary offence. Any further punishment will obviously involve a loss of remission.'

'The culprit's word is as good as the complainer's.'

'But that's not so, sir, even in law.'

'How isn't it?'

'I am entitled to have my barrister attack the other man's credit.'

'You haven't got a barrister here,' the governor replied. 'I can't take your word against his. You are wasting my time.'

'I feel as if I am in the position of Christ before the judges,' complained Potocki.

The governor was becoming impatient. 'Christ's not here, de Montalk,' he shouted. 'Anyway, you'll go back to C Hall for your own good.'

'It seems very hard to be punished for an offence which other prisoners have committed, and of which I am the victim.'

'You are not being punished! You are being sent back to C Hall for your own protection. I wouldn't envy your situation in D Hall if I left you there. The men don't like "shopping", you know. Don't you know what "shopping" is by now?'

'No, sir.'

'Well, when you're at school the other boys resent sneaking. When you've grown up it's not much better!' The governor turned to the guards. 'Return him to C Hall and have him scrub out his cell!'

The cell was scrubbed out many times, he was ill with diarrhoea, and his notebook—his only means of recording his thoughts, saving words, phrases, lines of poetry—was confiscated. In due course he was transferred to the canvas shed, where he was ostracised for having complained, and put to work on a darning machine. He hated both the machine and the shed. Unlike most of the prisoners, glad to escape from their cells at any price, Potocki would have preferred to spend his day alone in his cell.

> The only ones who do not mind being in their cells are those whose mental life is rich. I came to the conclusion that the common prisoner in his cell begins to wonder whether his existence is real, and in order to reassure himself he signals on the wall to the next man, who repeats the signal on the far wall for the next, and so on. Also they count the bolts in the door, and the bricks in the wall.
>
> Besides, the prisoners amuse themselves inventing the most absurd rumours, both about affairs outside, and about each other.

Not surprisingly, he was the subject of several rumours. One held that he was not a poet at all, but a confidence trickster, its inventor declaring,

'I couldn't think of a better pose than that myself.' Another had him in the habit of seducing girls aged seven—'Why this particular age was fixed on I know not, except maybe that seven is an occult number'—and to his concern this rumour gained credence. A third said his surname was really Smith.

By now the prison, so dispassionately observed before his appeal, often appeared very gruesome to Potocki. During drill, the sight of the grey prisoners walking aimlessly around and around the exercise ring reminded him of a 'danse macabre—the very opposite of that Dance of Life as which Havelock Ellis so rightly sees the Cosmos'. And at visiting time, with a grating and thick glass between himself and his friends, unable to have 'anything approaching a normal conversation', he was liable to find 'the whole affair . . . heartbreaking'.

At night, as the rifle range spattered and the black flap of the 'All-Seeing eye' in the door clicked and other prisoners, disturbed by their dreams, called out and banged on the floor with their buckets, perhaps he turned his back to the door and pictured himself in the halls of Admetus, the young King of Pherae, in whose court Apollo in servitude was treated with kindness. Perhaps he imagined Apollo making music and allowed the sounds of his lyre to lift him over the Moorish walls of the prison to trees slowly gathering shade in the parks, to early tulips and gravel paths, and the blue and green Serpentine, river of his childhood, moving smoothly towards the Thames.

One morning he wrote on his bench in the workshop, in order to remind himself of that Dance of Life, Edgell Rickword's line: 'Fantastic ceremonial floods the world'.

As for letter-writing, his great release, restrictions rendered this almost impossible. To his dismay the first letter he wrote after losing his appeal—a love letter to Edwina—was not sent. A week after handing it over for posting, he was summoned by the deputy governor, who said: 'You mustn't write all this sexual slobber, de Montalk. I suppose you know these letters are read?'

'Yes, sir.'

'Well, it's your own affair, of course, but it's *not done*, that's all!'

Potocki then wrote to Edwina:

My dearest Edwina,
As I am obliged to rewrite my note to you, so I can only ask you to imagine I am saying to you things I have often said in the past.
. . .

I have prayed for you every day since I first met you: in Cathedrals, Abbeys, forests—and now here. I say my prayers to Aphrodite and Apollo at half past six in the morning and about nine at night: so if you think or dream of me at those hours you'll know what has brought me to your thoughts. And now with a thousand kisses I commit you to the keeping of those deathless Ones!
Love from your sweetheart
Potocki of Montalk.

The next letter went out safely, 'containing a number of poems written out straight to save space'.

The next, however, had him in the governor's office. He writes in *Snobbery with Violence*: 'Commander Foster said: "Look here, de Montalk, I can't have you corrupting my officers with this sort of obscene stuff." Corrupting my officers! This was, as near as I can remember it, the censored passage:

> I would not have believed that I could have adapted myself so readily to a monastic life. It is rather amusing, as the only sort of monastery I have ever believed in was Rabelais's "monastère de Thélème", where half the monks were nuns, where everyone dressed in the latest fashion and where the device written over the door was "FAY CE QUE VOULDRAS" (Do what thou wilt). Rabelais thought that the inherent honour residing in noble souls was a self-sufficient guide, and the passage in which he states this is one of the most significant in European literature.'

He recalls asking the governor politely to tell him to which part of the letter he took exception.
'This—er—quotation from Boccaccio.'
'Rabelais, sir.'
'Rabelais. Besides, isn't this an *ode* or something you've got here?'
'It's a series of sonnets, sir.'
'Sonnets, is it? Well, I'm afraid they can't go out. You know there's a rule that no matter may be sent out which is suitable for publication.'
'But my last letter contained a number of sonnets, sir. Besides, you definitely said you had no objection to my sending a sonnet in the letter before last.'

'Well, it's the Home Office ruling, de Montalk. We have no power to vary it.'

Potocki then pointed out that anything written by a poet could be held suitable for publication, 'but logic of this nature was lost on him'. In the end almost all the poems he wrote in prison were despatched uncensored, in the form of letters. Without the guidance of titles or roman numerals, the censors were not alerted to the unsuitable presence of odes.

Most of these poems were initially written on toilet paper. He invented a system whereby the letters were a key to the poems he had written, in case the authorities confiscated the toilet paper. He told me: 'I thought that, as I hadn't really got them by heart, I should send them out in my letters. So I had a key in these letters, which was one of the reasons why the letters sounded so barmy. They sounded as if they'd been written by Dylan Thomas, or someone.' In all, thirty-three sonnets and two Latin translations from Catullus were written in coded letters, and carefully preserved on toilet paper.

In the archive I found an uncoded poem, 'Warning to the Puritans', inscribed with a thin nib onto a square of grey paper. It begins:

You are the same low rabble that in days
past kicked against your Poets and your Kings
and earned the Earl of Surrey's keen dispraise.

In late June 1932, with a sixth of his sentence remitted for good behaviour, Potocki was released from prison. Not long before he was due for discharge, the Distressed Prisoners' Association Board sent for him. As a pagan, he was considered by the panel to be the property of the representative from the Church of England.

'Your name is de Montalk, isn't it?' the representative asked awkwardly.

'No, sir, it's Potocki.'

'I suppose we can't do anything for you?'

'No, sir,' he replied, 'not unless you can find me a pleasant little state that's looking for an intelligent king.'

This remark made them all very polite, and they wished me Good Luck in a surprisingly ceremonious way. I smiled ironically and bowed in as pompous a manner as I could in prison clothes (I had ultimately got fitted out quite well, owing to Cresswell's friend who was Leader in the Part Worn Stores) . . .

Practising the advice he would later give John and me about humour, Potocki concludes *Snobbery with Violence* with wit and surprising restraint. Mindful also of Sir Ernest Wild's reading of one of his poems in court, he writes:

> Although I was treated so badly, my prison record is a good one. I was never (theoretically) punished and never even reported. A board is put up outside each prisoner's cell, on which his marks are written for each day and a letter for each week. If you behave yourself you get 'G.' If you toady, you get 'V.G.' If you crawl——[up the screw's arse], you get 'Excellent.' If you misbehave yourself you 'get an F' as the phrase goes, and if you get three F's you are automatically reported. As I got G for both 'Shop' and 'Landing' every week consistently from the beginning to the end of my stay at the Scrubs, I shall be, after all, entitled to have inscribed on my tombstone:
> 'HERE LIES A POET WHO NEVER HAD AN F.'

Restraint, however, was not about to move beyond the page. Potocki was not prepared to take the injustice and punishment to which he had been subjected in a spirit of acceptance or meek resignation. Inside the Scrubs he had submitted, as far as he was able, to destiny. Released, he raged. He had endured deprivation and humiliation—for what? For placing a handful of bawdy words, conceived in a light-hearted manner, on paper and showing them to a typesetter. A playful body of work, a private joke among friends. Certainly a jury might be shocked by such words and of their own volition find him guilty. He could accept that. What he could not accept was the sentence, the blind eye of British justice, the closing of ranks around the Recorder. He had been a first offender and the offence had been minor.

Deserted by Minnie, but reunited with Edwina, he wasted no time in publishing *Snobbery with Violence* and drafting *Whited Sepulchres*, which he serialised in the *Right Review* and later printed—'badly printed, well written'—in pamphlet form. He also published the thirty-three sonnets and two Latin translations completed in prison as *Prison Poems* from the Montalk Press for the Divine Right of Kings (1933).

He was appalled to discover that 'Here Lies John Penis' had been published without his authority while he was in prison. It was published in Paris by his friend, bookseller and publisher Charles Lahr of the Blue Moon Press in London. Lahr, whom Potocki had first met through Glass on his arrival in London, had been erroneously advised by Glass that permission to publish had been given: 'I had told Glass that the only circumstances in which I would even consider giving permission would be if they undertook to print and sell a vast number for my privy purse. Otherwise he need not mention it further. The publication contained villainous misprints.'

The high-handed disregard for his wishes further fuelled his intransigence. Angered by those who had dismissed his Polish ancestry (including Woolf and St John Hutchinson), he pursued his claim to the vacant throne of Poland in an increasingly spectacular fashion. Calling on his second name, Wladislas, he adopted its kingly version, pronouncing himself Władysław V, after Władysław IV, son of Sigismund III.

On 13 July 1932 Fairburn, now married, wrote from Culley's Farm in Wiltshire:

Dear Geoff,
I was very pleased to have word from you, and to hear that you were well. I had fears that the rest cure might get so badly on your nerves that you might be in a 'condition' when you emerged. However, I judge from your letter that you have suffered no ill: and deduce from my knowledge of your affairs that the Messieurs the Guardian Trust have been piling up a nice little sum for you. If it is not prying—how are your affairs? Do you reckon to be able to keep going indefinitely?

. . .

When I got your letter this morning I took down 'Surprising Songs' again and read it through. You are a difficult person, Geoff, and I find it hard to get on with you at close quarters. But when I read your poetry I get something from it that emanates from few poems—something beautiful and reassuring. Maybe it's mainly nostalgia. But it's very real and potent . . .

Good luck to you—and I hope you manage to put across a

book . . . "The Importance of being Sir Ernest Wild".
Yours ever—Rex.

The letter was reassuring. Potocki needed nostalgia. He needed to be reminded that there was gentleness in life:

I lay on a lawn in the sun under a tree
with leaves made luminously astral by the sun
shining through them, and moving in the wind . . .

that there would again be beauty:

. . . I wondered on
(in a reverie delicately drawn, fine and far-limned)
if the race of man is greater than the divine
monad, bright son of morning, which puts forth
this beautiful prayer to beauty—almandine
shadows and bright green lights, more worth
than all our warship-coloured mass of virtue,
all our ungodly prayers to divinity,
our cringing fear of religion's curfew,
our snub-nosed pageant of respectability.
(from 'Songs About New Zealand')

But the moment passed. The gentle poet of 'Songs' was beyond nostalgia. He had been set on a course of such disaffection that he would resist so-called respectability hard-heartedly and even more vigorously than before, and would do so for the rest of his life. As he had written to Glass from prison, he would never again compromise. He would have his way 'whole and undefiled', or he would go under.

He developed an abiding hatred of the English, spurning their justice system, their arrogance, and the corrupt public school ethos he believed the British class system spawned.

He also began to express anti-Semitic views. The source of these was never directly explained. I would find that the subject, if argued, would provoke such a strong reaction that it became impossible to pursue it further. Indeed, the secret to retaining an even and long-standing relationship with Potocki was to sense that some of his more extreme views were of unreachable origin, immune to reason, and back off. But an intolerance of Jews, by his own admission not present before he went to prison, certainly surfaced at this point.

I was to find his anti-Semitism particularly distressing. Was it backgrounded, I began to wonder, in his simmering belief, after his release from the Scrubs, that he had been betrayed by Leonard Woolf, a concept he then extended to the Jewish printer de Lozey who had taken his manuscript to the police, and to his hated stepmother, described in the typescript as 'kinswoman of Hyndman the jewish socialist'? Or was it more directly related to the right-wing milieu he entered after his release from prison? Or to the anti-Jewish campaign he would encounter in Poland in the mid-1930s?

I would not be the only one to find the basis of his prejudice, and the anger associated with it, puzzling. The American writer and private printer R.T. Risk, in his memoir *Why Potocki?*, also noted that 'the subject was a touchy one, and in questioning it I [Risk] clearly courted an explosion'.

Here perhaps were the foundations of some of the self-proclaimed injustices and prejudices we had encountered in Draguignan: conspiracies, passion.

# TEN

## New Zealand

*There is no question of going back to the Victorian 'ideal'. (Though even it produced poetry far better than the typical vapourings of today.)*

It is midday in September 1987, and John and I are sitting in Sunday traffic with Potocki, halfway to Paraparaumu, where my mother is waiting with lunch, freesias and serviettes on the table, grace and all kindness, and every care taken in the kitchen.

She hasn't yet met Potocki. Her disapproval of him has remained strong. And the television documentary—the robes, the language, 'that dreadful story' about Fairburn—well, her neighbours were nice people, and she was known at the church, and even the woman at the bank had seen the programme and recognised the name.

Quite a surprise, then, that we're driving him north, a green sea to our left, a stubbled hill to our right, at pains to remind him that my mother is of staunch Scottish ancestry—and a devout Presbyterian, just in case he's expecting wine with his lunch. 'She'll serve grape juice,' we say, telling him the story of our very merry but supposedly dry wedding, at which my father had to ask the hotel staff to open the bar to provide soft drinks, but quietly offer spirits instead.

Now, John carves the roast lamb, Potocki admires the home-grown potatoes and beans, and toasts my father, sadly deceased, and my mother pours second glasses of grape juice and proudly announces there's no alcohol in the house and she never drinks wine, not even at weddings.

There's a pause. Potocki accepts a serving of fruit salad, and sips his juice thoughtfully. 'What about Jesus' mighty fine first miracle?' he asks, shifting a cherry to the side of his plate, taking his time. 'St John, Chapter 2, the wedding at Cana in Galilee?'

'It wasn't really wine,' my mother replies.

He teases her with a smile. 'Such a *huge* quantity of water was converted. Six water pots containing two or three firkins apiece. A firkin holds quarter of a barrel—half a kilderkin—eight or nine gallons. That's sixteen to eighteen gallons of wine. A mighty impressive first miracle, wouldn't you say?'

'It still doesn't mean it was wine.'

'But what about the evidence of the guests? The Bible says they were grateful so much *good* wine had been served: *And when men have drunk well, then that which is worse* was served. And his mother approved! Didn't she say to the servants who were asked to bring water: *Whatsoever he saith unto you, do it?*'

I'm clearing the table, shaking the tablecloth, waiting for the air to become frosty. My mother wheels the tea trolley into the lounge. She helps Potocki to sponge cake and cream, pours coffee, hovers, mildly amused. She agrees with him that Christians never like to be told this was Jesus' first miracle.

In September 1984, Potocki returned from France, moved into Jonathon's bedroom, and resumed the familiar pattern of writing and entertaining. Once again there was the light, rapid sound of his typewriter, the small tinkle of his bell, the monologues during the period of adjustment. In the afternoon, while many his age napped, he visited bookshops, set type, and printed and bound small publications in the rooms of the private press at the university up the hill. He fretted about time. There was so much to be done.

By now the documentary had been scripted. When Potocki was ready, filming began. His energy at eighty-two was unnerving. For ten days I held my breath as he repeated stories, placed himself again and again on carefully positioned markers in a range of locations, and waited patiently as all the boredom and perfection of film-making took place. He responded to Ian Paul's thoughtful interest and the easy humour of the crew, and he enjoyed the attention.

When shooting had finished, and the long process of the edit had begun and he was no longer needed, there was no call for time out. He simply rose each morning, carefully opened an avocado from the brown paper bag in his bedroom (he usually had an avocado for breakfast, drizzled with vinegar and olive oil, and heavily sprinkled with black pepper), buttered his toast, drank his tea, and returned to his ten-hour day.

After many late nights in an edit suite—the essence of Potocki's life was as elusive on film as it had been on paper—the process, which included obtaining permission from the Director-General of Broadcasting to broadcast Potocki's use of the word 'fuck' in prime time, was completed.

There had been a short period of uncertainty when he questioned *The Count* as a tentative choice of title. 'As a title for the film,' he wrote to me, 'I would consider it virtually insulting. You don't talk about a person as "The Count" unless it is someone like Count Basie—a Negro noise-maker as You probably know. You would say "the Count" maybe, where he is the only Count in the circle in question, and preferably where he is the Count of the Place in question.' I came up with an amendment: *The Count—Profile of a Polemicist*, and he declared himself satisfied. The title was the only difficulty I experienced with him, despite the project's considerable potential for disaster.

He was back in France when the film eventually screened as the *Tuesday Documentary* on TV1, but positive reports reached him. He wrote to friends: 'Everyone who saw the première of Stéphanie's film seems to be very pleased with it, excepting it appears, Saint Peg of Paraparaumu (Stéphanie's mother). But then, as befits a good Christian, she is never pleased with anybody.'

Several incidents from this period remain with me.

There was the afternoon a couple of Mormon missionaries called at the door. Eager to be invited in and make the acquaintance of 'my cousin who's a pagan', they were left in the lounge with Potocki, and were still there hours later, sitting politely on the window-seat absorbing lectures on sun worship, the Emperor Julian, and—a Potocki favourite—the repressive ethical code of English puritanism.

There was the evening I returned home, having just settled an outbreak of food throwing in the Weir House dining room, and told him that the students concerned had been put on notice and fined. 'No shit taken!' I'd said heatedly, and he'd agreed, suggesting tactfully that perhaps I should express the sentiment more elegantly in Latin and, given the nature of John's and my duties as wardens, adopt it as the family motto. We did so and, when the occasion dictates, still use his translation, *Nullum Merdam Accipimus*, today.

There was also his note on 'evictible'. In an attempt to improve student behaviour in Weir House, I had drawn up a list of offences for which trouble-makers might be asked to move out of the hall. The offences, which comprised specific levels of disregard for people and property, had been carefully defined—pending argument from first-year law students—and posted under the heading EVICTIBLE OFFENCES on the hall noticeboard. I was pleased with the word 'evictible'. In bold lettering it left no doubt as to its meaning.

But before long discussion arose as to whether the word was 'evictible' or 'evictable', or indeed was a valid word. As the inventor of the word I was in no doubt and, as my keen supporter, neither was Potocki. Ever ready to engage wits, he set about supplying me with a useful opinion. 'This word,' he stated on a page imprinted with the Potocki family crest, beneath the heading 'EVICTIBLE, a Note by Count Potocki of Montalk'

> is not to be found in the Shorter Oxford Dictionary . . . but there is no reason why it should not be invented and made use of . . . I may not be C.T. Onions, Esq, Editor of the Shorter Oxford Dictionary but I have always been considered to 'know my onions' where spelling was concerned . . . Thus I personally would write this word evictible, and a young man of noble birth at Victoria University who has a genuine knowledge of Latin and Greek, which is always a help, says he would write evictible, for firstly it is correct, and secondly he would do so instinctively for reasons of euphony.

A formidable treatise on word derivation followed, at which point argumentative persons capitulated. To anyone still hanging on, he wrote sternly:

> The first thing thus is to get out of one's head that the -ible or -able termination corresponds to the word able. For that matter, in a word like horrible (from Latin horribilis), what is he, or she or it 'able' to do? And how about soluble or voluble? It almost looks as if we are in the presence of something like the Hungarian law of Vocal Harmony! In the meantime I hold that the word should be surely EVICTIBLE.

And there was the entertaining matter of his essay, 'The Ospedaletti Fellowship'. The essay, which became a topic of intense conversation in the house for some weeks and was composed with much humour, laments 'the utter neglect of the Ospedaletti side of Katherine Mansfield's life where she was so delighted with her surroundings, in favour of Menton where she never had a place of her own and whither she went much against her own will'. (In 1986, when Potocki reprinted the essay in pamphlet form, he castigated the proprietors of the 'Menton Racket', who, he quipped, 'seem to be vying with the Mormons, who baptize your ancestors for you, as many as they can get hold of'.)

Written intermittently over six days in 1984 at Jonathon's desk, the essay, which was submitted to the *New Zealand Listener* for publication, highlighted the place Mansfield held in her heart for this house and wanted to know 'why such a perpetual fuss should be made over her exiguous shanty in Menton, when in Ospedaletti she had a proper leasehold house...' It was found by the *Listener* to be amusing but was rejected, much to Potocki's annoyance.

His interest in Mansfield's hitherto unrecognised dwelling had been raised over a decade previously, in 1971, when he had made the acquaintance of the Menton writer-in-residence that year, referred to as the 'dishonest person who had procured for herself the "Menton Fellowship"'. The essay recalls a meeting with this 'Privileged Tourist', who had 'never so much as read the *Letters* nor the *Journal* of Katherine Mansfield' and admitted to being ignorant of the existence of the Ospedaletti property—'proof positive, of total ignorance of the *Journal* and the *Letters*'.

Acting on this admission, Potocki's story continues, he had produced books from his own library for her enlightenment and driven her in his 2 hp Citroen, together with Cathleen Owen and her young son, then living at the Villa Vigoni, to Ospedaletti to inspect the property, only to find the neighbourhood (which he photographed) had become a concrete jungle, covered with 'monotonously horrible and horribly monotonous blocks of flats'. Undeterred, and after the 'Tourist' had departed, he had made a note of every reference in the *Journal* and the *Letters* which might help to establish the whereabouts of the house, and returned to the town where, with the assistance of an official from the town hall, he had located the property 'cowering amid the concrete horrors'. He had photographed it from all angles so that Katherine Mansfield scholars could 'carry on controversies' about it, and concluded that letters written by Mansfield from the property (which he had found covered 148 pages of print) showed a 'very lively preference for the Casetta at Ospedaletti over the atmosphere of Menton'. 'If I ever went to Menton,' he quotes her as having said, 'I might meet an old dying American there who for sufferings-nobly-born might well leave me twice the sum. But I don't want to go to Menton, Boge.'

The essay concludes by suggesting that a scholarship or bursary be set up, to be called the Ospedaletti Fellowship. The first 'Bursar' should be himself, for all the trouble he had gone to on his own initiative, and the second should be 'Jonathon Miller of Wellington College, who is a fantastically gifted draftsman'. It envisages that Jonathon, who was taking art for School Certificate, would complete paintings and drawings for the Katherine Mansfield records, including the 'shanty at Menton, for which travelling expenses should be added', and quips that 'All sorts of persons who know nothing whatever about either Katherine Mansfield or Literature as such could be appointed at a later date, at Somebody or Other's convenience.'

The 1986 pamphlet version, printed in Hamilton, included a trademark foreword on people who had displeased him:

> We had tactfully referred to the dishonest person who had procured for herself the 'Menton Fellowship' . . . as a Privileged Tourist. But stay—does the New Zealand Listener belong to the Scott family? Which would not matter if they were talented people. For her name was Margaret Scott, which we reveal out of sheer indignation. (It appears she made a complete mess of her mission in any case.) Scott is the maiden name of Lauris Edmond, who recently received twelve thousand dollars as a well-deserved reward for not having an ounce of Troy weight of poetry anywhere in her person. Mark Scott is an utterly objectionable journalist, who wrote a long vulgar article in The Listener libelling the Police over the lamentable Battle of Queen Street. Plus Rachel Scott, Deputy Chief Sub-editor. And since I wrote the above last year, now we have Rosie Scott, see page 46 of present Complaints Against Broadcasting issue.
>
> Is all this just a co-incidence? Are these Scotts not related to each other? Or are they? . . .
>
> Or are we in the presence of a conspiracy by a group of nobodies to establish a dictatorship over New Zealand literature, which in the earlier part of this century had been so very promising?
>
> Anyway, there you are; Scott, Scott, Scott, Scott and Scott.

Dictators of what I understood was a public institution, The New Zealand Listener.

Unable to pass up a chance to denounce communism, he had added:

> Oh, by the way. Lauris Edmond informed me very firmly, that she is 'Left of Centre'. This is a cowardly catch-word, really meaning crypto-Communist, and is much favoured by some University people and literary hangers-on. Just in case the Bolsheviks, as such persons hope, 'come to power'.

Such was the industry, humour and outrage by which he still sustained himself. In May 1985 he once again put his car into storage in Auckland, and returned to Provence for the summer. When he returned in October, he moved into a bed-sitter beneath the house of a friend in Hamilton and installed a small press in the garage. Superannuation had been granted, a sense of belonging had returned, and a pattern for the next eight years had been established.

## ELEVEN

## The Later London Years

*Certainly the satisfaction of unfettered self-expression is worth a great deal of trouble.*

How different the years following Potocki's release from prison in mid-1932 and his departure for Draguignan in 1949. These were unsettled years, filled with political and legal activity, and driven principally by his contempt for anything left-wing and English.

He met Leonard and Virginia Woolf. Perhaps he imagined Woolf could yet be of assistance to him, for he writes in *Social Climbers in Bloomsbury*:

> When I was released from prison I naturally wanted to pay a visit to Mr Leonard Woolf, who had directed the defence in my case: the more so as Douglas Glass had reported him as having said: Why on earth didn't he come to me? We would have printed them for him in the basement at Tavistock Square.

The visit was not a success. Virginia Woolf records the occasion (which took the form of an after-dinner party on 10 November 1932) in her *Diary* without comment, but her dislike of Potocki is evident in *The Sickle Side of the Moon*, in which she writes to Ethel Smyth: '... I sat up till one thirty howling with laughter and rage at L's Polish Count—the man who wrote the water closet rhymes, and turns out to be an appalling bore, dressed in flowing purple, with hair down his shoulders, conviction that he is King of Poland; and the accent and manners of a Cockney stable boy.'

Potocki told me: 'They never invited me again and I don't think I would have been all that keen on going. They were a pack of snobs the lot of them. They thought I'd turned communist because I'd been ill-treated by the capitalist judges of England, but I had enough sense to see that, if the capitalist judges of England are no good, the communist ones are a great deal worse! They thought I'd go left, and help them with their leftist propaganda. Wishart thought the same and offered me money down—£50, which at that time was a lot of money—just for the sheer promise to write books that he wanted me to write.'

His account of the visit, which appears in a chapter entitled 'Quack Quack' in *Social Climbers in Bloomsbury*, never varied, and like all his good stories would be relayed at times almost word for word as written. 'I went to their place,' he would say, 'where there was a lot of very good old English furniture—chesterfields and that sort of thing, and decorations on the walls—and they were all talking in would-be Oxford accents. After a few preliminaries about cigars, which I refused, and Vermouth *mehde* specially for us by Mrs Montagu, in Turino, which I accepted, Virginia started in on Woolf's ancestry.' Virginia's remarks, played out by Potocki, who would straighten his back and lift his nose, would be delivered slowly in a pronounced Oxbridge accent, as recorded in *Social Climbers*:

> You knöö-oo Count Potocki, Aie always think may husband's race is söö-oo merch more civilayzed than ahs. They had their fenced citiz and their litera-tewer two thousand yeeahs before we did, in fact when our ancestors were dancing round with woad. Dohn't you think soh?

'She sat there,' he would say, puckering his lips and languidly waving two forefingers around his mouth, 'smoking a cigar, sticking straight out in front of her, and she looked really ridiculous with this virginal face and this great cigar sticking out. I said, "No, I don't, to be perfectly frank. I don't agree with that version of it at all."'

He would recall the conversation turning to those who were living the 're-arl layfe' in 'distressed areas', about whom one of the party of five was writing, and with whom another—William Plomer, plump and elegantly dressed with long clean cuffs—was corresponding. In particular, there was a 'minah' from whom 'an unsualleh long lettah' had recently been received. The conversation went something like this:

'And what sort of topics do they wraite about?' asked Woolf.

'Oh, you knoh, they—they wraite about all sorts of things. Realleh it's astonishing. *Fraightfully* interesting . . . onleh *extreemeleh* incoherent. Very undigested, so to spee—eek.'

'Re-arleh! and whe-ah, do you think, do they get hold of all this, as you seh, interesting matt*ah*?'

'Owe! Aye expect theh get it from the local librareh. And, perhaps, from talks on the Bibisi.'

'And, do you think, that theh hev aneh ho-oop?'

'Ho-oop? . . . No-oo: they jerst drawer the dohl and wraite these lett*ahs*!'

We would be invited to consider the *minah*, who, if he 'were hidden in one of the Georgian cupboards at 52 Tavistock Square would burst out and wring their ::::::g necks! And quayte raight too.' But, we'd be reminded, 'the poor minah isn't there. He is at home in his Distressed Area, his ear ringing as he reads his book from the local library.'

He had as little time for Virginia Woolf as she appears to have had for him. He would say to me: 'Well, she was older than I was. And her work—her work was half the trouble. I couldn't entertain any sincere admiration for it because it was all this elaborate stuff in prose with nothing behind it. She was just clev*ah* with words. Most of it should have been stuck in the dustbin. I'd much rather sit down and read Horace or Julius Caesar in Latin, or something like that. But the novel—I despise the novel as such, unless it's also an allegory or tale, or something written by Swift. It's not literature.'

His contempt for the English drove him from England. In the spring of 1933 he made his way via France, Italy, Austria and Czechoslovakia to Poland.

His hair, which had continued to grow in prison, was by now well below his shoulders, and he wore a velvet cap emblazoned with the Polish white eagle and the Potocki coat of arms. He also wore robes. 'When I came out of prison,' he explained, 'I was so *enraged* at having been put in prison that I thought, very well, I'll dress exactly how I like, and I went to the British Museum and examined a lot of old manuscripts and decided that I was going to have the Richard II style. Then I cut it out myself on the table and it was sewn up for me by Edwina. They were all simple tunics rather like university gowns with long sleeves in which I could put things. And then later in Poland I bought a great length of hop silk—thick, heavy, raw silk. It was off-white with glints of straw in it, and I had it dyed crimson—actually it's been dyed more than once—and it was made up for me by a professional seamstress in Poland. Like the cloak, the robes didn't really have anything to do with the claim to the throne, though of course they were in fact royal robes.'

He was welcomed by the Polish literary community, who suggested he translate the classic poetic drama *Forefathers* (*Dziady*) by Adam Mickiewicz into English. He started the translation in October 1933, but the need to earn a living left little time for unpaid work and the project was deferred. His earnings came mostly from a *Pologne Littéraire* commission to translate Polish poetry and prose into English: 'I got a złoty a line for poetry. You could get a three-course dinner with a great slab of meat in it in Warsaw for less than a złoty, so for each line I got a dinner, you might say. And then for prose—they were very short lines indeed for prose—I got a złoty for four of those and I translated quite a lot of prose. The paper also published a version of my life story, for which I was asked to write a sketch. I wasn't capable of writing Polish at that stage.'

He was also pursued by the Polish press, which reported on him with enthusiasm. 'When I first went there I stayed in a cheap hotel, where I was interviewed regularly, and the attitude of the press—the gutter press—almost rose to great heights in reporting their interviews with me. They would say things like "This aristocrat living in a worm-eaten hotel combines with an aristocratic appearance a truly monarchical, mild personal approach." I was written up in a number of papers, but I had no complaints about that. Well, there I was marching around Warsaw in fourteenth-century robes and bare feet in sandals—even in the snow.'

Perhaps his anti-Semitism was finally realised here. The 'age-old Polish–Jewish symbiosis', as Adam Zamoyski's *The Polish Way: A Thousand-year History of the Poles and Their Culture* refers to the comfortable 'political, economic and cultural framework' within which 'four-fifths of the world's Jews' had traditionally sheltered in Poland, had disintegrated irrevocably by the time of Potocki's visit, and it is not inconceivable that in this environment Potocki's anti-Jewish sentiment, initiated by experiences related to his trial and appeal, extended to his childhood and strengthened by his move to the extreme right, gathered pace.

Certainly his conviction and imprisonment were still heavy on his mind, for he drafted a long letter to King George V setting out his ancestry, recalling his trial and appeal in intense detail, and requesting a pardon. It was an anguished letter, handwritten, in a scratched and heavily corrected state. As I didn't find a clean copy in the archive, I assumed that, as with the typescript, Potocki had been attempting to exorcise the experience and had not taken it further.

In 1935, he returned to London to report on George V's Silver Jubilee. Press credentials (featuring a photograph of Potocki in robes) from the Chief Editor of the *Ekspres Poranny* in Warsaw, dated 18 April 1935, confirm his status as the paper's correspondent. In fact, he had been given written contracts with several Polish newspapers. While he was in England, however, the Polish patriot and statesman Marshal Józef Piłsudski died and, with the jubilee no longer news, the contracts, including his return fare to Poland, were abandoned.

Obliged to remain in England, he attempted to build on the genealogical research he had undertaken in Poland, hoping that Cedric, who was by now living there and also following the ancestral trail, would permit him access to his papers. But Cedric would not co-operate. The relationship between the brothers had begun to sour as small notes of rivalry, not apparent as children when they were comrades-in-arms, had crept between them. In 1929 Potocki had written fondly of his brother: 'It is hard to imagine anyone disliking Cedric, either then or now. [He] is surely one of the nicest people I have known in this earthly life.' Now Cedric, who was also writing poetry and would marry and convert to Catholicism in Poland, was tiring of Potocki's claim to the throne and increasingly impatient with his brother's conduct, which he found 'unbecoming'.

Dispirited, without funds, and trapped in a country which he believed had betrayed him, perhaps he sought a passage home. His archive produced a letter, dated 24 August 1935, stating that his father was 'unable to pay or refund the cost of the passage'. Perhaps Robert, like Cedric, had passed beyond the point at which he was willing to assist Potocki.

This was Potocki's most public and turbulent period, the period in which he was reported most often and in which, fuelled by the polarities of bolshevism and fascism in Europe, his eccentricity and combativeness asserted themselves most strongly.

This was the period I struggled with as I researched the

documentary. Its detail, dense and confused, jammed in my mind, hiding the images I needed to work with. I tacked up flow charts and made sketch boards, but the stories stayed on the wall. I re-ran my tapes, but all I heard were my questions: 'Yes, but didn't you just say . . .' and 'What year was that again?' and 'Which gaol (or county court) was it this time?' And later, although the archive reduced the rumours, the political and legal pictures remained indistinct.

These were also the years in which the heightened sense of personal injustice imposed by his childhood, and fed by his imprisonment, assumed elements of persecution, the boundaries of which would become permanently blurred. The result of this was most obvious in Potocki's belief, following his release from prison, that a conspiracy based on 'political prejudice and prudery' was the cause of his literary oblivion, the 'boycott . . . unheard of in the annals of world literature', the fact that he 'didn't exist'. While his suggestions of a conspiracy regarding his trial and appeal were not unfounded, it seems to me that Potocki failed to accept the possibility that the quality of his verse had deteriorated, or to understand the extent to which his intransigence and extravagant right-wing behaviour provoked a wary response from those who did not understand him. It was here that the essence of his eccentricity—the childlike preoccupation with self, and the sense that the world was against him (which, as Weeks postulates, may contribute to an eccentric's evolving originality and creativity)—was ultimately realised.

'God,' Fairburn had written to Lahr as far back as August 1932, 'he does live in a hell of a fairyland, doesn't he? All Kings ought to be put in circuses. They'd be funny without being dangerous.'

The civil war in Spain broke out. As large sections of the London literary and intellectual community moved to the far left, Potocki's anti-establishment views and royalist convictions, together with a belief that bolshevism would undermine the foundations of Europe, involved him in a move to the extreme right. In 1936, with financial assistance from Aldous Huxley and Brian Guinness, he purchased his first printing-press and established his intermittent and controversial right-wing political and literary journal, the *Right Review*. The publication, which he described as 'quite frankly founded to advertise my own genius', lambasted democracy, which he considered 'a hypocritical system for flouting the wishes of the people', argued in favour of a monarchy with a plebiscite, and 'generally served as an intellectual counterblast to bolshevism'.

In his first editorial, October 1936, he explains his political point of view:

> It is our aim to show that the Divine Right of Kings is the sanest and best form of government . . .
>
> We are as much opposed to Capitalism, if by that term is meant Plutocracy, as any communist could be—but we are not opposed to capitalists so long as they function as such without damaging the interests of the whole State . . .
>
> Neither do we consider Fascism as anything but a very bad form of government, being as it is based on demagogy, but we point out that it is a natural reaction, based on a thoroughly justifiable instinct of self-protection, whereby nations rid themselves of the socialist and communist plague . . .

This first edition also includes a clear expression of anti-Semitism and indicates the basis of his thinking:

> The matter of race is another question where we do not agree either with the Fascists or the Communists. Men are to be judged by their worth as members of the human race as a whole—by their beauty, breeding, wisdom, and good will. This applies even to Jews; but it is our duty to be very suspicious of a race whose dealings with outsiders are such as recorded, firstly in the Old Testament, and later in various books of history written as often as not by themselves, wherein they boast of exploits which entitle them to the name *hostes generis humani* . . . In the meantime it is the Jews themselves who invented inhuman racialism, and who stick tenaciously to it to the public and private detriment of all outsiders: and Aryan racialism is nothing but a reaction to this. There is no doubt at all in our mind that the Jewish nation is at the present exercising a very bad influence on all countries where it is strong; and not the least of its crimes is its desire to foist on to the world the wicked scheme called Communism.

In some later editions he would attack the Jews strongly, describing communism as 'Jewish fascism' and Jews as 'enemies of Poland'.

In the March and June issues of 1940, Potocki included his 'Speech from the Throne'. Describing his monarchical views on the running of an imagined kingdom, this covers topics ranging from state revenue and trade to religion and morals, Potocki declaring that private morals are of no concern so long as they 'do not involve any violation of persons or their rights'.

The *Right Review* published social comment, satirical prose and poems by Potocki and others, reviews of books and concerts, and woodcuts, most notably by George Hann. Between October 1936 and 1949, when Potocki left London to live in the south of France, he published seventeen numbers of the journal. Two further numbers were published from Provence.

The printing-press was an important means of making himself heard, the need for which had been appreciated by Aldous Huxley when he first met Potocki after the latter's return from Poland. 'Huxley came to see me,' he recounted, 'when I was living in Tavistock Square, in the basement, and he sat in an old peasant chair which belonged to me, and he just listened to me telling him my life story. He sat there in profound silence, and when I had finished the general all-round sketch of my life he said, "That's the most extraordinary story I've ever heard. Your family must be mad." And I said, "Well, you know Huxley, they would say that I am mad." And I'm sitting there all in crimson robes, and he went like this—put his hand across his face as if he were brushing away a fly—and he said, "Oh yes, I know, but they must be *really* mad to be so devoid of all human feeling." And he picked up a book on my mantlepiece, when he was going, and stuck £2 under it, and said he was going to send me more money. "We'll have to lift the lid of your coffin," he said.' Huxley donated Potocki all the profits on his 'famous pacifist pamphlet', and persuaded Guinness to contribute £30. 'He suggested to Guinness that, after all, I had a right to express my opinion, even if he and Guinness didn't agree with it.'

With Huxley's 'extremely exiguous funds', Potocki rented an unfurnished flat at 39 Lambs Conduit Street in Bloomsbury, and set about finding a press. As he was unfamiliar with the craft of printing, this took some time. Finally, in the late spring of 1936, he settled on a flat-bedded press with a very crude roller guided by steel rabbets (or grooves) and covered with rough felt. 'No one except myself could have printed normal letter-press at all on this primitive gadget, for it needed a patience no one but myself has been known to possess since

Job.' He assumed that the press had probably been used to print newspaper posters from huge 216-point wooden letters, or maybe only to take the proofs of such. 'There I was printing on it with 10 point, and that's why the stuff was badly printed. *Nobody* could have printed properly with it.'

He recounted the setting-up of this press one evening over dinner. Afterwards, as John and I did the dishes, and he stood at the stove heating milk to mix in a mug with a generous measure of whisky, he said: 'Did I mention the newspaper poster I had in my flat at the time? Soon after I got the press up and running, I saw this billboard with the headline MAN GETS THREE MONTHS FOR DUCKING WOMAN PC. She'd been going to arrest him and he'd pushed her into a pond. So I asked the newsagent if I could have the poster, and I took it home, and altered it by printing an F in similar lettering, over the D. It was one of my first serious and subversive attempts at printing, and it caused great amusement when anyone came round.' We'd all laughed, and Potocki had rinsed the saucepan, inclined his head, committed us to the care of his immortal gods for the night, and departed to linger over his nightcap alone.

Later, it occurred to me that, together with the strange little scene in the kitchen—Potocki dressed like a medieval monk pottering about with his milk, heating it, rinsing the saucepan, graciously placing us in the care of his gods—the story rather succinctly reflected the person John and I developed a sense of during our first meeting in Draguignan. It was only a small story, and artless at that, but in accordance with the photograph in *The Blood Royal* which was 'absolutely unretouched', and the letters I had seen him typing in Latin, even though he knew the recipients would not understand them, it called up elements of his personality which, given the immediate impact of his eccentricity and extreme views, were reasonably and frequently overlooked. Playful and impish elements, which also included the correspondence he directed to the Ministry of Stealth and Total Obscurity (the Ministry of Health and Social Security), the notepaper headed ETERNAL PAGAN RELIGION, CHURCH OF ENGLAND BRANCH which he wound into his typewriter (a heading I now assume related to the decision of the Distressed Prisoners' Association Board in the Scrubs that, as a pagan, Potocki was the property of the Church of England), the wearing of his small silver crown when breakfasting with a guest, or during photo opportunities.

Certainly his personality played up this eccentricity, but we had discovered that, alongside the talkative, sometimes frustrating, apparently egotistical and subversive persona, there was consideration, graciousness and, importantly, much humour.

By now word of Potocki's right-wing sympathies was spreading. He was courted by the British Union of Fascists and met Sir Oswald Mosley and William Joyce. Although his dismissal of demagogy meant that he was not enamoured of fascism, he accepted a number of the union's printing commissions.

In March 1937, Potocki and his journal were attacked in the left-wing periodical *John Bull*. Following publication of this article, his landlord gave him notice to quit. Potocki hit the bailiff who issued the notice, was arrested, and fined £6. Two separate legal actions ensued: an unsuccessful bid to sue *John Bull* for libel, and a successful action against his landlord. Wary of incompetent counsel, and without funds, Potocki conducted both cases himself. In the case of the landlord, his legal sidestepping saw the action run for two years, during which time he lived on in the flat rent-free.

*John Bull*'s unfavourable opinion of the *Right Review* was not shared by all. Critic and editor Hugh Gordon Porteous, who was then writing for the *New English Weekly* and T.S. Eliot's *Criterion*, observed in the former that, while the journal would be of value primarily as 'a collector's piece and an investment', the editor's prose contributions deserved reading, and that the serialised *Whited Sepulchres* was, as Huxley had already confirmed, of 'considerable sociological, and I think literary significance'. Porteous wrote:

> Count Potocki is undoubtedly an extra-ordinary fellow. No matter what one thinks of his poetry or politics, his Blake-like independence and righteous indignation command respect.

He notes Potocki's passion for royalism and 'fanatical dislike of all dictators, Jews, Christians and Communists', and concludes that his opinions, however irrational, are at least completely his own and 'expressed with a sincerity, vigour, humour and originality not to be found easily today on our Left'.

Porteous's comments in the *Criterion* arose out of his lament for the mediocre nature of the *Left Review*. Here he wrote of Potocki's journal:

it has the rare negative quality of not being boring at any point . . . his ideas are not all so foolish as they look, and his incidental criticisms are pungent and salutary, expressed with wit and vigour.

Potocki did not confine his wit and vigour, nor his talent for controversy, to his journal. When Edward VIII abdicated the throne in December 1936 amid widespread public demonstration, the avowed royalist produced a manifesto. Entitled 'The Unconstitutional Crisis', the pamphlet proclaims: 'Old Baldwin the ugly goes to the divine Monarch of these Islands and tells him he cannot marry the girl of his choice.' It also predicts the fall of the British Empire. Explaining his response, Potocki says on tape: 'I was *flaming* with indignation about the abdication itself. After all I was born a royalist, I'm a consequential royalist, and I just didn't hold with Baldwin chucking out His Majesty the King. So I wrote this thing in a great hurry and forgot to sign it— proof of my famous vanity, although the British Museum realised at once it was my doing and put it in my name. It was set in linotype and had a woodcut of Mrs Simpson by George Hann on the cover. And we ran off as many copies as we could on that flat-bedded machine, which was still all that we had. Then, at a quarter past three on 19 December, Nigel Heseltine, who was a fellow editor, and I took it out and sold it for one penny in Whitehall. We disguised ourselves as a couple of religious cranks in order to avoid arrest by carrying a placard mounted on a broomstick reading WHERE WILL YOU SPEND ETERNITY? And I was in my robes.'

A huge crowd had gathered in the Mall and the pamphlets sold rapidly. Potocki became separated from Heseltine. 'The crowd came surging around and said, "Yer pal's been pinched." And I said, "What do you mean, my pal's been pinched?" And they said, "The pal wot was wiv yer, ee's been pinched." I said, "Surely not," and they said, "Oh yes he is, he's over at the coppers' shop. You go over to the coppers' shop and you'll find him." So I went over to the coppers' shop and I said, "The crowd says you've arrested Mr Heseltine." And the policeman said, "Yessir, it's quite true we did arrest Mr Heseltine, but he's been released." So I said to the policeman, "May I ask on what charge he was arrested?" and the policeman said, "Yessir: obstructin' the traffic." And I said, "Do you mind telling me how you can obstruct traffic which is already obstructed in the highest degree conceivable?" He said, "Sah matter of interpretation sir." I said, "Oh I see. What you mean is that, just as Baldwin can abdicate his Majesty the King, they can do what they like with poor fools like us. Is that it?" And he said, "Yessir."

'Then we went along, at Charles Lahr's suggestion probably, to Freeman, a printer with a good, highly valued automatic German machine, and he printed a vast quantity of the second issue of the manifesto and didn't take a penny for it, and we went out on the street again. And we were in front of Buckingham Palace, and there were great crowds there, and after a while I saw a flat-foot carting Heseltine off in the direction of the palace. Shortly afterwards another one came and got me, and we were arrested on a holding charge of distributing a pamphlet or selling a pamphlet in a royal park—the Mall was deemed to be part of the Royal Park Gardens because it goes straight up to the palace—and taken into the palace and held. We waited somewhere on the ground floor, in what was probably a guard room, until they took us round to that posh police station in Cannon Row for aristocratic drunks and the like, where they locked us up. They held us there until quite late at night, until we were able to get hold of Aldous Huxley, who sent round his wife, and that Welsh writer Robert Nichols to bail us out.

'We were ordered to appear at the police court at 8.30 the next morning. The magistrate was moderately favourable toward us and, as the case was drawing to a close, the clerk of the court jumped up and said he had had a telephone call from Whitehall that the government wanted a remand in custody so that we could be charged further with the actual wording of the pamphlet. But the magistrate, who didn't want to be told what to do by the government, became annoyed, and said, "Oh no, I can't have that. Fined two pounds and ten shillings," and bundled us out of the court. And that's what happened about that, you see. It was my first political manifesto, but it was by no means my last.'

The events surrounding the distribution of the abdication manifesto was one of Potocki's favourite stories. Like the visit to Leonard and Virginia Woolf, it was a tale perfected, and recounted almost to the last word in dignified tones of outrage and amusement. The dialogue was always particularly effective. We were soon able to deliver the entire story ourselves, word for word, and even the children had parts of it off pat. They would chant among themselves when he wasn't present: 'Yer pal's been pinched . . . the one wot was wiv yer.'

The publication of his satirical serial *Social Climbers in*

*Bloomsbury* in the *Right Review* in 1938 (the exposé was also published as a pamphlet over the imprint of The Right Review in 1939) provoked further controversy. Woolf was so incensed by the unflattering report of his after-dinner party that he issued threats of libel action against booksellers stocking the *Right Review*, resulting in the appearance of pseudonyms in the subsequent exposés. Potocki responded with the following notice:

> Certain persons, who are or claim to be described in this book, have been going round the bookshops threatening to issue a libel writ if they stock it, though they would not dare sue the author and could hardly succeed if they did . . . If your bookseller is afraid, get it direct from The Right Review, 12 Winchester Street, London SW1.

Novelist Lawrence Durrell (who was not enamoured of the English either) wrote from Corfu:

> I don't always like what you think, yet I do always admire and subscribe to what you *are*. There is such brightness and warmth in your prose, and so much leisurely and wicked humour that I defy anyone not to be interested in and delighted by it . . . I love the self-possession which makes each thrust—like a good fencer's lunge—seem absolutely effortless. Power to your long right arm!

In addition to the chapter on the Woolfs, *Social Climbers* included amusing encounters with other literary people perceived to be intellectually shallow or pretentious. Poet, writer and Blake scholar Ruthven Todd was one. 'It was Todd who invented the story that my name was really Smith and I was the son of a milkman, because I put him in *Social Climbers in Bloomsbury*, under the name of Dryven Mudde.'

Dylan Thomas also featured. Potocki, who had met him in the summer of 1935 at a party in Parton Street given by the sculptor Hughes, told me that he knew Thomas 'quite well' during the entire period of the *Right Review*: 'I was present when he met Augustus John, the painter, intellectual and generally colourful character, in the Fitzroy Tavern, on 13 November 1935,' he said, 'and there is an account of this meeting in *Social Climbers in Bloomsbury*. It's all quite correct except that the person called Divine Thomas was Augustus John, Bill Bumption was Bill Empson, and I called Dylan, Andyl Motsah—it was a perfect anagram of his name.' He recalled the group 'baiting' Thomas into reciting a poem which he, Potocki, had written on his behalf—'a Dylan Thomas poem, which although we were good friends I wrote to poke fun at his doings. That thing that starts off:

> About the senile tops of level mountains
> in the fifth house of whoredom lies my loved one
> when, lost in love, the swilling ocean hollows
> the cup-crowned Hebe-heaven of her backbone'

Potocki always referred to Thomas—albeit affectionately—as a bogus poet, because he believed his work to be the result of a deliberate and manufactured, rather than an inspired, process. He maintained that Thomas agreed with this definition of himself. 'You know,' he wrote to me in 1982, after receiving a couple of poems sent by Jonathon, aged thirteen, which he had found to be 'clevah', 'the Romans said: "Poeta nascitur, non fit." To render this succinct Latin phrase fully in English, you would have to say: "You have to be born a poet and cannot become one." This is without any doubt true. No amount of effort will ever make a genuine poet.' The letter advises Jonathon that, if he wants to take up the 'trade' of poetry manufacture and produce verse that is 'extremely sophisticated and is a thousand per cent valueless, and get published by Her Majesty's Lit. Fund and the Milk Marketing Board', he should consider the method of the 'sedulous manufacturer of "poetry"', Thomas, who

> really did manufacture poems, you know. He would lock himself up in the Boat House and write down one line of a poem. He would then meditate for a long time, as to how to make this line more sophisticated. You have to get words into the most unnatural possible juxtapositions and fill your poem with oxymorons of the extremest kind. For instance suppose there is some milk in your poem, you had better call it black milk—you will get full marks for that. Then our Dylan does the same with the second line. Each line gets discarded a dozen times, until it is as sophisticated as you can manage. One of his acquaintances once picked up all this stuff. He'd write one line, and then he'd contemplate it a hundred times

and then change it and make it slightly different, and then another line, and then he'd chuck the stuff away and start off again. And he had paper all over the floor, and somebody found it.

He continued: 'I see Jonathon says "it takes years of devotion to make a good poet." Nothing could be further from the truth, and I hope he will tell his teacher I said so.' (Was it only coincidence that Potocki's example, 'black milk', echoed the 'Black milk of daybreak' repeated in the poem 'Death Fugue' by Jewish poet Paul Celan?)

Potocki remained firm in his view of the poet as a special person endowed with mystical powers. With his poetic allegiance firmly posted to classicism and the traditional, he never accepted what he perceived as the deliberate and ambiguous approach of the Symbolists, or their break with poetic tradition. He did not see the point of distorting grammar or using devices outside readily decipherable language to support meaning, arguing that poets like Thomas wrote in a flat and incoherent manner and would not be understood by ordinary people.

One afternoon in Edinburgh in 1983, while I was recording Potocki reading from his poetry, I noticed that the typescripts invariably included the circumstances in which the poems had been written. That, for instance, his meditation 'A Silent Pool'—

> God make my heart a silent pool sometimes
> and teach the busy mind to leave its labour:
> then when it lies as still as glass
> and there comes forth no tinkle of sweet rimes
> even from the gentle harp and merry tabor,
> Your likeness God over those deeps may pass.

—had been written on '26 ix 30. Sitting on the tomb of a Norman abbot in the Cloisters. Westminster Abbey'. I also noticed that frequently there were footnotes. His poem 'Salisbury Cathedral'—

> I said 'a great white flower'—that was Canterbury,
> and now I can say only the same thing again
> because no words could tell with all their pain
> beauty of tall spire and cold clerestory,

nor can the utmost music of my verse
speak of this cool fair unfolded bloom
sweet with all brightness and rich with all gloom
calm with the feet of angel thurifers.

I can only echo 'un rêve de pierre,'
worship the dreamer of this dream in stone,
and for a consolation make my own
these words from the dark rime of Baudelaire.

—for example, which had been written in 'The Close, Sarum, xi Sunday after Trinity, 1928', was followed by: 'Believe it or not, this poem was printed in the Observer, London who paid two guineas for it. Nowadays they are printing sheer rubbish.'

I liked these informative and personal touches. They suggested that, for Potocki, poetry was an art inseparable from his everyday life—his journal, if you like. In old age he collated a good deal of his poetry in thematic sections; but, read with an eye to chronology, this combination of poetry and comment not only offered glimpses of his inner life but also confirmed biographical detail and contained an appealing sense of him recording events as they unfolded, in words which, as he told me, came to him directly as if 'by divine providence'.

'Assuming,' he once said, 'that some of my poems are really good—and I think posterity will admit that they are—I wrote them in about five minutes, and that's what Byron says. Byron was accused of biting the end of his quill pen to write something and he said, "I wrote it while my valet was dressing me for dinner." There's Byron scribbling away on the sideboard while his valet's creasing his tie or his cravat.' I was reminded that, whatever impression of aristocratic nonchalance Byron may have affected, his manuscripts make it clear that he did work at perfecting his verse, and I wondered whether Potocki's assertion that he was a spontaneous poet was similarly misleading. Whether the inclusion of the additional details was an affectation, an attempt to create an impression that he did in fact write with divine guidance and only rarely needed to refine his work. Later, however, when he lived with us for long periods, I realised that in fact he did write urgently and immediately, assembling his thoughts in final form in his mind as he typed. And even later, when perusing his archive, I found that, although prose manuscripts had been heavily corrected, most of his poetry seemed to have arrived more or less intact.

By now Potocki was printing a poem each year for the Feast of Saturn, at Christmas. The *Right Review* states that a month after the reading in the Fitzroy Tavern, Augustus John had Caitlin Thomas read Potocki's poem for the 1935 festival aloud thirty-five times. Entitled 'Magic in Words', this sonnet reflects not only the extravagant and regal imagery that characterised much of Potocki's poetry following his release from prison, but also his developing interest in nature mysticism.

> The gentle wine of flattery makes men mad
> but also in good time it makes them kings.
> What power exists can make good men of bad
> but wizard words that some sly poet flings
> into the blest crucible of his song?

He really did believe there was a magic power in words. 'Cinemas, tape recorders, all this modern stuff is proof that speech is based on a vibration,' he said when filming the documentary. 'What is speech but a vibration. God spoke and the universe was formed.' He later placed curses of 'BAD LUCK' on those who displeased him, and I was all too aware of this belief in the infinity of nature as I struggled with the super-bug while examining his archive.

Although the London years were lean, the period between 1935 and 1939 was especially hard. Potocki wrote and printed in 'unbelievably miserable circumstances, and without almost everything one should have, including often sixpence to put in the electric light meter'. With his only sources of income small returns on printing commissions, sales of the *Right Review* and intermittent contributions from fans, he was living 'very very poorly.' This situation eased somewhat in 1939 with the establishment of The Right Review Bookshop in his flat in Winchester Street, from which he sold political pamphlets and second-hand books, and to which 'communists and racial enemies' were asked to 'please abstain from calling'.

Increasingly, he sought direction in astrology, to which he had first given serious consideration when reading Chaucer's *Treatise on the*

*Astrolabe* in prison, and had begun to study seriously, as a science, in Poland. By this time, too, sun worship had become the centre of his faith and philosophy of life. In 1938, mindful of the recent abdication, he published a booklet of poems entitled 'Abdication of the Sun' in which he explored his religious views. The underlying substance of these was his pagan belief in a natural order, based upon nature and nature mysticism, as explained in *Whited Sepulchres*:

> The Cross Itself is a Pagan Symbol, older than the parvenu religion which has appropriated It; being as old as the universe, no less. And we who are fighting against censorship, against Puritanism, against Calvinism, against Democracy and against Christianity, are the avengers of that great Apostle of Paganism, the Divine Julian, who, brought up in the new religion, turned back deliberately to the Light of the Gods, and tried to stem unaided the advancing tides of darkness.

In championing the sun, which he believed was proof of a god of life, and Apollo, the old God of the Sun, he rejected repression, 'practical denial of the world', and any religion which sought to symbolise its faith in dead rather than living things. The collection closes with a statement on his philosophy of life:

> Life is a dream, fired
> with images of calm, storm, wind, and snow;
> and all that is required
> is to have done with fear,
> to fill the heart with laughing peace,
> and know
> that the kind gods are near.
> ('Philosophy')

Much of his time was spent studying language, literature and European history at the British Museum. On 14 January 1939, an unidentified London newspaper in his archive confirmed his standing as a London identity. Describing him as one of London's characters for the last ten years, it speaks of his hair reaching to his waist, his robes, and the Roman salute he gives his friends and the commissionaires at the Reading Room of the British Museum, where he is often to be found. 'I call on the Count', writes the reporter, who was received in Potocki's bedroom:

> His bed has his crest painted at its head. Another gown of gold and crimson is flung over the bedhead. 'I say my prayers in that' he says. 'I am a Pagan. I pray to Apollo.' There is a fine arrogance about him. He can carry his long hair and his robe. 'I am one of England's major poets,' he says. 'I am as good as, say, Byron. I have never said that I compare with Shakespear. He is above us all.'

The same year, in a colourful ceremony for the Rites of the Sun, Potocki crowned himself 'Władisław 5th, King of Poland, Hungary and Bohemia, Grand Duke of Lithuania, Silesia and the Ukraine, Hospodar of Moldavia, etc, etc, etc, High Priest of the Sun.'

He also met Odile Morcamp, the petite fair-haired French schoolteacher with whom he was to spend the next four years, and for whom he was to yearn for the rest of his life. They married on 8 September 1939, a week after Germany invaded Poland, in a 'mystical pagan ceremony' written by himself. 'I performed it in the presence of witnesses, at our flat at 12 Winchester Street,' he told me, 'and we had a little lead Hitler on the altar. It's disappeared, I'm sorry to say. Ten months later we were thrown into prison. Over the Battle of Claverton Street.'

The Claverton Street incident occurred in 1940 when Potocki was summoned for an alleged black-out offence, 'when in fact my black-out was as good as anybody else's because the bombings hadn't really started. Later, when I started translating Mickiewicz, the black-out really did apply—

> Shut the door and mime the motions,
> Stand around and guard the potions!
> No lamp, no candle is allowed!
> Across each window hang a shroud!
> Let not the moon's pale gleaming tacks
> Filter in across the cracks.

—but no one was taking it particularly seriously at that time.' Asked repeatedly to present himself to the court on the black-out charge, he refused to go. Instead he rang up the police and said, 'If you come here in anything but a friendly spirit you'll be thrown out of the window of the top storey.'

Some days later six policemen arrived, demanding that he and Odile admit them to their flat. Potocki, however, shouted across the barricade of furniture they had piled at their door at the top of the stairs: 'Read the notice on the door and go away!'

The constables read 'Kingdom of Poland and Grand Duchy of Lithuania Chancery' out loud and departed, only to return with a dozen reinforcements. By this time the barricade, which had consisted of an iron bed and bookcases, had been strengthened with a partition, and Potocki and Odile, who had been preparing for a siege, were using a pulley and basket to pull up provisions supplied by Polish supporters down on the street. There was ground pepper in the basket and, as the entry contingent gathered on the landing and the detective inspector called out, 'Come out of there, de Montalk!', Odile filled 'a women's whirling syringe' full of pepper and sprayed them through a hole in the partition. Entry was then forced, during which the Potocki coat of arms on the door was smashed. As the sergeant and his men made their way through the barricade, sneezing, the leading policeman was cracked on the top of his helmet with a hatchet wielded by Potocki.

The pair were arrested—Potocki in crimson robes, Odile also in a long gown—and taken to the police station, where Potocki was charged with assault and Odile with being an unregistered alien. 'They wouldn't accept Odile's defence that she and I had been married and were in the process of trying to get a registrar to register the marriage. I had claimed that we were married in a manner analagous to the Hindus, and as 600 million of His Majesty's subjects were Hindus, we were entitled to have the marriage registered.' Their occupations were stated to be, and entered in the register as, King and Queen of Poland. They were tried almost immediately and sent to separate prisons. Potocki served two months in Wandsworth Prison, where he sewed mail-bags, and Odile was confined for a month.

They were officially married on 8 September 1940, the day Potocki was released from prison, 'in a registry office which specialised in marrying famous people'. Odile was twenty-five, he was thirty-six. The blitz had just begun. As Odile had not slept since it started and refused to spend another night in London, they collected what they could of their belongings, piled them onto a lorry and left for the home of an architect friend, a member of the Imperial Fascist League, in Bookham, Surrey: 'We went down to Ha Ha Ha Harvey's house, Half Moon Cottage, which he had generously put at our disposal. Harvey was supposed to be an absolute worshipper of the monarchy and in particular of Władisław V of Poland, but later I came to the conclusion that it was an MI5 house and we were under observation without realising it.'

At Half Moon Cottage, away from the bombing and blackness and the docks still burning, they resumed married life. Odile gave French lessons and Potocki returned to his translation of *Forefathers*. Mickiewicz's poem, one of the great works of European poetry, is based on the ancient pagan rite of the Warlock who yearly summons up the spirits of the dead and asks what they need. Its view that events in the material world are dominated by psychic realities was in line with much of Potocki's own thinking, and he immersed himself in the project, 'egged on by Odile', completing it—'three hundred pages of rhymed poetry'—by the spring of 1942. 'Although it lacks the synthetic wisdom and completeness of Faust,' he later wrote of *Forefathers*, 'it contains much higher flights of real poetry.'

When his father died on 2 April 1942, aged seventy-one, he freed funds previously tied up in Robert's marriage settlement and bought a new press, a crown folio Harrild platen machine run by an electric motor. He then set about printing the first three parts of his translation. Part four was not printed until the complete work was published by the Polish Cultural Foundation after the war.

In Surrey, as in London, controversies, headlines and flamboyant moments continued. Potocki attempted, unsuccessfully, to become registered as a conscientious objector and to obtain a diplomatic passport. He formed the Polish Royalist Association, and swapped his robes for a tailor-made russet-coloured uniform in wide-wale corduroy. This uniform was based on that of the Polish army, and Potocki wore it with the Polish eagle, fashioned from sterling silver by himself with the Potocki coat of arms on its breast, and a silver King Louis XVI sword.

He also began a legal action against his former publisher, the Columbia Press, for conversion of his printing-press on the day he was released from prison, following which it was damaged by bombs. This led the *Evening Standard*, in October 1941, to run the headline: CLAIM TO BE A KING: TOOK OATH BY APOLLO. The action, which argued that the police had arranged for the press to be uplifted from Claverton Street and stored (and, thereby, Potocki believes, silenced) dragged

Potocki in royal regalia in the grounds of the Villa Vigoni, Draguignan. The silk robe was spun near Warsaw in 1933 and later embroidered by Odile.

*Left:* Potocki typesetting at the Villa Vigoni.

*Below:* Potocki in a Draguignan café, with an unidentified female companion, circa 1968.

*Above:* Potocki with Cathleen, who lived at the villa for seven years and gave birth to her son Gwilym (not Potocki's child) there.

*Right:* Cathleen and Gwilym.

*Below:* Potocki holding one of his eight Siamese cats in the back garden at the Villa Vigoni, circa 1973.

Frederica, Potocki's lover for over thirty years, and into old age.

Frederica at Ventimiglia, possibly late 1970s.

The Villa Vigoni (top storey, back view) in the process of renovation at the time of my first visit in 1968.

Potocki wearing his chased silver crown, with William Broughton at the Villa Vigoni, July 1970. (William Stevenson Broughton papers, Alexander Turnbull Library, Wellington, MS-Papers-3976-2)

Potocki with me (and child's hand— lèse majesté!) in Edinburgh, 1983.

Potocki at a Victoria University student orientation programme in Wellington, 1984, where he read poetry with Gisborne poet Gary McCormick and told a lunchtime audience that he strongly disapproved of conventional men's clothing. (*Evening Post*, 4 May 1984)

The launch of Denys Trussell's biography, *Fairburn*, Auckland, 1984. Potocki is in the front row, next to an unhappily seated Eric McCormick. (Anne Noble, *Metro*)

Potocki and his Austin 1800. (Anne Noble, *Metro*)

Filming the TV1 documentary *The Count—Profile of a Polemicist*: Rod Cave, Ian Paul (director), Potocki and Malcolm Cromie (sound recordist) in the lounge of our 'hospitable mansion', Wellington. (Not in shot: Richard Bluck (camera operator) and Don Duncan (camera assistant).)

Potocki with my husband, John Miller, in the bedsitter at Hamilton.

Potocki, Draguignan, July 1996.

The burgled and scattered contents of the bindery and archive in the Villa Vigoni at the time of my last visit in July 1996.

on for the duration of the war. It was eventually won by Potocki, who collected £100 in damages from the War Damages Commission.

And he attracted the attention of the *Daily Express*. On 29 March 1943, a lengthy article headed 'PACIFIST FROM JAIL IS KNIGHTED BY SELF-STYLED KING WLADISLAV' appeared alongside a report on the fifty-ninth raid on Berlin and requests from farm workers for more meat, fat and sugar. It presented a detailed report of his knighting of pacifist and former 18B detainee Frederick Bowman, recently released from Brixton Prison (the 18B regulation allowed for the internment of those presumed to have enemy sympathies). The investiture had taken place in the monarch's palace—a partly timbered cottage of six rooms—before a large photograph of Sir Oswald Mosley on the mantelpiece, and following a morning service to the sun.

> A strange scene. There, in a cottage bedroom, sat the congregation of 12 in a semi-circle round a draped chair, 'the throne.' By it was a bedside table on which a candle burned. There was a stick of incense waiting to be lit, and an Easter egg painted red with the 'royal' arms.
>
> Ginger-bearded, 'Sir' John Harvey, an architect, and owner of the palace, who is 'Chancellor of the Orders of Knighthood', appeared. He wore a Robin Hood tunic with leather-belt, sandals and brown tweed tights. He carried music, which he propped on the mantelpiece, and a flute.
>
> Through a four-foot doorway 'the king' appeared, and everyone stood up. He was robed in scarlet, the embroidered fringe of his cloak reaching down to his sandals. His hair—wisps of it nearly gold—swept back from his forehead and hung to his waist.
>
> On his finger, a ring; on the shoulder of his zip-tunic, a decorative clasp; and on his chest, the 'royal' badge etched in duraluminium.
>
> As high priest of the sun, he lit the incense and intoned a prayer while 'Sir' John accompanied him, between gasps, on the flute. He prayed for the quick, for the dead, for his own 'sacred person.'
>
> His 'queen,' a petite, blonde Frenchwoman, shared her handwritten prayer-book with me. Like the others, she wore sandals.
>
> After the prayer, a reader in peacock purple stepped forward to read from the Egyptian Book of the Dead. There was a prayer for people who were working for peace. Then a list of the names of the

sun god as known to the civilisations of history. After each prayer the congregation chanted, 'Amen-Ra!'

The account continued with the knighting of Bowman, who was called to the throne 'in his black City coat and pin-striped trousers' to kneel, have a yellow silk ribbon pinned to his shoulder, and be invited, as 'Sir Frederick', to arise. The reporter observed that there was a stone altar to Apollo in the garden and that, at the gate, the royal standard of crimson and gold fluttered from a bamboo flagstaff.

A footnote to the article advised that 'A Polish Government official in London said last night that "King Wladislav" is not recognized nor regarded seriously. He said: "He comes from a side-branch of a well-known aristocratic Polish family. He himself was born in New Zealand, the son of an architect who gave up his title."'

The following week the knighting was reported, with disapproval, by Potocki's old adversary *John Bull*. Bowman was described as 'a rank pacifist', and readers were warned that Potocki's 'fantastic claims shouldn't be taken seriously—at least by people who prefer to give their spare cash only to deserving causes'. (Bowman would later be 'deprived' of his knighthood by 'Royal Rescript'. A bulletin in the *Right Review* in May 1946 announced that this action was taken in 1944 for 'lèse majesté and for gross breach of his oath of fealty'.)

## TWELVE

## Katyn

*No one in the Kingdom except Ourself printed
anything of the truth about Katyn in English.*

Frivolous though many of Potocki's 'royal' diversions were during the Second World War, they did not distract him from his ever-present concerns about Soviet Russia, whose long-term intentions regarding Poland he questioned. He regarded the Soviets as 'the worst possible, and most irreducible enemy of Poland', foresaw a Soviet Poland 'as no Poland', and believed that 'a Poland with a powerful Soviet neighbour would live in misery and fear and in perpetual risk of ultimate liquidation'. Increasingly he found himself printing material that supported Polish citizens in exile, including material censored in reports published by the British press.

Ever since the outbreak of war, government officials had been observing Potocki's pro-fascist activities with concern. Put simply, his politics arose most immediately from his abhorrence of bolshevism and his view that fascism, although undesirable, was the lesser evil.

Less immediately, perhaps, there was his response to Russia itself and the respective roles of Prussia and Russia in Poland's long history as an invaded nation. This is a complicated issue with its origins in the eighteenth-century colonisation and 'ruthless repression' of Poland by Austria, Prussia and especially Russia. In *The Polish Way*, Zamoyski confirms that this colonisation went beyond considerations of physical control to deeply disquieting efforts to impose moral control, particularly by Russia, and observes that, as the Polish mentality was 'saturated with the notion of legality and reciprocity . . . Russian rule in Poland offended not only by its aims but also by its methods'. He continues:

There was not a Radziwiłł or Potocki who did not at some stage between the 1790s and the 1860s experience a situation which revealed to him that in time of crisis he belonged not to some superior *internationale* of European aristocracy, but to a hounded nation.

There is a saying among Poles that, in the event of simultaneous invasion by Germany and Russia, they would put business before pleasure and shoot Germans first. While he found Russians individually 'likeable', Potocki believed that, in ideological terms, occupation by Germany was the more acceptable alternative: while Germans adapted, Russians obliterated.

Having rejected both New Zealand and England, he identified strongly with Poland. From the spring of 1941, when the worst of the Blitzkreig was over, the Battle of Britain had been won and Hitler was invading Russia, he was increasingly open in his support for Germany, believing that Britain had broken faith with Poland, since Britain was 'sworn to declare War on the inhuman Soviets and has not done so'. This despite Germany's savage occupation of Poland and its leaving the Ukraine, formerly the location of so much Potocki land, in flames. His hatred of the English may also have played a part. What greater anti-English stance could one take, what greater act of provocation, than to support Germany, to declare one's enemy's enemy as one's friend? When Britain and the Soviet Union became allies in 1941 his disillusionment was complete.

The extent of his contempt for the Soviet Union is perhaps illustrated in his refusal to be published by a pro-communist publisher, as a result of which what appeared to be a promising opening came to nothing. In 1938, Aldous Huxley, having read a draft of Potocki's life story (could this have been the corrected typescript I found in the archive?) had written to Potocki, saying that he had found the material 'intrinsically interesting', and 'skilfully' treated, and making some suggestions for improving it, including:

> a fuller and more elaborate description of the Vallombrosa garden and of your mother: this would serve to emphasize the difference between the paradisal beginning of the story and its hellish continuation.
>
> Also I think you might say a little more about your father's character while he was under your mother's influence and treating

you well . . . this would serve to bring out by contrast the monstrousness of the later behaviour . . .

He had also arranged for his own literary agents, Curtis Brown, to seek a publisher for the manuscript. The agents suggested offering it to Michael Joseph, who, after three years publishing as a subsidiary of Victor Gollancz, was in the process of launching his own successful publishing career. But as Potocki believed Michael Joseph to be 'the upper intellectual storey of Gollancz', and as Gollancz personally 'had just flooded the world with millions of copies of more or less pro-Soviet pamphlets', Potocki refused to have anything to do with him. 'So they all got the huff,' he explains in *Aristo*. 'I didn't want to do anything that would contribute in any way to the pro-Communist successes of Mr Victor Gollancz. After all, there was going to be world war, and I was on the other side.'

In 1943, alarmed by rumours among the Polish community of atrocities committed against Poles by Britain's ally, Russia, Potocki's political activism gathered pace. Among those from whom he sought assistance was the Duke of Bedford, another German sympathiser, who wrote from Woburn on 29 April 1943:

Your Majesty,
At the moment I am not quite sure where, by reason of my unpopularity, I should really be able to do much to help the Polish cause . . . What you say is confirmed by what more than one friend has told me of conversations with Poles in the Country. Very many seem to hate and fear Russia, even more than they hate and fear Germany, and consider that the Russian treatment of Polish prisoners has been more ruthless. Considerably more than a year ago a Polish officer told a friend of mine that the Russians had kept alive the private soldiers among the prisoners captured, but all the officers had disappeared and he believed that they had been murdered. The statement in the German propaganda seems now to confirm his supposition in a rather sinister fashion.
Yours very truly, Bedford.

And on 1 May: 'I quite agree with you that this business of the Polish officers is exceedingly fishy, and I cannot believe that they were murdered by Germans . . .'

This 'exceedingly fishy' business was a story circulating among Poles in England that, in 1940, the Russians—then allies of Germany—having taken 14,500 Polish intellectuals and officers prisoner, had massacred them, many in the woods at Katyn, near Smolensk.

'My inquiries revealed,' Potocki told me, 'that in 1939, a month after Stalin and Hitler had signed their then secret agreement to carve up Eastern Europe, and less than three weeks after Germany had invaded Poland, Russia had also entered the country, without any declaration of war, and in contempt of peace treaties still in force with Poland, on the pretext of saving Poland from Germany. It deported over a million Polish citizens to Russia on this pretext, and took 181,000 soldiers, including 10,000 officers, prisoner, detaining them as prisoners-of-war in three concentration camps, at Kozielsk, Starobielsk and Ostaszkow.'

His further inquiries disclosed that, following questioning by the Russians, 400 officers assessed as friendly to the Soviet system had been confined in a monastery at Griazoviec and a small number distributed among common prisons. Disturbingly, nothing further had been heard of the remaining men since mid-May 1940.

'In fact,' he continued, 'on 5 April 1940, Russian troops had commenced the liquidation of the officers left in the camps. They had told them they were going home, and transported them in batches every few days in the direction of Smolensk. Some were said to have been shot on arrival in the woods at Katyn. Others were rumoured to have been taken all the way to the White Sea, where they were loaded into barges which were sealed, towed off-shore and sunk. It was a deliberate act of extermination designed to deprive Poland of the cream of its military leadership. When Germany attacked Russia on 22 June 1941, and the Soviets entered into a treaty with the exiled Polish Government in London, with a view to forming a Polish army in Russia to assist with resistance against Germany, the Polish general, Władysław Anders, recently released from the infamous Lubianka prison and made commander, became aware that thousands of Polish officers, many of whom he knew, were not to be found.'

By now the Germans had occupied Katyn and, acting on advice that a large number of Polish officers had been buried there, they started digging in the forest. On 13 April 1943 Goebbels announced the discovery of the remains of thousands of Polish officers. The British

Government emphatically denied that the massacre had taken place and, as Potocki discovered, news of the atrocity—which was by now public knowledge in Europe—did not reach the public of Britain.

When Potocki first told me about the Katyn massacre in 1983, I had regarded his account with some scepticism. I wondered whether, given his political mindset during the war, the facts were as he had conveyed them. My own inquiries at the time were not conclusive. They revealed that a massacre may have taken place but the details were shrouded in uncertainty, and it had only ever been an issue with Poles.

It was not until June 1995 that I discovered from reports in the press that wartime intelligence reports, sealed for fifty years after the war, confirmed not only the full horror of the atrocity, but also Potocki's belief at the time that the British Government had been aware of the massacre. The official line had been 'to pretend that the whole affair was a fake' and that the Government had believed: 'This is obviously the most convenient attitude to adopt, and, if adopted consistently enough, will doubtless receive universal acceptance.' The reason was that 'Any other view would have been most distasteful to the public since it could be inferred that we were allied to a power guilty of the same sort of atrocities as Germany.' The Soviet Union had also emphatically denied Germany's assertions that it was responsible for the massacre, and continued to do so until 1990, when KGB archives revealed irrefutable evidence that it had been carried out on the direct orders of Stalin.

Details of the massacre are still coming to light. In May 2000, the *Times*, reporting on 'one of the worst single atrocities of World War II', revealed the investigation of 'new graves thought to contain the bodies of high-ranking Polish army officers shot by the dreaded NKVD on Stalin's orders 60 years ago'. It also disclosed the existence of a letter written in 1959 by 'the then head of the KGB to Nikita Khrushchev the Soviet president' which stated that 'another 10,000 Polish officers were shot in 1940 at two other western Soviet sites'. The article also states that the current Polish Prime Minister, Jerzy Buzek, had confirmed that, as Potocki had suspected, the victims were not only 'defenders of our country', but Poland's elite: 'professors, judges, engineers, artists'.

On 4 May 1943, at the request of Poles in London, Potocki, seeking to expose the atrocity and discredit Britain's bolshevik ally, wrote his

'Katyn Manifesto'—a pamphlet he claimed was 'the only statement of the truth in English about this matter until well after the war'. The Poles had wanted to write the account themselves, but Potocki, believing they would be seen simply as 'blowing off steam', insisted on writing it himself.

He sought maximum attention for the manifesto, boldly opening the text, which was accompanied by a map of Eastern Europe showing the camps and the known extermination site, with his credentials: 'HIS MAJESTY WŁADYSŁAW THE FIFTH, BY THE GRACE OF GOD KING OF POLAND, HUNGARY AND BOHEMIA, GRAND DUKE OF LITHUANIA, SILESIA AND THE UKRAINE, HOSPODAR OF MOLDAVIA, ETC. ETC. ETC: HIGH PRIEST OF THE SUN . . .' He then exposed the Soviet atrocities, implied a British Government cover-up and attacked the diplomatic protection of Bolshevism. Why, he wanted to know, may the Bolsheviks claim Polish lands, while the Poles may not claim lands formerly stolen from Poland by Russia? And why may the Bolsheviks break off diplomatic relations with Polish officials while the Poles may not retaliate? He concluded with a solution: 'It is HIGH TIME for a negotiated Peace, in which we hope the Germans will be persuaded to display a proper regard for the rights of Poland. Poland and Hungary to be united according to our map (with possible concessions to the Germans); the jews to be helped if they will even at this late hour repent and behave themselves; the Tsar to be restored in Russia and the King in France. Niech Żyje Polska!'

On 13 May, having run off 'thousands of pages' on his crown folio Harrild platen press, he went up to London with the first batch of pamphlets. It was widely distributed by both Potocki and the Polish government-in-exile, and it wasn't long before he was placed under British Government surveillance and the matter was raised in the House of Commons: 'A question was asked by some lackey who was at the service of the Soviets—a Labour Party member, of course', whether the Government was going to order him to be arrested for disturbing the relations between the Allies. Herbert Morrison, the Home Secretary, stated in a written reply that the manifesto was 'an imaginary projection from the brain of an individual, who styles himself King of Poland . . . The language of these documents is so extravagant, and their author's claim so preposterous that his eccentricity must be obvious to the reader.'

The press was unsympathetic. The *Daily Worker* pounced on the manifesto, describing it as 'poisonous filth' and Potocki as a 'crazy

Fascist Count', and even the hitherto sympathetic *Daily Express* was scathing. William Hickey spoke of 'war documentary *curiosa*' and wrote, 'This is the nursery or Bedlam version of the Bolshevik bogey.'

Warned by his friends that very soon he would be going inside again on any pretext whatsoever, Potocki waited to be charged with another alleged offence. Three months later, in September 1943, he was summoned to court to answer the charge of insufficient black-out for which he had been waiting. He refused to go. He wrote to the court arguing that, not only was the information against him improperly laid, but no British court had the right or power to summon him, 'the only lawful Sovereign and Ruler of one of the great Allied Powers, to wit, Poland'. A further communication, delivered by Bowman, who identified himself as Sir Frederick Bowman, Knight of St Stanisłas, Press Attaché to the King of Poland, advised that 'His Majesty is too busy to attend Court on such a small matter as his time is fully occupied with political work in connection with a negotiated peace.'

Presiding judge Tudor Rees was not amused. 'We will have no more nonsense,' he declared. 'An alleged breach of the law is never a small matter. Don't talk about His Majesty. He is no Majesty; he is a humbug. He calls himself the King of Poland. I consider him the king of humbugs. This man has got to be here a week today. If he is not, a warrant will be issued for his arrest.'

The order was ignored, and on 21 October Potocki was arrested by the Special Branch. In court he refused to speak English and demanded an interpreter. Evidence was given that on the night in question, 31 August 1943, on returning from London, he had allowed light to fall 'from a tiny window, on the wall of the neighbouring house', an action he declared to be a physical impossibility. He was found guilty and sentenced to two months' hard labour, reduced by a third, in Wandsworth Prison.

The *Daily Worker* described Potocki as dressed in 'a reddish-brown velvet suit, scarlet wool socks, red sandals, and natural coloured wool gloves', with his long brown hair fastened at the back with a clip, and his green sheathed sword on the police table. It gleefully reported that, on receiving his sentence, Potocki shouted 'Heil Hitler!' It was alleged, the *Daily Worker* went on, 'that when spoken to about the light, he replied: "Your bloody laws and your bloody courts have nothing to do with the King of Poland," and added that he "would like to see the Germans overrun this country".'

By now Odile had left him. Alarmed by his violent hostility to the Government, and anxious about where it might lead, she walked out on him two days after he published his 'Katyn Manifesto'. She had, after all, already spent time in prison on his account. He was devastated. 'It was Odile who made the wonderful embroidery which she put, as if on ecclesiastical apparel, in a great band around the bottom of my somewhat worn Polish hop silk robe,' he once said to me wistfully. 'And also on the sleeves and around the neck. She was a wonderful musician—she wrote the music criticisms for the *Right Review* under the name Margaret Townshend—and she could do anything: repair cloth, embroider . . .'

He told me that the reason they had no children was Odile's fear that, given his fiercely anti-government policy, he would be imprisoned and they might not be able to provide for them, or even to keep them. 'She was an extremely intelligent woman,' he said. 'She was the little mirror of my soul. She was also attractive, sensual and humorous. She'd refer to herself as the Piggle, a slightly modified form from Chaucer's poetry where *pigges nye* comes in as an endearing nickname, and one of our friends sent her a beautiful piglet made of gold, on a tie pin, with tiny ruby eyes. After she left me she ended up living with someone else and had two children by him. Finally I divorced her in Draguignan, because publicity about divorces is forbidden by French law and by that time she was teaching in a Roman Catholic college in England and could not afford the publicity. We remained on good terms until she died. I was very much in love with her.'

He believed that, apart from his obscenity trial, his attempt to expose the massacre at Katyn was his most significant moment. Certainly in terms of personal cost it rivalled the trial. It ended his marriage, and caused him to be imprisoned and reviled. It would be fifty years before its truth was known.

On release from prison towards the end of 1943, he was ordered by the Ministry of Labour to serve six months in an agricultural camp in 'the British Soviet punishment republic of Northumberland'. He ignored the order. The conduct of Sir Ernest Wild at his obscenity trial still strong in his mind, he was busy instituting court proceedings against Judge Tudor Rees for remarks made against him at his black-out hearing on 7 October.

Orders to report to Northumbria kept coming, and he continued to ignore them. 'They were foxing themselves,' he told me. 'One department was trying to conscript me for the army, and the other one was sending me these mandatory orders to go to this camp. In the end I thought, well, I'll go to the camp because every time an order arrived, the astrological descendant was very strong, as if a hint from the Gods. So in 1944 I went, and I turned up there with the beret and the Louis XVI sword and everything.'

The camp was 'horrible'. 'We lived in huts, and we were sent out to different farms in a lorry where we would have to occupy ourselves with threshing wheat, and go out on these corn stacks and things, and there I was with the Order of the White Eagle flashing in the sun. The others were mostly people who wouldn't have been much use for anything else. They would say "coom an' get yer beit", when you were supposed to get your food. It was technically an agricultural hostel, but everyone considered it to be a concentration camp without barbed wire.'

He stayed only a month. In January 1944, he received a summons from the solicitors acting for Judge Tudor Rees and left for London. He didn't bother to return. The camp manager, 'Mad Mathews', refused to give him permission to go, saying he would have him brought back as a runaway slave, but Potocki said 'Heil Hitler!' and left.

Back in London, he took a flat at 10 St Peter's Street, hoisted his standard on the roof, and installed his press in the basement. For the next four years he eked out a living, here and elsewhere in London and Surrey, undertaking translations and printing commissions for the Polish government-in-exile, and maintained a vigorous presence in the press and legal system.

His case against Tudor Rees—cited soberly in court documents as 'WLADYSLAW the Fifth, King of Poland and Hungary, Plaintiff, and JUDGE TUDOR REES, Defendant'—was struck out when the judge, after a series of adjournments, successfully argued the judicial defence of absolute privilege. Potocki was informed by the High Court of Justice, King's Bench Division, that his case disclosed no cause of action and was frivolous and vexatious.

His attempt to defend his tenancy at St Peter's Street also foundered when, in November 1946, he was successfully sued by the landlord for possession of his flat. The landlord had removed his flag from the roof and Potocki had been withholding his rent. The headline in the *North London Press* read: THE KING MAY HAVE TO LEAVE HIS PALACE—HE HASN'T PAID THE RENT.

At around this time he received £542 from his mother's estate, together with shipment of one-third of the chattels. With the war finished, and his financial situation more secure, he was now eager to leave Britain. However, his passport had been confiscated and attempts to renew it were proving fruitless. In 1947 he put the matter in the hands of his friend the Duke of Bedford, and at the end of the year was finally issued with a new passport. 'But it was without our ancestral title of Count,' he fumed, 'and the profession of Poet which had figured on my passports for twenty years, and also on the national register. I told them they would bring England *Bad Luck* by having done this.'

A letter from Uncle Ted—now known as Uncle Toad—in Auckland, dated 29 December 1947, left him in no doubt that returning to New Zealand was not yet an option:

> I feel that it is useless my giving you any advice but what you want to acquire is a merit exclusively British—mental balance and sound judgment . . .
> Now Geoffrey, it is time that you achieved some mental balance—some 'commonsense'. Of what use is it being able to speak six languages if you have nothing sensible to say? Why be a disgrace to the family and avoided by all members of it when you might be a credit to it?
> Your affectionate Uncle Ted.

He made inquiries about obtaining work elsewhere. Invoking the royal 'We' he wrote to a university in India, asking whether

> there would be any possibility of Our earning Our living by teaching at your University. We were born in New Zealand, and We think most people will admit that We speak and write english as well as anyone alive, but We have been unable to become famous as a writer owing to the trouble We have always been in with the british. During the war We were violently pro-Axis and for this went to gaol twice and had all sorts of other troubles.

Another letter, addressed to the American Ambassador, advised that 'We should like to be in a position to use Our gifts in the fight against Soviet Russia'. His feelings at this time were expressed in a savage poem entitled 'Ritual Clobber':

The murderous, savage, hypocritic brit
makes up in wickedness for lack of wit.
The entire structure of his social life
and the aggressive rudeness therein rife—
religion, propaganda, legal screeds
are rituals to excuse his wicked deeds.
The brit's a ritual murderer, ritual robber
and ritual swine done up in ritual clobber.

On Saturday 14 August 1948, he departed for Europe, where he spent the next two months in Switzerland, Italy and southern France. 'I went to see if the stuff they were saying about the state of Europe was true. They were spreading rumours that you couldn't live there, that they would chop your fingers off to take a ring at every street corner, and that kind of thing.' His sense of relief at having left England was expressed in a letter to a friend written on 22 August in Paris:

> At Brighton, while I was in the buffet, there were from twelve to twenty explosions in the station which sounded either like one of those bombs that explode piecemeal, or like the maniac firing from powerful small arms like a tommy-gun . . . I did not believe I was free from that prison-island until the ship began to move.

In Switzerland he sought out the aged Countess de Bioncourt, daughter of Count Bernard d'Harcourt and granddaughter of the Duc d'Harcourt. He had been told that her father had been French Ambassador in London, Moscow and Switzerland, and had known his great-grandfather, Count Józef Potocki. The countess provided him with a signed declaration stating that she and her family had known all the persons in the drama of Potocki the Insurgent and his marriage to Judith, and confirming that it was well known that Judith and her sister Norah, foster daughters of the Marquis Townshend, were in fact the natural daughters of George IV, King of England.

The countess, who appears to have been charmed by Potocki, urged him to settle in Europe. He decided provisionally on Provence, because the climate was agreeable and land was said to be cheap. He wrote to a female admirer in New Zealand: 'I am now doing all I can to make arrangements to leave England for ever . . . I do not read anything in English these days, not even Shakespear, as I hate the english too much, but I have made an exception in favour of your poems . . . I reciprocate the loving thoughts you send. Laszlo R.'

Back in England he sold his press and started packing. But the 'british' had not yet finished with him. In March 1949, he was arrested and charged with assault after a female admirer, alarmed to find he was moving to Europe, entered his flat, refused to leave and was pushed through the door.

In a process now very familiar, he was remanded in custody. Only this time a psychiatric assessment was called for. 'When I was in court I claimed I was above their jurisdiction. I said that as King of Poland they could not judge me, and the magistrate said, "Well, in that case I shall have to send you to Brixton Prison for a week to have your state of mind tested." They'd never done that before, you know. I said I was King of Poland from the beginning of the war on all occasions, but because they'd won the war they thought they could be funny.' He spent a comfortable week in Brixton, in the psychiatric ward: 'It was a lovely clinic. It had a beautiful bathroom, a marquetry floor, a great old table as long as this room, and a wonderful old Cockney warder.' He was observed for a couple of days, and then questioned. As with all his good stories, his verbal account of the interrogation followed the written version almost word for word.

'Now, then, why do you say you're King of Poland?' the psychiatrist asked.

'Well, it seems to me that Poland needs a king,' Potocki replied.

'Perhaps, but why should it be you?'

'Well, for one thing Poland needs an intelligent king, not like what you have here.'

'Yes, but why should it be you?'

'Well, the Poles have a constitutional adage which says every Polish gentleman is a candidate for the throne.' Potocki repeated the adage in Polish. 'It's quite true that it exists, you see.'

'Oh, is that so? Yes, yes, I daresay, but why should it be *you* and not some other Polish gentleman?"

'Well, anyone who knows anything about Poland has to admit that we are among the greater Polish gentry. Besides which, I have published my genealogy several times showing that I have the hereditary right to the throne.'

'Do you imagine that by signing a paper you could put the Polish army, fleet and airforce in action?'

'No! Of course I couldn't. It's a great pity I can't, rather than those thugs you've set up over there.'

'Do you think that in any circumstances you might actually reign as King of Poland?'

'It's not impossible.'

'Well, in what sort of circumstances do you imagine that might happen?'

'One of these days you'll have serious trouble with your beautiful Soviet ally,' said Potocki, 'and then it may become a question of urgent interest to Europe, and perhaps to the entire world, to get the Poles to co-operate with the Germans. How do you think you're going to manage that after all the lies you've told? You've created a situation where no Pole dares to say that he's pro-German. You will have to find somebody who will not be distrusted by the Poles, nor by the Germans.

'Who is this person?'

'I can tell you what will happen: the Germans will find some person who has a Polish name, and speaks better Polish than I do, but is really their agent, and they will say to the Poles, "This gentleman is your king, your führer, anything you like, he's your chief." And the Poles would say, "Hah, heard that before," and bump him off, and quite right too. The next thing is you people would say, "Oh yes, but your wonderful free Polish government in London, which represented you throughout our war for freedom, and which we most unfortunately had to disavow, and besides admit we shouldn't have done so, is once more your free, marvellous, democratic Polish government." And then the Poles in Poland will say, "*What?* That gang in London who stole our money, and bought themselves with it laundries and printing shops and hotels and forests and castles and farms and everything you can buy with money, those people? You must be laughing!" And they'd be quite right too.'

At this point I pictured the psychiatrist looking thoughtful, playing with his pen and deciding that the argument, although unlikely, was lucid. That the patient was articulate and surprisingly charming and, although he played out a day-dream, he showed no sign of delusional mania: he was able to look around himself, to know he was not really the King of Poland.

Doubtless Potocki smiled and shrugged, disarmingly, as he finished: 'Where are you going to find your man? Any Pole who has anything against me has a flaming cheek because I did not have to be a Pole—

I'm a New Zealander. And any German who has anything against me after all I've done for Germany would also have some cheek. You may find that you have to make me King of Poland yourselves because I am anti-English.'

A report was made to the court. At the conclusion of the case the magistrate said: 'Well, prisoner, as you know, I have before me the report of the psychiatrist of His Majesty's Prison at Brixton, and he declares that you are perfectly healthy in every respect, both in body and in mind, and for this reason I am going to fine you £2.'

Outside the courtroom Potocki said to the police: 'You gentlemen know I never pay fines, but on this occasion if I pay this fine, will there be any objection to my taking the next suitable boat-train to Paris?'

'No,' they replied, 'you will be quite free. You can do what you like.' Thereupon in the third week in March 1949, he left the 'Kingdom of the Half Mad'. He deposited most of his belongings with cousins in Paris, made his way to the south of France, which he had been told was littered with houses which were falling into disrepair and which, with a bit of energy and a few sacks of cement, one could do something with, and installed himself in the Var, in Draguignan, quite close to the Mediterranean coast.

# THIRTEEN

## Draguignan and Dorset

> *Wether report: Thick snog & freezing drivel on the B.B.C., with patches of moonshine, low audibility. There will be Shahs from the East, and precipitations at see level. There is wether all over England & Wales. Britannia will have funny periods and squawling Shahs.*

Samarkand had become hazy. Its frescoes and portals were fading, its markets had lost their glitter, the route to its ancient marble and gold was impassable. If he had had the fare for the voyage home, would Potocki have returned to New Zealand?

And what, I wondered, was New Zealand? Was it as he might have remembered it in the Scrubs, as he later wrote in the typescript, as it was before Lestes—a holiday alongside the sea? He and Cedric running down to mudflats overgrown with mangroves, crabs which bit their bare feet, patches of sand to which they rowed in a dinghy when the tide came back? Games of war on clay roads, swampy valleys of raupo, learning to ride beneath wattle?

Or was it law firms: conveyancing deeds, counters, the stain and ink of dead wood? And schools—those anxious months as a teacher on horseback, seventeen kilometres between Greenhithe and Deep Creek, three days in each, £5 a week, and the horse he couldn't mount without fear of being thrown?

What of the war? Cousins injured, careers and sweethearts abandoned? (Although Cedric would fit in, having joined the Polish Air Arm in Britain.) Perhaps he told himself that he was no hardy participant, no seeker of solidarity; that, like Leonardo da Vinci, on his own he was himself, in company he was half of himself, and still best suited to exile. Safer, he may have concluded, the life of the writers and artists who had moved to Provence before him, the German intellectuals who had settled near Toulon before the war, Huxley who had built a villa there. Marseille had become a centre for surrealists, the troubadours' poetry of impossible love had thrived. Giono had written: 'Provence has a thousand faces, a thousand aspects, a thousand characters.' There was a history of difference there. And it was hotter and cheaper than Paris.

In April 1949, with financial assistance from the Countess de Bioncourt, Potocki purchased a *cabanon*, formerly an olive harvester's hut, in the Vallon de Gandi in the Draguignan countryside. The property, which cost £100, also comprised three-quarters of a hectare of fig, olive and almond trees on walled terraces, and was obtained cheaply he believed because the owners—printers who had bought it during the war in order to have olive oil—did not have time to carry out the improvements necessary in order to sell it.

Although the cottage (built during the reign of Henry IV) was solid, with stone walls fifty centimetres thick, it was badly in need of repair, and Potocki immediately set about sealing it for the next winter. The countess, who by now had constituted herself his aunt, offered to contribute to its renovation.

Without a press and the financial assistance of printing commissions, he knew life would be hard. That having spent his share of his mother's estate on resettlement, and with his only immediate income a small remittance from the family trust, donations from the countess and the proceeds of occasional grape-picking, he would barely be able to sustain himself.

Until such time as he acquired a press, he told himself philosophically, he would carry out the renovations himself. And live off his land. He could print, play the piano and read Sanskrit—all self-taught—now he would learn to make walls, install windows, construct beehives and sell olives. He would distil wine from figs and keep hens, goats and rabbits. 'People were very pleased to buy my roosters,' he later wrote to my father, 'because they knew jolly well that they hadn't been fed on any chemicals, and the same with the eggs.'

In late September 1949 he took time out from cementing and tiling and travelled to Germany. Here he met Marja Merkowna from Poland. Marja, aged forty-two, suggested that she join him in Draguignan as his 'servant woman' and, attracted principally by the prospect of speaking Polish on a daily basis, he agreed. It took him some time to arrange official permission for her to live and work in France, and she did not arrive until April 1950, 'which was just as well because the cottage was taking time to get into a quasi-habitable state'.

Marja, or Marysia as Potocki also called her, was pregnant when she arrived, and a month later gave birth to twin girls in the local hospital. Potocki, surprised by the seemingly advanced state of her pregnancy, argued that the twins could not possibly be his. As he later explained in a letter to a friend, he had not met Marysia until 24 September 1949, at which time she must already have been pregnant—a supposition confirmed by the entry permit in his passport. He wrote: 'She maintained persistently that the German doctor who issued her with a medical certificate prior to leaving Germany, which said she was in the fifth month before Christmas, was wrong, and thus I was taken unprepared. It was evident why she did this. She began to infer that I was the father.'

Potocki always vigorously denied fathering the twins, and I had never doubted him. It is true that he had abandoned Wanda, but he was happy to claim her as his daughter. Why, then, deny the twins? Issues of responsibility and financial support? He lived from day to day, his means meagre. The prospect of commitment to Marysia, with whom he had envisaged only a casual relationship as housekeeper? I had seen a letter to a friend which suggested he did not find Marysia appealing.

The Countess de Bioncourt, who visited Draguignan soon after the twins had been delivered, urged Potocki to put them in a home. Despite his limited means and distrust of their mother, whose domestic limitations were now obvious, he refused: 'I wouldn't have dreamt of such a thing,' he wrote to his friend. 'I couldn't see what harm they'd do here.' Was he recalling the effects of his own maternal separation? Or had he decided he was obliged to support the twins? Whatever the reason, they were removed from the hospital, 'where they would certainly not have lived many weeks', at the earliest opportunity and were provided for by Potocki for the next five years.

Meanwhile, he had started work on a second dwelling. The countess, having inspected the cramped arrangements in his Shack, as she called his harvester's hut, had purchased a derelict peasant's cottage on an adjacent piece of land. The two-roomed, double-storey cottage had belonged to and was 200 metres from Monsieur and Madame Payan, his nearest neighbours. The countess suggested he name it after the Villa Vigoni, home of his great-great-aunt Norah, on the shores of Lake Como.

His early years in Provence would be centred on improving these properties, visiting his benefactor in Switzerland, and entertaining her when she was in town—the countess frequently travelled to Draguignan, where she took a room at a hotel and had Potocki join her for conversation and meals.

Letters to (among others) his executor in London, 'Old Clarke', indicate that by August 1950 Potocki had finished the first volume of Bhandarkar's *Sanscritt*, acquired a second-hand Citroën courtesy of the countess, and met her Swiss German friend Frederica (Fritzi):

> The Countess de Bioncourt bought the car because she alleged that I was ruining my heart with the daily trip to Draguignan on my bicycle . . . The other day I had a fever of nearly 40 degrees Centigrade. And also there is another annoying matter. The Countess de Bioncourt wants me to divorce Odile with a view to marrying a friend of hers, a Swiss girl, who looks very young but isn't. I consider this a perfect outrage. If people wanted to bring the world luck they would try to marry me with some nice little German Princess—or Hungarian or Polish—but not with a Swissess. She is quite nice as far as she goes, but I am astonished at the depravity of the Countess, who while she is always lamenting the disappearance of the great nobility, tries to bring about mésalliances of this sort . . .

On 11 September he wrote from Canton de Vaud, Switzerland ('anniversary of my marriage with Odile as a matter of fact'):

> Yesterday the Countess insisted on my doing the Tour du Haut Lac with a pretty Swiss woman who is one of her friends . . . I think I told you, the Countess is one of the few remaining links with the affair of my great-grandparents . . . She is a very old lady, but is extremely cultured and reads an enormous number of books in several languages. She is also a student of precious stones, botany, and many other subjects. She speaks Russian, German, English, Italian, Spanish, and her French is the French of a great French aristocrat, and not the rubbish one usually has to listen to. She used to own the Villa Belvedere on the Lago di Como, where my great-grandparents met . . .

By now Potocki, exasperated with Marysia, had moved out of the Shack and installed himself in the unfinished villa. Starting with the top floor, he set about renovating it in earnest. The roof and floor were renewed, the staircase and central beam replaced, and by the end of the year there were new windows and French doors, a garage under construction in corrugated asbestos and a room for storage and wood. All this in addition to cultivating his land, which now encompassed 120 feet of olive trees. 'A "foot" of olives,' he explained in a letter, 'is one tree, or several, between the trunks of which an animal cannot pass with a plough. There were probably about three hundred trees.'

When Old Clarke proposed a visit the following spring, Potocki believed the Villa Vigoni might be almost ready for house guests. He suggested Clarke bring 'a few Utility sheets' with him and a couple of good second-hand blankets, and pay a few francs for food if Potocki happened to be out of funds. He warned that Marysia was not a good cook but, as she peeled potatoes and prepared the vegetables, only 'the artistic side of the cooking would have to be done', and promised very good wine for about a hundred francs a bottle.

Meanwhile, his friendship with the long-legged, fair-haired Frederica, who was around ten years younger than Potocki, was developing. In 1952 he persuaded her to come and stay, writing to her in English after she left:

> My love,
> ... The curious thing is that ever since you went away I have had the impression that you were thinking about me in a nice naughty way. I am convinced it is you—I have thought about you every day, about your good character and sweet presence, but also have thought about you very sensually. Is it mutual? ...
> Tuesday afternoon I was gathering olives at the Shack property, and also pruning the tree, which I think I have learnt how to do quite well. And the trees are therefore gradually improving. Each year also it is less difficult to gather the olives. I was thinking about your idea that you would like to help me gather the olives. And I was also thinking that it was not work particularly suitable for you (nor for me either). However, on condition that the weather is nice and that there is no wind, it is not bad. Naturally there is only one way to gather olives, and it is how the professionals do it. They never work alone—there are always at least two persons. The whole

of the ground under the tree is strewn with large cloths, and therefore the workers do not have to bother to grasp the olives—all they have to do is to make them fall down. I have only two cloths and one of them has been damaged by rats at the Shack . . .

Fritzi and Potocki exchanged hundreds of letters between 1950 and her death in late 1980, usually in French, Fritzi in a soft round hand and Potocki in type. Potocki also wrote her many poems. Their correspondence suggests an erotic, yet easy, even homely relationship and his visits to her orderly and efficient home in Chesières in the Vaud Alpes, and later, when their relationship was well established, her twice-yearly visits to Draguignan to clean the villa, cook and mend clothes, were eagerly anticipated interludes in his life. She provided the comfort and companionship of the home life he had known only briefly, during his four years with Odile, and an environment in which he felt free to write. He in turn was an attentive and appreciative lover.

Within five years of his arrival in Draguignan, the freedoms of country living, so appealing at first, were palling. Subsistence farming was imposing its own pressures—the olives were late, the goats were not giving milk, the hens did not lay—and the renovations, hampered by the diversion of the countess's donations into household expenses, were proceeding only piecemeal. When Fritzi, who regularly supplied tea and biscuits from Switzerland, sent money for roof tiles and a door, and Potocki had to spend it on butane gas, bread, buttons, a hair-cut, candles, a sharpening and pruning knife, sugar for jam, 'and a Nestlé case for a hen's nest', he told her: 'if I am to stay here my situation must improve very considerably'.

Furthermore, life at the Villa Vigoni lacked intrusion and, as much as he sought solitude and complained when interruptions caused him to fall behind with his writing, he also needed issues to rail against, a political life, lovers, literary exchange. In addition, while there may have been time for translation, poetry and correspondence, without a press he was unable to deliver himself to a wider audience: 'I didn't yet have another printing-press. You see, for a long time I wouldn't think or write or read in English if I could help it. I didn't even want to have English spoken about my person. But after a time I thought, "Well, after all I am a master of the English language, and it's a weapon, and I'd better pick it up and use it," so I decided I wanted a press. Frederica said that I'd got into trouble having a press and she didn't want me to have another one. I said, "That's not the case. I got into trouble through *not* having a press."'

In 1954, increasingly in need of diversion, he wrote to Fritzi:

My love,
. . . Are there any hopes that you might turn up here one of these days? You say you are glad that I am pleased with the Citroën, but the next thing is to have you in it. It was just lovely driving you across France

. . .

There has been a great controversy in the (exiled) Polish press about the relations between Chopin and the Countess Delfine Potocka. It appears that this lady was about as sexy as it is possible to be, and that Chopin wrote her a lot of outrageously sensual letters

. . .

The piano has recovered somewhat from the winter, though there are still a few mute notes. And the instrument makes a noise when one is playing it like an old tracker-action organ. . . . It is however only half a tone below pitch . . .

Before I forget: next time you come here, could you think of bringing me a pattern, of the simplest sort, for making house-slippers out of skins? And for that matter out of other materials. Some of the best slippers are made out of bits of carpet. And also some of the wool, if you have any left, with which you made this wonderful jacket . . .

There are lots of things I wanted to say to you, but I must see if I can gather a few olives before going to town. If by any chance you took it into your head to come here before I have finished the olives, I should get someone else to gather them 'à moitié.' I am longing to be able to flirt with you again, and kiss your sweet lips. It is a pity you are not like Delfine Potocka—I would add something naughty.
Lots of love and kisses, dearest.

He was also corresponding with Dorli—small, dark-haired German-born—with whom he had once had a very different relationship. They had met in London either during or after the war, and their frank, highly charged correspondence between 1948 and 1959 suggests an intense and secret affair. Indeed, Potocki sometimes addressed Dorli, upon whom he would bestow the title of Baroness, as 'My Secret Wife'. In 1955 they met discreetly in Paris, and in 1956, when frost ruined his olive harvest, he returned to her in London, staying for six months.

His affair with Dorli, as conveyed in a collection of explicit letters written in English and German and sent in 1955 and 1956, reveals a hard-edged interest in sex not apparent in his other relationships. 'At 9am,' he writes in October 1956, 'I gave my right thigh four cuts with a cane and was thinking so hard of You that I wondered whether in spite of all You say about not bearing pain, You sometimes do flagellate yourself.' Anticipating their meeting in Paris, for which Dorli is purchasing canes, he writes: 'In Paris I think I can take the 30 even if you apply them hard'. They also speak of any other adventures he might be having, including a 'triangular' encounter conducted locally, and of his sexual isolation: 'There do not seem to be any fucks in the offing,' he complains in November 1955, 'but one never know what may suddenly turn up.' And he writes of Aunt Emily's thrashings with his mother's riding whip. Were there connections here to his abrupt response to my question about explicit depictions of sado-masochism on video, and to Cedric's warning in 1968 to be 'careful of Geoffrey. He thinks of nothing but sex'?

These letters, which I found towards the end of my examination of the archive, caused me to think again about Cedric's concern, and to wonder to what extent—discounting the verses and translations for which Potocki had been tried, the endless writing of erotic poetry, and his reputation for amorous pursuits—had his preoccupation with sex resulted in behaviour that might have been considered unacceptable. Or whether there had been any such behaviour and Cedric's comment had simply reflected his own morality. I reached no conclusions about this.

The letters also raised the issue of his sexuality. Questions had so often been asked. I had heard it said that homosexuality could have been Potocki's great secret, that the accusation at primary school by his father might alone have triggered a lifetime's repression and forced displays of heterosexual activity. What of his benefactors? I had been asked. What of his Lithuanian idyll? I can only say here that my own sense of Potocki, together with the evidence of his archive—all those letters, manuscripts, poems, all those words written by women—does not support this view. It is true that I knew him only as an older man, but there was nothing in his frank and, circumstances permitting, propositional point of view, even then, that suggested concealment. 'My biographer should note,' he once told me firmly, 'that *I was not homosexual!*' and, triangular sex aside, I had no reason to believe otherwise.

Yet I was intrigued by another connection: his behavioural similarity to Casanova. Here were two amusing, charming, learned and flamboyant men, who flouted convention, sought literary recognition (unsuccessfully) and pursued aristocratic acceptance (although, unlike Potocki, Casanova had no aristocratic ancestry). Both wrote prolifically but published only a fraction of their work (the first edition of Casanova's original manuscript, *Story of My Life*, was not published in French until 1962), were imprisoned more than once, lived in exile, translated major works of verse (Casanova the *Iliad* into Italian verse, Potocki *Forefathers* into English), and had obsessions about Poland (Casanova wrote a 'vast, well-documented *History of Unrest in Poland*' in Italian). More specific and significant, however, was the extent to which they were devoted to and admired by women, the manner in which their reputations as amorists appeared to connect with the unresolved grief of maternal desertion in their childhoods (Casanova by the theatrical Maria Farussi, Potocki by Annie Maud Vaile in death), and the seemingly irreversible effects of these desertions on the rest of their lives.

The London interlude appears to have been helpful, for Potocki returned to France resolved to remain, and eager to find a press. Although it would be three years before the Marinoni press we had seen on our first visit to Draguignan was installed in the printery, he recommenced publication of his annual poem for the Feast of Saturn: 'I'd use a milk bottle. I'd roll the ink onto the thing, and then I got the rollers out of a discarded washing machine at the tip, and then pushed them over it. Of course the result was quite bad, but those things are probably very valuable.'

By 1958, writers revisiting the literary world of the 30s and 40s had revived interest in Potocki. Journalists called, keen to investigate his exile and current activities—this explained the newspaper articles I'd seen when I was at college—and his publications began to attract collectors of rare and unusual books.

He was regularly in touch with Richard Aldington, a friend since 1928 and a supporter at the time of his trial, who was keen to see him set up with a press. Like Potocki, Aldington wrote in searing terms about the hypocrisy of modern society and literary pretentiousness (Aldington's 1933 novel, *The Colonel's Daughter*, had been so direct that two libraries had refused to stock it, and his biography, *Lawrence of Arabia*, had reviewed the controversial adventurer in a similarly uncompromising manner). Furthermore, as a translator of Greek and Latin poetry, Aldington shared Potocki's admiration of ancient civilisations.

Potocki's letters to Aldington were lengthy, frequently comprising detailed descriptions of his domestic arrangements. Potocki was unfailing in the documentation of his living conditions. Why? Probably because, in the first instance, his precarious financial state necessitated a considerable degree of practical self-sufficiency. He had to undertake car maintenance, apply himself to building and plumbing and carry out household repairs. This is not to say his work was always, or even usually, of a professional standard. He did not build to a code and, as we had seen when we first visited the Villa Vigoni, some of his work, although functional, lacked finish and made use of materials such as tiles and irregular slabs of marble found at the tip. The sight of bottles in the stone walls of the villa was especially intriguing. On subsequent visits we never felt sure about the safety of the building. We were alarmed to notice, for example, that the main weight-bearing beam which ran the length of the living room—the beam which held up his bedroom with its weight of books, bed and piano—was riddled with borer and to find, on prodding, that it was soft in places.

Potocki, however, was very pleased with his work. Like his father, he favoured the use of concrete and stone, and frequently spoke with pride of the strength of his walls or the fit of his frames. And he was alert to domestic possibilities. I recall in particular the nicely shaped outgrowth of a bush or tree he had smoothed and nailed to a door as a handle. As the process of recycling and renovation occupied much of his time, not only at the villa, but wherever he lived—for there were always bookcases to be made from old crates, small filing boxes to be cut down from used wine casks, and tables, household appliances and storage cabinets to scavenge and adapt—it seemed inevitable he would want to write about these achievements and his plans for further improvement.

However, it was also my impression that his inventiveness went beyond financial considerations. That in part it stemmed from a need to create—a need reflected in my impression that he was a home-maker at heart. He cared about his surroundings, scouring markets and second-hand shops for rare books, silver, old coins and the odd piece of good crockery—sometimes as much for the ambience they would bring to his rooms as their value—even though his summer grass and the stems of his pink and mauve wildflowers would be growing long and stringy, and the villa ever more messy and dusty. 'In London Odile and I had a long elegant table,' he once told me, 'which I made from the door of an antique gentleman's wardrobe. People couldn't believe it wasn't a genuinely antique table.'

Furthermore, he gave thought to the small comforts of others, and while he did not appear to notice that his domestic arrangements were often odd and inconvenient, and in the case of his bathroom practically non-existent for a long time, he genuinely hoped to make his guests comfortable.

Having laughed and marvelled at Potocki's inventiveness for years, I was interested to read that Weeks's study of eccentricity had found similar examples of extraordinary creativity. 'Creativity is at the heart of eccentricity,' he explains, noting that many eccentrics are typically driven not by aesthetics or science, but 'by a powerful need to create in its purest, generalised form'.

Thinking further about conditions at the villa, it occurred to me that its combination of off-beat and unexpectedly conventional domesticity mirrored Potocki's personality—his extremes and the middle ground he frequently met. For amid the clutter of household effects and the apparently random acquisition and scattering of printing and building materials there were many small moments of economy and efficiency demonstrating an underlying desire to guide his life in an orderly and conventional direction.

I had found neat piles of used razor-blades, labelled, in Swiss matchboxes; old nails and screws, scrupulously sorted and saved in tea tins; hair brushes hanging conveniently alongside the villa's only mirror; and endless pieces of card tacked to bookshelves, cataloguing and cross referencing his library. I had also found, when following the instruction that, for example, Polish Literature might be located 'Above the Piano' and 'Above the Mirror' and on numerous shelves in different directions, that the system, which had presumably worked well in his mind, had either been changed or disturbed, or was not yet complete.

And it seemed to me that the villa as a metaphor for Potocki's life extended even further. It encompassed his view of poetry and his preoccupation with beauty, and while it sheltered profound works of literature, it also exemplified his belief that there was true beauty in the elemental aspects of life, such as milking cows, growing plants, feeding pigs—and building a dwelling. 'These are much more closely related to poetry than a middle-class suburban existence,' he had once said. 'I don't see there is any link between the middle-class life and art, but there are strong bonds between poets and pigs.'

Letters written to Aldington in February 1959 also discuss the costs and issues related to buying a press in Draguignan, and express gratitude for his financial assistance:

> Your kind letter with the cheque came today, having crossed my second express letter which I went to town to send yesterday . . . It certainly is very good of you to take so much interest in setting me up with a press. I sincerely hope the whole of the funds really will come from these other people, for that would be much more agreeable than depriving you of money, however much I may need it, which you need for your daughter, and also for yourself . . .

That summer Potocki once again owned a press. With the additional financial assistance of Fritzi, a 100-year-old Marinoni platen foolscap had been purchased and manoeuvred into position on the semi-sealed floor of the printery. The new operation, which was christened The Mélissa Press, took its name from Fritzi, whose pet name was Honey, 'in accordance with Liddell and Scott's Greek lexicon, which held that Melissa was a bee, a priestess of Apollo, honey itself'.

Despite 'unspeakable' operating conditions—the printery, which faced north, was freezing cold at least half the year, and had no heating or artificial lighting until 1969, when he bought a Honda generator—Potocki wasted no time in despatching translations, pamphlets and small booklets of poetry. Aldington wrote:

> Dear Geoffrey,
> Your most welcome book of poems arrived in the snow, bringing such warmth into the place that the snow has all melted and the

green world re-appeared! . . . All my congratulations . . . What matters is that your creative work should be again available—it is the best, the only answer to the lavatory-seat wipers of literature who naturally don't recognise a poet and a gentleman when by chance they meet him.
Affectionately, Richard.

Potocki was also writing to Lilian and Wanda, and to members of the wider New Zealand family, including my father. But he was rarely in touch with Cedric, who considered him to be morally corrupt. In a short admonition to his brother, dated 'Vernal Equinox 1958', Potocki had declared:

Punkie
You will be punished by God for your
outrageous and wicked words, reeking
with Uriah Heep-like arrogance.

However, family interests—previously safeguarded by distance—were about to become more complex and pressing.

In May 1959, a letter had arrived from Susan Powys, adopted daughter of the writer T.F. Powys and his wife, Violet, introducing herself as Potocki's daughter. Susan, now aged twenty-seven, had recently discovered she was the natural daughter of Potocki and Minnie, Potocki's mistress before he was sent to prison and maker of his second cape.

When Potocki entered Wormwood Scrubs in the winter of 1932, Minnie had just become pregnant. Unwilling to wait for Potocki's release, she had invited Francis Powys, son of T.F. Powys, to live with her in Potocki's rooms, at which time she had told Potocki of her condition and her new lover:

> She wrote me letters which were full of lies and lying promises, and asked me to provide her with information of a highly illegal order, which meant the letters were liable to get me into further trouble in prison. Friends went out of their way to inform me of Minnie's goings on—for perched up on the slopes of the Powys Mountain, she could scarcely act unobserved, even had she not been the very soul of indiscretion. When I came out of prison, a mutual friend

who had supplied her with the address of a chemist's shop, reported that she had gone into the shop surrounded with Francis Powys, and had said in front of clients in a loud voice and a la-di-da accent: 'Er-ew, Ahee héah you dü abawtions!'

The story of Susan's adoption is explained by Potocki in *Dogs' Eggs*, a four-part series subtitled *A Study in Powysology*, published by The Mélissa Press in 1968 and distributed by his invention, The Shack Press at Draguignan, from 1972. The title recalls Violet Powys's observation to Potocki that 'The dog's laid on the table again', and the series relates the strange, almost incomprehensible story of his ten-year association with the Powys family.

Regarding Susan's adoption, he writes:

> . . . I went to Provence and after a few months there went to Poland, where Minnie wrote me ludicrous letters (still extant) boasting of her proceedings.
> And upon these inter-facts, as the French say, Minnie and Francis Powys got the baby adopted by Theodore Francis Powys. Naturally I took it for granted that T.F. Powys's wife was a person of more or less the same social category as himself, he being a cousin of Lord Lilford, a Peer of no worse quality than nine-tenths of the 'older'(!) title-holders in England.

He surmises that Francis and Minnie gave T.F. Powys to understand that Francis was the father of the baby, as a result of which the baby was adopted by the writer and his wife, and the couple were forbidden to see each other again. Instead, they were secretly married in the lunch hour at the registry office, and T.F. Powys learnt of it through the daily papers. Minnie, who then identified Potocki as the baby's father, was forbidden all access to her daughter, and T.F. Powys gave an interview to the press in which he said, 'My only son having been eaten by a lion in Kenya, I had adopted Susan, the Perfect Child.'

From the beginning T.F. and Violet Powys made it very plain that they did not want Potocki to be in any sort of relationship with Susan. 'They also went to extraordinary lengths to prevent her from ever finding out who she was, and this without any doubt had a very bad effect on her mind . . . For instance, she grew up not knowing that Minnie, her sister-in-law, was her mother.'

Susan, who later renamed herself Theodora (Gift of the Gods) Gay Potocka, had discovered the identity of her mother during a visit to Powys cousins in the United States. After she returned, Louis Wilkinson, a family friend, confirmed that Potocki was her father, but had added that unfortunately he was dead.

And there the matter remained, until Louis Wilkinson got a letter from the poet Kenneth Hopkins... Kenneth reported that he had had a Poem for the Feast of Saturn (sometimes known as Christmas) from Count Potocki of Montalk, who had been reported in newspapers and reviews as having been killed by the communists in Paris in 1950. (And then for good measure, again in Poland a few years later.)

Life in Draguignan was gathering pace. Marysia, unable to persuade him that he was the father of the twins (on whose behalf, perhaps, she had been pursuing the Potocki name), had given up and returned with them permanently to Germany. No longer encumbered, Potocki was enjoying a steady relationship with Fritzi and, with the installation of his press, a renewed commitment to printing. Now, at the age fifty-six, he had the added interest of an adult daughter. 'Dear,' he wrote to her, 'I am sorry you were lonely, unhappy, and nervous as a child. I had an appalling childhood myself.'

After corresponding for over a year, Potocki and Theodora met when she visited the villa briefly in August 1960. Reluctant to make her acquaintance in the 'Powys entourage', he had invited her to Draguignan, paying for a first-class ticket, and arranging for her to come on a specific date, carefully selected 'for astrological reasons'. The pair appear to have been pleased with each other, for Theodora left insisting her father come and stay in Mappowder, Dorset, where she was still living with Violet—an invitation Potocki promised to accept as soon as he could 'park' his Siamese cats and finished printing a couple of books he was publishing on his press. However, as he was about to discover, his visit was not to be purely social. Theodora was in need of his help. As she writes in her own account of this period, *Potocki: A Dorset Worthy?*, Violet, who was now widowed and, following the death of her husband, had built and moved into a new house in the village, was 'proving a disastrous housekeeper and I was proving disastrously unable to help her . . . we were desperately in debt.'

He arrived in Dorset just before Christmas 1960, and here, in the environs of *Mr Weston's Good Wine*, *Mr Tasker's Gods* and *The House with the Echo*, begins the saga of Potocki's vexed and lengthy association with the Powys family as related in *Dogs' Eggs*.

His first impression was of 'an utterly uninhabitable house, where violent smells knocked you down before you could get inside the front door, where there was not room to turn around inside, and where the cooking was the worst in England, which is saying something'.

In *Potocki: A Dorset Worthy?*, Theodora recalls that, in addition to herself, Violet and Violet's Aunt Gert (Gertrude Cox, aged ninety), the house was occupied by Violet's two dozen cats, Violet's collie, a 'hutch full of guinea pigs on the landing' and, in the downstairs toilet, a wild rabbit. *Dogs' Eggs* adds the presence of 'a green parrot called Timmus' which was 'attempting to exist' in a cage and, in the bathroom, a hamster 'which was mostly not even on view, for it covered itself up with little bits of paper', as well as 'a kitten Violet had chosen to bring up in the bath'. In addition there were Theodora's two Alsatian dogs, and, outside in the stable with Theodora's mare, Violet's Labrador, plus pups.

Violet immediately prevailed on Potocki to help her with the payment of her outstanding accounts, and while he did not agree to settle any directly, he sorted her files, reduced some of her debts and arranged for a tax refund. When he realised the extent to which Theodora, although working hard as a herdswoman, was also 'up to her neck in debt', he reluctantly extended his stay. As a man who hated dogs, whose enthusiasm for animals generally did not extend beyond cows and well-trained cats (preferably Siamese), and who was further discomforted by the absence of a functioning stove, 'no hot water' and an abundance of fleas, he would not have made the decision to stay lightly. Indeed, it was made only after he had tried to persuade Theodora to leave Violet and the animals and return with him to Provence. He writes in *Dogs' Eggs* that, with 'the large plate glass windows on the ground floor' battened from within to prevent the dogs smashing them, scratched doors and 'seriously damaged' paintwork and wall plaster, the house was 'an absolute Bedlam'.

During this period Violet continued to pressure him for financial assistance. 'The moment came,' he told me indignantly, 'when she owed me £400. This might not seem like a huge amount of money, but for me it was a very serious matter. One day when she was pretending to moan about the money she owed me, I said I would buy the house at Mappowder from her if she liked, at £3000, and the £400 she owed me could be my deposit on the purchase. She had been trying to sell the house, which she alleged cost £4000, and had been offered £1500, not for her equity after the Powys mortgage, but for the whole freehold, which considering its condition was a fair offer.'

His undertaking to buy was provisional on Violet signing a covenant to spend £850 of the money she received—'mainly money I was virtually giving her'—on a bungalow of two rooms and a kitchen which he personally would build on Theodora's five-acre (two-hectare) holding two miles into the country at Lovelace's Copse, where Theodora grazed her mare and Violet a jenny donkey and foal. Violet was also to ensure that the Powys Trust mortgage remained on the property. These dubious arrangements were confirmed in an agreement signed before a Mr Street, a retired major and the local postmaster.

In the meantime, in the summer of 1961, Violet had been moved, with 'Aunt Gidge' and 'innumerable cats', into what *Dogs' Eggs* describes as an 'aluminium caravan with a very pleasant interior woodwork including a central folding partition, all in a spotlessly clean and virtually new condition', beneath a hawthorn tree at Lovelace's Copse. Theodora, who liked her privacy and independence, had installed herself in a 'garden hut' (previously the revolving hilltop sanatorium of essayist and novelist Llewelyn Powys), and Potocki had taken up residence across the field from Violet and Gidge in a self-converted deep litter chicken house, to which he proposed to add an annexe for printing. With the dogs confined to a fenced area, the purchase of a golden Jersey heifer, re-named *Złota*, for milk, butter and cream, plans to have a press installed in the annexe and visits from Dorli and Frederica, presumably he believed he would resolve his daughter's problems in some comfort. Once he had cleaned, renovated and sold the Mappowder house, he would use the profits to pay Violet's and Theodora's bills, build them a bungalow, pay whatever he still owed on the house, and be left with a small sum—effectively money recouped. 'He really felt it his duty to give me all the help he could,' writes Theodora.

Having settled the small community at Lovelace's Copse, he once again directed himself to supporting his daughter and resolving her affairs. On 23 November he sent the following letter to the local laundry, after it refused to accept her herdswoman's washing:

> In re Mrs 'Arris and Hassociates Ltd.,
> A company with paid up capital of 100,000 pounds, trading under the style 'The Argyle Laundry', at Latimer Rd., Winton, Bournemouth.
>
> Dear Ltd Co.,
> When Miss Powys, adopted daughter of the celebrated writer T.F. Powys, received, a couple of months ago, your insolent letter refusing to do her laundry on the grounds that it was too dirty for your august staff to handle, the first reaction in the neighbourhood was: 'It seems they expect the clothes to be laundered before they are sent to the laundry.'
> I myself, however, advised Miss Powys to send this stuff forthwith unaltered to your rivals in the trade, who accepted it without demur and did it extremely well, being about the best laundry I have ever had to do with, in my life in various parts of the globe. Their only defect appears to be, that they do not call at Monkwood.
> I have the honour to draw your attention to the fact that these big industrialised laundries are nothing better than mechanised washer-women, which is doubtless why your letter was couched in such bad English. Some live washerwomen however are good-looking, attractive and squeezable, which is more than can be said for any Limited Company whatever.
> If you have a look at the enclosure you will see that by addressing yourself, my dear unattractive Limited Company, to a suitable Antiquarian Bookseller (if you know what that means), you can sell the present letter, and distribute the price to your fortunate shareholders.
> Mit arischem Gruss . . .

But, despite levity and best intentions, relations between the households in the copse were becoming strained. Violet, Gidge and their cats were cramped in the caravan, and Violet, previously enamoured of Potocki but now disapproving of his romantic liaisons with Dorli and Frederica, turned on him and started accusing him of deceitfulness (despite each woman knowing of the other's visits).

Matters deteriorated considerably when, in cold weather, Theodora moved into the annexe with the press, and Violet put what Theodora describes as 'the worst possible construction' on the move and caused 'a terrific row'. Added to this, there was the problem of obtaining health department approval for the proposed bungalow, the plans for which could not be approved until a fail-safe water supply had been found, and the increasingly urgent need to clean and improve the Mappowder house so he could sell it. There was also his ever-present awareness that, having entered into the agreement with Violet, he had put his small amount of capital at risk.

In *Dogs' Eggs* he writes that the agreement cost him 'five years of grinding, black, grotesque slavery, almost worthy of some Soviet joint, drowned in loathsome smells, marooned in mud . . . and my own properties in Provence going to waste meanwhile . . . Obviously I had no desire to make a house of this sort my dwelling, even in perfect condition—quite apart from the fact that I had no desire to live in England at all.'

First he had to divest the house of its contents: boxes, rubbish, furniture, even the harmonium 'at which it seems Violet used to sit in former days, artistically swaying her bottom, and soulfully playing Nearer, my God, to Thee'. He writes that 'An appalling amount of time and trouble was wasted cleaning dog and cat excrements and general dirt' from the contents of the house.

> In the end a great deal of what was in the house was sold at quite good prices . . . Violet did nothing whatever toward this beneficial result, except to sit on her wide arse and collect the money, which she then proceeded to squander as before. Naturally I charged her nothing for my work, efforts, and negotiations, nor the wear and tear on my car and type-writer, which former was very considerable indeed—for several years the unfortunate little two horse-power Citroën was used as a veritable lorry for long distances on Violet's business, transporting huge quantities of timber, for instance, which in the end necessitated many repairs and replacements, finally including the whole transmission system.

Next, he applied himself, with Theodora's help, to the rest of what he termed 'Violet's sordid mess':

During the whole period when we were coping with Pongo House, as I used to call it (from the Angolan noun, pongo [orangutan], the New Zealand noun Pongo [derogatory term for an English person], and the verb 'to pong', neither of the two latter being in the snooty Shorter Oxford Dictionary) we had to keep taking disinfectant throat pastilles . . .

They cleaned and redecorated for nearly two years, at which point, although improvements were not yet complete, he decided the property was advanced enough to put on the market. The For Sale notice read:

> . . . Mappowder is a very beautiful Dorset village, from which the Dukes of Bedford claim to spring, and has an exceptionally lovely Parish Church, in the graveyard of which lies buried T.F. Powys, author of Mr Weston's Good Wine and many other renowned books—it was with his money that the house was built, by his widow. . . .
> The house was built in 1955 at a cost of nearly £4,000 and has recently been thoroughly redecorated. The telephone lines are in the house but the instrument itself has been disconnected . . .
> The water reserve tank in the roof did not freeze during the big freeze-up last winter, being heavily lagged and intelligently made . . .
> There is a fine view over meadows, for eight miles or so to High Stoy (a hill the name of which has a strange Polish flavour) . . .

But the house did not sell. At this stage Potocki discovered that he was not in fact the owner of the house, and that the complicated agreement he and Violet had reached was not sustainable, because it was conditional on the mortgage which she covenanted to grant, but which in her other capacity as trustee she was refusing to grant. 'Therefore I did not own the house, but she owed me £1300 odd, and would not do either one thing or the other. As a result, for the time being at least I was being done out of the use of my money.'

All the while, at Lovelace's Copse, conditions were deteriorating further. There was an uncommonly cold winter (said to be the worst in a hundred years), a piped water supply was proving difficult to find, the bungalow had not been (and would never be) started and Violet, who according to Theodora 'exaggerated the least thing into high drama', was going out of her way 'to make', as Potocki writes in *Dogs' Eggs*, 'at least one row every day with Theodora . . . Her influence over Theodora had plainly been bad, except insofar as Theodora had reacted against her.'

He continues: 'The late Richard Aldington has said in one of his books that in England they positively prefer people who are bogus. Anyway what I had to put up with from Violet—thus what Theodora had obviously had to put up with ever since T.F. Powys died—was such that I printed a work on my press at Draguignan that the remaining Powys's did not swiftly recover from.' He was referring, of course, to *Dogs' Eggs*, confirmed by Theodora in a letter to me as 'simply the flat truth'. She added: 'I don't think it was diplomatic [of] Father to write it, nor do I think it helped his case . . . but for a man who'd just lost pretty nigh every penny he possessed it was understandable, I think.'

He also began legal action to recover his funds, an action the Powys family resisted so vigorously that settlement was not achieved until 1971. Initially he acted for himself, acquiring the assistance—and inconvenience—of a legal-aid lawyer only when it became clear the case would be long running, even by his own protracted standards:

> It was extremely onerous doing anything through a solicitor practising in Dover, a place I was never in except momentarily passing over to France. The journey from Dorset was long, devious, difficult and expensive—for a matter which had arisen in Dorset and was to be tried in London . . . Once one has been fool enough to accept what calls itself Legal Aid, it is virtually impossible to regain control of one's affairs . . . Quite certainly I would have been far better off had I issued the Writ in this case myself . . .

In 1966 he finally returned permanently to Draguigan, where, with no settlement in sight, he made good his threat to the Powys family and began to document the saga. The slim, digressive series *Dogs' Eggs* is highly amusing, probably libellous, and descriptions of Violet's house should not be read before dining. It appeared between hard covers, accompanied in Part I by a couple of murky black and white photographs captioned:

Violet's Lervly New House I, View of the interior after it had already been very considerably cleaned.
Violet's Lervly New House II, Another view of the interior—2 doors & 2 bits of wall: in a straight line, made to appear to ziz-zag because one bit partly cleaned!

Some parts also contained delightful corrigenda and comments, including: 'This page is printed with one roller instead of three.'

The Powys family were understandably upset about their portrayal in *Dogs' Eggs*, and when, after nine years, the court decided that Potocki should receive £500 in full and final settlement from the Powys estate (Violet had since died), payment was made conditional on his agreement that he would not

> make any further publication in England or elsewhere of the booklet entitled 'Dogs' Eggs', and that he was not to publish any booklet or pamphlet which was of a similar nature to Dogs' Eggs containing material which would harm or injure the character or reputation of any member of the Powys family.

'What,' he asks in *Dogs' Eggs* Part I, 'is a Powys? Is Mrs Powys-Keck (see London Telephone Directory) included?'

Ten months later, having received only £300, Potocki prepared to offer Parts I and II of the series for sale. His solicitor was then forced to disgorge funds held 'in escrow'. However, this meant that, after all the time and money Potocki had put into the publication of the booklets, he was bound by the terms of the settlement and they could not now be sold.

Conveniently, at this moment a book thief was visiting Draguignan and one afternoon, while Potocki was away in Italy buying printing paper, the thief and an accomplice broke into the Villa Vigoni and stole the copies of Part I which were ready for sale. In due course, Part I was issued as a stolen and pirated edition under the imprint of The Shack Press, Draguignan. Later, the subterfuge was repeated and Parts II to IV appeared, under the same imprint, much to Potocki's public delight.

## FOURTEEN

# Realisation

> *When we had left the site Theodora informed me that she considered the mosaic a fake. And in spite of our Scots Ancestors (through my Grandmother Macalister) we decided to spend another five shillings to see it again and investigate certain points.*

The six years in Dorset were by no means centred on the Powys house at Mappowder. When improvements assumed less urgency, Potocki and Theodora moved between England and France. A small card printed by Potocki indicates they had hopes of renting either the deep litter house or the villa:

> Would like to contact couple, preferably literary, who would find it worth their while to look after small holding in Dorset while we are in Provence—& house with acre of olive trees (and printery!) while we are in Dorset. All advantages and snags frankly discussed by letter . . . For astrological reasons, please give dates of birth.

As time passed, however, he and Theodora became less compatible. She writes that 'He was city' and she was not. While she wanted to ride and spend time with her animals, 'His idea of a lovely day out [was] to sit in Salisbury Cathedral and listen to the organ, preferably being played Bach.' It seems that, after three or four years, their relationship started shadowing that between himself and his own father. A controlling aspect to his behaviour developed. He scrutinised and disapproved of her male friends, did not find her habit of wearing jeans feminine, insisted she desert her animals, and Violet, and move permanently to France. Theodora recalls that increasingly he 'openly and loudly' disapproved of all she did, tried 'incessantly' to change her character, and attempted to persuade her to marry a man of his choice.

By now Theodora was a woman in her early thirties. 'In the long run, I can't be told what to do,' she wrote to me. 'I can't take orders, or even advice! And I most certainly can't be told who to marry . . . I enjoyed his conversations and actually found him quite good company for quite a while, but in the end the differences were too great.'

He also established a printery in Dorset. In 1962 the distribution of his grandfather's estate enabled him to purchase a Gordon crown folio press with an electric motor which he installed in the makeshift building at Lovelace's Copse, the location of which he pinpointed as 'through the first gate to the right past the Brace of Pheasants on the road from Plush—also known as Plush Bottom—after Mappowder and Folly.' He announced himself to the district in a pamphlet entitled 'A New Dorset Worthy', printed at the copse.

> I do not claim to be as good a Poet as William Shakespear, but he had nothing to do with Dorset anyway and I am a good deal more like him than anyone whose voice has yet been heard on the B.B.C. during its disgraceful existence.
>
> It is true that I am opposed to virtually every movement or line of thought triumphant at present, but does not the fearsome and uncertain state of the world show that I am right in this? Besides, no genius was ever born to advertise the successful follies of the time: a genius always has something genuinely new and newly genuine and this is why he usually has a lot of trouble.

As ever, his press was controversial. He undertook printing commissions which included Colin Jordan's *National Socialist*, and one pamphlet printed at this time, 'Two Blacks Don't Make a White: remarks about Apartheid' (1964), drew an injunction against its sale. The 23-page pamphlet, which sold for three shillings, quotes William Blake's 'One law for the lion and for the ox is oppression' (which also appears in *Snobbery with Violence*) and argues against equal rights for South African blacks. Potocki believes the South African Government's attitude to apartheid was the correct one. While he does not preclude the possibility that 'a given Black Man might be superior to a given White Man', that 'certain Black Men may be worthier individuals than some White Men' and that 'in certain matters the Negroes might be superior to the whole White Race', 'they are, nevertheless, in a general way inferior'. Describing himself as having become 'at very great personal expense to Ourself the Prophet of Truth in our time', he asks why have indigenous Africans

> not produced great civilisations such as ours have been in their hey-day . . . the immense poetical, literary, musical, architectural & scientific heritage of our forefathers? . . . Who prevented them? They have had through the millennia the limitless riches of Africa, the sun, the forests with wonderful wood, stone, jewels, gold; & the remains of the great non-Negro civilisations of the past, of the Pharaohs, of people like Juba, King of Numidia; of Carthage, Morocco. These princes and these peoples were at one time their neighbours.

He explains that his argument, which he develops in some depth, does not encompass considerations of 'actual colour' but focuses on the level of civilisation and learning.

> The Mongolians, the Hindus, and allied peoples are not white either. Yet the culture of the Chinese is renowned, that of Japan ought probably to be far higher esteemed than it is, while the literature of the Hindus is one of the very greatest of the world, their architecture is of the highest interest, & their arts & crafts as good as ours or better.

Rereading the pamphlet while writing this memoir, I realised that previously I had dismissed it. I had glanced at it, ignored the complex subject of culture, and pushed Potocki's support for apartheid, together with his other racially unacceptable statements, towards the convenient pile in my mind marked Eccentricity. I had done so without arguing with him, or even murmuring opposition to his view. But now questions were arising: given such assertions, how had I tolerated Potocki, laughed with him, even liked him? Had there been any more to my acceptance of him than blood ties, sympathy, his amusing stories and charm?

I thought hard about this. The question was fundamental to my regard for him, and to the tone the memoir was adopting. My most immediate response was that, day to day, Potocki in person—as I and my family had known him—had not presented as a bigot. We had never personally heard him speak in support of apartheid—an issue of significance in New Zealand during much of the time he was staying with us—and, once he had realised how much we found his occasional anti-Jewish remarks objectionable, they had ceased. It's true that his apartheid pamphlet and other examples of intolerance sat on our bookshelves, but then so did dozens of other views we did not subscribe to.

However, defining Potocki as an atypical bigot, and accepting that (certainly in old age) his views were a small part of his overall mood, did not answer the question. The intolerance was still there: it just wasn't immediately expressed or visible.

Or did it? The concern about racial intolerance is its expression, and its potential for harm when it moves beyond thought to the controlling context of its time. It seemed to me that, while the pamphlet on apartheid had once held this potential, and there was no doubt about his bigotry during his post-prison years in London and later in Dorset and Draguignan, when I came to form my impressions of Potocki twenty years on these expressions had become distanced. Furthermore, although reports of sporadic outbursts in New Zealand reached me, such opinions were less frequently stated—indeed, he was more concerned with chastising his own race as he considered the future of, and declared his support for, Maori. Time, and mellowing, had tempered the troubling aspect of harm.

Still, the issue of his racial attitudes remained. Once again, context seemed relevant—the context, that is, of his wider life, his non-conformity, his thwarted disposition. His stated opposition 'to every line of thought triumphant at the moment'. His vigorous rejection of almost anything: democracy, Christianity, puritanism, communism, all things English, even the decimal system and modern men's clothing. Here, I believed, I might be closer to the heart of the question. For, although Potocki had held and argued his opinions strongly, some of them had been so wayward or strange, so connected to his role as a dissident and provocateur, that, frankly, for the most part I hadn't taken them seriously. American writer and private printer Terry Risk appears to concur: 'these ideas,' he writes in *Why Potocki?*, 'provocative as they were, were of little real consequence to me, or anyone else'. So does Gordon Porteous, who wrote of the *Right Review* in the *Criterion* in 1937: 'It appears to be produced rather as a gesture of defiance than anything else: defiance of Catholics, Communists, Jews, Legal Administration, anti-Monarchists and Mr Rickword.'

The additional relevance of context, or Potocki's immediate

circumstances, to the issue of his racial intolerance was brought home to me when he was staying with us at Weir House. Here, he was interacting daily—in the dining room, the common room and as he strolled along Kelburn Parade to the printery—with students of all ages from twenty-six countries: from Africa, Asia, China, India, the Federated States of Micronesia, the tiny Pacific island of Truk . . . Here we discovered that his history of intolerance was at odds with his behaviour. For, invoking his wide knowledge of culture, he mixed readily, and with what we observed to be genuine interest and warmth, with all the students, especially those from abroad. He had long discussions with them over lunch and dinner. He enthusiastically recounted to us the knowledge gleaned.

'He was great,' remembers Karun Lakshman, one of the deputy wardens and a law student from Fiji. 'I mean, how often do you get to meet a pretender to a throne, especially one who can read Sanskrit? He was very learned, had enormous knowledge, and was easy to talk to—even though most of the time you had to listen to him!'

It can be argued, of course, that Potocki was simply aware of his place. He knew that, in order to remain as our guest at our convenient and 'hospitable mansion', charm and discretion were needed. It can also be said that he liked to talk and the students were a captive audience. However, because he stayed regularly with us, for up to five months at a time, and given his age and famous tendency to temper, I believe it is unlikely that an act at this level could have been so effortlessly sustained, or that we would have failed to see through it.

'How did you find him?' I asked the children, now adults.

Jonathon, the eldest, remembered him briskly as 'a character', as 'interesting with a good sense of humour. He was always in my room.'

'He was a great talker,' said Melissa, who was named after his press. 'And he always made a serious effort to come out and have a chat when I was sunbathing. He had a lovely smile. I'll always remember his smile.'

'He ate all our butter,' said Donovan, who didn't miss much.

'I remember him as a funny old man,' said Dylan, the youngest. 'But I found it fascinating to enter his room and see all his books, and papers, and bells.'

Further questions arose. Was I becoming an apologist, too ready to explain him? In attempting to understand the processes by which his life had been shaped—the cosmic circumstances, as he might have described them; the not so random 'synchronicities', as Robert Dessaix calls them in his account of his own life—had I become over-sensitive to the myths that surrounded him, the false reports, the many small pieces of his life misrepresented by rumour?

More intriguingly, was I moving from the mental to the physical and becoming possessed by him? Only the previous evening, Dylan had slapped his thigh and exclaimed to John: 'She looked just like Geoffrey when she said that! Did you see her! The way she went like this with her mouth?' And he'd made some small biting motion which I hadn't recognised, but which he, when younger, with the sharp eyes of a child, had sometimes seen Potocki make when he was preparing to speak. Had I even attempted to become him? In 1997, when renewing my passport, I'd reverted to using my maiden name—a step I'd been planning for some time. Or so I thought. But now I remembered that I was listing the archive that year. Could the name change have in fact been an act of less than random synchronicity?

I flicked past the treatise on apartheid to the back of the pamphlet, where there was a promotion for 'One More Folly', also published in Dorset from his 'P.G. Wodehouse address', as Richard Aldington called it, also the subject of an injunction. I went in search of this pamphlet, which was somewhere in the pile of his publications sent regularly since 1968. It was an amusing and cogent piece in which he suggests that a mosaic, found by a smithy, Mr White, in a field at Hinton St Mary in 1963 and declared to be Roman, 'is neither ancient nor christian (being a copy of some sort)' and that '"experts" as such are nobodies anyway'.

It was also wonderfully irreverent. I was reminded that, although Potocki's views were frequently not my views, his uncompromising honesty, dismissal of humbug (in the manner of Uncle Bert, perhaps) and humour, together with his love of language, were among the reasons I liked him. I began to see then that it was because I liked him that I was attempting to understand him, and that because I was beginning to understand the forces which had shaped him, I wanted to explain why he behaved as he did.

I knew that my biographical voice was not his voice. How could it be? There were too many differences between us. But I also knew that the better I saw the shape of him, the more I was becoming a mediator. I wondered if I was beginning to experience a subtle process in biography in which the fact of one's subject—the well-worn stories and details—become less important than their newly perceived truth? Truth which I was seeing as small breathing moments not previously noticed, forced by the accumulation of fact to the surface. Private moments which were gathering lightly like dust and tapping my hand as the narrative grew.

It struck me again how different the fact, or public view, and the private truth of Potocki, as I interpreted it, really were. The public view was divided. On the one hand there were those who likened him to F.W. Rolfe, the incisive writer who styled himself Baron Corvo, whose life was similarly rich in incident, who also engaged in long and vituperative correspondence with his many enemies, and who was rejected by his own and the next generation. And there were those who likened his vigour, penetrating mind and aptitude for amorous adventure to that of the politician, rake and wit John Wilkes, who also suffered imprisonment and persecution for publishing obscenity. There were even those who described him as an eccentric genius. On the other hand there were many who saw him as a bigot, a racist and a snob; as vain and flagrantly self-promoting; as homophobic and unhinged (or lacking balance, as his father and uncle put it); as a poetaster and a bore.

If the latter views were understandable—Potocki could be his own worst enemy—they were also incomplete. Yes, he was an egotist, but, unusually for an egotist, he was well mannered. And his sense of humour meant that, as his close contemporaries, including Mason, had observed, he was also likeable. Furthermore, he could be considerate: one didn't always have to play his game. This is not to say that, when criticised or provoked, he could not be 'appallingly and unnecessarily rude', as Theodora once remarked. In fact, I soon became aware that the secret to a harmonious relationship with Potocki lay in accepting that certain games did have to be played—games which related to his inability to discuss rationally such matters as his Jewish paranoia, a defence of Leonard Woolf, a word of reason about his father. The games also included the incorrect use of his name and failure to use his title or recognise his aristocratic ancestry.

The latter transgressions, if seen as deliberate, would bring forth a particularly strong response, as C.H.R. Taylor, Chief Librarian at the Alexander Turnbull Library, discovered in 1959. Potocki, responding to Taylor's suggestion that the library 'relax formalities' with regard to his title and name, despatched to Taylor five irate, closely typed pages with an extended postscript, decrying his 'disgusting' attitude and any other attitude he, Potocki, had hitherto found wanting in life. Reading and enjoying this letter—Potocki was the master of the vituperative response—I could see that the origins of the tirade lay in his childhood and the dismissive treatment he had received at his trial. These experiences had permanently scarred him and, if someone touched one of the scars, he let them know about it. He could not help himself, hinting as much in the letter to Taylor: 'I am certainly quite unusually good-natured, far more so than ever Rex was... And I am philosophical from day to day while reserving the future. But once any of the matters in issue are stirred, I am full of perfect oceans of furious rage...'

I also knew it was important to use caution when contradicting him, for he reacted strongly against any suggestion that he was being told what to do. This reaction too was likely to have had roots in the bullying and powerlessness he experienced as a child, reinforced by his time in the Scrubs.

This is not to say that suggestions could not be made. He could be very biddable, particularly if he perceived himself to be bestowing a favour, or if the bidder was female. Melissa once asked him directly, 'When are you leaving? I'd like my room back,' and he immediately and graciously made arrangements to move on. Like most people, he responded to 'Do you think...' and 'Would you mind...', and as long as we remembered this we avoided the intransigence and seemingly unprovoked outbursts for which he was famous.

I was aware too that game-playing contributed to our mostly harmonious relationship. My combined closeness and distance as a cousin and the protocols we observed as hostess and guest meant that, although I was related and ready to accommodate him, I wasn't affected by or tied to him in confusing and emotionally complex ways.

The differing faces of Potocki were also present in his writing. Reading through some 200 poems from his vast collection, and contrasting them with the provocative, albeit often humorous, edge of his pamphlets, I was reminded how frequently he confounded the precept of essential eccentric. While he met Weeks's tests in so many ways, he was not, unlike most eccentrics, immovable at the centre of his universe. As his poetry (and behaviour) often showed, he was also capable of gentleness, attentiveness and a lyrical appreciation of nature, beauty and life's smallest pleasures. And, just as he could be talkative and time-consuming, he could also be thoughtful and patient. I recall especially the letter he took the time to send to the teenage daughter of friends of ours (with whom he usually stayed when he was in Auckland) when she took up smoking. Suggesting that she think of the effects on her body, he wrote:

> You can't get another body till your next incarnation, and even then, the new body You do get will be influenced by what You have done this time round.
>
> It is not so terribly uncommon to be a beautiful and kissable young girl, but your object should be to be a beautiful old lady, whom boys will want to kiss when You are Ninety.

Reflecting, as I often did, on his success with women—although not necessarily with wives—it occurred to me that, beyond his good looks and the charm of his archaic other-worldliness, perhaps the poetic side of his personality was the key here. Unlike some New Zealand male poets of his generation who asserted their masculinity by engaging in exaggerated male behaviour, he was secure in his role as a poet, and as a participant in what he perceived to be the male poetic heritage of classicism, learning and the study of language. He was not concerned with promoting his maleness in acts of mateship or the rituals of beer drinking, or other overt behaviours. For him art was all, poetry was the pinnacle of art, and the poet, 'at the back of written poetry', as his foreword to *Surprising Songs* proclaims, was 'the outrider of the hordes of men . . . the avatar bearing in his own being a light against the darkness'. There was no higher masculine calling. He showed his strength, therefore, in subtle ways: in assurance, manners and an appealing independence of spirit; in humour and a genuine liking for women. He listened to women, looked at them, made them feel they were special. He acknowledged their spirit as well as their sexuality:

> Most men have union with a woman's flesh,
> and nothing else: I with her whole being.
> I find you more attractive when your fresh
> intelligence and wit inform your seeing.
> (from 'Saint Valentine's Day', written for Fritzi, 1972)

And what of his poetry? 'I write three forms,' Potocki said in old age, commenting on his prolific output, his tongue lightly in the side of his cheek: 'satirical poetry in order to castigate my enemies, love poetry in order that I may praise the charms of female admirers, and serious poetry in order to fathom what I feel are profound spiritual issues.' He also said: 'All manner of poetry is possible, all modes, except that practised by the profoundly ungifted modern intellectual proletariat.'

Comment on his poetry varies. While there have always been small presses keen to publish him, modern mainstream opinion has mostly been negative, when it hasn't ignored him entirely. Even his early work, once well regarded, is now seen by some as more indicative of a youthful facility for good imitation (a facility which might explain his success as a translator) than an original talent. It is my view that, with the leaving of New Zealand, the lifting of restraints and the freeing of his latent eccentricity in London, this facility—this talent, perhaps—eventually became trapped inside the folds of his cloak. The poet as a writer was overtaken by the poet as a person. 'Let us talk less about poetry and more about the Poet,' he wrote in *Surprising Songs*. 'For poetry without the Poet is as stale and empty as a land without a king.' Ortega said that the great poets are those who have listened greatly. Well, Potocki was a talker, a thinker and certainly a watcher, but how effectively, I wonder, as his eccentricity flourished and, later, as he emerged from prison forever wronged, defiant and political, did he listen and see? As Cresswell observed, he was at his best as a poet when he was satirical, whimsical, playing with words. I cannot determine when 'Chorus of Poles' was written, but its lines are typical of Potocki when he was not on his best poetic behaviour:

> Rat-traps for satraps,
> samovars—poison-jars
> for commissars and red tsars;
> pot-hooks for politruks,
> preambles, shambles,
> rambles mid brambles,
> jakes for snakes,
> and wakes for fakes.

I also found the simplicity of some of his love poems appealing:

> You are in fact the same girl, the same
> in life, in death, in the dreaming sleep between . . .
> (from 'That Treasure', written for Fritzi, 1973)

and, like Fairburn, who wrote to Allen Curnow in 1945 that poems by Potocki (and Cresswell) carried 'romanticism to the length of a contortionist act' yet saw 'some virtue in them for all that', I acknowledge Potocki's resolve that his poetry, above all, affirm the importance of feeling.

His talents as a translator of poetry, on the other hand, were highly praised. Wiktor Weintraub of Harvard University, for example, introduced his English translation of *Forefathers* as 'the first translation which the reader can enjoy as true poetry'. While the celebrated French literary critic Orion, writing in *L'Action Française* on 13 April 1939, believed that Potocki had translated the work of poet and political theorist Charles Maurras into English verse of the same standard as the originals: the rhymes were better than one wanted to believe possible, he said, while the sense, the sound and the rhythm were incredibly faithfully rendered. The Maurras translations were similarly praised by Pierre Pascal, translator of Edgar Allan Poe and editor of the review *Eurydice*. Pascal wrote the same year that they were beautiful, and extremely successful, and that the virtuosity with which they had been executed was so powerful that one remained truly astonished by it. Even Maurras himself expressed admiration: he had been able personally to admire the elegance and precise truth with which both the sense and the rhythm had been captured, he wrote in *L'Action Française*, 6 November 1939.

As to the other 'facts' or public views—yes, he was a monologist, and as such could certainly be a bore. When he came to stay, we would find the first couple of weeks difficult, and the evening meals particularly taxing as wine only increased his volubility. Each evening midnight would roll by as, eyes glazed, plates empty, we would quietly yawn and wait at the table for an appropriate moment in the conversation to excuse ourselves. '. . . an eccentric will maunder on relentlessly, regardless of fire or flood, and if his interlocutor walks out of the room, he will follow him', confirms Weeks, who found that, in terms of thought, language and communication abnormalities, 'derailment and loss of goal' are significantly less frequent among eccentrics than non-eccentrics. However, if Potocki was given time to settle, some sort of 'inner audience' would assert itself and he would fit comfortably into family life.

In fact, monologues aside, I often felt grounded, even reassured, when he was around, responses I attributed to his encyclopedic knowledge, confidence and general air of invincibility. These responses I now also see in terms of his entelechy or particular talent for motivation, a quality often seen in eccentrics. Being near someone with strong self-determination and vision is said to give others hope and determination, and this is one of the qualities that makes many eccentrics engaging and endearing.

Was Potocki homophobic? I believe not. In response to suggestions that he might himself be homosexual—as a child accused by his father, as a young man in prison, as a close friend of Fairburn—he vigorously and disparagingly rejected the claims. But, as he told me himself, and as his response to Cresswell at a time when society was strongly homophobic suggests, the sexual orientation of others was not an issue with him—a view consistent with his moral code.

Mentally unstable? Discounting his flashes of anger, I believe Potocki accommodated more of the world than one might think, and while it is very likely that he suffered from depression as a child ('a most frightful nightmare . . . and it seemed interminable, but at last with adolescence I began to waken, and slowly to live'), his adult life demonstrated that in fact he was an extraordinary survivor. Here again, Weeks's study seems relevant. Identifying what he personally considers to be the single most defining value of eccentrics, Weeks cites 'their courage and resilience under fire, on an ongoing basis'.

At this point it occurred to me that the issue of truth was becoming a preoccupation. It kept rounding the corner, asking: 'How is it that you think you knew Potocki? You were a late-comer to his life, an occasional participant. Where are you finding this truth? In the transcripts of interviews? Dialogue? In letters (the true "fossils of feeling" that Janet Malcolm speaks about in her meditation on biography)?'

One day, my mind went back to the small room in the city where I had unpacked the archive. Here, quite early on, as I was kneeling on the floor—back stiff, knees sore—from beneath the dust, and pages still damp with the earth and rain of France, a sense of Potocki I had not previously recognised had begun to emerge. Here in the quiet room with his letters, the small notes to himself, the invoices, lists and receipts, the 'fact' of him had become overlaid with his familiarity—the scent and fine ash of incense he left in circles on his desk; his hands and feet, lean, always tanned; the small movement at the side of his mouth when he was concentrating or reading. I recalled his quiet way with paper, his light step, and each morning, as he left the house and I checked his room, the undented stillness of his bed.

Had the process of biography and memoir begun with my first

awareness of him? With my mother's impatient remark, or the photo with the cat he called Franco—the first time I noticed him?

In 1966, before Potocki returned to Draguignan, Rigby Graham, on assignment from the *Private Library* to investigate the forthright yet sparsely documented world of Potocki and compile a checklist of his work, traced him to Lovelace's Copse. In a feature article for the spring 1967 edition, he described his arrival:

> I reached a five-barred gate leaning drunkenly open, halfway up a steep slope leading into a field. Turning in before quite realising where I was, the car lurched and bounced to a shuddering halt, hub deep in a rut, beside an assortment of corrugated and asbestos sheeted huts, and a heap of brick ends, broken pipes, bits of wire, wood and old iron bars. An outburst of frenzied barking from a bevy of alsatians kennelled in an engineless old Austin reverberated across the vale. It did not seem at all likely that this could be the place, so reversing hastily to escape the noisy dogs, I started to slip and slide back down the slope.

As he passed the gate, Graham noticed a small paper sign above the letter box, bearing 'in faded typing the legend "The Mélissa Press"'.

> As I was trying to decide whether to go forward or back, a figure strode through the gate in the wire fence. He wore a pink shirt and riding breeches and his bare feet were in sandals. Despite the incongruity of this dress in these surroundings, it was obvious before he spoke that this was the Count. Courteously and graciously I was welcomed and invited into his home.

Graham found himself in an enclosed field with a couple of Jersey cows, a copse of trees and a 'long low building of the kind used for deep litter chicken houses'. Inside there were the usual Potocki accompaniments: books, piano, Siamese cats and printing equipment. A litter of kittens miaowed on a bed 'and a young bull calf looked wistfully into the room from the other side of a low window'.

The room was sparsely furnished and the double bed, which was covered with a gold bedspread, also served as table, chairs and settee. Graham noted that food had been placed out of reach of the cats in baskets which hung from the roof, and there was a jug of milk 'still warm and frothy' on a small chest by the bed. As the cats jumped and thundered overhead in the space between ceiling and roof, tea, bread and honey were served, 'the tea from a Japanese porcelain teapot on which the broken spout had been carefully replaced by a rubber antisplash extension for a water tap'.

Some of Graham's impressions of his Dorset visit coincided with my own visit to Draguignan: the uncertain access, the scattered building materials, the gracious welcome and off-beat hospitality. Even the colours of the shirt and riding breeches were similar, and I acknowledged his use of the word 'strode': my own first impression of Potocki had been the long assurance of his stride.

Graham obviously found Potocki good copy, for he made two visits to Lovelace's Copse (the second with Rod Cave, editor of the forthcoming edition of *The Private Library*) and the article which followed offered a deftly observed account of Potocki's circumstances (although, as Cave tantalisingly noted in his preface, many questions remained unanswered).

The concluding description of the second visit has Graham, Cave and Potocki 'struggling for three-quarters of an hour' in calf-deep mud, frantically trying to free his car 'from the morass into which it had sunk during the hours we had been there'. Graham writes:

> We put brick ends, pieces of wood, old sacks into the slimy ruts and under the wheels, trying to give them something on which to grip. As the front wheels spun, hissed and burnt we were splattered—our clothes and faces thickened and grimy. Eventually the Count harnessed his little Citroën (476cc, complete with French, Polish and English nationality plates) with a coil of wire to my front bumper on the Morris. I thought if it tears the bumper off it will be worth it to get out of this mess.

In a scene which might have been a sketch of his life, Potocki's Citroën strained resolutely over and over against what seemed like impossible odds, finally breaking the wire, but moving the Morris far enough for its wheels to take hold. Graham and Cave had departed abruptly and thankfully, their last view of him 'in his wide skirted green tweed coat, knee breeches and clogs, smiling and waving before striding back to his printing press'.

# FIFTEEN

## Resolution

*Wild Oats (1927) has been sold lately [1974] in Tasmania at 150 dollars. Odd Numbers of the Right Review have been selling at over ten pounds each (four hundred times the published price).*

Potocki, once again resident in Draguignan, moved beyond late middle age in excellent health. He attributed his energy and absence of illness to his pagan prayers; his consumption of garlic and raw onion, honey, milk, olive oil and red wine; his naked sun-baths, during which he believed exposing the groin to the sun was beneficial for encouraging the production of cortisone; and his conviction of the truth of astrology. The herb comfrey—'it was called *conferva* by the Romans, from the Latin verb *confervere*, to grow together'—also featured. He always carried some in his car, convinced of its healing properties, 'particularly its ability to heal or knit damaged or split bone . . . for it heals through the skin and across the flesh'.

Perhaps his preoccupation with having himself heard, his endless schedule of writing, printing and stirring himself up against anyone who opposed him, was also good for his health. Well into his eighties he still worked more than a ten-hour day, adamant that his dislike of exercise and his regimen of regular sex was also in part responsible.

In 1967, however, at the age of sixty-four, he was obliged to have prostate surgery. On 9 October he wrote to his friend the Harley Street specialist Hindenach, from Chesières, Fritzi's home in Switzerland:

Lieber Johann!
. . . Well, I had to be operated for the prostate also . . . Mademoiselle Jaggi [Fritzi] who had come hastily down from Switzerland, decided to take me back (by train) to Switzerland where I was operated on by a fashionable, and I think very competent surgeon . . . He seemed

very surprised at my rapid recovery but he said an enlarged prostate is 'not a disease, but a state'. The whole thing has cost me a small fortune but at least I have been properly looked after . . .

He returned to Draguignan three weeks after surgery by train, accompanied by his Siamese cat Owka. Given to him as a kitten in 1952, Owka travelled everywhere with him, usually by car. Much as he indulged her, he was particular about her behaviour inside the villa and, when he stayed with us, our own cat Peta, when she ventured onto the bench or the table, was always gently admonished with 'Even Owka was not allowed on the table'.

After the operation, he learnt to his profound disappointment that he was now sterile. But the disappointment did not linger: his wartime translation of *Forefathers* had attracted the favourable attention of the Polish literary establishment, and the Polish Cultural Foundation in London had made arrangements to publish it, advancing him £50 on royalties at twelve per cent. 'A jewish professor at Harvard . . . has written superlative praise of it,' he told Hindenach. 'He is a Polish jew and knows quite well I am anti-jewish.'

During the next two years interest in Potocki deepened. Commentators began to notice that his seemingly wayward life in the twenties, thirties and forties had not been out of step with the sexual revolution, freedoms and climate of protest of the sixties. With this recognition, and small presses in Britain and Canada keen to print his poetry, he was able to write with satisfaction to his former benefactor and since sometime detractor, Brian Guinness, now Lord Moyne, about his encouraging revival. 'I always had the impression,' he wrote, 'even in the old days, that you were afraid of making a fool of yourself, and that it was only Huxley's moral support that enabled you to help the *Right Review* . . . Anyway, you no longer risk so much making a fool of yourself by helping that long-haired, crimson robed crank, Potocki, not so much because for long past I have my hair short and hardly ever wear my robes, as because the tide seems to be turning anyway.'

While his search for recognition was proving fruitful, he was finding his personal life less fulfilling. In 1969, dejected because he had been unable to persuade Fritzi to marry him or to move permanently to Draguignan, he suggested that a Welsh girl, whom he had met in Dorset, come and stay. Cathleen Owen, aged twenty-four, enticed by an extended vacation as cook-housekeeper-conversationalist in the Provençal countryside, left her small daughter in Dorset with her mother, and moved in at short notice. 'She was divorcing her husband, an English chappie who was completely unfit for her,' Potocki wrote to me. 'She lived with me from 1969, but she and I were lovers before she went and got married.'

Cathleen found the south of France 'lovely to live in' and, although on arrival she became embroiled in an argument with Potocki that was so heated she nearly took the next boat back to Britain, she remained at the Villa Vigoni, on and off, for the next seven years. She quickly became aware, as we had, that the secret to living with Potocki lay in accepting that certain subjects could and should not be argued.

It was Cathleen who was responsible for obtaining and distributing the pirated editions of *Dogs' Eggs* from The Shack Press at the Vallon de Gandi. She appears to have embraced life in Provence, showing an interest in and flair for not only printing, but the ongoing renovation of the villa and the Shack, and unlike Theodora, who, having argued with her father, drifted out of his life, she remained on good terms with Potocki after she left Draguignan, losing touch with him only after he returned to New Zealand.

In 1971, she gave birth to a son, Gwilym—not Potocki's child—in his large comfortable bed in the upstairs bedroom. She had found the induced birth of her daughter in hospital distressing, and had decided that this delivery would take place at the villa. The hospital was only ten minutes' drive away and she had every confidence in Potocki, to whom she had given full instructions. Potocki was similarly relaxed about the impending event. On the morning in question, Cathleen having been in labour only an hour, he finished his breakfast and safely delivered Gwilym, his godson. 'He was terribly proud,' said Cathleen. He announced Gwilym's birth in an eighteenth and occasional issue of the *Right Review*, dated summer 1973: 'Gwilym George Owen, who was born on the 25th April 1971 with His Majesty as *accoucheur*, was presented at the Altar of the Sun . . .'

The trio spent seven 'mostly happy' years together. 'I stayed that long,' Cathleen told me, 'because there was a whole different atmosphere. He was the only person who'd ever encouraged me to write, to extend myself. I pruned olive trees, made stone walls, discovered how to build . . . learned there was nothing to building.'

The villa, moreover, despite its architectural shortcomings, was in many ways a relaxed environment in which to raise a child. There was no television, no traffic, no demanding telephone and, although the plumbing and power supply were inadequate and there were no labour-saving devices, neither were there many of the strictures of society. The neighbours were well spaced and pragmatic, meals were simple affairs, and dust and disorder did not matter. Besides, it would have been a disaffected child who could not be happy in Potocki's kingdom of household animals, sun and wilderness. Potocki might also have been writing of Gwilym's freedoms when he wrote of his Siamese cats, at ten am, in 1973:

> Some cats
> live in flats
> and the back yard
> is hard—
> but for ours, space abounds:
> they have ample grounds
> they climb trees
> as they please
> in the donkey's pepper they creep
> over the wild thyme they leap.
> They go where they like
> in the rosemary and spike
> they roam everywhere
> in the perfumed air
> unlike those cats
> who live in flats.
> ('Our Eight Siamese')

Just as Cathleen had trusted Potocki to deliver Gwilym, she was also comfortable about leaving him in his care, even when she travelled as far afield as England. 'Yes,' he wrote to me, 'I was landed with the exclusive care of a baby—well, he was aged about twenty months—and I was ill as well, so that when I wanted to stay in bed I had to get up to change his nappies, feed him and the like.'

By 1971 the electricity lines and water supply extended as far as the cottage and, after arranging for an electrician to put in a couple of lights, he completed the installation over the next two years himself. With the Shack property also improved, he advertised it as holiday accommodation under the heading: 'DO YOU WANT A CHEAP & UNUSUAL HOLIDAY?'

Count Potocki would let you a picturesque, primitive, small, stone house in a large olive & pine grove—no mod. cons. but very comfortable bed(s). 14 miles to coast. Lovely surroundings, sunbathing 'in the altogether' cannot be observed nor interrupted. Say £5 a week, less for longer. Owner lives round the corner, could be helpful . . . ACRE OF GROVE FOR SALE ALSO.

It seems there was at least one would-be taker. An irate letter from a lady in Surrey, who had confirmed that four adults and a number of children would 'rent the shack' for a week, only to have the arrangement fall through, expresses 'frustration and anger' at the inefficient handling of her booking, and the fact that 'at no time . . . was mention made that we would be sharing certain facilities in the house with you'.

Now past seventy, Potocki was working as never before. In between writing, printing and translating he was completing the garage, adding a room and attempting to catalogue his archive. Although his pamphlets still tended towards the political and polemic, a less preoccupied note was finding its way into his poetry. He wrote of his garden, his goat, his rooster, his pig in Dorset—a pedigree Wessex Saddleback sow. After Owka's death, at twenty, in 1972, he published a booklet which collected the verses he had written about cats.

With writing and printing finally providing a living, Potocki was finding that there was less time for correspondence. As far back as 1971 he had sent me a letter indicating frustration with this new situation:

. . . I mean I have so much to do that I don't know where to begin. How can I sit down to the typewriter when I am folding sheets, sewing up books, or making covers for them? Or when I am printing? Printing is a craft which demands infinite patience and uses up a great deal of time. I am probably the only person round here who has virtually no spare time at all. Or while I am mixing cement and building picturesque stone walls? Why doesn't the Prime Minister of New Zealand come here and do some of this for me? I feel posterity will say I was more fitted to rule a country than he was.

Star rising or not, he continued to pursue unfashionable causes, despatching his views to mail-order *aficionados* and enemies on a range of issues, including his old hobby-horse heredity ('Blue Blood in the Butter Republic') and Britain's ill-advised adoption of the decimal system ('The Decimal Superstition'). A satirical poem, written in 1940 by 'Prince Bobowski Poet laureate to the Bank of Poland', chastising Lord Moyne for addressing him as Mr Wladyslaw ('Guinness is Good For You') was also released.

There were many other pamphlets with intriguing titles: 'Columbus Discovers Ireland', 'Were Bach's Ancestors Polish?', 'The Polish Daily Prefers Lies', 'Ungallant Gallantry', 'Some Future Butler' and 'The King of Poland's Plan for Rhodesia'. In 'That Impossible Fellow' he fumes about the disinclination of 'publishers to publish works by Us' and recalls the affair of the anthology of New Zealand verse, *Kowhai Gold*, in which a poem 'of Ours ... was included without so much as a By-Your-Leave, and without the family patronymic Potocki, while infamous poetasters had pages & pages', as a result of which he had 'insisted on their taking this poem out'.

The *Kowhai Gold* affair further illustrates his assertion of principle against his own literary interest, as with Gollancz and Wishart. Were such stands taken, I wondered, purely as a matter of principle, or was there also some sort of subtext? He did it again and again, alienating those who might have advanced his literary career. Was there more mileage, perhaps, in being a candidate than a player? In sustaining personal myths? Were the principled stands just great stories—or was a sense of personal liberty the real issue? 'True eccentrics are never acting,' writes Weeks. 'They are strong individuals ... They repudiate nothing. They refuse to compromise.'

He also took time to defend his literary reputation when 'some megalomaniac calling himself an expert' introduced 130 unauthorised changes into the text of his translation, *Forefathers*, at the time of its publication by the Polish Cultural Foundation. 'There will simply have to be a row about this,' he declared as he made arrangements to take the foundation to court. 'Suffice to say that none of the alterations were really necessary, most of them were clumsy and incompetent, a large proportion of them abolished the rhythm or the rime or both, and some of them were downright disastrous.'

In January 1970, the case of *Potocki v the Polish Cultural Foundation Ltd* was heard before Judge Granville Slack in the West

London County Court. As was his habit, Potocki conducted the case himself. On the morning of the hearing, the *Times* previewed the suit. In a lengthy article which recalled his obscenity trial, wartime politics and private press, it reported that:

> The Count will wear long crimson robes at the hearing at West London County Court. He claims his title through his great-grandmother Princess Czarporyska [*sic*] from the Silesian Piast family which, he says, as the oldest surviving line of the original Polish dynasty, gives him a better claim to the throne than the Queen of England to hers... He says his religion is 'beauty and one's friends.' Some of his friends, he adds, liken him to John Wilkes: 'but I think they're mad; all I have in common with him is the love of freedom.'

There was standing-room only in the courtroom, and much laughter was reported. 'Even the Judge was holding his face between his palms so as not to burst out laughing,' Potocki told me by letter. Later, he produced a pamphlet, 'Printed by hand and foot at the Mélissa Press', which detailed the proceedings, including his cross-examination of the foundation's chief witness, who had agreed to remove the changes but failed to do so before printing took place:

'Apart from the Judgement itself,' he writes, 'the most important moment of the case was when Dr Czerwinski ("the Bald-Headed Old Crocodile", as the Baroness von Zittau [Dorli] persisted in calling him) was in the witness box. He was wearing a theatrically conspicuous Hearing Aid, a real Beggar's Opera effort. When he signed the undertaking at his solicitor's office he was wearing no such thing.'

'When was the book printed?' Potocki asked him.

'In August.'

'So you were lying all along, and never at any time intended to keep your written promises?' Czerwinski did not reply.

'Is it not the case that you have all along pretended that the book was printed during the riots in France, and now you admit it was printed a couple of months later?'

Czerwinski, fiddling with his hearing aid, appeared confused and did not answer. Potocki, unable to get an answer out of 'this bumptious old donkey', then addressed the judge: 'It seems to be useless questioning this witness, Your Honour. He reminds one of the ghosts in the play itself, whom the Warlock is unable to exorcise:

Good God! How horrible! He balks,
he neither goes away nor talks!'

The editor responsible for the changes to the translation, who is described in the pamphlet as 'lurking in cowardly anonymity', was not identified in court. 'However,' the report continues, 'the Royal Polish Counter-Espionage has discovered, from sources right within the orbit of the criminal group that We were mistaken in the sex of Sir Mighty Nitwit, Ph.D. It never occurred to Us that a woman would be such a fool.—Sir Mighty Nitwit, Ph.D., in reárl layfe is merely Mrs Marja Danilewicz, A.L.A., & you can go & have a look at her at the Polish Library, 9 Princes Gardens, London, S.W.7.'

On 5 February 1970 Judge Granville Slack, who had reserved his decision, found in Potocki's favour. Potocki was awarded £40 damages and costs, which he elected to forgo in favour of possession of the remainder of the edition. He had the books sent to the Villa Vigoni, and sold them from there. He corrected them in over a hundred places by hand. In my own copy, printed 1968, he noted on the back of the title page: 'Abominable improvements deleted for Stéphanie and John', and made the changes boldly in blue biro.

With the foundation case settled, he turned to the task of cataloguing his library and archive, and made arrangements to have an interim valuation made of his papers: 'The valuers [a Dr McCoy and his colleague from London who spent eight days studying the material] put its value at around £6000, and said I should on no account accept less than half that sum.' This valuation did not include 'any of the New Zealand stuff, which contained letters from Walter D'Arcy Cresswell and R.A.K. Mason, nor a set of poems in manuscript by Maxwell Rudd.'

As for his library, he hoped that someone in the family would be intelligent enough to want to use it. 'Isn't there one of you who is going to learn Polish, French, Italian etc and become a proper cultured European?' he asked. 'The fact that I have a private library in twenty five different languages proves that brains are lurking round the family somewhere, I think.'

By now he had entered into negotiations with the Alexander Turnbull Library in Wellington over letters he had received from Rex Fairburn. 'They offered me [NZ]$750 for his letters from July 1926 to July 1927. Initially I asked for £1,000, but I changed this in the end to ten thousand Swiss francs.' His relationship with the Turnbull Library had been awkward, partly as a result, as his earlier correspondence with Taylor demonstrated, of the suspicion with which many in literary New Zealand regarded him. Take, for example, a note from Denis Glover to the library on 15 November 1959 about Potocki's own letters, which comments: 'They make a fascinating story of the flowering and final ripe-rottenness of a rare eccentric . . .'

The awkwardness continued. Beset by poverty and pressure of work, and affronted partly by the fact that the library's interest lay with Fairburn and not with him, but mostly by offers he considered insulting, he rapidly lost patience, writing to me on 15 February 1971 that he had remade his will and left all his New Zealand manuscripts, including the letters, to the Polish Library in Paris.

The correspondence between Potocki and the Turnbull makes entertaining reading. While the Turnbull cajoles and flatters, Potocki responds sharply and with vintage indignation. He is unimpressed by the library's assurances that $750 is 'a not unreasonable counter proposal' in line with 'the current international market price for New Zealand manuscripts of this kind', and scathing of its expressed hope that he will accept the offer 'in your [his] interest, as well as for the future of our own Fairburn collection'. He ignites the usual preoccupations—his trial, his royalist convictions, his own unrecognised greatness—adds the customary accelerants—democratic oppression and the war against Germany—and repeatedly decries its attempts to mislead him. His letter on 21 July 1970 to A.G. Bagnall, Chief Librarian during this period, is typical:

Dear Sir,
. . . In my letter of 21st May to Mrs Margaret Scott, I did not say I was willing to sell Fairburn's letters to me for $2,000. What I said was, that I was willing to send a list of them as a preliminary, 'provided that there is no question of anything less than a thousand pounds'. 2,000 N.Z. dollars is not a thousand pounds, but is five percent less, as you know. Thus you have had the list of the letters by false pretences, just as you have illegally, in breach of my copyright, photocopies or microfilms of my letters to Fairburn.

I therefore re-state the matter: I am willing to sell the letters for one thousand pounds, or ten thousand Swiss francs, whichever be the higher on the Swiss market at the time of payment . . . You refer to the price at which you have purchased 'similar letters' but you know very well that no 'similar letters' exist. You yourselves out there have made Fairburn into a Little Tin God, so you cannot expect to buy this Tin Godhead's letters at a derisory price . . .

And the long letter of 12 January 1971, in which he advises Bagnall of his decision about the Polish Library in Paris, is a Potocki classic. It concludes:

. . . Wherefor [sic] WE, Władysław the Fifth King of Poland and Hungary and other Territories (as the Nazi radio used to say) being further Poet, Prophet, magician, and correspondent with the illustrious Dead and even the Living, took thought and decided to foil the plans of the wicked. Namely We are now sixtyseven, and the Turnbull might think unto its dishonest self, that We might shortly Kick the Bucket, whereupon it could swizzle the various MSS and the like, out of our innocent Daughter, the Princess Maud Wanda of Poland, for little or nothing. We therefore drew up a new will, wrote it out in Our Own Hand, and signed it before reputable English witnesses at Bussana Vecchia in Italy. It contains the following words: 'Further in view of the general mean and avaricious attitude of the Turnbull Library which I esteem to be an anti-cultural institution, and of an Act of the New Zealand Parliament which it has procured to prevent the exportation of manuscripts and the like from New Zealand, a parallel to which in the pre-War Polish republic operated to the great detriment of the nearest heirs of Frederic Chopin, and which I consider illegal immoral and contrary to the real interests of the human race; in order to check-mate this sort of blackmail I bequeath all the manuscripts and typescripts of the late Arthur Rex Dugard Fairburn, Walter D'Arcy Cresswell, Ronald Alison Kells Mason, Maxwell Billens Rudd and other New Zealand writers of which I may die possessed to the Biblioteka Polska (Polish Library) . . . with the proviso that N.Z. citizens should be required to pay for access to them'.

The scene that winter is easily set. While Potocki struggles with a thin sky and an indifferent harvest, and breakfasts on an egg boiled over bottled gas, in Wellington 'autocrats' such as Bagnall 'live well on the heritage given to the world by people like me'. They sit at comfortable desks, their coffee, air temperature and retirement schemes constant. They ask him to 'give' them the assets he has struggled to preserve from dampness, mice ('the dirty democratic beasts') and the 'frightful misery' in which he has lived. They do not agree that he should try for the best price he can get. So, the 233 pages of Fairburn letters, clippings and envelopes which he has spent his life protecting—even transporting to Poland and back—are contained in a wooden box in the basement, and they will stay there. Were it not for people like him 'there just wouldn't be any libraries'.

Cathleen Owen, present throughout his later years of negotiation with the Turnbull, put his position succinctly: 'He was living poorly,' she told me, 'and they were expecting him to accept poor offers. They would say, "If you're not willing to sell el cheapo, you're a load of shit." They wanted those letters for tenpence.'

In the end, however, despite informal advice in 1970 from his valuers—who were 'emphatic' the Fairburn letters listed in the inventory compiled for the Turnbull 'were worth a thousand pounds'—poverty, flattery and the library prevailed. In 1976 Lauris Edmond, who was about to begin editing Fairburn's letters and needed to secure the Potocki collection, was encouraged to approach him directly during a visit to London and Europe. In *The Quick World*, she explains that Denis Glover, who had introduced her to the project, had arranged with Jim Traue, the new Chief Librarian, that she could increase the Turnbull's offer from $750 to $1000. She traced Potocki to London, where he had taken a flat while he arranged the sale of his small property in Dorset, and found him charming in slippers, 'economising' on the heating and talking 'impenetrably' and at length on the customary subjects. Having endured a burnt meal of parsnips and chops, Edmond broached the subject of the letters, and by flattery and cajolement persuaded him to agree to their sale. However, Potocki suddenly asked, 'Who are you buying them for?' and, caught off guard, she replied, 'The University of Auckland Library.' Traue, who remembers Edmond's anxious call in the middle of the night asking 'Can we cover this up?', quietly took care of arrangements. The letters were despatched to and paid for by Auckland, and copies made their way to the Turnbull.

Later, Potocki would discover the subterfuge and, while he maintained relatively cordial relations with Traue, Edmond became *persona non grata*: 'It isn't that I don't want the letters published,' he would say to me angrily, 'I just don't want them published by *her*!' (I have little doubt that Edmond's uncomplimentary inclusion in the introduction to the Ospedaletti essay in 1986 was related to the Turnbull's unmasking; as was his indignant outing of the 'Privileged Tourist' as a former correspondent, the Turnbull Manuscripts Librarian Margaret Scott.)

A letter sent to me at the time of his stand-off with the Turnbull confirmed the increasing value of his work. 'I mustn't forget to tell you', he wrote, 'that recently Sotheby's, so famous in London, sold for fourteen pounds, a mere pamphlet of my poems, published for about seven shillings and sixpence about five years ago by Savage of Leicester, a man I have never even met.'

Potocki's financial burden was gradually easing. As the decade progressed, a bequest from the now-deceased Countess de Bioncourt, small but regular remittances from his father's estate in New Zealand, profits from his press and the occasional sale of archival material meant that he was finally feeling a degree of financial assurance. There was also security in knowing that, with the nearby military academy expanding and Draguignan itself creeping closer, the value of the villa and Shack properties—together with the piece of land he owned in the suburb of Flayosc—was rising.

This reassuring state of affairs did not mean, however, that Potocki had abandoned his frugal lifestyle, nor the meticulous checks and balances he had imposed on expenditure. Take, for example, the following entry in a ledger from this period:

| | |
|---|---|
| 1 Jan. | not in town |
| 2 Jan. | tip to telegraph boy 1.00 |
| | vegetables 2.50 |
| | meat for Owka 2.50 |
| | two spark plugs 8.60 |
| 6 Jan. | hook for window 1.50 |
| | After dinner at night main gas bottle expired = 15 days |
| 7 Jan. | was in town but spent nothing. |
| 8 Jan. | Air poste letter to Stéphanie Miller (Mrs) 80 |

The page had a supermarket ticket clipped to it, each item checked and ticked.

When I came upon detail of this nature in his archive—endless lists, cheque butts, financial records—I found myself wondering to what extent the exactness, at odds with his chaotic surroundings, was the result of living on the edge of poverty, and to what extent the legacy of his childhood and his trials—experiences which had created anxieties about access to food and reinforced a need to remain in control. And whether there was a connection with the hitherto unexplained termination of his previously amicable relationship with Terry Risk, which soured suddenly and for all time during their trip to Venice in late summer 1974.

This incident had been on my agenda for years, ever since I had discovered Risk's slim, hand-printed memoir *Why Potocki?* when researching the documentary. At the time Risk, who was clearly fascinated by Potocki, had attributed his abrupt dismissal to Potocki's eccentricity. He had supposed that Potocki inhabited a world peopled by foes, that 'it was a lonely battle he fought' and that it was enemies, not allies, he needed in life. But I had not been convinced that eccentricity in a broad sense was necessarily a factor.

The trip to Venice had taken place at Risk's instigation. He was staying at the villa at the time, as he had twice before, investigating the 'enigmatic' Potocki and his legendary Mélissa Press. Hoping to extend his research further, to the fifteenth-century Venetian printer Erhard Ratdolt, he had suggested that Potocki drive him to Venice so that Cathleen could see the city, and offered to pay half the expenses. Potocki, who was planning to travel to Ventimiglia in Italy to replenish his stock of paper and have his passport stamped (when his French residence permit expired in 1966 and the French bureaucracy 'made a fuss' about renewing it, he opted to become a tourist, thereafter leaving the country every three months and re-entering on a temporary permit), consulted his horoscope and agreed to take Risk the considerable extra distance to Venice.

The party, which included Gwilym, aged three, made the journey in Potocki's small Citroën, accompanied by supplies of water and food, camping necessities, and a rubber mattress strapped to the roof. With the car capable of a top speed of only 70 km/h and its erratic performance necessitating frequent stops for repairs—made by Potocki—the journey took two and a half days.

Tension between the two men appears to have been reasonably high. Risk remembers that he was 'breathless with nervousness' for much of the journey as Potocki took them through the dense Italian traffic up and down hills, along freeways and through interminable tunnels—in which Risk 'felt particularly vulnerable'—but was unable to assist with the driving because he was not covered by insurance. He found their overnight camping arrangements, which included mosquitoes, similarly frustrating.

In Venice, he did his research, only to find that when it was time to depart for Draguignan he was not wanted on the return journey—a dismissal for which no explanation was given. A month or so later he received a letter from Potocki accusing him of being a confidence trickster, and demanding payment of the small sum he owed Potocki for letters and publications he had sold on his behalf in the United States. A second letter from Potocki, dated 19 January 1975, fumed:

> I like your flaming effrontery: after the way you have behaved. You ought to have your neck wrung, in the most literal sense of the word, nor need you have any confidence that you will not undergo some such fate or analogous.

I had puzzled over Potocki's dismissal of Risk for years. Once I had ventured a question, only to receive a vague answer. Risk had been dishonest and Potocki was not inclined to discuss him further. However, the morning I came upon those meticulous columns of minor expenditure—which I found myself examining with the same sense of realisation that I experienced when reading the typescript—something clicked into place. Here were more chinks—more scars—in Potocki's seemingly subversive and unyielding persona. Here too was the effect of his struggle to stay free of conventional employment for the sake of his art, to make himself heard, and of the impoverishment and frugality necessary to his commitment. 'As private printers go,' Risk wrote, 'Potocki probably stands apart. Whatever can be said of him, it would never be that he was a hobbyist. For him printing was an act of commitment and of conscience.'

Placed alongside his enhanced sense of personal injustice—a flashpoint since childhood—and his anxiety about food, the columns pointed to the reason for 'the calculated insult at Venice'. Perhaps Risk had been seen as taking advantage of Potocki's hospitality; perhaps he had failed to account for a meal in a café, forgotten to pitch in with a camping fee, experienced a weak moment with the large basket or cool box in the back of the car. The reason, I decided, might have been as simple and as complex as that.

Despite the acrimonious footnote to their friendship, Risk's account of Potocki concludes on a generous note. He remembers his extraordinary vigour, his capacity for story-telling and his hospitality—particularly recalling the trouble Potocki went to one winter trying to improve the sealing in the guest room, and providing a heater which he would turn on before Risk went to bed. He declines to dismiss him as the 'arrogant crackpot' many believed him to be, acknowledges 'an ever-enlarging group of admirers, not his contemporaries, who see him as a rather lonely, romantic figure, possessed of an appealing nobility', and believes he will be remembered for his eccentricity, his obscenity trial and a number of his translations. He writes:

> ... granted that he was difficult, irritable, opinionated, and irascible, I also remember him as hospitable and generous in his own way, a wonderful talker, sharp-witted, and a master at letter-writing. He was undoubtedly one of the most interesting men I have known.

Potocki was entering old age. Indifferent health and diminished circumstances were circling his friends. A long-time friend, the poet and critic Kenneth Hopkins, wrote in 1975:

> My literary fortunes, despite my prestigious professorship, continue dicey, or (to be frank) don't exist at all. Nobody will publish my works any more and I am become a cipher and an hissing. However, I am too old to care and have been busy writing parodies ... I hope you are going happily in the world and I send you my best nearly forty-years-old affection.

Four years later Hopkins wrote in similar tone:

> Dear Geoffrey,
> Thank you for your letter and for the delightful cat poem ... Thank you also for the Christmas poem ... I don't issue cards at Christmas, keeping my slender means for drink instead, to drink the health of my dwindling circle of friends—who would have thought that Death would have undone so many? as the chap says (now also dead)

... Meanwhile, it is generally considered that I am unemployable. I have a little book on Llewelyn Powys coming out with an obscure publisher, otherwise I have no publishers any more and no prospects of getting one. ... I review books for the Norwich newspapers, read bad mss for a literary agent, and occasionally visit schools at £25 a time to tell children on no account to go into poetry writing for a career ...
Yours, if not forever, then for as long as may be ...

But Potocki had no literary fortune to lose, no declining career to lament. Encouraged by the recent interest in his work he was still pursing the fame he had failed to achieve as a young man. He was working furiously from dawn until dark, rising at six, cleaning up the terraces, doing work on the house, sorting his papers: 'So much sheer work in addition to the writing and printing.' He had also begun publishing his life-story in Polish—a defiant response to those in New Zealand who were seen to have professed interest in and then offended him.

He wrote to me on the back of a poem for the Saturnalia: 'That it is in Polish and not in English, is the fault of the Gang of Four—Dr Broughton, Alister Taylor, Keith Matthews, and "Lauris Edmond".' Matthews was the New Zealand lawyer who, in 1977, finally paid for and collected the Fairburn letters on behalf of the Turnbull Library, and delivered them to the New Zealand Embassy in Paris; and Taylor was a publisher who, having visited the villa at the request of the Turnbull, made plans to publish Potocki's life story—a proposition which folded when Taylor failed to provide a financial gesture of goodwill, and Potocki 'became irascible and made demands which couldn't be met'. Broughton was a Massey University lecturer whose mail went astray. In July 1970, when the troubled negotiations with the Turnbull Library were at their height, Broughton (now a professor of English at Massey), his wife and their two children spent four days in Draguignan while the academic, who had an interest in early New Zealand poetry, perused the sensitive collection of Fairburn letters. The family stayed in the Shack and ate at the villa and, in the manner of Risk, Broughton found Potocki to be 'friendly, charming and a genuine and generous host, even though he was living on very little'. He also found him to be 'highly eccentric, overpoweringly egotistical and extraordinarily intelligent'. And typically volatile, with a propensity for switching unexpectedly, almost mid-sentence, from urbane conversation to offensive tirades on subjects which included Bolsheviks, Jews and New Zealanders. The family's departure was amicable and, after their return to Palmerston North, Potocki wrote to Broughton. But the letter never arrived. When he failed to reply, Potocki took umbrage. A letter in Latin was sent expressing outrage that Fairburn was seen as the more important poet, and the incident, which prompted an ever-widening resentment that Potocki, financially stressed, was expected to contribute to the Fairburn legend at his own expense, saw Broughton join the cast list of those who conspired against him.

In 1979, the London-based *Art Monthly* published a tribute to Douglas Glass. It recalled their friendship in factually inaccurate terms and suggested that, as Potocki's name appeared in every memoir of the period, the Arts Council should consider asking him to open its Thirties Exhibition, 'provided of course that he wears the old regalia'. Responding to *Art Monthly*, he again demonstrated that he had lost none of his capacity for comeback. He said would *not* be dressed up and paraded around and, furthermore, he was tiring of public rumour and misrepresentation by the press, particularly as it so often appeared in tributes to others:

> ... neither I nor Glass were ever prosecuted in New Zealand for publishing allegedly pornographic poems (or prose) ... Glass never published anything whatever in his New Zealand days, and until I, with great skill and tact tutored him otherwise, spoke such execrable English, that there could be no question of his writing anything whatever that was publishable. There is no mention of Douglas Glass in the catalogues of the British Museum (British Library) as the author of any texts whatever. Just as a matter of interest, there are 68 entries relating to me ...

Despite its length, and many protestations, it was mild letter—by Potocki standards, a polite letter. With age and greater financial security, was a more temperate side emerging?

On 20 February 1982, a year before he set out by car to visit us in Edinburgh, he drafted the following poem at the Villa Vigoni at one pm on the back of a Westminster Bank account, having 'had the idea a couple of days ago':

We learn at last, when growing old,
how to live, the foe to fend,
the girl to approach, the means to acquire—
when to be, when not to be, bold,
how to arrive whither we tend,
how best to use the vital fire!

It could appear, the time's too late
our own mistakes to put to rights!
But yet I think, in another life
we shall have time to chisel Fate,
to correct our aim, adjust our sights,
and make amends to friends and wife.

## SIXTEEN

## Final Impressions

*O great unquiet world of men, be still!*
*Round you in the sun the green lawns lie golden,*
*the trees sigh comfortingly.*

It is July 1996. In the Draguignan countryside, on the other side of the small wood which meets above the middle of Le Chemin des Faïsses (formerly Le Chemin de St Martin), there's a numbered stake set in a pile of small stones. To the right of the stake there's the driveway, still only a track, still overgrown like the rest of the land. Our cab stops, and the driver winds down his window and peers uncertainly at the stake, the long grass, the mottled tiles struggling between trees in the distance.

'La maison?'

'Oui. Oui, la maison.'

The sun is hot enough for us to be sleeveless by mid-morning. The road is white and pleasantly dusty. There's a scent of pine and herbs in the driveway, a scattering of wind in the trees, only a breeze on the land, silent, deep with secrets, much as we remember it. We lift our lunch from the back of the cab—a green bottle of Badoit, baguettes filled with tomato and cheese, bananas, a packet of biscuits. 'Return at four,' we tell the driver, pointing to the stake, beckoning, stabbing our watches, steering wide mock-wheels in the air. Imitating the sound of his motor. 'Quatre heures, s'il vous plait.'

We had arrived the previous evening by train and checked into the Hotel du Parc, a pension on the edge of the old town in the Boulevard de la Liberté, near the Place du Dragon. I had telephoned Potocki immediately. We'd spoken twice since he had returned to France permanently in 1993, and he had not written. Sitting on the side of the bed waiting for him to answer the phone, I was anxious. News of him over the past three years had been sparse. He had rambled on the phone, spoken of having pizza delivered by taxi all the way from the town, and of people who entered the villa and threw away his papers. Telephone conversations with his nearest neighbour, Annie Larminach, had been limited by language difficulties, and we knew only that since his return a guardian appointed by the French courts had been taking care of his finances and assumed responsibility for his care. From time to time we had had a French friend in Wellington phone the guardian, a retired army officer, but feedback had been limited. In 1995 Potocki's land in the Vallon de Gandi had been sold to cover his living expenses and his likely admission to hospital or a home for the elderly. Meanwhile, Annie was doing his shopping and washing and providing an evening meal.

The telephone continued to ring. I was about to replace the receiver when a weak voice said, 'Oui?'

'Geoffrey,' I said, 'it's Stephanie.'

There was silence, and then only breathing.

'It's Stephanie, and John, from New Zealand.'

'Oh.' The reply came absently, as if from a distance.

'We're in Draguignan. We're coming to see you tomorrow.'

More silence, more breathing, and then a thin click from the receiver, as if being placed on a hard surface, and the sound of shuffling, as if he were looking through papers or moving about in his bed. The phone stayed off the hook. 'I don't think he'll know us,' I said to John.

The beehive looks lonely. The garage is empty. We find the Renault near the road in long grass, some distance from its battery and front seat, its windscreen shattered. Thick bushes cover the front of the cottage where a chair is trapped in the undergrowth, still upright as if it stumbled outside and forgot to return—wrought iron, white, ghostly. Annie's dog barks in the distance, her cockerel can be heard closer at hand. Her house can't be seen through the trees but the wire mesh of her hen-run is coming up, to the left of the villa, straight ahead on the boundary.

Potocki appears to be hidden away. The front door has been locked with a large key, and the living room is dark. There's a dusty overcoat on a nail in the porch wall, and an unfurled umbrella covered in cobwebs.

Access to the unlocked bindery, where he was once easily seen folding sheets and sewing up booklets, is blocked by gas bottles, water containers and half-empty cartons. In the printery and archive, the earth floor is damp, stones have been sent through the window, papers sprawl on the floor and in the typesetting corner glass has sprinkled itself in the type and the trays are askew. John picks up the invoice for a printing commission in 1953, and a handful of poems and creased letters. The black body of his press sits in a corner. The porch, which was never properly finished, crumbles beneath a disorganised insurrection of vines. We move around the side of the cottage to the upper level and the back garden, and call out and peer through the white lace curtains on the French doors to his bedroom. We knock, try the handle. The door is not locked.

He is there, but we hardly see him at first. He hovers in dim light between his piano and wide bed, and a table still set with the remains of a meal, holding a cane. His hair is untrimmed, he has a beard—white, long and surprisingly thick—and his legs are shiny and thin beneath a nightshirt and short dressing-gown.

I take his arm and assist him to a soft chair. He sits and looks at us, the light of interest gone from his eyes. 'I'm Stephanie, from New Zealand,' I say. He remembers only a house with a sea wall and a beach, a country with a beach the colour of sand, and his mother who painted the Waikato River which hangs in oils on his wall. He believes we are all on the bridge of a ship, and I see that on the table alongside his bed the telephone receiver has not been replaced.

It is Guy Fawkes night in Wellington, 1993. The air is chilly. Potocki and I are side by side on dining chairs watching the celebrations from the window.

'Sitting here like royalty,' I say as the family light crackers on the lawn and wave sparklers at the sea.

'The King and Queen of Poland,' he replies. He's been talking all day. This morning he didn't like the mug he kept his toothbrush in, at lunchtime the tuna sandwich was too salty, this evening someone was stealing his socks and he wouldn't believe they were being washed.

'You tell lies,' he told me. 'I'm leaving for Nice on Sunday,' even though he had a booking for the following week.

A skyrocket disappears in a shower of stars and a silver dragon turns to smoke. We watch ourselves in the glass. Close to the verandah a roman candle and a golden forest light up the room in the rich tonings of an ancient court.

When Potocki returned to France for the last time in November 1993, his health was good but he was frail, and his short-term memory was fading. Sometimes he was confused. I was worried about him making the journey alone—worried about the effects of jet lag on his fragile mind, the isolated villa cold and damp on arrival, an early frost on the ground. I offered to find him a small flat in seaside Plimmerton, near Wellington, where we were then living, and placed an advertisement in the local papers and shop windows: 'Bedsit Wanted For Elderly Writer and His Books.'

But once he had decided to return there was no dissuading him. He made his travel arrangements by phone and had John drive him to the city to pay for his ticket. I remembered a letter he had sent me a couple of years previously: 'On purely astrological grounds,' he had written, 'I have never believed that I was likely to die in New Zealand. Draguignan would fit the bill fairly well, and Cracow even better (in both cases on account of the Dragon).'

Over the last eighteen months he had become progressively tired, and his New Zealand base in Hamilton—the bed-sit beneath the house of a friend—increasingly chaotic. As far back as February 1992 he had written:

> I have been much annoyed by having to sleep during the daytime—although strangely enough I have been sleeping very well as well at night. I sleep right through the night, without even dreaming to any extent. But it has never been my style to sleep during the day. It is only in the last couple of years that I have found myself falling asleep in the daytime.

We had called on him a month or so later and been alarmed to find him lying in bed in the middle of the day, a rickety one-bar heater blazing perilously close to his bedclothes. He had confessed to turning the heater on its back and using it as an element for cooking. And his friend, who was also his landlord, had told us that he frequently boiled his electric jug dry, oblivious to the smell of burning, which was filtering up through his ceiling and the floorboards of the house above.

This decline appeared to have been reasonably swift. In the five years after he had taken the bed-sit in 1985, he had maintained an astonishing pace, writing and printing pamphlets and poems for the Feast of Saturn, travelling around New Zealand, delighting his friends and chastising those who fell foul of him. The comparative mildness of the late Draguignan years had dropped away as fresh issues arose to challenge him, and, as his correspondence suggested, his response had been as excellently unpleasant and vigorous as ever.

When David Dowling, editor of *Landfall*, declined to publish his impressions of New Zealand after fifty years' absence, he had replied: 'Well, as far as Dowling is concerned, his no. 152 of LANDFALL is chock full of unmitigated rubbish, pretentious rubbish at that.' His ire raised, he had pursued the journal further. In 1985, he had written in a foreword to 'Making Tracks', a poem by Weir House student Darryl Ward printed by Potocki, that it had come to his attention that poems by Ward entered in a competition, the winners of which would feature in *Landfall* 152, had not been successful. He had 'already noticed' that the issue contained

> twenty pages of alleged poetry, by nine alleged poets, plus 26 pp. of pseudo-learned, pretentious disquisitions, largely written by Dr Broughton, concerning a couple more 'poets', with extensive quotations from their works; and that all of this was marked by a very extreme lack of talent.

'Not a single sentence of it approaches Poetry within miles by any conceivable criterion', he continued, adding that 'The whole blessed lot is complete, total, and unmitigated worthless rubbish and Darryl should be "chuffed" at not being included.'

He had also abandoned the lectures in Maori he was taking at Waikato University, writing to Hemi Kingi that he had not expected 'these university lectures to turn out to be a succession of Christian prayer meetings . . . I shall probably continue to learn Maori on my own as I have done with Sanskrit, German and other languages . . . you ought to know better than to espouse a religion which has done your race so much harm . . .'

Social and neighbourhood issues received similar attention. When a female member of the Hamilton Lodge of the Theosophical Society, to which he had belonged, had among other misdeeds allegedly referred to Poles as 'Tadpoles', he demanded 'a full written apology' within ten days from the date of his letter, failing which the curse he had placed her under would come into effect. Demanding that she also apologise for lies she had (allegedly) told, he warned: 'If you do not add an apology for your lies, any apology for the tadpoles will be insufficient to avert the curse which you deserve.'

A female neighbour who, presumably inadvertently, had burnt a patch of his landlord's overgrown garden, including a clump of comfrey, also came under fire: 'It is abundantly clear why you did it,' he admonished her by mail, 'for you have done the same thing before. Your purpose was to destroy a clump of comfrey':

> There are many medicinal herbs which do heal but have to be used with care. Comfrey is however an exception. Of course fools can do themselves harm with anything whatever, such as bread or carrots. But you would have to go to a fantastic amount of trouble to do yourself any harm with comfrey . . . It so happens, that I ate a fair amount of comfrey last year myself. This was specifically because I wished to prove to a friend of mine who is a high-up in the DSIR, that whatever the DSIR itself might say if paid enough money, comfrey is completely harmless. Would you explain why I have not been poisoned by the comfrey I ate? . . . take notice that if you do anything remotely resembling your incursions to date on to this place, you will run into serious Bad Luck from which nobody can save you, not the Pope himself. And you will have richly deserved it.

His pamphlets, too, had lost none of their humour and sting. 'Kahore, Kahore!' ('which is what the chieftains said when the pakehas wanted to buy Remurera'), published from Hamilton in 1988, warns about the future of race relations in New Zealand and gives considerable thought to Maori disaffection over lost land. It urges setting up tribunals to 'determine whether the lands were wrested or cheated from the Maoris or not' and suggests that, as the impartial constitution of such tribunals would be a problem, 'participation by Japanese and Hindus'. It also presents a means by which 'a unit of value (say of the value of a hundred present-day dollars) could be determined' based on the current cost of 'definitely essential items':

... for example, a pound weight of rye bread, ditto of alleged white bread, ditto of first quality beef, ditto of butter, of sugar, of good tea e.g. Earl Grey, a litre of milk, a pound of potatoes, of cabbage etc., a yard of good suiting material, ditto of shirt material, the weekly rent of a four-roomed house in a medium district, the weekly rent of a shop of given size in the main streets of a hundred localities ...

Naturally art was given an airing. 'Draft of a Foreword', a cardboard-covered booklet printed the previous year, laments the 'bad' state of world culture. 'The few genuinely gifted artists who have led the way to this shambles, who themselves knew how to draw or paint, such as Picasso and Salvador Dali,' it opines, 'have simply opened the doors to hordes of art criminals, to join whose well-paid ranks the only real qualification is boundless impudence.' Music is described as 'a howl of horror (highly paid),' poetry as beneath 'all possible contempt', architecture 'very remunerative to the criminal pseudo-architects' and paintings and sculptures 'an insult to the rubbish-van'. It sees no reason why a renaissance 'should not be launched from New Zealand'—with his assistance.

There had been a trip to Melbourne in December 1987 to attend the exhibition 'The Private Press work of Count Potocki of Montalk', a display of his writing, printing, ancestry and lifestyle mounted at Monash University; in April 1990 he had travelled alone to Poland; and in 1991 he had followed the sun, as usual, to France for May to September.

The documentary, the continued attention of the media and his rediscovery by small-press enthusiasts had encouraged him. While acceptance by literary New Zealand continued to elude him, he now accepted that the question of his recognition might not be addressed until after he died.

Yet perhaps the signs of deterioration were already there. Favourite phrases such as 'bottomless ignorance' and 'boundless insolence'— often used interchangeably—were appearing more frequently in his letters, and the pamphlet account of his 1990 trip to Poland, 'In April of this Year', although well written and charged with his usual outrage and verve, told a tale of incarceration at odds with my understanding of the trip, and the postcard sent from Warsaw at the time:

The first time I have been in Poland since 1935. The way the Poles have restored Warsaw is perfectly astounding. The Russians seem to be gone without leaving a trace but I fear they have a large army somewhere further East. Not a word of Russian in the streets or shops, yet they all learnt Russian obligatorily . . . The restoration of Warsaw is a genuine miracle. Best wishes to You and my young Cousins from Władysław, R.

I had understood the trip to be a pilgrimage to his spiritual homeland, at the invitation of Dr Andrzej Klossowski of Warsaw University and the Polish National Library. After his return, however, Potocki had spoken only of a quest to advance his claims to the Polish throne. And, although he had reported enthusiastic and well-attended readings and meetings, he had also complained of having been kept under house arrest by Klossowski, who he now believed was a Soviet agent aware of his 'Katyn Manifesto'. 'I did not at once tumble to what had happened, but after a while, it was only too obvious,' he said. 'I would sincerely suggest to the Poles that the whole Library service should be investigated for Soviet machinations. The Library Service! What a perfect hideout!'

This was strange, because he had been corresponding in a friendly manner with Klossowski for at least six years. Furthermore, in 1986 Klossowski had written approvingly about him in a lengthy piece in the *Ossolineum* of Warsaw, describing the Mélissa Press as enjoying 'a considerable reputation among book-collectors and literary people', and commenting that, although Potocki's publications were eccentric in the highest degree, 'there is no lack among them of quite good poems and of good translations (including some from Polish works)'.

As Potocki tells the story in his pamphlet, between meetings Klossowski, together with his 'obvious subordinate Golski', kept him 'sequestered in the fullest sense of the word', warning him that 'Warsaw was a hotbed of violent crime, where people would kill you to steal whatever money you had on you—but where, in fact, the only violence that was done me was done by this pair of scoundrels.' He surmises that perhaps the old communist system of assigning tourists a 'Guardian Angel' or 'warder' was still in force. This may have been so, but it seemed to me that the 'sequestration' probably had more to do with the fact that the librarian, finding himself responsible for a frail, jet-lagged and possibly confused old man, had seen a need to keep Potocki secure, as conditions in Warsaw at the time were indeed as Klossowski described them. It is also likely that, to minimise Potocki's costs, arrangements had been made to accommodate him privately, with Golski.

Potocki writes that he was driven by Golski to the 'very singular place which he occupied' and required to remain there. He describes the accommodation (in a dacha, which at that time was likely to have been the equivalent of a 1950s New Zealand bach) as 'worse than primitive':

> The so-called toilet was away round the third side of the house, and was what used to be called in New Zealand a dunnikin. There were no means of washing one's hands at all, except that Golski would produce a small saucepan of allegedly warm water, which he would pour over my hands while I made an attempt at washing them. There was no pretence of any means of washing any other part of the anatomy. To get to this fabulous dunnikin one had to get through grass and trees, which were worse than annoying if it rained or if it had been raining. In this marvellous dacha I was very poorly nourished, and at irregular and inconvenient hours, and all the time I was being charged up with it.

He recalls that contributing to his sense of sequestration were an iron fence and a dog. And the physical presence of Golski, whose appearance was not found to be pleasing. His response to Golski, who is described as 'hideous in a country where the looks of the people are far above the European average', recalls his deeply seated sensitivity to beauty 'in all its forms', and his early childhood antipathy to the family's 'star Christian', Judith—the aunt who had 'emanated a bad magnetic influence'. Not only was it 'no advertisement to be seen in [Golski's] company', he declares, but 'his inexcusable habit of pushing himself against me, and attempting to paddle my hand on idiotic pretexts [was] particularly offensive'.

This strong aversion to Golski caused the visit to assume elements of high farce in Łódz, to which Potocki had been taken by car for further readings. Unwilling to remain in close proximity to his host, he insisted on returning to Warsaw by rail. A row broke out (presumably because at that time robbery was common on Polish trains), during which a member of the group 'turned on quite a lot of prolonged histrionics', promised to 'die of heart failure!' and required the 'ostentatious' administration of two cups of water and four white pills in order 'to save him from altogether collapsing or having a mortal fit'.

So much for the hospitality and best intentions of the eminent librarian. 'Dr Klossowski,' Potocki writes in his pamphlet, 'who is an absolute ignoramus in comparison with me, is a doctor of librarianship. Librarianship is useful, but is no subject for a Doctorate.'

Had Potocki published this pamphlet ten, or even five, years previously, I might have interpreted it as a wry piece on glasnost or the downsides of a plural society. But I was slowly becoming aware of other small episodes of paranoia consistent with ageing. Increasingly he was misplacing his papers and other important belongings—irreplaceable documents relating to his ancestry, a coat, a ring, a purse full of cash—and accusing others of stealing them. I was told that on one occasion, having lost his diary in the Hamilton library, he accused the librarian of taking it and demanded that he come to the bed-sit to apologise in person. The diary had later been found on a bookshelf.

His relationship with John and me so far remained intact. After a visit when passing through Wellington in 1992, he had written touchingly inquiring about my Achilles tendon, which I had ruptured for the second time:

> My dear sweet Cousin,
> Could You perhaps find time to let me know how your Achilles' tendon is getting on? I have been sedulously and religiously saying prayers for it twice a day and it would be wrong practice to continue doing so, if the necessity had disappeared. But the Achilles' tendon is never, I fear, child's play so I expect it is too much to hope that it is already cured. Still let me have news of it.
> And . . . is my memory serving me rightly—I seemed to think that Ritchie told me that you were going to move out to the Kapiti Coast?
> You were certainly beautiful as You were chatting there, and the expressions on your face were delightful and charming. Also the tones of your voice . . . I have often thought that You and John were as good an advertisement for marriage as could be called to mind. I hope You are both being well looked after by the deathless Gods . . . May all go well with You and John and your children (and the tendon).

His five-month trip to France in 1991 was the last time he would commute. He was very tired throughout 1992 and spent the winter in Hamilton. He fell behind with his correspondence and, although in February 1993 he typed me a long letter, concerned as always about my Achilles tendon, some of the content wandered and words which had been misspelt had been corrected in a shaky hand.

Dearest Cousin,
Thank You for your beautiful and long letter. There are a lot of things I must answer or anyway advert to. For instance—it seems that even our typewriters must be cousins as well. I am writing this on what calls itself a Sperry Rand Remington—it must be one of the last to have been made entirely of metal as opposed to plastic. And is correspondingly heavy. Like You I use it when I have trouble with my electric typewriters, which is only too often. I bought it at the Presbyterian Op Shop, for $35 and it has been so far most reliable . . .
  Before I forget—I take it You know that Stéphanie in ancient Greek means a diadem? I am really ashamed to be so slow, or inexistent in answering letters. I am not ill at all—though if I reach my birthday I shall be ninety. I am sleepy and I fall asleep in the day-time which enrages me. I never was a person to sleep in the daytime. Anyway I do sincerely hope that your leg and foot are both going to be absolutely all right. I hope You will not insist too much in trying to use them . . . Try swimming perhaps . . .
  It is rather fun about our typewriters being cousins . . . I really must get round to answering your good letter of nearly three years ago. I think it must have arrived when I was in Poland . . .

A weak afterthought ran across the top of the page: 'Booked flight for Europe 31st May. Return about mid October.'
  But he didn't leave, and seven months later he called me from Hamilton. His landlord was poisoning him. The landlord's son was a nitwit. His landlord was the most fundamentally evil person he had met in fifty-six years. He had fallen and hurt his side, and couldn't get out to buy food. He was worried about the safety of his books and papers in the bed-sit. People were entering the room and might be stealing them. The paranoia of age was encompassing his past. In the manner of many in this state, he was reliving his old horrors and fears:

starvation, incarceration, conspiracies, censorship and literary oblivion perhaps in the form of loss of documents.

With his landlord and his more immediate relatives unable to assist, I arranged for someone from Presbyterian Support Services to visit and report back. A volunteer rang me that night from Hamilton Hospital. Potocki was being admitted, under duress, with pneumonia.

Between his admission to hospital in September and 12 November, the day he left New Zealand for the last time, Potocki wandered between states of placidity and paranoid confusion. I went to Hamilton to assess the situation. The social worker appointed to his case left me in no doubt about the course that had to be taken. 'His living conditions are deplorable,' she said. 'He can't return to the bed-sit. It's damp and dangerous—a health hazard. He's been assessed as no longer able to look after himself. His family will have to do something.'

In the hospital I found Potocki in a four-person cubicle, sitting high in bed, well supported by pillows. There was a pile of books on his locker, and outside his window spring trees danced in the wind. After the bleak disorder of his lodgings, it was a comfortable scene. He was calm and rational, and charming. Delicately I broached the subject of his ongoing care—the possibility of 'retirement accommodation' near me in Wellington, or cousin Ritchie in Palmerston North. 'Security,' I suggested. 'A nice room with your typewriter and books, and your papers safely in storage.' Regular meals—no poisoning. He was agreeable, enthusiastic even. Yes, he would go to Palmerston North. There was a Polish community there which had expressed interest in him. I should arrange for the contents of the bed-sit to be packed into a truck and moved there immediately. I could also book his flight. He would stay with Ritchie until a suitable establishment had been found.

It was too easy.

A house surgeon entered the cubicle and sat on the end of the bed. Young, female. His face brightened. She needed to conduct a little test. Run a few questions past him in order to assess the state of his mind. I caught my breath. 'Routine,' she added, 'for patients who are elderly.' She arranged a sheet of paper across a book from his locker and handed him his fountain pen. 'Words mainly, and a little general knowledge.' He looked interested. I retreated discreetly to the side of the room.

'Firstly,' she said, 'I'm going to give you three words, and I want you to try and remember them. Then, when we've finished talking, I'm going to ask you what they were.' He leaned forward expectantly. In Draguignan he had ninety-seven dictionaries in twenty languages.

'The words are *dog, tree* and *apple*.' I scrabbled in my bag for a notebook and biro.

'Dog, tree and apple?' he asked in astonishment.

'Yes, *dog, tree* and *apple*. And when you think you've memorised them, I want you to write me a sentence.'

'Write a sentence? In what language? Really, this is the most shocking impertinence.' He unscrewed the cap from his pen. 'Why don't you ask me a proper question like "What was the beginning of Caesar's Gallic wars, or who was the wife of Cepheus, King of Ethiopia?" Really this is not up my street at all. In fact it's *bloody stupid* if I may say so!'

Silence. The sentence was composed, reluctantly, and the young doctor squinted at a spidery line: 'Once more unto the breach, dear friends . . .' Her voice fell away.

'William Shakespeare,' said Potocki impatiently. 'Don't I get any points for another language? Or an opening line from Ovid?'

The doctor slipped the sentence into a folder. 'I'm afraid not. But you will if you tell me what day of the week it is.'

'How about something from Juvenal?' The doctor raised an eyebrow. 'Well, if you must know,' Potocki exploded, 'it could be Tuesday, and it might even be Monday, depending on which side of the world you're in!'

'Good. And who do you think the Prime Minister of New Zealand is?'

'*Think*! I don't *think*, I *know* for a fact!'

'And his name is?'

Potocki turned in the direction of his neighbour, a mound attached to a blood transfusion on the other side of the screen. 'Really, can you beat this for bottomless ignorance?' he said to the curtain. 'All this psychiatric rubbish is a *flaming cheek*! They really do need their brains tested, these people.' He put his pen on the locker, pushed back the bedclothes and, leg by thin leg, lowered his feet to the floor. 'The words are *dog, tree* and *apple*,' he said to the cubicle at large, holding onto the cord of his pyjama pants and shuffling towards the door. 'And experts are *dangerous lunatics* who on no account should be trusted!'

After this he accused the medical staff of trying to 'incarcerate' him and insisted on leaving for Palmerston North. A couple of days later I took him to the bed-sit so that he could retrieve his cheque book and pack a suitcase. This was achieved with difficulty. The room was clogged with files, books, loose paper, empty food tins and old typewriters. The shower, the wardrobe and the spaces beneath the table and the desk were filled with empty spirit and port wine bottles, plastic bags and newspapers. Eight years' accumulation. Potocki just sat in a soft chair and looked yellow, and said he was weak on his pins.

The next day, I sent forty-six cartons to storage in Palmerston North. Potocki followed by air, and within two weeks Ritchie had placed him comfortably, and with his full agreement, in a spacious retirement home with an established garden. He was calm and quiet, liked his room, and was looking forward to unpacking his typewriter and some of his books.

Meanwhile, Christchurch publisher Greig Fleming was planning the launch of *Aristo*, a recently compiled collection of essays by, and interviews with, Potocki, which he was publishing as 'A tribute to the Count at ninety'. The launch had been timed for October, the month of his birthday. Somewhat against his better judgement, Ritchie agreed to take him to Christchurch for a few days. But the lights, excitement, rush of recognition and departure from routine unsettled him, and after his return Ritchie reported a marked deterioration in his mental state. He had become increasingly bad-tempered, and declared Ritchie was part of a plot to 'incarcerate' him in that 'zoo where people pinch things from your room'. He wanted to return to the 'Holy City'. One night he threw his dinner plate on the dining-room floor, rang Fleming and asked if he could come and stay with him in Christchurch.

He had been in the South Island only six days when he wanted to be in Wellington. His hosts spoke to me urgently on the phone. They described him as forgetful, irrational and paranoid. He had accused them of starving him. And now, it appeared, the plot to poison and incarcerate him had thickened to include all the Potocki cousins, even me. They would be putting him on a plane the following day. The family groaned.

He arrived at 5.30 pm, delighted to see me despite my alleged complicity, and was docile until darkness fell, when he became heated about 'the plot, on account of Katyn' and declared his intention to return to France and the safety of his own home.

Over the course of the next two weeks he became calmer. He ate well, sat in a sunny spot in the lounge and looked at the sea, and read

*The Bone People* in snatches. 'I'm quite enjoying it,' he said, 'although some of the coarse language is unnecessary. It's only there for effect.' There were a lot of books in the house and he seemed comforted by the ink, the paper and the neatly ordered spines. He moved among them as he might among friends, removing them, holding them, replacing them exactly where he found them. He slept a lot. He needed routine and time to settle. But he was adamant he would leave. He liked the idea of being at the villa again. 'I'll be surrounded by my own library,' he said. 'Just imagine, there are hundreds of books in Polish alone, and a great deal of poetry, from as far back as 1562 AD.' Only occasionally did he become irrational. A letter was sent to New Zealand Post, whom he accused of stealing his mail, and another to his bank, the Westminster Bank in London, upon whom he placed a curse of 'Bad Luck' for some alleged misdemeanour. He didn't remember the launch of his book— 'More lies!' he shouted at Donovan one day when he mentioned it.

On Thursday, 11 November I packed his two suitcases and washed his hair. He sat on a stool at the basin, enjoying the trickle of warm water on his head and the scent of the shampoo, appreciative of my time. Stronger now, he was looking forward to leaving, to being free— free of the bed-sit and the 'pig islanders' at whose hands he now believed he had been treated so badly. I bought him some woollen vests and a new black beret. He thought Provence would be warm. He kept forgetting he would arrive in late autumn.

Two days later, dressed in his robes, with his front-door key and passport, and cash in sterling and francs deep in the long pockets attached to his sleeves, he was entrusted to the care of an airline. He left, grateful for our help, and vowing to see to it that those responsible for his 'starvation, illegal arrest and attempted murder in New Zealand were brought to justice'.

We spent four days with Potocki in France in 1996, arriving in a taxi around ten, and leaving at four. I sat with him as he lay on top of his bed, dozing or slipping away as if into a dream, birds, maybe mice, scuffling in the roof, Annie's cockerel, upset by all the unfamiliar activity, crowing incessantly from the hen-run nearby. Each day he became more lucid. From time to time we spoke about London during the war, Odile, who was on his mind, and his father, at whose feet he laid the blame for much that had gone wrong with his life. He was still very bitter about his father and his 'treatment of his eldest son', voice would rise and become fierce when speaking about him. The room was dark and cool, and he lay relaxed as if floating just above his blankets.

On the fourth afternoon, while Potocki was sleeping and John was in the basement packing the archive, I slipped down the narrow staircase from the bedroom to the living room to browse among his files. Although we had decided we would pack only the archival material most directly at risk, I wanted to be sure the files inside the house were secure. The room hadn't been used since Potocki's return. It was muted, dusty and damp—unquestionably mice and spider territory—and the electric light wasn't working, so I hastily scanned the shelves, removed a box at random, and took it into the garden.

The contents were disappointing—mostly greeting cards and handwritten letters of an occasional nature—but it was pleasant in the sun, so I continued to sift through them. Then, towards the bottom of the box, I came across a cache of longer letters in a transparent plastic folder. There was something about the light, well-formed yet free-flowing hand that suggested they might be of interest. I slid them onto my lap. In the top letter I caught the words 'lymphosarcoma' and 'I have learnt to live with the constant danger of this incurable disease . . .' These had to be letters from Odile, sent long after she and Potocki had separated.

The letters, mostly in English, were written between 1949 and 1971. They began 'Dear Geoffrey' and ended affectionately with 'Blessings' or 'All love and Blessings' or 'Blessings upon your head'. They frequently discussed practical matters relating to the divorce, which Potocki resisted until 1955, by which time Odile had a partner and two sons. They also spoke of her return to university, her BA with Honours in French, her MA, her PhD, and the shadow of lymphosarcoma. On 20 July 1957 she had written from Devon that she 'should go to Exeter to have an unusual lump removed from my tummy', and on 7 October that she had had surgery at the Royal Devon and Exeter Hospital for two enlarged glands.

Earlier, on 22 May 1956, she had replied to a request from Potocki that they meet:

> . . . the simple plain fact is that I have neither the time nor the energy to amuse myself with any diversions or even with thoughts of the same—I have a very exacting job, a heavy social life, a

household to look after, a very loving husband and two demanding and affectionate sons and believe me, that leaves no place in one's life or mind for 'fancy work' however pleasurable. Besides I am getting old. You know my age as you know your own and you can judge. I hope you have a successful time over here—does it feel strange after so many years away?

Although I detected a note of exasperation, the tone was friendly. Odile wrote as if she understood and was still fond of her former husband. In 1969, the sarcoma, apparently controlled for twelve years, resurfaced. In January she wrote: 'I am being looked after for the old lymphosarcoma in Leeds', and in May: 'I have had a very bad patch of health'. On 15 January 1971, seemingly in good health again and now aged fifty-six, she had written that 'apart from minor health worries all seems o.k. . . . we hope to be in France again for the summer'. This was the last letter in the folder.

That night, our last in Draguignan, I slept badly. A headache had started to gather behind my left eye and I found myself drifting in and out of a dream in which Potocki stood on the bridge of a ship, smiling.

I took a couple of Panadol and tried to get back to sleep. But I couldn't stop thinking about him, alone on his bed day after day, the villa silent, shaded by trees, submerged by vines, no radio or ringing telephone, no conversation, no longer a desire to read, the room dim by day and dark early, his eyes twitching behind their lids, rolling, suggesting a life now lived in the mind. Too weak to walk beyond the door. Was he waiting for his reincarnation? He was strongly persuaded that re-birth was a fact. A God also. A God above his immortal gods. He had written of a God who spoke 'and the whole universe was formed', that there was 'the most beautiful burst of music when he spoke':

> Round that harmonious Song
> great suns began to form
> ecstatic worlds to throng;
> Love was the milk-white norm.
> Night melted: from the dark
> all shapely beauties came,
> and Love, a shining Ark,
> and Loveliness, and Fame.
> (from 'In Principio')

'Although what is God after all?' he had once written to me. 'If he's capable of doing things no decent human would do, then they've got the wrong version.'

At around two am I heard the rumble of thunder in the hills. Had he heard it? Then the sound of rain pattering into the plane tree outside our window—soothing summer rain. Rhythmic. Was he aware of the rain, the sun, the seasons? 'October,' he'd said suddenly that afternoon from his bed, waking, blinking as if he'd been dreaming. 'Odile. She'll come for the autumn. Go to the border. Visit the caves at Ventimiglia.' Comfortable in a foam-rubber chair, I had entered what I wanted to believe was his reverie: Odile taking a train from Nice, cool in the carriage, *climatisée* on the brown seat against the window, her hair close to her head, a coat laid across the top of her case; carrying gifts she had bought him in London: biscuits, a tin of tea, a gold charm which dangled from a ring on her wrist.

I'd wanted a sense of completion. Something to lessen the sense of loss which had permeated his life. Consolation before I left him.

The train moved through the city—sun, palms, the slim shadows of balconies. It stopped at Antibes and gathered speed beyond Cannes. The parade flickered. The pebbled beach became a long stretch of sand as it climbed to the top of the bay.

I'd glanced at Potocki. His eyes were closed, but his toes were making small movements beneath the blanket, and he was clasping and unclasping his fingers around the handle of his cane, which lay on the bed.

The train rocked and rushed inland. The walls of the room slid into darkness, emerging on the plain beneath the red face of the Esterel range on the other side of the tunnel.

I shut my eyes. Clouds today, rain tomorrow, and soon the first real winds of the season. The living room was cold and there were cracks in the stone he should have cemented this summer.

The headache was still there but it was being subsumed by the dream of the afternoon: Odile at the bench in the living room, pouring sugar into a saucepan, stirring it with a wooden spoon, coaxing it gently to a brown heat; layering oranges, sliced, in a shallow glass dish; smudging them with the caramel; preparing a meal: a small fillet of beef which crackled and spat and smelt good as she turned it, sediment which smelt good as she browned it; softening mushrooms slowly in butter. On the gas ring a clump of asparagus tied together with string quivered and bent gently in the steam. She took a bottle of milk from the small fridge. 'A béchamel sauce for the asparagus,' she said, stretching past him.

They lay in the garden and talked about tasks that awaited them: the shaking of branches, the gathering of olives in coarse wide blankets. They considered the possibility of a mule and a simple Roman press— a system of stones they could operate by hand. There was a fig in the grass, and he placed it in her pocket. The breeze freshened and a leaf settled between the pages of his book. He left it there for the winter.

I returned to the bedroom, to the bridge of the ship. Odile was rainbow bright. Vivid in a long blue gown. She was filling a wine glass with burgundy, raising the glass against the window in the bedroom— its small light—and laughing. She sipped the wine, drawing a small quantity carefully onto the front of her tongue; passed the stem of the glass through her fingers, raising the temperature of the wine with the warmth of her hand. 'I am the Temple of Poseidon,' she whispered, her mouth shining like a pearlfish, waving like a column of water, the smooth length of a curtain, the long tail of a breeze. She took Potocki by the hand and they danced, waist to waist. Her English was excellent. Her hair gleamed in the sun. Her body was gold at the edge of an ocean, and the sky had become too distant to be relevant:

I slept soundly for a couple of hours. When I awoke the next morning, the headache had become a migraine. We delayed our flight. That evening I rang Annie Larminach. She had taken Potocki his evening meal and he was fine. Brighter than she had seen him in months.

In April 1997, Annie called me and told me Potocki had died. He had passed away the previous week, on 14 April, in a nursing home in Brignoles, once the summer residence of the old counts of Provence, near Draguignan—the place to which they took their wives to give birth. He had fallen in his room some months earlier and been admitted to hospital for assessment. Although he was uninjured, the decision had been made to commit him to care.

It was July before we could travel to France to find out at first hand the circumstances of his death, and speak with the notary who had been assigned the task of winding up his estate. Having lived continuously in France before dying (unable to assert his temporary status as a visitor), Potocki was deemed to have been domiciled in that country. The result was that his property now came under the jurisdiction of French law.

We checked into the Hotel du Parc, and the next morning took a taxi to the office of the notary in nearby Trans en Provence. We knew the provisions of his will were complicated, and the notary confirmed, through a translator, that the estate would indeed take years to settle. And there were additional complications. For one thing, the beneficiaries as named by Potocki were no longer the major beneficiaries. Under French law, immediate descendants shared three-quarters of the estate, regardless of whether or not they had been named in the will, and the named beneficiaries shared only the remaining quarter. His daughters, Wanda and Theodora, neither of whom had been named, would now share the significant portion of the estate; this meant Theodora would have to be traced and then she would have to prove Potocki was her father. We knew all this. The notary paused. The twin daughters of Marysia, last heard of in Germany, would also have to be traced, she said. We expressed surprise. 'One daughter has already proved Potocki was her father—in a French court in 1983,' she said, producing certified documentation. 'This twin, and possibly her sister, are also major beneficiaries.' We were shocked. Potocki had denied fathering the twins so strongly.

We borrowed the key to the villa and after lunch took a taxi on the now familiar route past the American War Cemetery to the École d'Artillerie, where we turned left onto the sealed portion of the Chemin des Faïsses. Dry summer grass, trees, and from a distance the cottage unchanged. We could smell the rosemary and thyme, but the land and the air felt different. Everything was left to memory. There were no more secrets.

We let ourselves into the back bedroom. The small window was patterned with vines, the sun was directly overhead, and the room was dark. We tried the bedside lamp and the light but the electricity had been disconnected. As our eyes adjusted we saw that the room had been up-ended and ransacked. There were bare stretches of shelving where many books of value had sat, and small circles on top of the piano where the delicate tea-set in Japanese porcelain had been arranged. The oil painting his mother had made of the Waikato River was an empty patch in a frame on the floor.

The other rooms upstairs—the new bedroom over the garage, and the small room off the porch—had also been dismantled, and mirrors, windows and furniture smashed. I found some large filing boxes on the floor, and opened them. They contained clothes carefully packed in tissue paper and labelled in English: 'Brown shirt for summer suit . . . Best blue shirts . . .' Fritzi's work, presumably.

Downstairs in the living room, more bare shelves. Drawers hung from cabinets, their contents scattered, and the cutlery boxes which had contained his mother's silver were empty. There was paper everywhere: what was left of the archive.

The next day, on the notary's instructions, we supervised the packing of the contents of the villa, including the remainder of his archive, and accompanied them in a van to storage in Draguignan.

That evening we dined out with Annie and her partner, Alain. Annie, pert and vivacious in her early fifties, had lived next door to Potocki all her life. Her grandfather had sold him the land and dwelling which became the Villa Vigoni, and as a child she had played with the twins. When Potocki had returned to the villa for the last time in 1993, incapable of looking after himself, she had agreed to provide an evening meal and basic care. It was true, she said, that Potocki had always denied fathering the twins. He had been contemptuous of the attempt to prove paternity, refused to have a blood test and, when the case came to court, either failed or refused to attend. He had believed it would come to nothing, knowing that, as long as he retained visitor status in France, his estate could be left to whomsoever he chose.

We asked about the last years of his life—his arrival by plane from New Zealand, the train and taxi from Nice. Conversation by phone had always been difficult, but now, over dinner, it was easy. Annie had a mobile face and expressive hands, and with the assistance of wine everyone's language skills were improving. She told us he had arrived in darkness, that in his confusion he had misplaced his key and spent the night under a bush. She confirmed that he had fallen a few months after our visit the previous summer, and had been too weak to lift himself from the floor. With winter coming on he had been admitted to the 'house for old people' in Brignoles. He had remained in bed there, and before long had forgotten who she was. In time he had started to stiffen—Annie closed her eyes and became a chipmunk, elbows bent, arms tight on her chest, hands closed, close to her chin.

\*

Before leaving Draguignan to take the train from Les Arcs to Nice, we visited Potocki's grave. The old cemetery, inside the town, was cramped, with gravel walkways and tightly spaced gravestones. It was bounded by busy streets, and extension had been possible only by excavating a chalky hill at one end. A caretaker in a small building at the gate checked a logbook and gave us a number. We didn't understand. He wrote it on a slip of paper—266—and pointed at the hill.

We found Potocki buried beneath a slab of grey speckled granite into which G. *Potocki de Montalk 1903—1997* had been etched. No headstone, no title, no Latin, no mention of Apollo or his other immortal gods.

'What is important,' he had once said, dismissing private printing as an ancillary art and his press as a vehicle for fine book-making, 'is what one finally manages to get on paper.'

Despite disapproval and ostracism, and his claim that only a small percentage of his writing had ever been printed, he had succeeded in this. His commitment to free speech, to being heard, had showed what was possible. His legacy would be his writing and his printing. And the astonishing stories of those who remembered him.

I took some photos of the scene. Wanda was unlikely to travel to France. A group was gathering at a mound of newly-dug earth nearby. Fewer than a dozen mourners. Small bunches of flowers had been placed on the earth, and some of the women had covered their hair with lace. A priest stood among them. His murmur mixed with the sound of the traffic. A group of a similar size had attended Potocki's burial. And a priest from England had spoken about him at the graveside in English.

AUGUST 1989, HILLCREST ROAD, KIRIKIRIROA
ON AN IMPUDENT MESSAGE LAST XMAS

Horace, Ovid, great Ennius, have all
proclaimed what lengths of human time their song
would hold the folk of distant lands in thrall.
The events are far from having proved them wrong,

rather indeed they rate their fame too low!
They have outlived since Sumer a third part
of history. Thou carping knave, just know
the same is true of Us and of our art.

When there remains no track nor trace that once
you lived on earth, my writings shall be read
my poems sung, my legend heard, thou dunce
thousands of years after the flesh is dead.

# Sources

## A NOTE ON SOURCES

Principal sources for this recollection of Count Geoffrey Potocki de Montalk were my correspondence, conversations and interviews with Potocki; my diaries and personal collection of family records and Potocki memorabilia; and papers (including legal documents and previously published and unpublished correspondence and manuscripts) found in Potocki's archive.

Other important sources were poetry, pamphlets and booklets written and printed by Potocki—works which I found valuable as much in understanding him as in documenting his life. A selective checklist of his work is provided below. (Given the prolific and somewhat unsystematic nature of his output, the definitive list of Potocki's work, including poems for the Feast of Saturn, awaits the attention of more serious scholars). Many Potocki publications—including single poems and some pamphlets more accurately described as leaflets—appear in bound or booklet form. For purposes of categorisation here, however, works of fewer than 24 pages have not been italicised.

## CHAPTER EPIGRAPHS

| | |
|---|---|
| ONE | Conversation with author. |
| TWO | *Right Review*, Number 13. |
| THREE | 'Return to Apollo' (draft typescript). |
| FOUR | 'Songs About New Zealand, III', 1927, *Surprising Songs*. |
| FIVE | *Aristo: Confessions of Count Geoffrey Potocki de Montalk*. |
| SIX | 'Draft of a Foreword'. |
| SEVEN | Conversation with author. |
| EIGHT | Conversation with author. |
| NINE | *Snobbery with Violence*. |
| TEN | 'Draft of a Foreword'. |
| ELEVEN | Conversation with author. |
| TWELVE | 'Second Katyn Manifesto'. |
| THIRTEEN | From 'Parish Notes, Mainly Jottings from 1966', *Right Review*, Number 18. |
| FOURTEEN | 'One More Folly, Observations on the Hinton St. Mary mosaic'. |
| FIFTEEN | *Check-List of Publications by or concerning COUNT POTOCKI OF MONTALK, PART I*. |
| SIXTEEN | 'Nunc Dimittis, VI, Meditation before a golden Buddha, after a walk in the Gardens', 1927, *Surprising Songs*. |

## Works written (mostly printed) and published by Potocki:

'The Opal Studded Diadem', leaflet of poems (Auckland, 1923).
*Wild Oats: A Sheaf of Poems* ('By the Author', Christchurch 1927).
'Against Cresswell', lampoon (London, 1930).
*Prison Poems* (The Montalk Press for the Divine Right of Kings, London, 1933).
*Whited Sepulchres, Being An Account of My Trial and Imprisonment For a Parody of Verlaine and Some Other Verses*, pamphlet (The Right Review, London, 1935).
'The Unconstitutional Crisis', pamphlet (London, 1936).
*Blest Clay*, poems (London 1937).
'Abdication of the Sun', poems (London, 1938).
*Social Climbers in Bloomsbury, Done from the Life*, pamphlet (The Right Review, London, 1939).
'Katyn Manifesto', pamphlet (Little Bookham, Surrey, 1943).
*Right Review*, Numbers 1—17, journals (The Right Review, London, October 1936-June 1947).
*Mel Meum*, poems (The Mélissa Press, Draguignan, 1959).
*The Fifth Columnist: A Short Story by Jim Goodleboodle ex convict*(The Mélissa Press, Draguignan, 1960).
'YTT YZZ', poem, promoted as: '. . . the first surrealist poem to be issued by this anti surrealist press . . . Tariff post free to Japanese 3d., to Hungarians, Balts, Germans, eighteen Bees [18Bs], and sexy women 6d., otherwise 1/6 (The Mélissa Press, Draguignan, 1960).
'A New Dorset Worthy', pamphlet (The Mélissa Press, Dorset, 1963).
'One More Folly: Observations on the Hinton St. Mary Mosaic', pamphlet (The Mélissa Press, Dorset, 1963).
'Clara Petacci', 'Three two-penny broadsheets issued by The Royal Polish Society for the Enlightenment of the Clergy' (The Mélissa Press, Dorset, 1963).
'Two Blacks Don't Make a White: remarks about Apartheid', pamphlet (The Mélissa Press, Dorset, 1964).
*The Whirling River*, poems (The Mélissa Press, Dorset, 1964).
'Some Future Butler', pamphlet (The Mélissa Press, Dorset, 1965).
'Ungallant Gallantry', pamphlet (The Mélissa Press, Dorset, 1965).
*The Blood Royal of Ireland, Scotland, Wales, England & Other Countries*, genealogies (The Mélissa Press, Draguignan, 1966).
'The King of Poland's Plan for Rhodesia', pamphlet (The Mélissa Press, Draguignan, 1966).
'Blue Blood in the Butter Republic', pamphlet (The Mélissa Press, Draguignan 1968).
*Dogs' Eggs*, Part 1 (The Mélissa Press, Draguignan, 1968).
'Hymn to Wilson', pamphlet (The Mélissa Press, Draguignan, 1968).
'Letter to Har vey [sic]', pamphlet (The Mélissa Press, not located, 1968).
'Were Bach's Ancestors Polish?', pamphlet (The Mélissa Press, Draguignan, 1969).
'The Polish Daily Prefers Lies', pamphlet (The Mélissa Press, Draguignan, 1969).

'Roger and Angelica', poem (The Mélissa Press, Draguignan, 1969).
'Guinness is Good for You: A Christmas Jingle by PRINCE BOBOWSKI poet laureate to the Bank of Poland', poem (The Mélissa Press, Draguignan, 1969).
'Miraculum Secundum Naturam', pamphlet (The Mélissa Press, Draguignan, 1970).
'Potocki Versus the Polish Cultural Foundation Ltd', pamphlet (The Mélissa Press, Draguignan, 1970).
'Text of a Resolution', pamphlet (The Mélissa Press, Draguignan, 1970).
'That Impossible Fellow', pamphlet (The Mélissa Press, Draguignan, 1970).
*Dogs' Eggs*, Part 2 (The Mélissa Press, Draguignan, 1971).
'The Decimal Superstition', pamphlet (The Mélissa Press, Draguignan 1972).
'The Jinx', pamphlet (The Mélissa Press, Draguignan, 1972).
'Sete: Images of Provence', poems, with drawings by Marjorie Jackson-Pownall (The Mélissa Press, Draguignan, 1972).
'Columbus Discovers Ireland', pamphlet (The Mélissa Press, Draguignan, 1972).
*Right Review*, Number 18, journal (The Mélissa Press, Draguignan, summer 1973).
'Our Verdict', pamphlet (The Right Review, Draguignan, 1973).
*Cats*, poems (assumed to be The Mélissa Press, Draguignan, mid-1970s—publication page missing from author's copy).
'Check-List of publications by or concerning COUNT POTOCKI OF MONTALK, PART I' (The Mélissa Press, Draguignan, 1974).
*Dogs' Eggs*, Part 3 (The Shack Press, Draguignan, 1975).
*Dogs' Eggs*, Part 4 (The Shack Press, Draguignan 1975).
'Notes by Richard Bielicki and Count Potocki of Montalk for Chopin and Mickiewicz Recital' (The Mélissa Press, London and Draguignan, 1977).
'Notes for Chopin Concert by Richard Bielicki And Chapter One of Work in Progress—Szopen—by Count Potocki of Montalk' (The Mélissa Press, London and Draguignan, 1977).
'Let the Rhodesians Not', pamphlet (The Mélissa Press, Draguignan, 1977).
'Whereas With You', poems (The Mélissa Press, London and Draguignan, 1977).
'The Hungarians', poem (The Mélissa Press, 1978).
*Right Review*, Number 19, journal (The Mélissa Press, Draguignan, October 1979).
*Dzieciństwo Moje: 1903 & 4* (The Mélissa Press, Draguignan, 1980).
*Dzieciństwo Moje: Tomik II 1906 & 1907* (The Mélissa Press, Draguignan 1981)
*Dzieciństwo Moje: Tomik III* [undated] (The Mélissa Press, Draguignan, 1982).
'Second Katyn Manifesto', pamphlet (The Mélissa Press, Draguignan, 1983).
'Tama-inu po', poem (At the Printing-Office on the Parade, Victoria University, Wellington, 1984).
'The Fat Woman of Peckham Rye', poem (printed by Walter Lemm at the Imp Press, Auckland, probably mid-1980s).
'The Ospedaletti Fellowship', pamphlet (Hamilton, 1986).
'Draft of a Foreword', pamphlet (The Mélissa Press, Hamilton and Draguignan, 1987).
'Prisoner in Buckingham Palace', pamphlet (Hamilton, 1987).

*Isten*, poems (The Mélissa Press, Hamilton, 1988).
'Kahore, Kahore!', pamphlet (The Mélissa Press, Hamilton, 1988).
'In April of This Year', pamphlet (The Mélissa Press, Hamilton and Draguignan, 1990).

**Unpublished Potocki manuscripts of particular interest:**

'Here Lies John Penis', verses and translations (although these works have been published in the appendix to *A Long Time Burning* (1969), the collection reproduced here is from Potocki's typed version, 1933, as originally written).
*Return to Apollo: In the Halls of Admetos*, incomplete draft typescript (London, 1937)
Draft typescript of obscenity trial (London, undated).

**Selected published translations by Potocki:**

*Music Within Me*, poems by Charles Maurras, mostly from *La Musique Intérieure* (The Right Review, London, 1946.)
'Dear Garment', poems by Charles Maurras and one poem by Charles d'Orleans (The Mélissa Press, 1965).
'Her Wonderful Shoulders', sonnet 'Dame Vor Dem Spiegel', by Rainer Maria Rilke (The Mélissa Press, Draguignan, 1967).
*Forefathers* [*Dziady*], classical poetic drama by Adam Mickiewicz (Polish Cultural Foundation, London, 1968).
'No English Horse', poems by Sandor Petofi with illustrations by Rigby Graham, translated from the Magyar (The Mélissa Press, 1972).
'Magali', poem from *Mireio* by Frederi Mistral (published for the Royal Polish Cultural Foundation by The Mélissa Press, London and Draguignan, 1977).
'Sonetto All'Italia', poem by Vincenzio da Filicaia 1642-1707 (At the Printing Office on the Parade, Victoria University, Wellington, 1985).
'Little Jokes', poems by Mikołaj Rey (At the Printing Office on the Parade, Victoria University, Wellington, 1986).

**Other published works by Potocki:**

*Surprising Songs*, poems (Columbia Press Ltd, London, 1930).
*Lordly Lovesongs*, poems (Columbia Press Ltd, London, 1931).
*Snobbery with Violence: A Poet in Gaol*, pamphlet (Wishart & Co, London, 1932).
'Poems & Translations', with drawings by Rigby Graham (Pandora Press, Leicester, 1966).
'Cicadas', poems with linocuts by Bill Powell (New Broom Press, Leicester, 1968).
'Pastorale', poems with illustrations by Tony O'Dwyer (Offcut Press, Leicester, 1968).

'Lammas Day', poems with illustrations by Rob Armstrong (New Broom Press, Leicester, 1969).
'Myself as a Printer', French fold with drawings by Rigby Graham (Daedalus Press, Stoke Ferry, for the Brewhouse Press, Leicester, 1970).
'Meillerie', poems (Cuckoo Hill Press, Pinner, Middlesex, 1973).
'While Howls And Grunts', poems (The Messrs Eastgate, Palmerston North, 1979).
*Recollections of My Fellow Poets* (edited by Donald Kerr, Prometheus Press, Auckland, 1983).
*Aristo: Confessions of Count Geoffrey Potocki de Montalk*, essays, and conversations (with Greig Fleming; Leifmotif, Christchurch, 1991).

**Selected works by others, printed and published by Potocki:**

'A Letter from Richard Aldington and a Summary Bibliography of Count Potocki's Published Works', pamphlet (The Mélissa Press, Dorset, 1962).
'A Tourist's Rome', Richard Aldington (The Mélissa Press, Dorset, 1961/1962).
'Balls & Another Book for Suppression', Richard Aldington (The Mélissa Press, Dorset, 1962).
'Thomas Hardy from Behind and Other Memories', P.J. Platts (The Mélissa Press, 1965).
'The Sale of Manhattan Island—A Huge and Historical Confidence Trick', Cathleen Owen (The Melissa Press, Draguignan, 1973).
'Making Tracks', Darryl Ward, poem (At the Printing Office on the Parade, Victoria University, Wellington, 1985).

**Works about or mentioning Geoffrey Potocki or his family:**

Broughton, W.S., *New Zealand Profiles: A.R.D. Fairburn* (A.H. & A.W. Reed, Wellington, 1968).
Cave, Roderick, *The Private Press* (Faber & Faber, London, 1983).
Craig, Alec, *Above All Liberties* (George Allen & Unwin, London, 1942).
Craig, Alec, *The Banned Books of England and Other Countries: A Study of the Conception of Literary Obscenity* (George Allen & Unwin, Great Britain, 1962).
*Cyclopaedia of New Zealand*, Volume 2, Auckland (The Cyclopaedia Company, Christchurch, 1902).
*Dictionary of New Zealand Biography*, Volume Two (Bridget Williams Books and the Department of Internal Affairs, Wellington, 1993).
*Dictionary of New Zealand Biography*, Volume Three (Auckland University Press with Bridget Williams Books and the Department of Internal Affairs, Auckland, 1996).
Edmond, Lauris, *The Quick World* (Bridget Williams Books, Wellington, 1992).
Fairburn, A.R.D., *The Letters of A.R.D. Fairburn* (selected and edited by Lauris Edmond, Oxford University Press, Auckland, 1981).

Mason, R.A.K., *R.A.K. Mason at Twenty-five* (Nag's Head Press, R.A.K. Mason Papers Trust, New Zealand, 1986).
McNeish, James and Helen, *Walking on My Feet: A.R.D. Fairburn 1904-1957, A Kind of Biography* (Williams Collins Publishers, Auckland, 1983).
Leckie, Frank, M., *The Early History of Wellington College* (Whitcombe & Tombs, Auckland, 1934).
Potocka, Theodora Gay, *Potocki: A Dorset Worthy?* (Typographeum, Francestown, New Hampshire, USA, 1983).
*The Private Library*: Quarterly Journal of the Private Libraries Association, 'Geoffrey Potocki and His Press', by Rigby Graham (Spring 1976).
*The Private Library*, 'A Private Library in Provence', by John Macalister (Spring 1984).
Rex v G.W.V.P. de Montalk, The Central Criminal Court, Old Bailey (copy, shorthand notes; 8 February 1932).
Risk, R.T., *Why Potocki?* (Typographeum, Francestown, New Hampshire, USA, 1981).
Risk, R.T., *Four Private Presses* (Typographeum, Francestown, New Hampshire, USA, 1981).
Rolph, C.H., *Books in the Dock* (André Deutsch, London, 1969).
Scott, Margaret, *Recollecting Mansfield* (Random House NZ, Auckland, 2001).
Thomas, Donald, *A Long Time Burning* (Routledge & Kegan Paul, London, 1969).
Thornton, Geoffrey, *Cast in Concrete: Concrete Construction in New Zealand 1850-1939* (A.W. & A.H. Reed, Auckland, 1996).
Trussell, Denys, *Fairburn* (Auckland University Press/Oxford University Press, Auckland, 1984).
Vaile, E. Earle, *Pioneering the Pumice* (Whitcombe & Tombs, Christchurch, 1939).
Woolf, Leonard, *Downhill All the Way: An Autobiography of the Years 1919-1939* (The Hogarth Press, London, 1968).
Woolf, Virginia, *The Diary of Virginia Woolf, Volume IV: 1931-1935* (ed. Anne Olivier Bell, The Hogarth Press, London, 1982).
Woolf, Virginia, *The Sickle Side of the Moon: The Letters of Virginia Woolf, Volume V: 1932-1935* (ed. Nigel Nicholson, The Hogarth Press, London, 1979).

**Additional background sources also helpful in preparation:**

Alvarez, A. (ed), *The Faber Book of Modern European Poetry* (Faber & Faber, London, 1992).
Davies, Norman, *Heart of Europe: A Short History of Poland* (Clarendon Press, Oxford, 1984).
Dessaix, Robert, *A Mother's Disgrace* (Flamingo, Harper Collins Publishers, Australia, 1994).

Dorling, Captain H. Taprell, *Ribbons and Medals: The World's Military and Civil Awards* (Doubleday & Company, New York, 1974).
Eby, Douglas, 'Eccentricity and Creativity', http://hometown.aol.com/douglaseby (August 2000).
Elgrably, Jordan, 'Wilder at Heart', http://www.metroactive.com/papers/metro (Metro Publishing and Virtual Valley, February 1996).
Flem, Lydia, *Casanova: or the Art of Happiness* (transl. Catherine Temerson, Penguin Books, Great Britain, 1998).
Hamilton, Edith, *Mythology: Timeless Tales of Gods and Heroes* (New American Library of World Literature, New York, 1962).
Huxley, Aldous, *Letters* (ed. Grover Smith, Chatto & Windus, London, 1969).
*Literature and the Arts: New Zealand* (University of California Press, 1947).
Malcolm, Janet, *The Silent Woman: Sylvia Plath and Ted Hughes* (Vintage, New York, 1995).
*New Encyclopaedia Britannica*, 15th Edition (Helen Hemingway Benton, Chicago, 1979).
*New Scientist*, 25 February 1995.
Pushkin, Alexander, *The Letters of Alexander Pushkin* (transl. J. Thomas Shaw, University of Wisconsin Press, Madison, 1967).
Rousseau, Jean-Jacques, *Confessions* (transl. Angela Scholar, ed. Patrick Coleman, Oxford University Press, 2000).
Shetreet, Shimon, *Judges on Trial* (North-Holland Publishing Company, Amsterdam, 1976).
Siegel, Allen M., *Heinz Kohut and the Psychology of the Self* (Routledge, New York, 1996).
Sparrow, Judge Gerald, *The Great Judges* (John Long, London, 1974).
*The Spectator*, 18 March 1995.
Thoreau, Henry David, *Walden; Or, Life in the Woods* (Anchor Press/Doubleday, New York, 1973).
Tripp, Edward, *The Meridian Handbook of Classical Mythology* (Penguin Books, New York, 1974).
Verlaine, Paul, *Femmes/Hombres* (transl. Alistair Elliot, Anvil Press Poetry, London, 1983).
Weeks, David and Jamie James, *Eccentrics* (Phoenix, Orion Books, London, 1996).
Yeats, W.B. (ed), *Oxford Book of Modern Verse* (Oxford University Press, Great Britain, 1960).
*The Years Between: Christchurch Boys' High School 1881-1981* (Christchurch High School Old Boys' Association, editorial chairman A.T. Campbell, Christchurch, 1981).
Zamoyski, Adam, *The Polish Way: A Thousand-year History of the Poles and their Culture* (John Murray, London, 1987).

# Acknowledgements

I am forever grateful to my husband, John Miller, for his unfailing support and good humour during the course of this project, and, for many years, his interest in and enjoyment of Potocki. Without John this book would not have been written.

I am also deeply indebted to Fergus Barrowman, Bill Manhire and Harry Ricketts for their encouragement and advice. And to Andrew Mason for his empathy and expertise during the editing of the book.

Others to whom warm thanks are due include: the National Library of New Zealand, Te Puna Matauranga o Aotearoa, for making its Hygiene Room available when I was listing the contents of Potocki's archive; the Alexander Turnbull Library for access to the Potocki collection when revisiting Potocki's archive for editorial checking seemed unwise, and the reproduction of photographs from the William Stevenson Broughton papers; the University of Auckland Library for access to the Joseph Wladislas Edmond Potocki de Montalk and A.R.D. Fairburn collections; my children: Jonathon Miller, Melissa Moon, Donovan Miller and Dylan Miller; Cathleen Allworth, Karen Anderson, Claire Baylis, Merv and Sybil Cooper, Tim Corballis, Tim Croft, Phillip de Montalk, Ritchie de Montalk, Kate Duignan, Gerry Evans, Wanda Henderson, Annie Larminach, Łukasz Łachowicz, Michael Laws, John Macalister, James McNaughton, Jane Perry, Vivienne Plumb, Andrew Potocki, Peter and Thérèse Potocki de Montalk, John Powys, John Priestley, K.B. Smith, Theodora Scutt and Louise White.

I also gratefully acknowledge the writers and the estates of writers from whose work or correspondence I have quoted brief passages in criticism, including: Richard Aldington, the Duke of Bedford, W.S. Broughton, Roderick Cave, Alec Craig, Norman Davies, Lauris Edmond, A.R.D. Fairburn, Greig Fleming, Douglas Glass, Denis Glover, Rigby Graham, Kenneth Hopkins, Jamie James, Donald Kerr, Frank Leckie, John Macalister, R.A.K. Mason, Odile Morcamp, R.T. Risk, C.H. Rolph, Theodora Scutt, Gerald Sparrow, Shimon Shetreet, Geoffrey Thornton, Denys Trussell, E. Earl Vaile, David Weeks, Ernest Wild, Leonard Woolf, W.B. Yeats, Adam Zamoyski. Lines from 'Tarantella' by Hilaire Belloc are reprinted by kind permission of PFD on behalf of: The Estate of Hilaire Belloc ©: as printed in the original volume.

# Index

*L'Action Française*, 273
Acton, Justice, 163, 164, 165, 167
Adams, Vyvyan, MP, 158, 174
Aeschylus, 165
Aldington, Richard, 121, 135, 152, 160, 250, 252-3, 261, 268
Alexander Turnbull Library, 269, 284-8, 292
Allen, J.A., 31
Alliance Française, Auckland, 52
Anders, General Władysław, 230
Arend, Dr Marjan Z., 109-10, 112, quoted 110, 112-13
*Art Monthly*, 293
Aristophanes, 165, 176
Auckland, views on, 95, 97, 125

Bagnall, A.G., 285-7
Baldwin, Stanley, 214
Barrie, J.M., 84
Barry, Gerald, 162
Bedford, Duke of, 229, 236, 260, quoted 229
Belloc, Hilaire, quoted 27, 28
Bevan-Brown, C.E., 79
Blake, William, 16, 17, quoted 22, 58, 264
*Bone People, The*, 309
Bowman, Frederick, 225-6, 233
Britain, in WWII, 22, 228, 229, 231, 232
British Museum, 221-2
British Union of Fascists, 213
Brooke, Rupert, 89, 97
Broughton, Dr W.S.: visits Potocki, 292-3; quoted, 82, 94; mentioned, 299
Butler, Samuel, 100
Buzek, Jerzy, 231
Byron, Lord, 160, 162, 219, 222

Caesar, Julius, 147, 206, 307
Cain, Detective Inspector, 152
Campbell, Mrs Patrick, 150-1

Campbell, Roy, 30, 160
Casanova, Giocomo, 249
Cave, Prof. Roderick: interest in Potocki, 126, 128-9; visit to, 276; quoted 12, 128-9
Celan, Paul, 218
Chaucer, Geoffrey, 135, 176, 220-1, 234, quoted 135
Chopin, Frédéric, 46-7, 247
Chrapowicka, Countess Zinka, 112
Chrapowicki, Count Adam, 101, 111, 112
Christchurch, views on, 97
Claret removal company, 14, 44
Clarke, C.H. ('Old Clarke'), 244, 245
Cock, Alfred, QC, 51
Columbia Press, 110, 112, 118, 154, 224-5
Connolly, Cyril, 34
*Country Life*, 107, 112
Cox, Gertrude, 256, 257
Craig, Alec, 21, 155, 156, quoted 146, 148, 156, 163
Cresswell, Walter D'Arcy: Potocki visits in London, 108-9; homosexuality of, 108-9, 274; Potocki lampoons, 109-10; views on Potocki's verse, 113, 272; recollected, 123; mentioned, 273, 284, 286
Crisp, Quentin, quoted 40
*Criterion*, 213-4, 266
Curnow, Allen, 273
Curtis Brown, literary agents, 229
Czerwinski, Dr, 283-4

da Vinci, Leonard, 241
*Daily Express*: article on investiture, quoted 225-6; on 'Katyn Manifesto', 233
*Daily Worker*, 232, 233
Dali, Salvador, 301
Dante Alighieri, 162
Davies, Norman, quoted 47

# Index 327

de Bioncourt, Countess Gilone Henriette Marie, 237, 242, 243, 244, 288
de la Mare, Walter, 112, 160, quoted 113
de Lozey, Leslie, 134, 138, 144, 145-6, 170, 177, 196
de Montalk, Alexandrina Williamina Sutherland (née Macalister) (grandmother): married, 51, 52; described, 56-7; dies, 65; mentioned, 62
de Montalk, Annie Maud (née Vaile) (mother): family of, 52; death of , 43, 53-4, 56, 116; relationship with Potocki, 43, 54, 84, 85; described, 55-6, 60-1, 76; memories of, 60-1, 297; estate of, 235-6, 242
de Montalk, Cedric, *see* Potocki de Montalk, Cedric
de Montalk, Dulce Maud (sister), 53, 54, 60, 66, 74, 78
de Montalk, Emily Littre (aunt), 56, 57-8, 248
de Montalk, Evelyn (née Hickson), known as 'Lulu' or 'Lestes' (stepmother): marries Robert, 65, 76; régime at Vallombrosa, 65-70; described, 68, 196; régime at Alfriston, 72-6; Robert's view of, 88-9; mentioned, 43-4
de Montalk family: origins of name, 49-50; in New Zealand, 20-1, 39, 42, 48, 51, 119, 253
de Montalk, Geoffrey, *see* Potocki de Montalk, Geoffrey
de Montalk, Henry Potocki (uncle; grandfather of author), 24, 52
de Montalk, Count Joseph Wladislas Edmond Potocki (grandfather), 21, 46, 50-2
de Montalk, Judith (aunt), 56, 58-9, 303
de Montalk, Kenneth (cousin; father of author), 19, 21, 33, 49, 197, 242, 253
de Montalk, Lilian (first wife, née Hemus): meets Potocki, 84; marriage, 85, 89-91, 97-8; gives birth, 86; assaulted by Potocki, 90; seeks restitution of conjugal rights, 97; relationship with Potocki, 98; later life, 98, 103-4, 125, 253
de Montalk, Margaret (mother of author), 33, 70, 197-8, 199
de Montalk, Odile (second wife, née Morcamp): marriage, 222, 223; arrested and imprisoned, 223; described, 234; relationship with Potocki, 234, 246; divorce, 234, 244, 310; letters to Potocki, 310-11, quoted 310-11; mentioned, 36, 224, 225, 251, 309, 312, 313
de Montalk, Ritchie (cousin), 304, 306, 308
de Montalk, Robert Wladislas (father): remembers first wife, 60-1, 70; remarries, 33, 65, 75-6; as architect, 61, 66, 69, 70-1; financial position of, 69, 70-1; moves to Alfriston, 71; moves to Mangaweka, 76; moves to Nelson and Wellington, 79; death of, 224; estate of, 288; relationship with Potocki, 33, 54, 63-4, 71, 73, 74, 75, 84, 87, 88-9, 98-9, 102-5, 107-8, 120, 208, 263, 269, 309-10; advice to Potocki by letter, quoted 84, 86-7, 98-9, 102-5, 107; letter to Lilian, quoted 88-9
de Montalk, Stephanie (cousin; author): RELATIONSHIP WITH POTOCKI: makes contact with, 19-23; visits in Draguignan: (1968) 26-32; (1996) 13-14, 295-7, 309-13; (at grave) 316; letters from, quoted 19-20, 21-2, 33-5, 304, 305; provides hospitality to: in Edinburgh, 36-9; in New Zealand, 122, 125, 197-8, 267, 297-8; as trustee of estate of, 14, 313-16; attracted to, 21, 32, 265-6, 267-8; responses to, 32-3, 40, 41-5, 59-60, 69-70, 77-8, 84-5, 115-16, 181-2, 195-6, 212-13, 231, 241, 250-2, 265-71, 272-5, 282, 290-1, 293, 311-13; reflections on trial and appeal of, 140, 143, 144-5, 147, 155, 165-6, 168-73 AS BIOGRAPHER OF POTOCKI: writing life

of: 15, 16-17, 40, 44-5, 77-8, 181, 265, 268-9, 274-5; records interviews and poems with, 36-7, 209, 218; produces *Kaleidoscope* documentary on, 37, 39, 128, 129-30, 197, 198-9, 208-9; discusses public and private perceptions of, 226, 232, 264, 269-74, 291; dealing with archive of, 13-14, 15-16, 42-3, 268, 274, 310, 315; physical reaction to archive, 13, 15, 16, 170, 220
PERSONAL LIFE: in France and Spain (1968), 23-4, 32; with Video Recordings Authority, 58; as warden of Weir House, 126, 199-200, 267
de Montalk, Victoria (aunt), 56, 62
de Montalk, Wanda (daughter): born, 86; as child, 97, 98, 103-4, 120, 243; reunion with Potocki, 124, 125, 243; mentioned, 253, 286, 314, 316
Denning, Lord, quoted 169-70
Dessaix, Robert, quoted 268
Dettman, Prof., 80
Donne, John, quoted 132
Donnelly, Ian, quoted 94, 113
Dorli ('Baroness' von Zittau) (lover), 36, 39, 247-8, 257, 258
Douglas, Lord Alfred, 155
Dowling, David, 299
Draguignan, town of, described, 25
du Cann, C.J., barrister: conduct of Potocki's defence, 137, 139, 143, 145-6, 148, 149, 150-1, 152, 160, 166, 178
du Parcq, Justice, 163, 164
Durrell, Lawrence, quoted 216

Earl, Kent and Massey (Auckland law firm), 81, 82
Eccentricity, discussed, *see* Weeks, David
Edmond, Lauris, 202, 203, 287-8
Edward VIII, King: as Prince of Wales, 180; abdication of, 214-5
Edwina (lover), 36, 132, 161, 174, 175, 186, 190-1, 193, 206
*Ekspres Poranny*, 208

Ellis, Havelock, 160, 190
Eliot, T.S., 160, 213
*Empire News*, quoted 138
Empson, William, 217
Ennius, 317
Esher, Lord, 160
Euripides, 165
*Eurydice*, 273
*Evening Standard*, 224

Fairburn, A.R.D.: at Remuera Primary School, 67; as member of 'poetic aristocracy', 82, 94; resumes friendship with Potocki, 89; collaborates with Potocki on sonnet, 89, 92-3, 94; *Wild Oats* dedicated to, 91; with Potocki and Mason in Auckland, 99; in New Zealand, 114; in London, 116-19; publishes *He Shall Not Rise*, 118, 132, 133; marriage, 118; amorous adventure, 131, 132-3; Potocki's affection for, 116-7; letters to Potocki, 94, 95, 194-5, 284-8, 292, quoted 94, 95, 194-5; views on Potocki's poetry, quoted 119, 177, 194, 273; recollected, 123, 270; reaction to Potocki's trial in letters to Mason, quoted 154-5; views on Potocki, quoted 177, 194, 209; views on Glass, quoted 177; views on Auckland, quoted 95, 97; views on New Zealand, quoted 114; mentioned, 100
Firth, Clifton, 118-19
Fleming, Greig, 308
Foster, Commander, prison governor, 188-9, 191-2
Forster, E.M., 160
Fritzi, see Jaggi, Frederica

George IV, King of England, 49
George V, King of England, 208
Germany: occupation by, 228; in WWII, 222, 228, 229, 230-1, 232
Glass, Douglas: meets Potocki in Auckland, 82; in London, 100; arrested and imprisoned for theft, 100-1, 136; re-

fused service in restaurant, 105-6; with Fairburn and Potocki in London, 117, 118, 132; accompanies Potocki, 133-5; arrested, 136; in Brixton prison, 136-7; bailed, 137; quoted at preliminary hearing, 138; discharged, 139; supporter at Potocki's trial, 143, 153; seeks support for Potocki's appeal, 159, 160, 161, 162; fails to provide meal before Potocki's appeal, 163-4, 178; writes to Potocki after appeal fails, 173-4; blamed by Potocki, 177-8; advice to Lahr, 194; later prominence as photographer, 168, 293; tribute to, 293; Potocki's later view of, 293
Giono, Jean, quoted 242
Glover, Denis, quoted 285, 287
Goebbels, Josef, 230
Gollancz, Victor, 229, 282
Golski ('Guardian Angel'), 302-4
Gould, Gerald, 160
Grabowski, Dr Zbigniew, quoted 112
Graham, Rigby, 275-6, quoted 275-6
Grant, Alison, 123
Guinness, Brian (Lord Moyne), 209, 211, 278

Hall, Radclyffe, 34, 135, 143, 155-6, 168
Hann, George, 187, 211, 214
*Hansard*, 158
Harvey, John, 224, 225
Hemus, Lilian, *see* de Montalk, Lilian
Heseltine, Nigel, 214-5
Hewart, Lord Chief Justice, 163, 165-8, 171, 172-3
Hickey, William, quoted 233
Hindenach, Johann, 21-2, 277, 278
Hitler, Adolf, 228, 230
Hogarth Press, 159, 174
Homer, 162, 165
Hopkins, Prof. Kenneth, 255; quoted, 33, 291-2
Horace, 206, 317
Housman, Laurence, 160
Hudson, Stephen, 160
Hutchinson, St John, barrister: conduct of Potocki's appeal, 147, 162, 163, 164-5, 167, 171, 174-5, 194; as friend of Woolf, 159, 171, 172; as 'left-wing liberal', 172
Huxley, Aldous: supports Potocki, 160, 163, 209, 211, 278; praises *Snobbery with Violence*, 181; visits Potocki, 211; bails Potocki, 215; seeks publication of Potocki typescript, 228-9; mentioned, 158, 241-2

*Ilustrowany Kurier Codzienny*, quoted 112
Imperial Fascist League, 224
*Irish Statesman*, 107

Jaggi, Frederica (Fritzi) (lover): meets Potocki, 244; relationship with Potocki, 23, 245-6, 247, 255, 257, 258, 277, 278; pet name, 252; mentioned, 36
John, Augustus, 155, 160, 216-7, 220
*John Bull*, 213, 226
*Jones v. National Coal Board*, 169-70, 172
Jordan, Colin, 264
Joseph, Michael, 229
Joyce, James, 34, 150, 160
Joyce, William, 213
Juvenal, 176, 307

*Kaleidoscope* TV documentary on Potocki, 37, 39, 128, 129-30, 197, 198-9, 208-9, 220
Katyn massacre, 19, 22, 229-33, 234
Kerr, Donald, 123-4
Kingi, Hemi, 299
Klossowski, Dr Andrzej, 302-4
Kohut, Heinz, 115-16
*Kowhai Gold* anthology, 282
Krushchev, Nikita, 231
*Kurier Poznanski*, quoted 109-10, 112-13

Lahr, Charles, 112, 177, 194, 209, 215
Lakshman, Karun, 267

*Landfall*, 299
Larminach, Annie, 296, 313, 315
Lawrence, D.H., 34, 134, 135, 150, 160, 181
*Left Review*, 213
Lindsay, Jack, 129
Lithuania, 101-2, 112
*London Review of Books*, 172
Longford, Lord, Report on Pornography, 34
Lowenfels, Walter, 106, 111
Luck, Jean, 132-3

Macalister, John, 29-30, 31
MacDiarmid, Hugh, 137
Malcolm, Janet, 274
*Mangaweka Settler*, 76
Mansfield, Katherine, 107, 201-2
Masefield, John, 151
Mason, R.A.K.: meets Potocki, 82; with Potocki and Fairburn in Auckland, 99; in New Zealand, 114-15; appraises *Wild Oats*, 93; letter to Potocki, quoted 93, 114-15; mentioned, 94, 95, 117, 118, 123, 154, 155, 269, 284, 286
Matthews, Keith, 292
Maurras, Charles, 273
Mays, Jocelyn, 118
Merkowna, Marja (Marysia), 242-3, 245, 255, 314; twin daughters of, 243, 255, 314, 315
*Methodist Times*, 134
Mickiewicz, Adam, 34, 207, 222, 224; see also entry for Forefathers, under Potocki de Montalk, Geoffrey: PUBLICATIONS
Miller, Donovan (son of author), 38, 122, 267, 309
Miller, Dylan (son of author), 37, 122, 267, 268
Miller, John (husband of author): accompanies author to visit Potocki, 13-14, 26-32, 295-7, 309-13, 316; as trustee of Potocki's estate, 14, 313-16; and *Kaleidoscope* documentary, 128; views on Potocki's trial and appeal, 169-72; quoted, 30, 49; mentioned, 20, 23, 24, 31, 35, 126, 193, 197, 212, 268, 298, 304
Miller, Jonathon (son of author), 37, 122, 126, 198, 202, 217, 267
Miller, Melissa (daughter of author), 38, 122, 267, 270
Milne and Choyce department store, 81, 82
Milton, John, quoted 61
Minnie (Upfield) (mistress), 115, 143, 161, 174, 193, 253-4
Morcamp, Odile, see de Montalk, Odile
Morrison, Herbert, quoted 232
Mosley, Sir Oswald, 213, 225
Mulgan, Alan, 94, 95
Mussolini, Benito, 147

*Nation*, 159
*New English Weekly*, 162, 213
*New Scientist*, quoted 41
*New Statesman and Nation*: views on Potocki's trial quoted, 153-4, 176-7; mentioned, 181
*New Zealand Artists' Annual* (1929), 114
*New Zealand Herald*, article on Potocki, 123, 124, quoted 124
*New Zealand Listener*, 201, 202-3
*New Zealand News*, quoted 102
*News of the World*: report on Potocki's trial, quoted 143; mentioned, 154
Nichols, Robert, 215
*North London Press*, 235

*Observer*, 107, 219
Old Bailey, 139, 142-3
'Old Splash' (benefactor), 101, 106
Orion (French literary critic), 273
Ortega, José, quoted 272
Orwell, George, 181
*Ossolineum*, 302
*Otago Daily Times*, article on Potocki, quoted 127
Ovid, 307, 317

Owen, Cathleen (lover), 201, 278-80, 287, 289
Owen, Gwilym (godson), 279-80, 289
*Oxford Companion to Law*, quoted 172

Paderewski, Ignacy, 95-6
Parr, Blomfield, Alexander and Burt (Auckland law firm), 85
Pascal, Pierre, 273
Paul, Ian, 128, 198
Payan, Monsieur et Madame, 243
Picasso, Pablo, 301
Piłsudski, Marshal Józef, 208
Plomer, William, 205, quoted 206
*Poetry* (Chicago), 107, 112
Poland: as elective monarchy, 121; Russian colonisation and repression of, 49, 227-8; Prussian colonisation of, 227-8; in 1930s, 196, 207; in WWII, 222, 228, 229, 230-1, 232, 239; Soviet intentions for, 227; under communist rule, 48, 239; re-emergence as independent nation, 48; in 1990, 302-4
Polish Cultural Foundation, London, 34, 36, 224, 278, 282-4
Polish Library, Paris, 285, 286
*Polish Daily*, 182
*Pologne Littéraire*, 207
Porteous, Hugh Gordon, quoted 213-4, 266
Potocka, Countess Delfina, 46-7, 247
Potocka, Judith Charlotte Anne (née O'Kennedy) (great-grandmother), 49, 50, 51, 237
Potocka, Theodora Gay, *see* Powys, Susan
Potocki de Montalk, Cedric (brother): in childhood, 43, 53, 55, 59, 64, 70, 72-4, 77-8, 80, 208, 241; with stepmother, 65, 66, 68, 69, 74; cadet reporter with *NZ Herald*, 103, 105, 114; as adult in Europe, 21, 22-3, 114, 120, 161, 208, 241, 253; author visits in Portugal, 24-5, 30, 248; relations with Potocki, 103, 105-6, 137, 208; on family genealogy, 48-9, 50, 51, 120

Potocki de Montalk, Geoffrey Wladislas Vaile:
CHILDHOOD & ADOLESCENCE: 43-4; birth and first five years, 53-6, 59-60, 241; death of mother, 45, 53-4; after death of mother, 56-9, 60, 62, 249; reacts against stepmother, 65, 66-7, 70, 74, 75; starvation of, 66, 67-8, 74, 76; meets Fairburn, 67; at Alfriston, 72-6; belief in specialness of, 54, 62, 64, 78; effects on later life, 77-8, 81, 104, 249, 270, 289
EDUCATION: at King's College, 62, 63-4; at Remuera Primary School, 67; at Alfriston, 73; at Manurewa, 74; performance in entrance to secondary school exam, 76-7; at Christchurch Boys' High School, 21-2, 79, 80; at Wellington College, 79; matriculates, 79; private study at Victoria University College, 80; at Canterbury University College, 81; at Auckland University College, 81; at St John's Theological College, 82-3
YOUNG MANHOOD: as pupil-teacher at Berhampore, 80-1; as teacher, 81-2, 83, 241; joins Auckland law firm, 81; dismissed, 82; meets R.A.K. Mason, 82; returns to law, 82, 85, 86; joins Theosophical Lodge, 83-4; marriage to Lilian, 84, 85-6, 89-91, 97-8; becomes milkman, 85-6; moves to Christchurch, 86; resumes friendship with Fairburn, 89; meets Paderewski, 95-6; with Fairburn and Mason in Auckland, 99; leaves for England, 99
EARLY YEARS IN EUROPE: meets Glass, 100, 101; impressions of London, 100-1; in Paris, 101; visits Lithuania, 101-2; refused service in restaurant, 105-6; visits Cresswell, 108-9, lampoons, 109; on origin of Dorothy Cannibal, 115; with Fairburn in London, 116-18; responds to family criticism, 119-20
ARREST, TRIAL, APPEAL & IMPRISONMENT: writes 'obscene' verses, 131-3;

seeks compositor for, 133-5; room raided by police, 135; arrested, 136; in Brixton prison, 136-7; bailed, 137; at preliminary hearing, 137-9; trial brief prepared, 139-40; trial at Old Bailey, 143-153, 155; sentence, 153; prepares for appeal, 160-3; at appeal hearing, 163-5; reaction to failure of appeal, 174-5; blames Glass, 177-8; in Wormwood Scrubs: 161, 163, 180-1, 253; daily routine, 182-4; prison diet, 184-6; ill health, 184, 185; on prison life, 186-7, 189-90; sexual molestation, 187-9; letter writing, 190-2; encounter with Distressed Prisoners' Association Board, 192-3, 212; discharged, 192-3; wants pardon, 208; effects on later life, 175, 194, 195, 270, 289

LATER YEARS IN LONDON: visits Woolfs, 204-6; visits Poland, 206, 207-8; as Polish press correspondent in London, 208; moves to right, 209; arrested for assault, 213; arrested for distributing 'The Unconstitutional Crisis', 214-5; in poverty, 220; establishes Right Review Bookshop, 220; as London identity, 221-2; marriage to Odile, 222-5, 234; imprisoned for assault, 222-3; at Half Moon Cottage, 224; forms Polish Royalist Association, 224; conducts investiture, 225-6; printing censored material, 20, 227; open support for Germany in WWII, 228, 229, 233; investigates Katyn massacre, 229-31; produces and distributes 'Katyn Manifesto', 231-3, 234; arrested and imprisoned, 233; at Northumbrian agricultural camp, 234-5; sued by landlord, 235; obtains new passport, 236; seeks employment in Indian university, 236; visits Switzerland, 237; arrested for assault, 238; psychiatric assessment, 238-40

IN DRAGUIGNAN: at Villa Vigoni, 13-14, 19, 22, 26, 28-32, 34-5, 36, 243, 245, 246, 250-2, 279-80, 292, 295-7, 309, 315; at Vallon de Gandi, 30, 242, 243, 280-1, 296; joined by Merkowna, 242-3; birth of twins, 243; meets Frederica, 244; acquires Citroën, 244; affair with Dorli, 247-8; letter from natural daughter, 253; visit of daughter, 255-6; returns to live (1966), 261; joined by Cathleen Owen, 278-80; delivers and cares for godson, 279-80; catalogues library, 284; papers valued, 284, 287; negotiates with Alexander Turnbull Library, 284-8; rising value of properties, 288; trip to Venice with Risk, 289-90; dismissal of Risk, 290-1; death of, 15, 255, 313; estate of, 285, 286, 313-14; grave of, 316

IN DORSET: arrival and first impression (1960), 256; agrees to help daughter, 256; agreement to buy Mappowder house, 257, 260; at Lovelace's Copse, 257, 260-1, 275-6; deteriorating relations, 258-9, 261; renovates Mappowder house, 259-60; tries to let properties, 263

RETURN TO NEW ZEALAND: fails to secure Burns Fellowship, 33; expresses desire to, 39; arrives (1983), 123; at author's, 122, 125, 126-7, 198, 199-200, 267, 297-8, 308-9; reunion with daughter, 125; seeks New Zealand pension, 127, 128; visits Christchurch and Dunedin, 127; visits author's mother, 197-8; making *Kaleidoscope* documentary, 198-9; in Hamilton, 298-301, 304, 305-6, 308; visit to Poland (1990), 301-4; in hospital, 306-7; psycho-geriatric assessment, 306-7; in Palmerston North, 308; visit to Christchurch, 308; returns to France, 309

ANCESTRY: 20, 21, 22, 31, 46-51, 52-3, 120-1, 124, 208, 269; claim to Polish throne: 19, 22, 120-1, 124, 194, 207, 222, 224, 232, 233, 238-40, 283,

302; title of count: 21, 22, 102, 120, 152, 162, 199, 236, 269

AS POET: beginnings, 62-3; first poem published, 76; member of 'poetic aristocracy', 82, 94; first collection published, 82; poetic calling, 89, 90, 95, 110, 148, 160, 217-20, 271, 272; burgeoning career, 89, 107; collaboration with Fairburn on sonnet, 89, 92-3, 94; publishes *Wild Oats*, 91-5; publishes *Surprising Songs*, 110, 112-3; publishes *Lordly Lovesongs*, 112; writing poems in prison, 191-2; literary 'oblivion', 209; and *Kowhai Gold* anthology, 282; increasing value of works by, 277, 288; themes of, 91, 92, 94, 111, 273, 281; forms of, 91, 271-2; prolific output of, 270, 271; appraised by others, 93, 94, 95, 107, 110, 112-13, 119, 129, 139, 272; among founders of New Zealand literature, 94, 107; as verse translator, 34, 131-2, 149, 164, 207, 224, 272, 273, 278, 282, 291; views on Fairburn's poetry, 116-17, 133, 286, 293; poems quoted: 'Chorus of Poles', 272; 'Credo in Unum ...', 111; 'Evelyn', 112; 'Evensong', 111; 'Here Lies John Penis', 140; 'In Memoriam, Maxwell Rudd ...', 91-2; 'In Principio', 311; 'In the Manner of Paul Verlaine ...', 141-2; 'A Lyric', 93; 'Magic in Words', 220; 'On an Impudent Message ...', 317; 'Our Eight Siamese', 280; 'Paris', 110; 'Philosophy', 221; 'Praeludium', 106; 'Rex', 117; 'Ritual Clobber', 237; 'Saint Valentine's Day', 271; 'Salisbury Cathedral', 218-19; 'A Silent Pool', 218; 'The Song of the Braguette', 142; 'Sonnet' (with Fairburn), 92-3; 'The Song of the Dead Rat', 92; 'That Treasure', 272; 'Warning to the Puritans', 192; '"We learn at last ..."', 294

AS PRINTER & PUBLISHER: introduced to printing, 83; purchases first press, 209, 211-12; purchases new press, 224; produces 'Katyn Manifesto', 232; commissions for Polish government-in-exile, 235; at Villa Vigoni, 28, 29, 246-7, 249, 252, 254, 255, 261-2, 281, 297; The Mélissa Press, 29, 31, 252, 254, 275, 283, 289, 302; The Shack Press, 254, 262, 279; at Victoria University of Wellington, 126, 198, 299; in Dorset, 264, 275-6; described by Cave, 128-9; revival of interest in work of, 39, 249, 278, 292, 301; exhibition in Melbourne (1987), 301; commitment to, 255, 290; views on, 316; see also Publications

PUBLICATIONS: 'Abdication of the Sun', 221; 'Against Cresswell, A Lampoon', 109-10, 119; *Aristo*, 44, 308, quoted 55, 100, 229; *The Blood Royal*, 19, 30-1, 212; 'Blue Blood in the Butter Republic', 282; 'Celebrities Who Have Met Me, I. Paderewski', 95-6, quoted 96; 'The Decimal Superstition', 282; *Dogs' Eggs*, 254, 256, 261, 262, 279; quoted 256-62 *passim*; 'Draft of a Foreword', 301, quoted 122, 204; *Forefathers* (verse translation of Mickiewicz's *Dziady*), 34, 207, 224, 249, 273, 278, 282-4, quoted 222, 284; 'Guinness is Good For You', 282; 'Here Lies John Penis', 131, 132, 136, 194, quoted 140, *see also* ARREST, TRIAL ...; 'In April of this Year', 301, quoted 302-4 *passim*; 'In the Manner of Paul Verlaine', 131-2, quoted 141-2, *see also* ARREST, TRIAL ...; 'Kahore, Kahore!', 300, quoted 301; 'Katyn Manifesto', 231-3, 234, 302; *Lordly Lovesongs*, 112, 135; 'A New Dorset Worthy', 264, quoted 264; 'One More Folly', 268, quoted 263; 'The Opal Studded Diadem', 82; 'The Ospedaletti Fellowship', 200-3, 288, quoted 202; *Prison Poems*, 128, 192,

193-4; *Recollections of My Fellow Poets*, 123-4, quoted 79, 99, 108-9, 118, mentioned 45; *Social Climbers in Bloomsbury*, 168, 215-8, quoted 204, 205-6; 'The Song of the Braguette', 131, quoted 142, *see also* ARREST, TRIAL ...; *Snobbery with Violence*, 181, 193, quoted 179, 182-93 *passim*, mentioned 149, 180, 264; *Surprising Songs*, 110-13, 116-17, 135, 194; 'That Impossible Fellow', 282; 'Two Blacks Don't Make a White', 264, 268, quoted 264-5; 'The Unconstitutional Crisis', 214-5; *Whited Sepulchres*, 134, 181, 193, quoted 134, 136-7, 138, 144, 149, 151, 160, 163, 164, 168, 221, mentioned 168, 169, 181, 213; *Wild Oats*, 84, 89, 91-5, 277; *see also Right Review*
UNPUBLISHED WRITINGS: 'Evictible', 199-200, quoted 200; letter to laundry, quoted 257-8; 'My Private War Against England', 19; poems for the Feast of Saturn, 19, 33, 220, 249, 255, quoted 124-5, 220; 'Return to Apollo', 43-5, 58, 68, 70, 71, quoted 54, 56-9 *passim*, 62, 65-9, 72-77 *passim*
PERSONAL ATTRIBUTES: appearance: as child, 54, 56, 59-60, 66; in London, 115, 133; in court, 138, 143, 146, 150, 155, 168, 233; in prison, 136, 182, 193; capes, 115, 136; robes, 38, 115-16, 122, 124, 234, 277, 309; hair and headgear, 21, 56, 60, 115, 124, 206, 233, 277; uniform, 224; as king, 225; as older man, 20, 21, 26-7, 32, 37-8, 275, 276, 277; eccentricity: 20, 40-2, 62, 77-8, 208-9, 213, 251, 265, 273-4, 282, 285, 289, 291; habits: 32, 34, 37, 126, 198, 212, 218-20, 251, 274, 277, 288-9; health: 123, 277-8, 298, 306; increasing frailty: 298, 301, 304, 305-9, 313, 315; as linguist and translator, 36, 38, 96, 101, 107, 200, 207, 224, 235, 242, 268, 302, 307; personality: 32-3, 115-16, 212-13, 251, 265-6, 267, 268, 269-71, 273, 290; rituals: 37, 38, 122, 191; sensitivity to beauty, 59, 60, 62, 66, 75, 89, 92, 153, 252, 303; sexuality: 38, 73, 85, 116-17, 248-9, 274; as talker, 28, 30, 31, 37, 39, 124, 205, 215, 267, 273, 293

VIEWS: national: on England and the English, 31, 34, 38, 147, 172, 183, 187, 195, 204, 228, 237, 246-7, 261, 266; on Germany and Nazis, 21, 22, 228, 229, 232, 233, 239-40; on New Zealand, 95, 97, 100, 110, 111, 125, 152-3, 228, 241; on Poles and Poland, 227, 228, 239-40, 299-300; on Russia and Soviet Union, 22, 227, 228, 236, 239-40; on Vietnam war, 22; personal: attitudes to women, 38, 84-5, 107, 112, 271; on nature and natural products, 37, 85, 86, 128, 221, 242, 252, 277, 300; on sex, 57, 58, 81, 109, 139, 186-8, 248; philosophical: on astrology, 32, 53, 116, 220-1, 235, 255, 277; on fiction, 206; on heredity, 31; on puritanism, 199, 266; political: on bolshevism and communism, 39, 118, 203, 205, 209, 210, 227, 228-9, 232, 266; on capitalism, 205, 210; on censorship and freedom of speech, 20, 58, 143, 317; on democracy, 127; on fascism, 210, 213, 227; on monarchy, 209-10, 211, 214; racial: anti-Semitism, 39, 135, 187, 195-6, 207, 210, 266, 269, 278; on apartheid, 264-6; on Maori, 102, 266, 299, 300; religious: 38, 221, 311-12; on Christianity and the Bible, 39, 58, 59, 81, 82-3, 111, 117, 135-6, 146-7, 152, 198, 266, 299; sun worship, 20, 22, 30, 85, 117, 147, 199, 221
LEGAL ACTIONS: against Polish Cultural Foundation, 34, 282-4; against *John*

*Bull*, 213; against landlord, 213; against Columbia Press, 224-5; against Judge Tudor Rees, 234, 235; against Powys family, 261, 262
Potocki family: 46-51, 87, 96, 98, 124, 226, 228; coat of arms, 26, 47, 206, 223, 224
Potocki, Herman (great-greatuncle), 49, 50
Potocki, Count Józef Franciszek Jan (the 'Insurgent') (great-grandfather), 46, 49, 50-1, 76, 95, 237
Potocki, Stefan (cousin), 50, 51
Powys, Francis, 253-4
Powys, Llewelyn, 257, 292
Powys, Susan (later Theodora Gay Potocka) (daughter): adopted, 253-4; discovers parentage, 255; visits Villa Vigoni, 255; in Dorset, 255-61; deteriorating relationship with Potocki, 263-4, 269, 279; as beneficiary, 314
Powys, T.F., 253, 254, 258, 260, 261
Powys, Violet, 253, 254, 255-62
Priestley, J.B., 160
*Private Library, The*: articles on Potocki, quoted 29-30, 129, 275-6; mentioned, 31
Provence, attraction of, 241-2
Prussia: colonisation of Poland, 227-8; *see also* Germany
Pushkin, Alexander, 47

*R. v. de Montalk*, 173
Rabelais, François, 131, 135, 149, 151, 152, 156, 191
Ratdolt, Erhard, 289
Renner, Fritz, 79
Rees, Judge Tudor, 233, 234, 235
Rickword, Edgell, 30, 117, 118, 149, 153, 164, 266, quoted 190
*Right Review*, described, 209-11, 213-14, 266; attacked, 213; threatened with legal action, 216; quoted, 40, 50-1, 53, 54, 55, 60, 210, 279; mentioned, 44, 45, 59, 193, 216, 220, 226, 234, 277, 279
Risk, R.T. (Terry), 196, 266, 289-91, 292
Rolfe, F.W. (Baron Corvo), 269
Rolph, C.H., 140, 148, 182, quoted 136, 140, 148, 182
Rousseau, Jean-Jacques, quoted 12, 85
Rudd, Maxwell Billens, 81-2, 91-2, 123, 284, 286
Russell, Bertrand, 160
Russia: colonisation and repression of Poland, 49, 227-8, 232; *see also* Soviet Union

Samuel, Sir Herbert, 158
Saunders, R.L., 86, 95
Scott, Margaret, 201-3, 285, 288
Scott, Mark, 202
Scott, Rachel, 202
Scott, Rosie, 202
Shakespeare, William, 83, 133, 134, 135, 150, 151, 162, 176, 180, 222, 307
Shaw, George Bernard, 150
Shelley, P.B., 160
Shetreet, Shimon, quoted 173
Slack, Judge Granville, 282-4
Socrates, 164-5
Sophocles, 165
Soviet Union: intentions for Poland, 227; in WWII, 228, 229, 230-1, 232
Sparrow, Justice Gerald, quoted 173
*Spectator, The*, quoted 41
Stalin, Josef, 230, 231
*La Stampa*, 147
*Star* (Auckland), 94
Stephen, Sir James Fitz-James, 151
*Sun* (Auckland), 106
*Sun* (Christchurch), 89, 93, 96, 106, quoted 113
*Sunday Times*, 34, 100
Swift, Jonathan, 206

Taylor, Alister, 292
Taylor, C.H.R, 269-70, 285
Thomas, Caitlin, 220
Thomas, Dylan, 192, 216-18

Thompson, John Ross, 84
Thoreau, Henry David, quoted 42
Thornton, Geoffrey, quoted 71
*Time and Tide*, 154, 175
*Times, The*, 34, 231, 283
*Times Literary Supplement*, 149
Todd, Ruthven, 216
Townshend, Third Marquess, 49
Traue, Jim, 287
Trembecki, Stanisław, 46
Trollope, Anthony, 50, 150
Trollope, Frances, 49
Trussell, Denys, 99

Ukraine, 49, 50, 228
University of Auckland Library, 287
Urquhart, Sir Thomas, 135, 152, 156,

Vaile, Annie (née Earle) (grandmother), 52
Vaile, Blanche (aunt), 43, 54, 68-9
Vaile, Edward Earle (Uncle Ted), 52, 75, 88, 106, quoted 52, 71, 113, 114, 119, 236
Vaile, Evelyn (aunt), 68, 79-80
Vaile, George (great-grandfather), 52
Vaile, Hubert Earle (Uncle Bert) (godfather), 43, 81, 83-4, 86, 268
Vaile, Samuel (grandfather), 52, 53, 70-1, 86, 105, 106
Vallombrosa (family home), 53, 54-5, 60, 61, 71, 76, 78, 228
Verlaine, Paul, 131-2, 147, 149, 152, 156, 164
Vernon, François, 131
*Voices* (New York), 107
von Straubel, Carl, 123

Walpole, Hugh, 160
*Wanganui Chronicle*, 71
Ward, Darryl, 299
Warsaw, 49, 302-4

*Warsaw Voice*, 47-8
Watson, Bertrand, 139
*Week-end Review*, 162, quoted 158-9
Weeks, David, study of eccentricity cited, 40-2, 62, 209, 251, 270, 273-4, 282
Weintraub, Wiktor, 273
Wells, H.G., 160
West, Rebecca, 160, 162, quoted 175-6
West, Dr Louis J., quoted 42
White-Scott, Hessie, 67-8
Wild, Sir Ernest, Recorder of London: conducts Potocki's trial, 144-53, 234; distaste for Potocki, 146, 155; conduct of trial condemned, 147-8, 150, 155-7, 165-6, 169-72, 178; as poet, 156-7
Wilkes, John, 269, 283
Wilkinson, Louis, 255
Wishart, London publisher, 205, 282
Wolfe, Humbert, 107, 117, 160, quoted 113
Woolf, Leonard: described, 159; supports Potocki's appeal, 158, 159-60; assumes responsibility for defence, 162; 'Woolf clique', 163, 178; accounts for failure of appeal, 166-8, 169; motives for supporting appeal, 166, 168-9, 171; 'betrayal' of Potocki, 196, 269; visited by Potocki, 204, 205-6; threatens legal action, 216; mentioned, 156, 158, 172, 173, 194
Woolf, Virginia: describes Potocki, 168, 204; describes dinner party, 172; described by Potocki, 205-6; mentioned, 156, 158, 173
Wormwood Scrubs: described, 179-80; Potocki's experience of, 181-93

Yeats, W.B., 21, 30, 160, 162-3, quoted 31, 155

Zamoyski, Adam, quoted 207, 227-8